Cross-Readings

Philosophy and Literary Theory
Series Editor: Hugh J. Silverman

This series provides full-scale, in-depth assessments of important issues in the context of philosophy and literary theory, as they inscribe themselves in the developing archive of textual studies. It highlights studies that take a philosophical or theoretical position with respect to literature, literary study, and the practice of criticism. The individual volumes focus on semiotics, hermeneutics, post-phenomenology, deconstruction, postmodernism, feminism, cultural criticism, and other new developments in the philosophico-literary debate.

Stephen Barker *Autoaesthetics: Strategies of the Self After Nietzsche**

Robert Bernasconi *Heidegger in Question: The Art of Existing**

Véronique M. Fóti *Heidegger and the Poets: Poiēsis/Sophia/Technē**

Sabine I. Gölz *The Split Scene of Reading: Nietzsche/Derrida/Kafka/Bachmann*

Richard Kearney *Poetics of Modernity: Toward a Hermeneutic Imagination*

Jean-François Lyotard *Toward the Postmodern**

Jean-François Lyotard and Eberhard Gruber *The Hyphen: Between Judaism and Christianity*

Louis Marin *Cross-Readings*

Michael Naas *Turning: From Persuasion to Philosophy: A Reading of Homer's Iliad*

Jean-Luc Nancy *The Gravity of Thought*

Wilhelm S. Wurzer *Filming and Judgment: Between Heidegger and Adorno**

*Available in Paperback

Cross-Readings

Louis Marin

Translated by
Jane Marie Todd

HUMANITIES PRESS
NEW JERSEY

First published in English by Humanities Press International, Inc.,
165 First Avenue, Atlantic Highlands, New Jersey 07716

Cross-Readings first published in French as *Lectures Traversières* by
Editions Albin Michel, © Editions Albin Michel S.A. – Paris 1992

English translation © 1998 by Humanities Press International, Inc.

Library of Congress Cataloging-in-Publication Data
Marin, Louis, 1931–
   [Lectures traversières. English]
   Cross-readings / Louis Marin; translated by Jane Marie Todd.
     p. cm. — (Philosophy and literary theory)
   Includes bibliographical references and index.
   ISBN 0-391-04042-1
   1. Criticism. 2. Semiotics and literature. I. Title.
II. Series.
PN98.S46M376   1992   97-15543
809—dc21   CIP

All rights reserved. No part of this publication may be reproduced
or transmitted, in any form or by any means, without written permission.

Printed in the United States of America

Contents

1. Rue Traversière — 1
2. A Selvedge of Reading — 7
3. Punctuation — 15

Part One: Utopics

4. Rue Traversière, no. 59 — 24
5. Journeys to Utopia — 25
6. Archipelago — 34
7. Julie's Garden — 46
8. A Society of Machines — 68
9. Reveries: Utopian Practice and Fiction — 77

Part Two: Crossings

10. Rue Traversière, nos. 45–47 — 102

Politics and Seduction

11. The Right Choice as Remainder — 104
12. The Liar — 115

13. Gyges	123
14. The Sublime, the Obscene	137
15. The Caesura of the Royal Body	144

CHANCE AND SECRECY

16. Simonides' Memory Lapse	158
17. Falls, Encounters, and the *Premier Venu*	167
18. The Secrets of Names and Bodies	179
19. The Logic of Secrecy	195

PART THREE: FICTIONS

20. Rue Traversière, no. 48	206
21. The Bamboo Pole	208
22. "Hello, Who Is This?"	212
23. The Angel of Virtuality	219
24. Neither the True Sex Nor the False	228

END OF THE ROAD

25. Rue Traversière, no. 0	236
26. Echographies: The Crossings of a Conversion	238
27. The Place of the Point? Pascal	252
Notes	273
Index	285

1

Rue Traversière

> There are certain streets in Paris as dishonored as a man guilty of infamy; and then there are noble streets, and simply decent streets, and young streets about whose morality the public has not yet formed an opinion; and murderous streets, streets older than old dowagers, respectable streets, always-clean streets, always-filthy streets, working-class, hard-working, mercantile streets. . . . There are streets of bad company where you would not like to live, and streets where you would gladly stay. A few streets, such as Rue Montmartre, have a lovely head but end in a fishtail. Rue de la Paix is a wide, large street; but it does not awaken any of the graciously noble thoughts that take an impressionable soul by surprise in the middle of Rue Royale, and it is certainly lacking the majesty that reigns on Place Vendôme. . . . Is not Rue Traversière-Saint-Honoré a squalid street? There you find nasty little houses with two casements where, from one floor to the next, there is vice, crime, and bitter poverty.
> —Balzac, *La Comédie Humaine*

> cross, adj., (1) that which crosses, *cross street*
> —Littré, *Dictionnaire*, s.v. *traversier*

> Traversière (Rue)—Sector Quinze-Vingts. Last odd number: 95. Last even number: 80. Begins 84, Quai de la Rapée. Ends 100, Rue du Faubourg-Saint-Antoine and 88, Avenue Ledru-Rollin. Length: 835 meters. Width: 11 or 12 meters.
> —Jacques Hillairet, *Le XIIe arrondissement et son histoire*

I know Rue Traversière [Cross Street] very well, for I live in the neighborhood: The use I make of it as a pedestrian or a rambler, and which I am wont to attribute to all the residents of the area, belies the indications given in Jacques Hillairet's topographical note. Rue Traversière, I assert without hesitation, begins where the note says it ends and ends where the note says it begins. Running backwards in relation to the cartographical code of urban *ratio* that stretches in numerical order from the river, it, in fact, begins at Rue du Faubourg-Saint-Antoine and ends at the Quai de la Rapée. In reality—and one has only to visit the site and accompany the street along its trajectory to be convinced of this—Rue Traversière begins with the uncertainty of a star-shaped intersection, not only the ostentatious crossroads of Avenue Ledru-Rollin and Rue du Faubourg-Saint-Antoine but also the veering to the left of Rue de Prague and Rue Théodore-Roussel. Thus, we find that one side of the street disappears, while the other continues to the Faubourg-Saint-Antoine. What is a street that has only one side? In examining things closely, in looking for a name on a plaque or a final address inscribed above a door at this intersection, we could say that Rue Traversière is an edge, simply a selvedge of the fabric of houses and shops. How, then, could we locate the place of an origin along this borderline?

There is the same uncertainty, the same ambiguity, at the other end. Rue Traversière is endless; rather, its end hesitates between the incessant flow of Boulevard Diderot and, after a few dozen meters, that of Quai de la Rapée, unless we can consider the morgue (the medical-legal institute) the monument where the street we are following culminates. Without origin or end, without beginning or terminus, without starting point or point of arrival, without cause or goal, Rue Traversière confines itself to crossing: It crosses the city. The pedestrian "borrows" it for part of his trip, as far as Rue de Charenton or Avenue Daumesnil, or to Rue de Lyon or Boulevard Diderot. The cross street has no meaning and no direction other than that temporarily given it by the passerby; a segmented direction, a fragmented sense that, in the space of its "rection," is not its own.

Its relatively long history—it was already in existence in 1672—demonstrates this: Beginning in 1806, the one name designated three "streets" that had been individualized until that time. The part included between the quay and Rue de Bercy was, at the time, called Rue des Chantiers [Yard Street] because of the large number of lumberyards situated between its two streets, as far as Rue Villiot. It even bore the name of one of the owners of these lumberyards and was thus called Rue Cler-Chantier. Like the Passage Genty, Rue de Bercy, and Rue Villiot, it is a pathway opened between the lumberyards on the bank of the Seine. "The part between Rue de Bercy and Rue de Charenton was at the time the *Rue Pavée* [Paved Street]."[1] But it is the last section that holds the greatest surprise. "Situated between Rue de Charenton and Rue du Faubourg-Saint-Antoine, it was *Rue Traversine* in 1734, named after a gardener known as Traversire, the seventeenth-century owner of a piece of land that was sold in 1710 to expand the Hospital for Foundlings."[2]

Thanks to Jacques Hillairet's erudition, we find our street dispossessed of the "sense" of its name, simply echoing "Traversine," the proper name of the gardener Traversire. Unless, in this instance, what is involved is the surprising encounter between a proper name and the common term referring to a certain kind of street (as Littré notes in his *Dictionnaire* and Balzac in *Ferragus*), a *rue traversière*, a street that crosses, that confines itself to crossing, a street without origin or end. Between Jacques Hillairet, Balzac, and the dictionary, a childhood memory of mine opportunely comes to mind: the existence in Lyon of a street (it, too, a *rue traversière*) that was perpendicular to the large and very bourgeois Rue de la République and was in the postwar years a "red light" district, with its "houses" and prostitutes. It seems one of the prostitutes was legendary; she had a wooden leg and her entire body was tattooed with a serpent whose mouth opened around her genitals. Where does an aimless, endless journey lead? To the phantasmic *vagina dentata* of a peripatetic woman, a streetwalker with a wooden leg? Traversire or Traversière. Or perhaps the gardener's name refers to the "sire of crosswise or shortcuts"; in short, to the owner of a piece of land situated on the bank of a "street that crosses."

The street that crosses, that confines itself to crossing.... This morning, sitting at my desk writing this, I tried to trace Rue Traversière from my memory, or more exactly, to accompany its crossing in my mind. Nowhere in this journey do I find anything notable, a noteworthy trait that would deserve being written about and that would stop the passerby as he passed, the stroller as he strolled along. No historical curiosity, no memorable remains of the past, no picturesque moment in the present. Hillairet confines himself to noting a nursery school at number 41, a chapel of the Immaculate-Heart-of-Mary at number 48, and the former opening to the Passage Traversière that ended at 83, Rue de Charenton. The chapel, solemnly blessed in 1920, had replaced the François-Coppée hall where Abbot Lenfant, parish priest for the Church of Saint-Antoine-des-Quinze-Vingts, put on operettas such as *Niquette et sa mère* or *La petite chocolatière* as a way of reaching people who would not come to church. For my part, I would have added to this list the police station, the grocery that sells only Yugoslavian specialties, and the "little Arab" who stays open on Sundays till ten o'clock at night; even so, you would not think that Rue Traversière would one day attract tourists. A bit farther on, below street-level, between Rue de Lyon toward the Seine and closed off by a guard rail, there is a rather strange space, where some blacks used to propose a shell game to passersby; the area was perfumed with the spicy effluvia of a West Indian restaurant. But the gamblers, like the restaurant, disappeared a few years ago, and this place today welcomes only patrons coming out of the UGC cinemas on Rue de Lyon. With the gamblers gone, it seems as if Rue Traversière decided three or four years ago to conform to its destiny, the destiny of crossing, which was sealed in 1672. Today, I find in my memory only the blind walls of storehouses and workshops, dusty bistros whose neon and plastic flashing lights are sadly banal.

You have no doubt caught on that Rue Traversière is the itinerant emblem for my travels through texts, ramblings that have attempted to mimic in their writing, in writing themselves, various responses to what Latin grammar books term the fourth-question-of-place: *Qua?* Across?

Ubi is the most primitive and most essential question because its proper concern is place. This question corresponds to stasis, the immobility of a presence here and now: "The *place* is the order (of whatever kind) with which elements are distributed in relationships of coexistence. It thus excludes the possibility of two things being in the same location."[3] The copresence of things, everything in its place. "The law of the 'proper' rules in the place: the elements taken into consideration are *beside* one another, each situated in its own 'proper' and distinct location, a location it defines. A place is thus an instantaneous configuration of positions. It implies an indication of stability."[4] *Ubi?* Right here, for example, a text written in its completeness, the gray density of its present signs in the powerful permanence of their system to which the page, the chapter, and the volume grant a unique configuration, in the expectation that in reading through it you will realize its ephemeral virtuality.

Quo? Unde? The two "following" questions are said to be only very improperly about the place since they deal with space: "A *space* exists when one takes into consideration vectors of direction, velocities, and time variables."[5] Hence, *quo* (where to?) and *unde* (from whence?) presuppose bodies in motion toward a goal, an objective, an end, toward a place that can be posited as a journey's endpoint that is to be rejoined, where the body in motion will come to rest in the refound serenity of its natural location. Or it begins at a place of origin, a beginning from which it takes its impetus toward somewhere else, carving out a space, which opens up as a result of the force in this initial action.

Quo? To tell, to write toward what goals, toward what ends, a reading of *this* text, readings of the same text? Such readings have oriented their journeys in different ways, and, in this diversity, through it, no doubt, they seek to demonstrate the same thesis, assert an identical belief, aim toward a single resting place, find in the end the calm of repose.

Unde? To tell, to write from what grounds and foundations, from what secret bases and principles, from what posited or a priori postulates, from what systems of reference, preestablished conditions, or potentialities? Trajectories begin and continue, bearing the weight of their origins throughout their course; interpretations find, in the texts they apply to, markings and beacons that are so many recollections of their origins, a partitioning and surveying of signals and traits of this a priori memory.

We must, therefore, conceive of readings and written interpretations of texts as travel narratives that, to use the categories set in place by Certeau, incessantly transform places into spaces (*unde?*) or spaces into places (*quo?*), narratives that also organize the changing relationships places and spaces maintain among themselves. This play is endless, ranging from the setting in place of a motionless order where nothing moves except discourse itself—a discourse that passes over that order panoramically (*ubi?*)—to the accelerated succession of actions that produce their own spaces. Sometimes interpretations conserve the memory of a place of origin from whence they came (*unde?*), a more or less buried memory that nevertheless always governs their trajectories. Sometimes they head toward a point of arrival (*quo?*), toward the location where they reach their apogee, which, as a result, becomes the end that has instigated their course.

In its topics of "departure" and "arrival," the travel narrative in its journey is, in some sense, the dialectic between *unde* and *quo*, the passage, or even the transformation, from a topics of origin to a topics of end. Or, even better, it is a way—an often complex way—of rediscovering the origin in the end. We could say the same for the itinerary of textual interpretation: In a way "proper" to any particular text, unique to it, it tends to recognize, once it has reached its end, the motionless, essential, achieved meaning, the initial and secret injunction, the a priori principle that provoked it. Nevertheless, this meaning, this injunction, and this principle are no longer virtual or regulatory but are made into a stable reality: a unique truth that these texts enclosed before the readings came along to awaken them and give them their definitive place in the writing of the commentary, the gloss, the exegesis.

There remains, finally, the last question-of-place: *Qua?* [Through where?] Might we have enough imagination to employ it, or better, might we simply use a mode of textual interpretation that puts it to work? In its urban fabric, Rue Traversière suggested to me the emblematic trait of this practice. Why write *about* a text? I'll answer that question with another question: Why describe or rewrite *this* text? Slippage from one to the other, from scription to description to reinscription, with the help of a prefix; the displacement of one sort of reason, which explains and justifies with its principles and/or its ends (principles, *archai* and *dunamais*, finalities, objectives, and goals of a discourse in the form of a text put in the place of the text that was read and "worked on"); substitution of one theory for another in which the first is summed up and consumed. Might we not bring about a slippage in this reason, a displacement of this reading toward an art of means that would endlessly bracket its origin and its end, a technique of writing on the edge of a text to be described or reinscribed? Art for art's sake or one art for another, with a theoretical stake nonetheless, with no other end than the desire that the one art rise to the level of the other.

Where to begin from, or through? The precise art of means—not writing *on* or *about* a text, but writing, scripting, reinscribing, describing the text—begins only with the choice of this first path where the beginning of the discourse, of the text, is indicated by a crossing: Through where, *qua*? The fourth question-of-place is asked not about a stasis *here* nor about movements *toward* a goal or *from* a point but about a pure body in motion, without origin or end, a body that does not rest, that does not define its location except in terms of the trajectory that visits it without designating it as a dwelling. It is simply a transit, an intrusion without introduction, a departure without farewell: "We do not care about our reputation in towns where we are only passing through [*par où on passe*]. But when we have to stay some time we do care. How much time does it take?"[6] What exact measurement can we come up with to separate *ubi? quo?* and *unde?* from *qua?* How to write, script, describe, reinscribe?

Where to begin from, or through? How to intrude on the text without the violence of a transgression that opens the borders by tearing them, rupturing them? How to leave the text without sadness or melancholy, without the desire to remain, to tarry in the luminous shadow of its beauty? *Where* to end, to have done with this rewriting without positing an end from the outset? In a word, how to cross this text, this poem, this page, this volume, without breaking and entering into its home, without tearing it to pieces as we leave, at the moment of leaving it? We would have to use the text in the way the passerby customarily uses the Rue Traversière (twelfth arrondissement), by "borrowing" with a lively step a section of its itinerary without lazing about out of curiosity or dawdling out of interest. Simply passing as quickly as possible to other places, using it to have easier access to other spaces. That is also one of the meanings of *"traverse"* [shortcut]: "a particular route that is shorter than the main road or that leads to a place where the main road does not lead." It leads there, no doubt, but causes surprise or astonishment in doing so. The shortcut I take, oddly enough, leads me somewhere else, where the "main road does not lead," to another end I did not suspect: discovery. It was not where I wanted to go, and, yet, secretly, this place reveals itself as the place of a true desire, the desire for truth. The shortcut or the cross street of "interpretation" mysteriously confines itself to *indicating* this place, to allowing it to be experienced, precisely because it deviates from the main paths of discourse, because it takes a detour or a diversion from the method. "We do not care about our reputation in towns where we are only passing through." No worries about recognition; no concerns about legitimation. To respond "truly" to the question *qua*, to the question of pure crossing with all its figures of break and digression, of diversion and sidestepping, we would have to *practice crossing*, rupture, syncope, sidestepping. But to do this, a certain lightness of step is required, "lightness" in every sense of the term: agility, unconcerned swiftness, vivacity in stepping aside and leaving no trace, an art of means without authority or authorization, without depth or *consistency*, often a bit careless and casual, and, yet, the beginning of a writing, of a multiple rewriting to fit the virtuality of meanings—to try to play, to replay.

> Zarathustra, the dancer; Zarathustra, the light one who beckons with his wings, preparing for a flight, beckoning to all birds, ready and heady, blissfully lightheaded;
> Zarathustra, the soothsayer; Zarathustra, the sooth-laugher; not impatient; not unconditional, one who loves and leaps side-leaps.[7]

2

A Selvedge of Reading

> selvedge: n. (1) the edge of a fabric, the part that bonds the width on both sides. The *selvedge* is the strongest part of the material. (2) the limits or extremities of a field, a forest, a province, a kingdom. Fields that adjoin a main road often have their *selvedges* eaten by sheep that graze there. Wild beasts are a grave danger to the lands that are on the *selvedges* of forests.
> A child is said to be led by the selvedge when he is restrained by a selvedge or by a cord attached to the back of his garment to teach him to walk. Nannies call it a *tata*.
> —Littré, *Dictionnaire*, s.v. "*lisière*"

We would like, therefore, to travel along the edge of a text, of this text that is called a tale, at its strongest part perhaps—how strong?—to discern its initial limit, or one of its extremities, and to measure the effects of this journey on the reading performed on it. We would also like, as one of these effects, to pull on the tale's selvedge in order to discover something like a lesson in learning to "read," and, more archaically, in learning to listen to the voice of the tale, to its narration on the edge of its narrative, something like a preliminary instruction, a threshold injunction. And, since we are dealing with the tales-of-Perrault, we would also like to explore, in its history and its structure, the *tata* effects of the frontispiece.

The frontispiece, of course, is a kind of prefatory picture, a picture on the selvedge of the book and its reading. From Furetière to Littré, that is, from the end of the eighteenth to the end of the nineteenth century, it is possible to trace a remarkable trajectory in the word "preface." It is not that the term undergoes any important semantic change: At issue, rather, is an implicit aspect of its definition. For Furetière, a preface is the "notice placed at the beginning of a book to instruct the reader about the order and arrangement observed in the book, and about what he needs to know to take advantage of its usefulness and facilitate understanding." Littré, more sparingly, defines "preface" as "a preliminary discourse placed at the head of a book." Yet, we know that the preface still retains its cognitive power over the work it introduces and its prescriptive force over the reading to which it commits us. Nevertheless, as if these strategic and tactical operations now go without saying, the dictionary no longer takes the trouble to designate them in the essential definition of the term.

The illustration of the frontispiece, though it stems from a different semiotic substance, image rather than language, participates in the same operations—this is, in any case, our working hypothesis—but according to different principles and different modalities, which we need to describe and analyze. It operates less directly in relation to the entire apparatus of the "perigraphy" that surrounds the work like a Vauban fortification—the preface, notice, or foreword—than in relation to the title, the author's name, the book's name, and the name and address of the printer-publisher.

The term "frontispiece" is imported into the book, or at least as far as its border, from the field of architecture. Furetière defines it, in the first place, as the "face and main entrance of a large building that directly faces the eyes of viewers," and evokes Du Cange and the original Latin *frontispicium*, which signifies *frontis hominis inspectio*. The frontispiece is part of the specifically orthographical representation of an edifice or, to cite Vitruvius as translated by Claude Perrault in 1684, to "the elevation of one of the faces of the work one wishes to build." It is, in this instance, the principal and frontal face of a volume, which it *illustrates*. It is no accident that Furetière illustrates this principal *illustration* with "the most beautiful piece of architecture in France," the frontispiece of the Palais du Prince, that of the Louvre.

In the second place, the frontispiece slips from architectural volume to the volume of a book, from the principal face of one to the first page of the other, from architectonic illustration to ornament and representation. Furetière traces this move, since the image that decorates his first page, on which the book's title is engraved, also represents the frontispiece of a building. In a remarkable reshuffling, the characteristics of the preface that Littré omitted from his definition of "preface" reappear in the definition he gives of "frontispiece": "engraving placed facing the title of a book whose subject is analogous to the goal and spirit of the work." If we listen closely, all these displacements, slippages, and exchanges mark off the historical and theoretical trajectories of the literary text's selvedges, both the evolution of the preface and that of the frontispiece. They mark what is at stake in the use and power of these figures: the evolution of the addition, of its styles and its aesthetics. There is, therefore, a history and an aesthetics of selvedges to be constituted or, at least, to be developed.

We would like to "recognize" these selvedges in a particular case, that of Charles Perrault's *Contes*.[1] What are the meaning-effects or reading-effects ("reading" understood in the sense of the grasping or appropriation of plural meanings) when a book, a collection of written narratives entitled "tales," is introduced by an engraving that illustrates its title and that may constitute the first in a series of images arranged in the volume as illustrations? A second question follows from the first and concerns the notion of illustration itself. According to Littré, the frontispiece is an initial engraving "whose subject is analogous to the goal and spirit of the work." What does this analogy consist in? The very term "analogy" implies within its definition a subordination of the illustrating image to the illustrated text; conversely, the illustration should be understood as what gives luster, price, and value to a book, not only at an economic or aesthetic level, but also in the sense that it heightens and sheds light on certain of its aspects, which are thereby privileged. Certainly, we rediscover here a phase that is derived historically from the frontispiece, an engraving placed *facing* the book's title. But, according to Furetière, the book's frontispiece was, essentially, the framing of the book's title by an architectural representation— to be precise, that of a large building's frontispiece—by means of which its value as illustration was reinforced. Yet, that value was reinforced not through the subject matter or content of the frontispiece—the architectural representation has no (mimetic) analogy to the subject, to the goal or spirit of the work— but, rather, through its manner and effect, its ornamental prominence, its manner of "emphasizing" the book's title and, in that way, the book as a whole. Hence, the important and, no doubt, decisive relation of the illustration to the framing of the written text and the book in general, that is, its function *at* the limit and *as* limit; hence, the necessary inquiry into the indexical, iconic, and symbolic values of setting forth the "limit" in this way, as a representation, by using the frontispiece as the frontal and principal illustration of the volume of the book, of this book entitled *Histoires, ou Contes du temps passé avec des moralités* [Stories, or tales of time past, with morals] (1697).

Placed facing this title (but not framing it), the frontispiece in this instance certainly represents an architectural structure, but not the one Furetière described as the frontispiece. It is, in fact, quite the opposite: not the "face and main entrance to a large building," but the closed interior of a room in a house. Within this enclosure, we do not find framed the book's title or even the characters from one of the tales of time past that the book claims to bring together in a collection; on the contrary, we find a staging, a *representation of the narration* of these stories, of their *enunciation*. The frontispiece image represents, as a picture, the mechanism that produces narrative and that produced these narratives in particular, these tales of time past. That is, it represents their oral enunciation. An old nurse, governess, or "nanny," is seated on a stool weaving the wool from her distaff on a spindle. Her mouth is open, and her left hand is making the ancient gesture of counting on her fingers. She is speaking to three young persons "of breeding": a young boy in a hat who is standing, one hand resting on the old woman's lap; an adolescent girl in a fontange, her hands slipped into a muff; and a young man in a hat, seated in an armchair, with his back to the fireplace where a wood fire is blazing. In this closed space of hearth and home, the old narrator is set against the background of a closed door whose keyhole is at eye level. This nocturnal, intimate space of an evening at home is signaled not only by the fire and the hearth but also by the lit candle, which is casting its light from the candlestick placed on the fireplace mantel, and by a cat curled into a ball, nestled, with its open eyes "facing the viewer." What we have is the staging of orality with its canonical representatives, the all-powerful mistress of narrative voice and her addressees, children and adolescents, girls and boys, listening with rapt attention.

Nevertheless, the principle of architectural framing that Furetière sees as governing the literary frontispiece by derivation surreptitiously reappears in the image we have just described. In the shadow at the back of the room, barely lit by the candle and the fire in the fireplace, a stone plaque attached by four nails is hanging on the closed door, a plaque that bears the following words engraved upon it: *Contes / de ma / mère Oye* [Tales of Mother Goose]. This title is at least as apt for this collection as the one printed on the page facing the frontispiece: *Histoires, ou Contes du temps passé*. This is, in fact, the title that appears on the 118-page manuscript held together by the family arms of Mademoiselle, the niece of Louis XIV, to whom Perrault had dedicated the prose tales in 1695.[2] In recapturing the *external* normative value of the "frontispiece" genre, the image in the 1697 edition loses part of its *internal* coherence as a representation of the setting of oral narration. At the same time, however, this return of the written text in the form of an engraved inscription, heterogeneous to the paradigmatic image of narrative orality, reveals the strategy of the writer, Charles Perrault. It reveals this strategy at the price of incoherence and, no doubt, by dint of it. For the author has erased his name from the facing title page. This strategy is made even more explicit by the fact that, next to the engraved plaque where the generic name of the anonymous narrator in the image—Mother Goose—can be read, another, smaller plaque, also fixed to the wall with four rivets, is represented. On this plaque, there is an inscription of signs that has been crossed out with engraved, slanted lines: an *unreadable* inscription of a cryptic name. The name of the engraver? Of the writer? Initials? A monogram? Perhaps it is simply a sign that here there is writing in its most memorable and *monumental* form, the inscription of an epigraph.

The frontispiece of the 1697 edition, as a "preface" to the collection, thus exhibits the two topoi of the book's genesis: On the one hand, the *transcription* of narratives into an *oral* situation; on the other, linked as it were to this plotting, the effacement of the *author-writer*, whose name should *sign* the work, in favor of an instance of oral enunciation, the voice of the tale whose most striking characteristic is that it is *without proper name*. But these two topoi, by presenting an image of the frontispiece and of its "incoherence," exhibit, in turn, the author's double strategy. The first dimension of this strategy concerns the author himself. It aims toward his representation, that is, the representation of himself that he proposes and imposes on his readers, his new—modern, we might say—status. In that way, it authorizes him in his modernity by legitimating him in his dissimulation. It is as if the frontispiece, acting as a preface, tells the reader, leads the reader to understand, through reading, the following: "In hiding behind the voice of an anonymous enunciation, of which I am writing the narrative utterances, I am nonetheless the author by absolute right and the writer of the tales or stories of time past." The second dimension of the same strategy concerns the way the collection is to be read. Its title facing the frontispiece and, especially, the image the frontispiece displays, announce the constraining—not to say obligatory—protocols of the book: "This is how you must read." Or, to be more precise: "To read properly, the reader must rediscover, in his imagination or in actuality, the same circumstances as those that the frontispiece represents for him. Reading must become listening, and the printed pages must become nameless voice."

From this, we better understand—as Jacques Barchilon and Marc Soriano have astutely noted[3]—the revisions Perrault made in 1697 in the earlier version of the preface to "Little Red Riding Hood." He replaced the words "those who listen to them [these tales]" with "those who read them" and left out the stage directions that accompanied the wolf's words: "'The better to eat you with, my dear!' (*These words are uttered in a loud voice to frighten the child, as if the wolf were going to eat him.*)" Perrault made these changes not so much because, in two years, the calligraphied manuscript had become the Barbin edition, as because of the meaning-effects of the frontispiece and the first page, and of those that resulted from the interaction between the initial image and the title. Perrault now found them explicit enough in constructing and proposing scenarios of the book's appropriation and in defining the types of probable and desirable readers and specific types of reading.

We insist on the fact that these are *types of reading*: It seems to us that the description we have attempted of the frontispiece to the 1697 edition in all its complexity adequately shows that it is not at all a question of a regression to a primitive phase of the voice at either the level of the history of the "reading public" for the *Contes* or at the level of their particular "consumption"; it is not a question of returning the literate public to popular orality, nor of their regressing from adulthood to childhood. It is, rather, a certain play of literate reading with itself. This play consists, first, in reading while looking at the pictures, since these are illustrated tales. These "vignettes" are so many "iconic prefaces" to the reading of each of the tales in the collection. We would need to analyze the nature and function of these vignettes in their relation to the frontispiece image, which is, as it were, the first in the series. Second, this play consists in reading out loud and possibly reciting: We have seen in studying the frontispiece that the staging of the nanny in her situation of narrative enunciation is not just the representative of the oral "popular" sources of the tales she tells. Third, and perhaps above all, it consists in adopting a different mental attitude, an imaginary attitude even, for receiving the proposed tales as a new kind of literature. It is less a question of becoming cognizant of the collection's originality than of recognizing, in each of the pieces that compose it, something that is already known, already familiar, something that stems from a kind of unconscious culture of childhood.

It is certainly beyond doubt that some of the strategies or tactics that the frontispiece, in its relation to the title page, brings about are indicated only at a virtual level. At the same time, the reading scenarios it proposes are only possibilities that await cognitive or affective cathexis, and a study that set out to document the way these possibilities have been realized would have to be indissolubly historical and semiotic. To demonstrate this possibility, we note that any element of the frontispiece, any of its figures, could function as an "empty indicator" ready to be filled by later readers. I will note two of these.

First, the candle. Placed on the mantelpiece, it is one of the sources of the scene's light (the other being the fire in the fireplace), as demonstrated by the distribution of the shadows of the figured characters and objects. But, unlike the fire, its light is not represented but is rather arbitrarily or abstractly signified by a kind of mandorla that the rays around the flame trace, bringing to mind the mandorla that surrounds supernatural figures, or their emblematic symbols, in religious representations. The candle in the frontispiece "functions" as a mystical monstrance and, in this way, serves as a starting point for meaning [*départ de sens*], as Roland Barthes would say, or as a vision, or reading-effect, that transforms the recitation of tales of time past into an oracular pronouncement, transforms the nanny into a prophetess (or at least a sacred or magical voice), and transforms the act of listening to her into miraculous enchantment.

The other indicator requires a more extensive remark. The classical representation of a narrative, in a large history painting, for example, presupposes that those who tell the story, that is, its actors, are represented in profile or at a three-quarters angle. In any case, they do not maintain any figural relationship to what lies outside the representation, that is, to the instance of narrative production, either through their gaze or through their gestures. It is in this way that the pictorial narrative finds its narrative autonomy and establishes its historical "objectivity." This point appeared so important to theorists of painting that they explicitly assigned any figure looking *beyond the scene* the function of "commentator," an iconic and no longer narrative function, the discursive function of establishing an affective and cognitive link with the viewer. By representing, in profile, the two figures on the extreme right and left—the nanny and the young man sitting with his back to the fireplace—the engraver of the frontispiece follows the classic system, but, in doing so, he narrates the narration of a narrative. He tells, through intermediaries, the story of an oral narration of a tale.

Nevertheless, he introduces into this narrative scene of narration two figures that, even though they belong to the narrative, *are looking beyond the scene*. Of course, they are so discreet that they might go unnoticed, but it is this characteristic of adventitious and minuscule detail that makes them "empty indicators." On the left, there is the keyhole, the black hole of the lock at the level of the narrator's head, shown in profile; and above the fireplace is the cat, the two black holes of its eyes gazing at the back of the young man who is seated in profile, listening. The first hole is the place of the indiscreet gaze, which comes upon a spectacle it is not supposed to see, like the young prince in "Peau-d'âne" who *by chance put his eye to the keyhole* of the servant girl's door and discovered she was a dazzling sun princess. On the right, the other two holes, the cat's eyes, possess no gaze. No doubt, in the picture as a whole, this connotes the values of the private, closed, intimate, reserved space, the space of the tale's recitation. But these eyes also open, though only microscopically, the place of a secret for an "other" gaze that, even as it sees all there is to see (we look at the picture naively and without encountering obstacle), is nevertheless excluded from it. We are on the other side of the closed door, looking through the keyhole. We are expelled by the maleficent eyes of the cat on the other side of the mirror (of representation), and yet at the same time, we are magically drawn into it. These empty indicators point to all the readings of fairy tales as textual places of transgressions that are both socially and culturally untenable and yet symbolically acceptable. We may, in fact, wonder whether Perrault has not caught a glimpse of such readings. They bring about selvedges of reading and listening, "selvedges" in the dual sense: as an indeterminate edge, a visual borderline (where wild beasts of the forest or desert roam about), and as a lesson to be learned, "injunctive" and "prescriptive" rules of textual appropriation and cultural *tata*.

These few indications on the functions and values of the frontispiece in its role as preface to the 1697 edition of Perrault's *Contes* would find their theoretical and historical validity only through a diachronic study of wider scope that would take into account the series of frontispiece editions of the work. The few surveys we have initiated, like other recent studies, show that at the beginning of the nineteenth century, a shift occurs that is, no doubt, decisive for the selvedge line and the trajectory of meaning of the frontispiece to Perrault's *Contes*. Take, for example, a "popular" edition of 1808 (but we know that so-called popular editions do not address only a "popular" public condemned to orality by a lack of education). It is attributed to L. Duprat-Duverger, 21 Rue des Grands-Augustin, and goes by the title *Contes de fées par Monsieur Charles Perrault de l'Académie*. The frontispiece we have been studying reappears, but as a kind of publisher's logo. The old woman with her spindle and distaff and the six children and adolescents who surround her are all certainly there, but, in this case, they have moved out of the reserved, intimate, and closed space of narration, the space of hearth and home, and are arranged on a kind of display unit made of earth, grass, and plants. The frontispiece, as such, has disappeared, becoming an autonomous and stereotyped sign whose strict meaning would be: "Fairy-Tales-for-Children." And L. Duprat-Duverger has, in essence, become a specialty publisher of such books. In contrast, facing the title page in the position of the frontispiece are two vignettes, representing a scene from "Bluebeard" and another from "Little Red Riding Hood": They introduce the first two tales in the collection.

In the nineteenth century, the old nurse, who in telling the tales held us entranced, this ageless and nameless mistress of the voice, of orality, disappears little by little from the book's illustration and from the iconic protocols for its use and consumption, to be replaced by characters from the tales in narrative situations (or outside the narrative). Among them, we often find the fairy: The reader witnesses her promotion to the beginning of the book. But, in moving from the pages of the collection of tales in which she actively intervened to the image on the frontispiece, the agent of the story told in writing loses her narrative dimension and its predicates to become the abstract figure for the predicate of a literary genre, the *fairy* tale. This foreshadows the moment when the name of the author-writer Charles Perrault becomes lost in the anonymity of a term used to modify that genre: "Tales-of-Perrault." In the end, perhaps it is in this that the seventeenth-century writer found one of his greatest illustrations.

3

Punctuation

> punctuation: the art of distinguishing sentences, the partial meanings that constitute these sentences, and the different degrees of subordination appropriate to each of these meanings from one another by means of conventional signs
> —Littré, *Dictionnaire*, s.v. "*ponctuation*"

In his praise of Lamotte, d'Alembert notes that he "put into his reading the kind of delicate punctuation that makes different kinds of merit perceptible by inflections as minute as they are varied." Inflections of the voice, I will point out, so as to dot all the i's.

"Punctuation" stems from *punctum*, point or period. Hence, in the very term that designates the art of distinguishing between sentences and parts of sentences by means of conventional signs, we find the term that will give birth to all these signs, traces, marks, markers or demarcators, notes and remarks, indexes and signals. Are they as arbitrary, as conventional, as the dictionary suggests? The period or point, "the little mark you put in writing to indicate the end of a sentence" (thirty-first of the fifty-seven meanings assigned to the term *point* in Littré) will bear not only the brood of legitimate children—the colon, the question mark, the exclamation point, and the ellipses—but also the bastard semicolon, the comma, the parentheses, and the brackets. Let us consider these offspring one by one. The colon ordinarily introduces a quotation or an explanation; the question mark "says" very well what it means; the exclamation point follows the last word of a sentence and expresses astonishment; ellipses indicate that the meaning is there, silent, beyond the linear succession of points. As for the semicolon, in marking the comma's pause more forcefully with the help of a point, it separates the parts of subordinate phrases logically but not grammatically. The comma, which began as a little diddly marking defective passages, today indicates the slightest of all pauses. Parentheses, those sweet, young twins, embrace phrases separated from the sentences in which they are inserted, as do their twin brothers, the aggressive brackets. Yes, even quotation marks [*guillemets*] are sons of the point, though they bear the name of the printer Guillaume—or Guillemet, according to Ménage. They secure quotations to the text where the honest writer introduces them and take on the formidable task of signaling irony in the use of a term.

There they are, the multiplying instruments of the art of plotting out meaning, the familiar tools of the original point, the minuscule foundation for the graphic distinctions of meanings, whether complete or partial, in the space of the page, their order and harmony in the time of reading or the architecture of thought: the cosmic matrix point. Punctuation, a cosmetics of meaning born of the successive pregnancies of this matrix, a cosmetics of writing transmitting its inflections, as minute as they are varied, to the gaze that silently skims the lines, inflections as numerous as those that, as d'Alembert reported, Lamotte communicated to his listener while reading.

But before arriving at the place where it would give birth to a world (of signs) and to the art of using and enjoying them in writing and reading, the term "point" had to make a long voyage, trace a sinuous course in the vocabulary of the language. Moving from biting pain to the prick made in fabric by a threaded needle, and from lacework to the hole made in a belt, "point" finally crossed over to line measurements, believing then that it had finally reached the calm serenity of geometry. Wrong! For, after Pascal and Bossuet, the good Abbot Delille saw in the point—the smallest unit of extension, a quasi zero of space, "a supposition, an abstraction of the mind, a chimera" (Voltaire)—the opening toward an agonizing infinity: "I shall not follow you / into that deep sea / where every star's a point / and every point a world." In its destination, the point is already cosmic. To control this flight into terrifying infinite spaces, the point finally becomes a fixed and determinate place, a point of contact and a central point; a reference point and viewpoint, a point of support that, once found, allows Archimedes and Descartes to lift the world; or the cardinal points where geographical space finds its articulation, points of the solstice, the equinox, the zenith, and the nadir; the point of a target for taking good aim, points of convergence where light rays come together, points of incidence, of reflection, and of refraction, where they fall and are dispersed or broken up by the center, the radius point that, like a minuscule sun, is their starting point. We arrive, out of breath, at the reckoned or even calculated place in the sea where a ship, at a given moment, inscribes its wake by piercing a hole of regrets and hopes on the deserted map of waters quartered by latitudes and longitudes. We might mention the points of tear ducts, small orifices from which tears stream out and where the humor that lubricates the eye is discharged; and also that living point, the protruding point, the first appearance of a heart in an embryo. We might also evoke the red and white points that make spots in a diamond, and the black point on the horizon, the menacing storm cloud that appears in the sky. We might inscribe on a stone block marks that *mettent la statue aux points* in such a way that the master has only to add the finish and expression to the sculpture that has been rough-hewed in this way. We might re-mark on the dead point in a body in motion when it no longer receives motion from the initial force, that is, when its continued movement is due only to its acquired speed; but also, on the secret point we discover in the lower part of the reverse side of our coins, minuscule letters that indicate the city where they were minted . . . and the final stop, before entering the typographic realm, to put the dot—the point—on the i, the point "in the brown night, on the yellowed tower, the moon" (Musset).

In its lexical voyage, the point is thus at the center of tensions. It is the point of application for contrary forces: *forces of the infinite*, even annihilation, on the one hand, and *forces of emergence*, of apparition and birth, on the other. In the first category, we might mention the vanishing point on the canvas that brings together painted appearances, only to have them disappear within it, this little hole that Brunelleschi pierced in his experimental panel representing the Florence Baptistery and that Desargues, two centuries later, conceived geometrically as the point of infinity. In the second category, there is the point of the eye; the point of the subject; the viewpoint that this same Brunelleschi situated on the back of his panel in the position of the vanishing point, but on the other side, and from which the paintings of beings, of things, and of palaces leap forth almost to the point of quasi reality; the *point principe*, or place of the prince, the great master of ceremonies of images on the scene of representation; the infinite vanishing point in the very instant and the very place where it is also a minuscule point of emergence; the point of an original punctuation at the rational foundation of the representation of painting, and through which it surpasses itself—doubly, at its end and its beginning.

In his grammar of the elements of form, Klee conceives of this polarity between infinity and emergence; he leads us to conceive it as well, because he lets us see the original punctuation.

> The point is not without dimensions; it is an infinitely small element of the surface which, *as an agent*, executes zero movement, that is, it merely exists. As soon as the pencil touches the sheet of paper, the line appears. . . . The point is cosmic, it is a basic element. Every sperm is cosmic in its nature. The point is cosmic because it is situated at the intersection of several directions. . . . The line results from the ideal tension between two points. The result: an arc. . . . The point is set in motion and gives birth to a constitutive figure resting on the construction.

Elsewhere, Klee writes—and I like to think of Brunelleschi's eye at the viewpoint—"For I was precisely at the place where the beginning is situated." And, perhaps, along with the Florentine master, we need to think that the place of the beginning, its site, its point, is always the other side of a hole, the hole at the end. "That is," Klee continues, "that I could be as fertile as possible. . . . I am beginning at the same place as creative form: that is, at the point animated by motion."

The same is true, in a humble way, for the point, the period, on the page of writing: a modest phenomenology that repeats on its own scale the grandiose beginnings of the Renaissance. As I read, my eyes skim the line and the groups of signs, the closely set grisaille, up to the blank space, an interruption marked with a point. After a minuscule instant of pause, my gaze settles on the initial capital letter of the new sentence, and my eyes are off again through the line of signs, following the meaning and parts of meaning and the various degrees of subordination that pertain to each one. What has happened during this minor accident that is so necessary to reading? The little black spot pierces a hole in the blank space of the paper, and the silent murmur of the *dictio* that accompanies the instantaneous decrypting of written signs by the gaze, here, in an instant, is extinguished and disappears. The point is the minuscule and imperious index of this blank space: It notes its neutrality; it neutralizes the eye's secret voice.

Variation. Take away the point: Surprise! The separating void becomes a graphemic potentiality, a virtuality of signs, a power of meanings, a palimpsest of blankness. The *dictio* breathes heavily in this void, stumbles over this absence. Even absent, the period that points out this void occupies it entirely: It radiates the adequacy of its existence, as Klee said of the cosmic point. The presence of the point represents the imminence of meaning; the empty mark anticipates this meaning and prepares the silent voice, the reading eye, and the accompanying thought for it. The presence of the point is the promise of reading in a sign that suspends reading for a moment, thus offering its first fruits.

Application. From Pascal's *Pensées*:

> ... It is the effect of power, not of custom, for those capable of originality are rare; those who are strongest in numbers only want to follow, and refuse recognition to those who seek it for their originality; if they persist in wanting recognition and despising those who are not original, the others will call them ridiculous names, may even administer blows with a stick. So do not be conceited about your subtlety, or keep your satisfaction to yourself.[1]

(It hardly matters to me that the punctuation is that of the printer Louis Lafuma, who published the *Pensées* in 1954 in his own way—or, as he believed, in Pascal's way—in the volume I am reading at the moment.) I listen to the voice of the *dictio* that accompanies my reading. It is gasping for breath because of the syncope, the placement of the semicolons (interruption and resumption within the interruption), and, to a lesser extent, because of the commas; so the "blows with a stick" are a real relief, a resting place, a pause, which diverges from the violence in the meaning. There is a gap here between the reader's thought and the voice accompanying the writing. There is a spark, a flaring up of the discourse, which we could also call Pascal's "fragment." Pause on this point ... "blows with a stick." But the real blow with a stick is to come in a moment. In the pause it marks for the voice, the point or period, far from concluding with the blows of the stick by the greatest number, instead anticipates the violence of direct address to the reader, which occurs in the next sentence. Suddenly, the voice is reconciled with the "content" of the signs: "blows with a stick. So do not be conceited about your subtlety, [comma, an admirable pause of disjunction] or keep your satisfaction to yourself." In this instance, the point is certainly final, an "astonishment point" that leaves the reader voiceless and speechless.

Variation. It appears, however, looking at things more closely and listening to the written text more intensely, that this entire causative motion of form, as Klee would say, this entire trajectory of the *punctum* that ancient rhetoric called a "period" finds its power, its impetus, its rhythm, only in an initial interruption that, for better or worse, Lafuma marks with three points, ellipses: "... It is the effect of power, not of custom." The question of "sense" is, What does this mean? *What* is the effect of power and not of custom? As readers, we will certainly not find an answer by simply reading what follows in the text. To do so, we will have to provide a commentary, explicate and gloss the phrase. In fact, the answer to the question is suspended "at the origin," in the blank space "conventionally" marked by the three points, a reserved space, in the sense of the reserve in painting. It is a virtuality (both *virtus* and *dunamis*, force and possibility, potential) that will remain reserved until the end of our reading. It is the reserve of rhetorical force, of discursive violence that breaks out with the "*it is* the effect of power," where the writing is what it writes, the effect, the trace in the graphemes, of power, of a power that is not, however, the one being spoken about and that moves in successive swells, by the repeated syncopes of the semicolons, to break like a wave on the "blows with a stick." The ellipses, the so-called points of suspension on the edge of the first sentence of the *pensée* are the indexes of this virtuality, this potency of meaning and of its expression. At the end of a sentence, by contrast, and often accompanied by an "etc.," ellipses instead mark exhaustion, something like the lethargy of the infinity of disappearance, which the (vanishing) point also signals. Compare this to "*Meanings*—A single meaning changes depending on the words that express it. Meanings receive their dignity from words, rather than giving dignity to them. We need to look for examples. . . ." (Pascal).

Application. At the beginning of Stendhal's *La vie de Henry Brulard* [The Life of Henry Brulard], we read: "That morning, 16 October 1832, I found myself in San Pietro in Montorio, on Janiculum in Rome, it was a magnificently sunny day. A light sirocco wind that was barely perceptible was pushing a few little white clouds over Monte Albano, a delicious warmth held sway in the air, I was happy to be alive." As far as possible, I have underscored the signs of punctuation that raise questions for me. They also raised questions among other publishers since certain of them replace the commas with semicolons, favoring a reading of the manuscript that is thought to be more grammatically correct. I read this text, therefore, as I have always read it, dazzled by an encounter in the sun and in Rome with my fellow native of Grenoble Henri Beyle (Stendhal). A comma or a semicolon? The semicolon separates the parts of subordinate phrases not grammatically but logically, by marking the pause more clearly than a comma would do, and, we should add, less intensely than a period. As we said, the comma indicates the smallest of pauses, hardly an interval at all.... Reread again the two sentences in the passage cited above, whose closure is marked by a period or point. I now grasp why, without really thinking about it, I have always preferred the comma. "That morning, 16 October 1832, I found myself in San Pietro in Montorio...." The "I" inscribes himself in time and space, with dates and place names: that very morning of 16 October, near Bramante's tempietto and the church where Beatrice Cenci was buried, one of the most beautiful views of Rome; that particular morning, that particular place, the magnificence of the sun and the "I" at the viewpoint.... In the gesture of writing, Henri Beyle *almost* erases the recollection, the distinction between the self, the moment, the place, and the luminous profusion that envelops him. The comma that stands in place of the point or the semicolon is the signal of this *quasi evanescence* favoring a rapidity of inscription that lets itself be *heard*. Two almost inaudible pauses occur again in the next sentence, and the reader "feels," in the life flow of the "entire meaning," the happiness of writing about the happiness of being alive, one moment, one morning in October, in San Pietro in Montorio.

Drifting or Transport. The first pages of *La vie de Henry Brulard* are the journey in writing of the memory of the panorama in Rome that the narrator had discovered on Janiculum, standing on the terrace in front of the church; this panorama is also the journey of a gaze over the immense urban landscape discovered from that place. The homology between the two journeys is so strong that, in the play between the hand writing the memory of this luminous morning—writing at night at the Palazzo Conti, Piazza Minerva—and the gaze that, seeing the city in its magnificence in the sun, creates its landscape at the viewpoint, one kind of punctuation moves toward another: from hand to eye, between two times, between memory and vision. The writing hand almost instinctively possesses the art of distinguishing with signs the ebb and flow of sentiment and thought; and this type of punctuation becomes another, namely, the art of scanning the space exhibited by the emperors and popes and architects of ancient and modern Rome, as the narrator's gaze moves back and forth from the viewpoint he occupies to the horizon that limits his view: ". . . I was happy to be alive. I could perfectly well make out Frascati and Castel Gandolfo, which are four leagues from here, the Villa Aldobrandini where we find that sublime fresco, the Domenichino Judith. I can see perfectly well the white wall that marks the repairs made most recently by Prince Francesco Borghese, the same prince I saw in Wagram as colonel of a regiment of cuirassiers, the day my friend M. de Noue had his leg taken off" (*La vie de Henry Brulard*).

I have called these few reflections "drifting": drifting from a punctuation of writing to a punctuation of architecture, from page to landscape, but also the drifting of Beyle's gaze from space to memory, and of my gaze, as a reader, from a white mark to a point, by way of a sentence that never quite reaches it. From the viewpoint, in a single bound, the eye reaches the limits of the horizon that *two proper names*, two place names, punctuate with the topographical equivalent of a point or period: a complete sentence of the gaze, a phrasing of space that the two names Frascati and Castel Gandolfo bring together, from the capitalized "I" (at the viewpoint) beginning the sentence to the two "horizon points" they punctuate.

The drifting begins there, on the horizon line the eye scans: the weak pause of the comma, "the Villa Aldobrandini." The toponymic points are both left behind; a new sentence of space begins, a simple horizon line, a slight disturbance in the flow of writing: ", [comma] the Villa Aldobrandini where we find that sublime fresco, the Domenichino Judith." The gaze ceases to see what it contemplates and sees instead what it knows, or rather, what it means, what it would like to say, inserting into the line of writing, on the horizon line, a woman showing the severed head of a man to two children. In the text, the caesura of the point ". . . the Domenichino Judith." that sets off the sentence and separates it from the following one punctuates a body by means of a cut, an unspeakable castration—that of the despised father by the adored mother—in the name of "the Domenichino Judith," a double name. The sentence, written at night by candlelight, on the Piazza Minerva, ", I was happy to be alive. I could perfectly well distinguish Frascati and Castel Gandolfo," et cetera, is finally summed up and closed . . . by this caesura-point, "the Domenichino Judith." New beginning at that *very point*, a beginning marked by a caesura in time: "I can see perfectly well. . . ." In contrast to the earlier phrase, "I could perfectly well make out . . .," the *present tense* is used here rather than the *imperfect*. But what present are we talking about? That of the description-utterance or that of the written enunciation? Undoubtedly both: In the blank space of the page marked by the point inserted by the hand that is writing *now*, there appears another blank, that of a wall that marks the reparations made by Prince Borghese. Caesura on top of caesura, blank on top of blank, a point—a cut: the head of Holophernes cut off by Judith in the villa "repaired" and marked by Prince Borghese, whose name is inexorably and inexplicably associated with a "leg taken off. [point]"

Remark. Punctuation, the art of distinguishing sentences and parts of a sentence by conventional signs, the art of *punctum*, is and will always be only an art of writing. It is because Henri Beyle is writing the "city of memory" in his memory of the luminous morning of San Pietro in Montorio that Janiculum and Rome punctuate a viewpoint with their names, and Monte Albano, Frascati, Castel Gandolfo, and Villa Aldobrandini punctuate the horizon of his gaze with theirs . . . . The points and commas of this space are transported (as metaphor) from the page to the city, a space that is always related to a gaze that scans it from a viewpoint and to a hand that traces it with its signs.

But I can imagine that the eye and the gaze, the hand and the pen, are a moving body transported into the landscape. The art of distinguishing the phrasings of space by the conventional signs that distinguish sentences in language is here the art of taking a walk, where an "I" creates the space of its errancies, or rather, composes it, as in the protrusions of rocks, the advent of prairies, the injunctions of roads and paths, the hesitations of intersections and roundabouts, and the breaks of ravines. And it would be easy to recognize, in these spacings of nature or culture, of garden or city, the hard or soft, insistent or evanescent, signs that mark and indicate to a body in motion the complex modalities and inflections of their pathways, as minute as they are various, inflections that Lamotte, according to d'Alembert, made in his voice while reading in order to make different kinds of merit perceptible.

Part One

◆

UTOPICS

4

Rue Traversière, no. 59

In his display window, next to the sausages, the pâtés, and the vintage hams, the Yugoslavian grocer on Rue Traversière exhibits slightly stale tourist posters from the Dalmatian coast. Time and weather have yellowed the images of his native land. The time that has passed in the history of this well-placed emigrant on the "street-where-you-only-pass-by" and the weather that beats down along its edges season after season, blazing sun and pouring rain, gusts of wind and cool nights, have all tarnished the colors, have turned the landscapes, which should have appeased the nostalgia of exiles or enticed them to return, into rather dreary grisailles that, in the spots that stain the paper and the mould that eats away at the mounts, bear witness to the deceitful artifice of representation, or even the lack of reality of these too-dazzling islands bathed in a too-blue sea, of medieval Venetian fortresses illuminated too harshly by electric light. Although the photographs bear witness to the geographical existence of these places, they acquire, through the degeneration of the images, the strange value of a fiction, the fiction of a slightly vulgar utopia. Yet, the moral disenchantment that insidiously eats away at them elevates them once more to the dimension of lost places.

5

Journeys to Utopia

Thomas More's "wondrous" little book *Utopia* begins with the narration of a journey made by its author. Sent by his king on a mission to Flanders, he arrives in Bruges for the preliminary phase of negotiations with the delegates of the Prince of Castile, the future Charles V. During a temporary suspension in the talks, the English diplomat is able to go to Antwerp. It is here that his real journey begins, a journey that will carry him far beyond Flanders.

We find that this journey to Antwerp is a parenthesis in the time of affairs and politics, a vacation, a vacant or intermediary moment, as More himself writes. It is also a gap in the official space of the sites of negotiation: London, capital of Henry VIII, His Invincible Majesty, King of England, the author's master; Brussels, capital of Charles, His Serene Highness, Prince of Castile; and Bruges, which welcomes the representatives of the two parties. The detour to Antwerp is "gratuitous," therefore, but it is also a meeting with his friend Peter Gilles, whose inestimable moral and intellectual virtues make this stay a moment of vacation, a "real journey" where the traveler forgets not only the mission he is charged with but also his concern about its success. He even forgets the journey itself, the separation from his own place—his native country—and everything that attaches and fixes him to it: his wife and children, from whom he has been separated for several months.

It is within this space and time opened up by leisure and friendship, between the public affairs of the state and the feelings for home, that the noteworthy event of this journey occurs, and with it, the occasion to write of it and to report another event that is incommensurable with the first in space and time. At the same time, this gap encloses the remarkable event within its own story; this detour frames it within its writing, a writing that finds in it something more than a pretext. This story is, in fact, the very reason for the text's production.

"One day" in Antwerp, after hearing the mass at Notre Dame (and More does not hesitate to play the tourist for his reader: "a magnificent building which is always packed with people"),[1] the author is preparing to return home [*redire hospitium*]—a "home" that is foreign to him in two ways (it is neither

London nor Bruges, neither native country and personal dwelling nor official place of his mission). At that moment, he meets a stranger [*cum hospite quoddam*], catches sight of Peter Gilles in conversation with the traveler. All the signs point to his identity as a professional traveler, a sailor: his face burned by the sun, his long beard, his coat carelessly thrown over his shoulders. We may, then, wonder whether all of Utopia is not inscribed from the beginning, from the first pages of the book, in this initial gap in space and time, in the author's pleasure trip away from the historical and political identity of Thomas More, future chancellor of England, on a mission to Flanders. The foreign traveler he meets there is both Cardinal Morton's interlocutor in book 1 and the narrator's persona in book 2 (Utopia itself). We may wonder, however, whether he is not *first of all* a figure: the textual *figure* for this de-viation by the statesman outside the geopolitical space of London, Brussels, and Bruges, between Henry VIII and Charles; a figure as well for this interim moment of drifting, of friendship with Peter Gilles, a friendship that takes a vacation from "reality," from economic and business affairs, and the confrontations of two great European states.

For centuries to come, every utopia will begin with a journey. But has not every journey always been a utopia? A utopia not just in the sense of the curious quest for an "elsewhere" that is only elsewhere in reference to a "here" from which the landowner takes his leave, exiles himself, only to better find it again and appropriate it for himself, if only in the extreme form of a return from exile or a nostalgia for a home that is forever lost. No. Is not every journey, first and foremost, the vacant moment or the space of vacation that interrupts the continuity of time and suspends the ordering of places?

There is a belief that the journey implies departing from one place and returning to the same place, a place whose identity the traveler, the "subject-of-the-journey," enriches with a booty of knowledge and experience. In this return to the *same*, he reaffirms his *own* consistency as a subject, *his own identity*, whose constitutive limits lie precisely in the circularity of this trajectory in space. In contrast to this view, can we not maintain that the properly utopian time and space consists in opening within this circle and in tracing along this trajectory a placeless place, a timeless time, the truth of a fiction?

We have only to accompany More's writing, give it an attentive reading, to discover, from this starting point and in this departure itself, the endless drifting that eats away at history and geography (the subsistence of time and the ordering of places) in many short journeys. Hence the portrait of this sailor conversing with Peter Gilles on the parvis of Notre Dame. "Who is he?" asks More. Gilles responds not by giving his name, his profession, or his nationality, but by designating him by the most common trait of the traveler in general, and yet also the trait most likely to lead Thomas More *astray*: "There's not a man alive today who can *tell* you so many stories about strange countries and their inhabitants as he can." And he adds: "I know what a passion you have for that kind of thing."[2] The traveler is first a narrator, and the journey is a narrative. He has *seen* things and beings in the reality of the world that the narratee has not *seen* and will never know except by *hearing* tales about them. From the eye of the one to the ear of the other, the experience of the world is communicated in stories, in order to constitute a knowledge that More terms "historia," a great totalizing narrative that brings together in this place, *here*, direct eyewitness accounts, the very presence of foreign things that are *elsewhere*. "Then I didn't guess too far wrong," replies More. "The moment I saw him, I thought he must be a sailor."[3] More's conjecture is both true and false. The traveler is a sailor, but not by profession. He has certainly sailed, but not like Palinurus; more like Ulysses, or even better, like Plato. In these three names lie three epic and historic figures: Palinurus, the carefree traveler in Virgil's *Aeneas* who perished when he fell asleep at the helm; Ulysses, the Homeric hero of a thousand ruses who learned of the world, of men, and of gods in his ten years of wandering; and Plato, who went to Egypt to know the truth of society and to Sicily to establish it. These three names designate three journeys in fiction and in history, three manners of traveling around the world. From these three names, Peter Gilles and More construct the figure of the utopian traveler: the one he is not, the one he resembles, and the one he represents in his own way.

It is among these three names of journeys and travelers that the "true" name, a "Greek" philosopher's name, is uttered, in transit between history and epic, between ignorance, *doxa*, and science, in the dialogue between More and Gilles of which he is the subject: "Raphael" is his first name, "Hythlodaeus," his family name. It is a double or triple name—Raphael, Huthlos, Deus—a name that, in these three references, marks out three loci of language that are conjoined in the unity of his name: Hebrew, Greek, and Latin. "Raphael" is the messenger angel, "God's healing," in Hebrew; "Huthlos" is Greek for "nonsense"; and "Deus," Latin for "God." This triple meaning can be rendered by the enigmatic sentence: "God heals through God's nonsense." And it might very well be that beyond, or on this side of, three cultures, the traveler-philosopher's name-in-transit, his angelic first name, Raphael, refers to a travel narrative, since the heavenly messenger was the guide for the young Tobias on the roads of Assyria and Media.

In drifting through the traveler's names, we have found in "Raphael Hythlodaeus" what has long been noted regarding the place names that mark out the phases of his travels. In the center of the subject-of-the-journey's name, we find a term (*Huthlos*) that, even as it neutralizes its immediately discernible meaning, also enigmatically declares, if not its higher sense or its polysemy, then at least a plurality of meanings. These meanings authorize exegesis of every sort, set it in motion, but also suspend its truth in the limitlessness of a signifying production that may "fictionalize" any of its products whatsoever.

Thus, well before Raphael's journey-within-More's-journey comes across Utopia and describes it at length, it is Raphael Hythlodaeus's name, in the text written by More, that, in designating the sailor, covers over his description. It is the subject-of-the-journey who becomes a fiction and carries into fiction all who approach him: Peter Gilles and, especially, Thomas More, since it is in narrating the journeys of this subject that More, the future chancellor of England, becomes a writer, the author of a "*libellus vere aureus nec minus salutaris quam festivus.*"

The drifting of the subject-of-the-journey's name introduces us to the fiction of its truth (or the truth of its fiction) only to lead us to the limit of this journey. It is this limit that we need to understand if we are to understand the utopia in every journey, if we are to interpret in precise terms the journey of every utopia. This limit is not the end of the journey, its point of arrival. Nor is it exterior to the journey. What would be "exterior" to a journey other than the limitlessness of spaces where the "I" has not traveled, the infinity of places the "I" has not visited: everything that is not marked by the narrow tracing of "my" course, which, though circular, though leading me back to my starting point, nevertheless encloses no space of which it could be declared the endpoint and the demarcation. In the end, the limit of a journey is the journey itself, the tracing of its course, the pure trajectory of a moving, unsituatable subject. This subject would be always on the point of disappearing, were it not for the occasional prints his feet leave on the ground, the furrows his ship makes in the sea, and an ever-present memory, or, at least, a few recollections.

Peter Gilles, in introducing Raphael to More, tells precisely of his journeys, their origin in his desire to see the world, their starting point (Portugal), and their means, his engagement with the companions of Amerigo Vespucci. Raphael's journeys could have been the same as Vespucci's and his narrative very similar to Vespucci's own. Instead, during the fourth journey, rather than returning to Portugal, he was among twenty-four men who were left at Cape Frio on the Brazilian coast. At this point on the American shoreline, the fiction is exactly tangent to the circuit of geographic travels in the reality of the world; it is a minimal space on the borderline between the known and the unknown. Gilles points to this point, the location of the fort "*ad mines postremae navigationis,*" at the limit of the last journey. And on this frontier, strangely, as on a threshold of initiation, are combined human abandonment, the desire for the journey, and the encounter with death. Here, too, Gilles and/or More summarize(s) this encounter in two classic sentences: Raphael, happy to be left at the farthest reaches of the world, is more concerned to pursue his journeys than to find a final home, a tomb. Isn't he accustomed to saying that "the unburied dead are covered by the sky" and that "you can get to heaven from anywhere"?[4] This edge of the world, we are made to understand, is adjacent to another edge, that of the next world; and *on* this edge, *between* the two edges, a space opens that belongs neither to one nor to the other, an interval between the interior of these journeys that enclose the *terrae cognitae* and their outside, the unknown elsewhere. This indiscernible gap is the journey's imaginary. At this limit, in this gap, Raphael Hythlodaeus is also the figure for this imaginary. Through his role models and his names, through his appearance in More's book and in Gilles's narrative about him, the narrator of utopia deploys the space of an itinerancy of the imagination. The wondrous island will be the product of this imagination. Do we not see him come back from this space as suddenly as he had appeared on the parvis of Notre Dame in Antwerp, on the Ceylon side, en route to Calicut, through a *mirabili fortuna*, and, finally, back to his native country, *praeter spem*, when all hope was gone?

Raphael provides a narrative of his wanderings. For the moment, however, we do not hear his voice; it is More who reports the story to us: "*Narravit ergo nobis* . . ." and tells us where it was recounted. It seems that, *in order to be told*, the journey requires the return "home"; not only the return, but an intimate locale, a dwelling's enclosure. It seems that the discourse of narration needs to accentuate the difference between stories of moving through space—encounters, discoveries, and surprises, the excitement of events and accidents—and their telling, whose listening conditions are rest, leisure, and the stillness of a peaceful community of language: "We adjourned to the garden of my hotel [a secular, philosophical version of the *hortus conclusus*], where we sat down on a bench covered with a layer of turf, and began to talk more freely."[5]

Nevertheless, Raphael's narrative does not so much tell of a journey as unfold a map and the regular generality of its articulations: the equator, the sun's borderline that divides the world; burning-hot deserts, desolate spaces inhabited by snakes, wild beasts, and men as wild as the beasts. Then the descent into the other hemisphere begins: The heat becomes more bearable, the land greener, the animals less ferocious; people, towns, and cities appear, then trade between societies by sea and by land. It is in that other world, the geographic mirror reflection of this world, that Raphael and his companions establish the starting point for their journeys in every direction to new lands. That is how they encounter the island of Utopia, whose description constitutes the main portion of the book.

Note the place and function of the travel narrative (the narrative of Raphael's travels) in the economy of More's writing and in that of his object "*de optimo reipublicae statu deque nova insula Utopia.*" The narrative sets out and constructs the framework of a description and the enclosure of a map. It is told on its own limit, which is double, that of a geographic "reality" where it is articulated and displaced, and that of a sociopolitical fiction that appears descriptively only as the "cartographical" figure for this drifting, this narrative de-viation. The journey during which Raphael and his companions discover the island of Utopia takes place on the edge of a map of the world that, in

Raphael's discourse reported by Gilles, corresponds to the level of knowledge held by the book's writer. Vespucci's account of his journeys authorizes the plausible unfolding of this map at the far limit of his explorations in space (Cape Frio in Brazil) and in time (his last journey), just as Vespucci's journeys had themselves occurred at the edge of the map of Europe.

Within these itineraries opening from one map to the next, from one edge to the other, More, Gilles, and Raphael are simultaneously the narrating subjects and the narrated subjects: Gilles as told by More, Raphael as told by Gilles, each becoming lost in the others, one might say, between enunciation and utterance, as one enunciative apparatus (of narration) slips into another that frames it. That is how, without any break in the continuity between journeys and maps, maps and journeys, the historical and political figure of More becomes his other, which is himself, Raphael. Thus, he "destabilizes" his history, which is also the history of England and Spain, transforming it into that of a mysterious traveler beyond the confines of the known world. Or perhaps it is rather the unstable identity of Raphael, possessed by the desire to travel, who finds his consistency, his verisimilitude, his weight of historical and social reality in Thomas More, Henry VIII's diplomat on a mission to Bruges.

In book 1, the reader sees the precise marks of how fiction casts off from "reality" (the fictionalization of the real) or is anchored in reality (the realization of the fictive). He finds these marks between journeys and maps, mapped journeys (the journey "realizes" the map in the reality the map represents) and unmapped journeys (the map is suppressed by the journey "to the unknown"), between enunciators of utterances and utterances of enunciators. As we know, book 1 was written after book 2 and reinforces the anchoring of the wondrous island in the social, political, and historical known world.

Or perhaps, conversely, it cuts, one by one, every tie with this world. First, it cuts its spatial ties: It seems, in fact, that Raphael, despite his wanderings in every direction, is in some sense drawn toward Utopia like a magnet. We know that he evokes, in turn, his visits to three "imaginary" nations. The first nation encountered, that of the Polyleritae, is, we find, a more-or-less independent province of Persia. The second, that of the Achoriorum, is situated to the southeast of the island of Utopia. The third, that of the Macarenses, is nearby. From the first to the last nation, the reference points have shifted: Persia has given way to Utopia, but conversely, the traveler has passed from absurdity to happiness by way of nonspace [*poluleiros* to *macairos* by way of *a-chora*].

Second, book 1 cuts its temporal ties: The Utopians have never met men from beyond-the-equator, that is, Europeans, until Raphael and his companions arrive. *Except for one time*, that is, twelve hundred years ago, according to their annals, when a vessel of Romans and Egyptians was thrown onto the island by a storm. The survivors never left the island. As a result of this single encounter with the ancient historical world, the Utopians learned a great deal.

Twelve hundred years later, the modern contemporary world, thanks to Raphael's miraculous return, *might* learn a great deal from the Utopians. This is a remarkable "structural" reversal between two journeys, a one-way trip and a return trip. But the lapse in the logical functioning of this reversal (Raphael comes back *after having gone*, unlike the Romans and Egyptians who went but *did not come back*) indicates that it may be that Raphael's return trip was not preceded by any initial journey. Similarly, the slippage in grammatical mood from the assertion of a *fictive "fact"* (it is a fact that the *imaginary* Utopians learned a great deal from the shipwrecked peoples from the real, known world) to a *"real" possibility* (it is true that *real* Europeans might learn a great deal from the ideal society) marks this strange temporal journey from reality to fiction and from fiction to reality.

To come to the limit of the journey: Utopia is a map, as we said, but it is a map that is not on the map or that is not locatable on the map, which means that only Raphael makes—or will ever be able to make—the journey. We know the story that Gilles tells Busleiden in his letter (which, we might note, is published at the edges of the book) regarding the geographical location of the island: At the moment when Raphael was indicating it to More, a servant had come and whispered in his ear. At the same time, one of the participants in the exchange, who had a cold, was coughing so loudly that Gilles could not hear the traveler's words. That is how the possibility of inscribing the island on the map disappears, in the ironic fiction of an accident. But did not the island appear on already-existing maps? Gilles does not find it among either the ancient or the modern cosmographers. But perhaps it existed under a name other than the Greek name "Utopia." Or perhaps it was unknown to them, which would not be surprising given the number of new lands they knew nothing about that are now surfacing on the horizon of the world and of geographic knowledge. Thus, the map of the island is in transit on the maps, in the process of inscription and effacement, among all the real islands that are marked on maps by travelers who have recognized them and among all possible islands that other travelers will recognize in the future. It is the limit of all voyages, their dream or their secret figure. The map of this island is summed up and condensed in its name, the word that introduces it into the lexicon of places that are named and known. Like the map, the name of this island is in transit, in transit toward a name through the journey of the letters that compose it: *Outopia, Eutopia,* and *Oudepotia*. These three names circulate at the edges of the book, from a hexastich written by a Utopian poet to the title of the book, and from Gilles's preface to the letter from Bude to Lupset.... In these names, the "e" of happiness (*e*utopia) replaces the "o" of nonplace (*o*utopia) to cross the infinite and minuscule distance that separates a geographical fiction from a political and social fiction; and the permutation of the "p" and the "t" (*potia, topia*) moves us from time to space, or vice versa. Utopia is the itinerancy of letters in the displacement of names (and their meanings), on a map that does not find its map or that finds too many of them. It is, as it were, the imaginary or symbolic flip side of all journeys, whether of cognition, of recognition, of pleasure, or of desire; it shadows every stage of journeys in the reality of geographic space and historical time.

The Louvain (1516) and Basel (1518) editions of *Utopia* were illustrated with two frontispieces, the first by an unknown artist, the second by the Holbein brothers, Ambrosius and Hans. They show, in their similarities and in their differences, everything we have tried to say about the journey to Utopia and on the map. In each of the illustrations, there is a ship, a figure of the journey, facing the map of the island. In 1516, the caravel is docked at the entry to the inner bay. A small silhouette stands on the deck of the ship with its brailed sails; having arrived at the end of his journey, he looks out at the island and/or its map: He contemplates the topographical view of its capital in the landscape and reads its name, *Civitas Amaurotum*, engraved on its map. The 1518 boat is an exact reproduction, but reversed, a mirror image: It is no longer docked, it is pursuing its course toward the coast where three men are standing on a cliff above the sea. By means of this reversal of the image, this reflection, the ship is coming toward us, toward our world. The small figure on the deck, his back turned to the island, is watching his native country approach. None of the men on the cliff looks at the island, but one of them, perched on a cartouche where his name—"Hythlodaeus"—is inscribed, wearing boots and a beard, his coat thrown over his shoulders, points with his finger to the island and/or its map, showing it to his companion, Thomas More. He *tells* him of his journey, he *shows* him, he *makes* him see the wondrous island, but only through his language. The third man, a soldier represented in profile, with his sword at his side, is listening to the conversation. Let us repeat: No one *looks at* the island and/or its map in the space of the world, in the space of the image. It has become an object of language, of listening and writing, a *text*, and if we—who are about to read Thomas More's *Utopia*—see its image and are able to dream of what the image represents, it is only through the mediation of the two figures, Raphael and More, through the dialogue, the narrative, and the description that these figures represent. We see it only as the "ekphrasis" that Raphael's narrative and More's writing have constructed: fiction.

The Holbeins skillfully and ironically engraved this play between the journey and the map, reality and its fiction. In 1516, the anonymous artist had written three "place names," *Civitas Amaurotum*, *Fons Anhydri*, and *Ostium Anhydri*, on or in the map of the island; in 1518, the Holbeins inscribed them on three cartouches that are held suspended by garlands *attached to the frame of representation*. On geographical maps, these place names are written on the represented places they name, so that the referent, the represented, and the named coincide. In the Holbeins' engraving, however, by means of the decorative apparatus that bears them, these names are brought forward visually, in front of the represented objects they name. They move in front of the image as a whole; they belong to its frame, its edge. They are posed, we might say, on the transparent plane of the screen of representation. They obliquely show the unrepresentable part of the iconic sign, the part that, if it were to be represented, would neutralize and nullify by its opacity what the representation represents. They show that Utopia (the island and the map) is only a representation, a discursive "ekphrasis," a fiction of things through words. But they also show, conversely, that every representation, at its edges and its limits, conceals a utopia, the fiction of a desire for elsewhere realized right here, the promise of happiness in a journey, and the fiction of a return to the native country.

6

Archipelago

> island: a piece of land surrounded by water on all sides
> —Littré, *Dictionnaire*, s.v. "*île*."

PARADOXES OF THE ISLAND

At this place, there is a pure confrontation of elementary forces: the motionless land and the water in motion; in the sky, the cyclical fire of the sun and the great haphazard blowing of the wind. Did I say confrontation? It is, rather, an encirclement or a siege, an imprisoned land surrounded on all sides, confinement. The island is a closed space without closure. Thus, a place is constituted that is doubly determined: First, by the circularity of its edge, bank, shore, beach, reefs, and cliffs that succeed and repeat and rejoin one another in their diversity; and, second, by the limitless expanse that encircles this place with a rim of foam, the motion of the waves that break, burst, die, and begin again indefinitely. The island, then, is a double edge, one of land, the other of sea: a shore closed around the place it limits, an open expanse that the earth manages to puncture.

From it are derived other figures that repeat the first: the encampment and the steppe, the clearing and the forest, the oasis and the desert, the planet and space. Each time, the same strange conflict between expanse and place, an open but broached space, a closed place without walls, the adjoining of two edges that come together only to be differentiated. Even more abstractly, it is the edge of the formless and the limit of a form, where both exchange places and separate. It is indefinition in motion, where, by chance, here or there, at one moment or another, one encounters a fixed point: a form that receives its shape from its own miraculous presence but also from the other, its crown.

The hole and the bulge, the bulge that makes a hole in the other and that reverses it into the one. Thus, Athena speaks on behalf of the sage: "The master mind of war, so long a castaway upon an island in the running sea; a wooded island, in the sea's middle, and there's a goddess in the place, the daughter of one whose baleful mind knows all the deeps of the blue sea—

Atlas, who holds the columns that bear from land the great thrust of the sky."[1]

Most islands are merely mountain ranges or mountaintops. (Georges-Louis de Buffon, *Histoire naturelle des oiseaux*)

Here, in the language of the Enlightenment, we rediscover the abysses of the sea and the tall columns that keep the sky separated from the earth. The column has been plunged vertically into the depths of the waters. Thus, its capital is flush with the horizon, and, along that surface exactly, the sky and the earth are wed. At this conjunction at one point in the expanse, the summit is no longer lost in the cloud like the Atlantic column or Mt. Olympus. It is a simple bump on a line, a protrusion on the plane, an omphalos. But, below this, invisible, lies the implicit depth of plateaus, of mountains, of a submerged valley, and the presence of a land reservoir, it, too, invisible. From one island to the next, then, there lies the secret of a geological continuity that the gaze can only suppose, a network without break of which it can discern only discrete fragments. In their random arrangement, islands are an uncertain reflection of the regular figures of the sky's constellations; an archipelago is the blurred image of heavenly geometries; hence, the sky is inscribed on the sea in little dispersed bursts. A strange reversal of the hollow and the bulge, the continuous and the discontinuous. On the surface, there is depth. The summit is at ground level, the abyss reaches the height of the beach, and, lying along the shoreline at sea level, I am lost in the middle of the sky. The island is the place for the conversion of the sublime, provided we know how to listen to the depths in the surface and, in the undertow, the confused and endless muttering of stubborn land. In this place, I can dream of a mountain that has no valley.[2] It is the fertile dream of knowledge, a drifting undersea geology: For in moving from collapse to eruption, from slippage to fracture, the archipelago, with the help of this almost motionless history, recovers the logic of its origin. It is a fantasy, since the shaft that is plunged vertically into the ground opens onto Nemo, mystery, and onto one mystery in particular: the sea, strangely at the foundation.[3]

The island is a figure wherein the imaginary becomes caught in the paradoxes of closed and opened, hole and bulge, formless and form, and in the paradoxes of their edges: depth and surface, top and bottom, continuous and discontinuous—in the exchange of their secrets.

THE DESERT ISLE: TWOSOME IN AN EYE

What is feared from a child who survives the loss of his father?

> Let me hide him on some desert isle;
> Through his mother's care, you can be assured
> That with me my son will learn only to cry.[4]

These three lines from Racine's *Andromaque* set up the scene of absence: The desert isle inscribes in its center the mother's desire to save her son. It is an island of fiction, a passionate argument in discourse. How to make the innocent threat disappear from the eyes and violence of all, how to nullify it and, at the same time, ensure salvation and a means of survival; in short, how to hide? The island argument that Andromaque puts into words unites opposites: Astyanax could be alive yet gone, sheltered yet forgotten, buried as in his father's tomb, yet protected as in his mother's womb. He could become the new incarnation of the omphalos in the insular place: both shaft and tomb, the hole through which the dead communicate with the living, and the bulge, altar, and central hearth where a maternal continuity is affirmed in the secrecy of a home. Whether imaginary topography or exact cartography, the island in its fiction, and not only in the mother's discourse, always opens a harbor of grace somewhere along its circumference. The closed circle is broken to allow an entryway, a bay, a mouth, a port, a narrow opening where lost ships drop anchor after the storm and before the resumption of their voyage. A secret, hidden shelter where the water is smooth and serene in a land whose arms welcome and envelop. A maternal figure of the internal fold, of symbiotic passivity, the sweetness of learning to shed tears ("That with me my son will learn only to cry"). For the island figuratively to fulfill this function, however, it must be deserted. That is the only chance for the mother-son twosome, for the child in the mother. There is no third term, except, perhaps, the insular place itself, a monument to its disappearance. The island is a space deserted by all, except by the incestuous couple. It is the presence of that absence: no gaze from any direction; no institution or society preexisting dual, face-to-face presence. No code other than the code the couple gives itself. These two are subject only to the rhythms of nature: sun and night, winter and summer, the tide's ebb and flow. The deserted island is, in itself, the presence of that absence; not the absence of gazes, encounters, or even traces, marks, or signs of presence, but the absent gaze in its absolute form, the domination of an omnipresence equal to the emptiness of the place, something that is everywhere because it is nowhere. The secret buried in the tomb is constantly exposed, incessantly revealed because there is no one from whom it is hidden. On this fantastic island, in this insular phantasm, this narcissistic place, I take up residence in my own eye. To be seen by nobody. *Nobody* is looking at me. Nemo's paternal presence is felt from the bottom of the crypt. The deserted island is the best hiding place for lovers to huddle, in the universal absent gaze; it is a figure for the eye on the surface of the sea.

Defoe stages this scenario at the center of the Island of Despair, when, on the sandy beach, the imprint of a human foot leaves its mark. Where to hide, where to see without being seen? In a cave, of course, a negative island, a hollow and fold in the earth, a phantasm of the empty eye socket, the locus of the self.

I perceiv'd that behind a very thick Branch of low Brushwood, or Underwood, there was a kind of hollow Place... and getting with Difficulty into the Mouth of it, I found it was pretty large; that is to say, sufficient for me to stand upright in it, *and perhaps another with me*; but... when looking farther into the Place, and which was perfectly dark, I saw two broad shining Eyes of some Creature, whether Devil or Man I knew not, which twinkl'd like two Stars, the dim Light from the Cave's Mouth shining directly in and making the Reflection. However, after some Pause, I recover'd my self, and began to call my self a thousand Fools, and tell my self, that he that was afraid to see the Devil, was not fit to live twenty Years in an Island all alone; and that *I durst to believe there was nothing in this Cave that was more frightful than my self*, ... But still plucking up my Spirits as well as I could, and encouraging my self a little with considering that the Power and Presence of *God* was every where, and was able to protect me; upon this I stepp'd forward again, and... saw lying on the Ground a most monstrous frightful old He-goat... gasping for Life, and *dying indeed of meer old Age*.[5]

ISLAND OR CONTINENT, PASCAL OR DESCARTES?

"Is it an island? Is it the continent?"

Every castaway asks the same question when he is thrown onto the shore. It is a topographical variant of that other question, "Where am I?" Deprived of everything, covered with salt, exhausted, prostrate, he cries, "Where am I?" That is, what am *I* in this corner of the world? It is a question of topics, the locus of the self: "I began to look round me to see what kind of Place I was in, and what was next to be done.... My next Work was to view the Country, and seek a proper Place for my Habitation.... Where I was, I yet knew not, whether on the Continent or on an Island, whether inhabited or not inhabited, whether in Danger of wild Beasts or not."[6] "A few words again escaped him, which showed what thoughts were, even then, troubling his brain. This time he was understood. Undoubtedly they were the same words he had before attempted to utter. 'Island or continent?' he murmured.... On the way the sailor could not help repeating,—'Island or continent! To think of that, when at one's last gasp! What a man!'"[7] The question is vital. The continent is an open space, and, by taking a resolute course toward civilization, a man can put an end to the solitude of the wild. He must be self-assured in the path taken, despite the obstacles of things and men, must pursue a rectilinear course that is equal to the firmness of the project and the permanence of the intention. Such is the Cartesian forest: The travelers who are lost in it have every chance of getting out through their determination. Step by step, in their long chain of reasonings, they trace the trajectory of a path.

"My second maxim was to be as firm and resolute in my actions as I could, and to follow no less constantly the most doubtful opinions, once I had determined upon them, than I would if they were very assured."[8] Here is a moral rule for a course of action at a time when all certainty is still missing, including the first, the most fundamental certainty: I think, I am. Who am I, then, who thinks?

> Imitating in this travellers, who, finding themselves astray in some forest, must not wander, turning now this way now that, and even less stop in one place, but must walk always as straight as they can in a given direction, and not change direction for weak reasons, even though it was perhaps only chance in the first place which made them choose it; for, by this means, if they do not go exactly where they wish to go they will arrive at least somewhere in the end where they will very likely be better off than in the middle of a forest.[9]

As a precaution, while waiting for the answer to the fundamental question "Who am I?" the will's straight and narrow path substitutes for that answer. It heads not for the place where the desire for knowledge may perhaps be satisfied in a happy and instantaneous adaptation, nor even—yet—for the fixed and ascertained Archimedean point that grants the power to lift the globe, but only for some place that has no other characteristic than that of being an end, an arrival point, and not a middle, a place where "I find myself" without regret or remorse, while waiting to "ground myself beyond doubt." Where am I? The continent: By always walking in the straightest line, in the same direction, at the very end I will know what I am. Yes, it is the weak and wavering minds that turn now this way, now that, finally stopping in one place. It is they who repeat the same question without ever finding an answer: Where am I? Island or continent? The Cartesian space is an open, homogeneous, isotropic expanse where I have the power to decide *my* place by tracking the coordinates of *my* path, by determining with determination *my* course, my place, the place I appropriate for myself as my identity. If it is an island, what should I do? Reconnoiter the country and seek out a proper place for my habitation. On a continent, I recognize the country and fix my place. In appearance, the two gestures are identical. But Robinson Crusoe's or Cyrus Harding's words only formulate a dilemma in the end: Island or continent? How to put myself in the position of answering? First, I will take a circular look around to get a view of my circumstances: For I am, first of all, this surrounding, the limit of a circle that extends from my body to other things that hide from one another, that block the power of my sight. Where am I? Who am I? A place, a being defined by its circumstances: time and space.

> There was a Hill not above a Mile from me, which rose up very steep and high, and which seem'd to over-top some other Hills, which lay as in a Ridge from it northward.... I travell'd for Discovery up to the Top of that Hill, where after I had with great Labour and Difficulty got to the Top, I saw my Fate to my great Affliction, (*viz.*) that I was in an Island environ'd every Way with the Sea.[10]

"So, my friends, you do not know yet whether fate has thrown us on an island, or on a continent?" "No, captain," replied the boy.... "While you were carrying me yesterday, did I not see in the west a mountain which commands the country?" "Yes," replied Spilett, "a mountain which must be rather high—" "Well," replied the engineer, "we will climb to the summit tomorrow, and then we shall see if this land is an island or a continent. Till then, I repeat, there is nothing to be done."[11]

Nature offers the possibility of another gaze: In the unknown land, a mountain dominates. The close view at ground level is transformed at the summit into a global gaze extending to the far horizon; the land is discovered to be an island, a middle that the double edge of the ocean and the coast encloses, enveloped and enveloping. The dominating gaze (for this reconnoiter of the country is, in the first place, a visual gesture) situates itself at the mountaintop, only to recognize, vertically, its finitude of place, whatever the expanse of its vision. The end is not the desired terminus in the straight trajectory of a resolute will in a limitless expanse. It is, in this case, an *isolato* middle, whose knowledge or course can only be pursued by turning now this way, now that, then by stopping in the middle of this middle, in a place. Such is the Pascalian island, the human island,

> a middle point between all and nothing, infinitely remote from an understanding of the extremes; the end of things and their principles are unattainably hidden from him in impenetrable secrecy. Equally incapable of seeing the nothingness from which he emerges and the infinity in which he is engulfed.... Such is our true state.... We are floating in a medium of vast extent, always drifting uncertainly, blown to and fro.... This is our natural state and yet the state most contrary to our inclinations. We burn with desire to find a firm footing, an ultimate, lasting base on which to build a tower rising up to infinity, but our whole foundation cracks and the earth opens up into the depth of the abyss.... Once that is clearly understood, I think that each of us can stay quietly in the state in which nature has placed him. Since the middle station allotted to us is always far from the extremes, what does it matter if someone else has a slightly better understanding of things? If he has, and if he takes them a little further, is he not still infinitely remote from the goal? Is not our span of life equally infinitesimal in eternity?[12]

CENTER EFFECTS

Once more, we are faced with the paradoxes of the island in the universe of knowledge, paradoxes between the finite and the infinite, motion and rest: The global leads invincibly back to the local; the enveloping middle leads to the enveloped middle, motion toward the extremes to a home in the center. We find a center, that is, a motionless place at rest, but it is only the result of a flight toward the principle and the end; a center that is only the *center effect* produced by the limit at the point of infinity, its ebb and flow. In view of the ocean surrounding this little corner of land on every side, on the mountaintop, there is no other outcome than to "seat imagination," theoretical imagination, in the middle where the shipwreck placed it. It is in this place that we need to live as if in a center. Where am I? Who am I? I am on this island *as if* I were in the center of the sea. I am *as it were* a middle of the world. "I saw my Fate," which is to be a simulacrum, a fiction of being, of knowledge: power. And survival will consist in living the fiction as reality, constructing the model as history, building the theory as truth. Is this continental ontology or insular pragmatics? The straight path or the simulacrum of turning now this way, now that? I think, therefore I am where I *will probably be* better off than in the middle. I understand that I am always at a distance from the extremes and I *name* this place *center*, this place that has fallen to me as my portion and this land beyond which I perceive nothing, the "indivisible point." I name: I produce effects and, in this, I gain power.

"They say . . . and one can actually see for oneself, that Utopia was originally not an island but a peninsula. However, it was conquered by somebody called Utopos. . . ."[13] The conqueror, the man in power, can be recognized by this gesture of making an island out of a continent. On Abraxa, a chaotic continent peopled by an ignorant and rustic mob, he makes the violent decision to cut off the isthmus that attaches the land to the continent, so that the sea surrounds it on all sides, and to give the monster or miracle his own proper name: Utopus—Utopia. That is how he enters this land of fiction, this land that has no place; that is how he assures himself of his absolute power as creator, king, and father, through the simple effects of insularity.

"There was my Majesty the Prince and Lord of the whole Island; I had the Lives of all my Subjects at my absolute Command. I could hang, draw, give Liberty, and take it away, and no Rebels among all my Subjects. Then to see how like a King I din'd too all alone, attended by my Servants."[14] This parodic motif recurs three times during poor Robin's stay on his island: "It was a merry Reflection which I frequently made, How like a King I look'd. First of all, the whole Country was my own meer Property; so that I had an undoubted Right of Dominion. *2dly*, My People were perfectly subjected: I was absolute Lord and Lawgiver; they all owed their Lives to me, and were ready to lay down their Lives, *if there had been Occasion of it*, for me."[15] "[The Captain] told them, they were none of his Prisoners, but the Commander's of the Island; that they thought they had set him on Shore in a barren uninhabited Island, but it had pleased God to direct them, that the Island was inhabited, and that the Governour was an *English* Man; that he might hang them all there, if he pleased."[16] The first time, his Majesty has no other subjects but his parrot, his old dog, and two cats; the second time, he has three men—Friday, his father, and a Spanish papist; the third time, he is the governor and generalissimo of a troop of eight men. But the parody is threefold: Robinson Crusoe disguises himself as a governor; he resembles a king and is a pseudorepresentative of the king; he really reigns as a king but over a people of animals. Each of the parodies parodies itself; they are simply language games that become more and more effective since the last of them is a combat tactic that will lead to "real" deliverance. Nevertheless, the first example, "There was my Majesty . . .," is the direct expression of the center effect (be it theoretical, practical, political, or social) that the figure of insularity irresistibly provokes. Act as if the prison were a conquest, the prison cell a kingdom, as if solitude were supreme power. This discourse is that of power: the simulation of a center, the simulacrum of a land that has cast off all the mooring ropes that attached it to the real world and to history—a self-sufficient, self-subsisting totality. "How mercifully can our great Creator treat his Creatures . . . and give us Cause to praise him for Dungeons and Prisons. What a Table was here spread for me in a Wilderness, where I saw nothing at first but to perish for Hunger. . . . There was my Majesty the Prince and Lord of the whole Island."[17] Here we find the divine figure of all wisdom, of infinite productivity, of omnipotence, of all goodness; the royal figure; the more and more real fiction of potency—power.

Theoretical Application. The model of insularity or the insularity of the model consists in isolating the experimental mechanism, the theoretical schema, or the system of hypotheses from all outside circumstances, in order to obtain in this closed place the greatest purity possible, and then to claim that what has been left out is negligible. The political discourse of the model is both metaphor and paradigm. The results of the operation conducted in this way are universally generalizable, and its unique products are valid for all. In this way, the real is rational and the rational real. The absolute monarch, the wise, all-powerful lawmaker for his human crew, is on his island. That is how knowledge communicates most obviously with power.

ENTRENCHMENT ON THE ISLAND

The dominating gaze from the summit of the insular mountain ends with the central enclosure of a fortress.

"What to do with my self at Night I knew not, nor indeed where to rest. . . . As well as I could, I barricado'd my self round";[18] "I block'd up the Door of the Tent with some Boards within, and an empty Chest set up on End without";[19] "I was gotten home to my little Tent, where I lay with all my Wealth about me very secure";[20] "My Thoughts were now wholly employ'd about securing my self against either Savages, if any should appear, or wild Beasts, if any were in the Island; and I had many Thoughts of the Method how to do this, and what kind of Dwelling to make, whether I should make me a Cave in the Earth, or a Tent upon the Earth: And, in short, I resolv'd upon both."[21]

This place is conceived after mature deliberation; it is the final term of a plan and not a haphazard and catastrophic encounter; the result of an ordered calculation weighing the advantages; a local, optimal action within insular space, its map charted by a geometer's gesture, its blueprint made by an architect's hand, on the surface and in three-dimensional space, by erecting and excavating. Through the delimitation and elevation of regular voids and solids, a home is established or instituted, where life is economical and reserved, ever prudent, a rigorously regulated schedule, a precisely organized space. But, first, there is an entrenchment, a place cut off, subtracted or abstracted, set apart; a closure in the middle of the island that reproduces the island's circularity exactly, but undoes its paradoxes. It is an enclosure not by means of an open expanse but by means of a solid wall, a double or triple wall with no openings for either windows or doors.

The entrenchment, the fortress on the island, is a place of an invisible, horizontal gaze at the vastness of the sea. "When this Wall was finished, and the Out-side double fenc'd with a Turf-Wall rais'd up close to it, I perswaded my self, that if any People were to come on Shore, they would not perceive any Thing like a Habitation."[22]

Two Poles, Two Islands

Once the habitation—the fortress—has been set up and instituted, the new space of the island can be constructed, "beaten" by trails and paths and marked by reference points and markers. Robinson Crusoe takes possession of the prison through cartographic knowledge, by unreeling space along his itinerary and reeling it up again in his practical memory, a memory of paths leading away from the fixed point of the dwelling and back to that sheltered place.

> I had been now on this unhappy Island above 10 Months, all Possibility of Deliverance from this Condition seem'd to be entirely taken from me; and I firmly believed, that no humane Shape had ever set Foot upon this Place. Having now secur'd my Habitation, as I thought, fully to my Mind, I had a great Desire to make a more perfect Discovery of the Island, and to see what other Productions I might find, which I yet knew nothing of. It was the 15th of *July* that I began to take a more particular Survey of the Island it self.[23]

Journeys of exploration displace the original dwelling from its central position, moving it toward the edge; and, thanks to the newly beaten paths, the center is doubled and reproduced—identity and difference. The center circle of the island becomes a spherical plenitude with two poles equally sheltered, similarly fortified by the double circular fence. Yet they are functionally different: On the edge, the viewpoint looks out on the sea, that is, the invisible eye is fixed on the possible event whose occurrence may one day break the enchanted circle of the motionless horizon, reopen the sea route and the hazards of history;

in contrast, at the heart of the insular space, generous nature offers a paradisiacal place of happiness, and the gaze turns back on itself. In this mysterious utopia, the product of human effort, the circle of the double fence is transformed by natural magic into a quick hedge of burgeoning trees, a secret utopia that precludes the possibility of the event.

From then on, the island will live, develop, and be built in the exchange between the two poles of its sphere, between the sea home and the earthly home, the potential for the event on the edges, and the overabundant plenitude of the hidden center. It is between these two poles, in the journey from one to the other, that the idea of a power as absolute as it is solitary comes into being: authentic and fantastic identification, true and fictive appropriation, equal to the distance between the fortress on the seafront and the entrenched shelter at the heart of the land. The locus of his Majesty the Ego lies between the two.

> At the end of this March I came to an Opening, where the Country seem'd to descend to the West, and a little Spring of fresh Water which issued out of the Side of the Hill by me, run the other Way, that is due East; and the Country appear'd so fresh, so green, so flourishing, every thing being in a constant Verdure, or Flourish of *Spring*, that it looked like a planted Garden. I descended a little on the Side of that delicious Vale, surveying it with a secret Kind of Pleasure, (tho' mixt with my other afflicting Thoughts) to think that this was all my own, that I was King and Lord of all this Country indefeasibly, and had a Right of Possession; and if I could convey it, I might have it in Inheritance, as compleatly as any Lord of a Manor in *England*. . . . Having spent three Days in this Journey, I came Home; so I must now call my Tent and my Cave.[24]

The island is thus often, almost always, centered twice; rather, its center is only the trajectory back and forth between centers.

In the same way, the island is solitary, but it is never—or almost never—"isolated." And this is not the least of the paradoxes of insularity. In *Robinson Crusoe*, the desire for exploration finds, in this discovery, its second fulfillment, after Crusoe has crossed the central utopia from one end to the other. From this secret place, enclosed in the middle of hills and woods, in the center of the island, does he not have (and consider the fantastic strangeness of the description) "an Opening quite to the Sea on the other Side of the Island"? A transversal, diametrical trajectory with, at its end, the ocean once more; but "it being a very clear day, I fairly descry'd Land, whether an Island or a Continent, I could not tell. . . . I could not tell what Part of the World this might be, otherwise than that I knew it must be Part of *America*."[25]

Similarly, in Rousseau's fifth revery, the Island of Saint-Pierre in the middle of Lake Bienne replicates itself:

> This beautiful pond, which is almost round, encloses two small islands in its middle, one inhabited and cultivated . . . the other, which is smaller, deserted

and lying fallow. The smaller island will be destroyed in the end by the transportation of land constantly being taken from it to repair the damage that the waves and storms have done to the larger one. That is how the substance of the weak is always used for the profit of the powerful. One of my most frequent navigations was to go from the large to the small island, to debark there and spend the afternoon.[26]

The other island, whether threat or retreat, complement or supplement, and usually both, lies on the horizon of the first. It has its place in the field of vision, or on the map, only to signify the inevitable insularity of the first. It offers the occasion for comparison or confrontation, only to efface it and close up the island once more in its splendid isolation. The little island disappears in favor of the large one in the middle of Lake Bienne. But Kencraf Island in *Matthias Sandorf*, peppered with nitroglycerine, goes up in a shower of flame and steam, carrying out Antekirtta's judgment as it disappears. And Lincoln Island, that miracle of technological civilization, is blown from the surface of the Pacific by a volcanic eruption, while its untamed double, Tabor Island, assures salvation to the colony of castaways and their return to the mother island. An identical double, a simulacrum, a phantasm, an exact or reversed image, an archaic or anticipatory image, the "other" island has its part to play in the economy of insularity "itself," as its external but nearby reference point: to constitute and institute a lair, properly speaking. Hence, the other appears only long enough to permit the same to be produced and, through it, to be established in its truth.

THE PHILOSOPHER'S URBAN UTOPIA

In certain cities, a number of houses forming a group and bounded by streets or well isolated from other houses is called an island; this is a translation from the Latin *insula*, which was used in this sense in the enumeration of Rome's sectors. (Littré, *Dictionnaire*, s.v. *"île"*)

I thought I ought to try by all means to make myself worthy of the reputation I was being given; and it is exactly eight years since this wish made me decide to leave all those places where I had acquaintances, and to withdraw here to a country where . . . in the midst of a great crowd of busy people, more concerned with their own business than curious about that of others, without lacking any of the conveniences offered by the most populous cities, I have been able to live as solitary and withdrawn as I would in the most remote of deserts. (Descartes, *Discourse on the Method*)

I can affirm . . . that I enjoy much more Solitude in the Middle of the greatest Collection of Mankind in the World, I mean, at *London*, while I am writing this, than ever I could say I enjoy'd in eight and twenty Years Confinement to a desolate Island. (Defoe, "Serious Reflections During the Life and Surprising Adventures of Robinson Crusoe")

A big city is like the ocean, and a group of houses bounded by streets is like an island (cf. *"îlot insalubre,"* unhealthy island). The philosopher, the sage, retreats into his house in the middle of the crowd, like the castaway thrown onto the coast, solitary, entirely occupied with his own survival. The metaphor is not altogether a metaphor. The big city provides support for its *insulae*, whose residents live side by side, each taking care of his own affairs. This individual isolation occurs at the most complex and active intersection of exchanges and cross communications.

"Every Thing revolves in our Minds by Innumerable circular Motions, all centring in our selves," writes Robinson-Defoe from London.[27] Every individual point, the center of the circle of its passions, affections, and ideas, is nevertheless defined only as the intersection of the multitude of others. The big city with its islands, its islets and reefs, is the propitious site for this guilloche of centripetal insularities, whose repeated and determinate overlapping defines the centers of pathos. As a result, the philosopher on his urban island, a circle in the network of intersecting circles, uses the conveniences to attend only to the search for truth, fulfilling in the solitary pleasure of contemplation the sublime desire for knowledge. "I do not know if I ought to tell you about the first meditations I pursued there, for they are so abstract and unusual that they will probably not be to the taste of everyone."[28] Meditations whose first and fundamental stage is the narcissistic insularity of the cogito: "Immediately afterwards I became aware that, while I decided thus to think that everything was false, it followed necessarily that I who thought thus must be something; and observing that this truth: *I think, therefore I am*, was so certain and so evident that all the most extravagant suppositions of the skeptics were not capable of shaking it, I judged that I could accept it without scruple as the first principle of the philosophy I was seeking."[29]

The Cartesian traveler left the forest—where the more wavering and less resolved minds would have turned now this way, now that—only to reach the big city and close himself off in his *insula*, the proper place of truth and the being of the Ego. It is a Hippodamian or American city—islands on a checkerboard, indefinitely repeated, and, ideally, with no possibility of limiting the number of squares—insular and urban utopia where the desire to think truthfully is fulfilled.

7

Julie's Garden

> Having written you a long letter on an important subject, I will now indulge in a long diversion on a frivolous subject.
> —Rousseau, *La nouvelle Héloïse*

> The Chinese scorn this way of planting, and say a boy that can tell an hundred may plant walks of trees in straight lines, and over against one another, and to what length and extent he pleases. But their greatest reach of imagination is employed in contriving figures, where the beauty shall be great, and strike the eye, but without any order or disposition of parts that shall be commonly or easily observed: and... they have a particular word to express it, and where they find it hit their eye at first sight, they say the *sharawadgi* is fine or is admirable.
> —William Temple, "Upon the Gardens of Epicurus"

> In gardens, an opposition of the same type exists between a French or Italian garden on the one hand (plants artificially arranged according to a design decided on beforehand and constantly pruned into geometrical shapes) and a Chinese garden on the other. In a Chinese garden, the grounds are extremely worked over; the earth removed to form the lake is used to make the hill, rocks are brought in and plants arranged in a manner that reconstitutes a natural landscape: and if you wish to have plants that are small in stature, instead of acting directly by pruning them, you act indirectly to obtain dwarf plants. Direct action seems to lead to artifice; indirect action looks like a return to nature.
> —André G. Haudricourt, *L' homme*

Let us take a stroll through a garden in the company of Julie, Wolmar, and Saint-Preux, through this place that has always been ambiguous, where societies have articulated nature and culture, plan and recreation, representation and pleasure, work and *jouissance*. In the theories and practices of contemporary urbanism, of green spaces and "natural" sites for leisure in the large postindustrial city, Julie's garden is a *traverse*.

17 June. "We only work to be able to enjoy; this alternative between travails and *jouissance* is our true vocation." These sentences are a prelude to entering the garden, to its fictive construction in the text. The garden appears in *La nouvelle Héloïse* as a digression, a narrative-descriptive excursion beyond the subject matter, into the margins of the epistolary narrative and, yet, at its center. In its apparition and itinerary, its placement and displacement, the garden stands in the same relation to the surrounding farmland and to "wild" nature as the digression stands in relation to the novel as a whole: central/marginal. Here, too, and through another repetition at another level, the writer gives himself the choice of *jouissance* in work, in travails, in the suffering of writing. Letter 11 in part 4 of *La nouvelle Héloïse* is a quasi slippage outside the text from within the text itself, the intrusion of *jouissance* into work. It is, in a word, a text-garden.

Let me add a word on my own discursive position. In what follows, there will be three inextricably linked scenes of writing, three repetitions: the garden, the letter describing it, and my own text. First, Julie's garden, or Elysium, is Clarens, a piece of property, but one that has been turned inside out, whose outside now lies within its own space, as the setting for its "other." Second, the textual digression (in relation to Clarens, described in the preceding letter) consists in the revery-stroll that brings the fiction of the garden into existence from the distance of a recounted past (the letter Saint-Preux writes to Milord Edouard) and that narrates or describes the garden at a distance from the narration or description of Clarens and the novel as a whole. The revery-stroll is a discourse that performs the fiction as text; that is how the garden makes its appearance. But it also appears as a digression, as the place of the writer's *jouissance* in his work of writing, repeating Julie's *jouissance* in the center of her property. Third, there is my own "commentary," which rewrites Rousseau's text as a revery-stroll, rewrites it in the margin of the novel. A certain laziness in writing is manifested in this gesture, a certain theoretical "passivity." The garden in itself, through its fictional appearance, invites us to be lazy and passive; and the slow motion of this laziness and passivity has, as its aim, the writing of my own *jouissance* in reading through the text. To this I have added, here and there, memories of other readings, experiences registered immediately. Thus, the fact that I am writing this in a garden in Southern California becomes the echo of Saint-Preux's exclamation, "O Tinian! O Juan Fernandez!" or of this sentence, discovered in Bernard Guyon's introduction to the Pléiade edition, regarding men who have reached or passed the age of forty: "Read your own life as you read a novel." I rewrite it today as "Read your own life as you rewrite a fiction, for *jouissance.*"

Suffocating heat inside and out, the extreme heat of a summer afternoon, or, perhaps, a "mystery" of the limit: Such is the place, the nonplace of this garden that is neither outside nor inside (both unbearable), the place of the neuter or of *jouissance*, the place of a *respite* rather than a *retreat* into a room. "The sole cause of man's unhappiness is that he does not know how to stay quietly in his room."[1] As a vacant place, the space of a vacation, the garden is a motionless journey, a journey without displacement that has itself been displaced to the margin of the text. It is a digression, but in this it may point to another center, or to the center's other, the inverted center that only shows up in a margin. "Elysium" is the name for a motionless and displaced journey: the stroll.

> The error made by so-called men of taste is to want art everywhere and to never be happy unless it looks like art. . . . What is the sense of those perfectly straight and graveled paths you find everywhere, or those paths leading in all directions from a central point which, far from giving the appearance of the park's expanse as they think, only awkwardly show its limits? . . . Finally, isn't it peculiar that, as if they were already tired of the *stroll*, they resolve to walk in a straight line so as to arrive at the end as quickly as possible? Wouldn't you say that by taking the shortest route, they take a *journey* rather than going for a stroll and are in a hurry to leave as soon as they have entered? (Jean-Jacques Rousseau, *La nouvelle Héloïse*, part 4, letter 11, my emphasis)

Let us make a substitution in the images and evocations, make way for the here and now, the California garden and its triple boundary line: a low brick wall with daisies, pinks, and irises; the sandy, circular path with its roses; and its hedge, thick with lemon trees, orange trees, and cypresses straight as an "i". At this triple limit of a semicircular scene, isolated and secret, a woman is lying out in the sun. The garden is the place for woman to seek recreation; caress.

Elysium, woman's place, neuter or *jouissance*: It is the name not of death in the present or of death's aftermath. It is not an end, even less a beginning. But as a gap between Eden and paradise, earth and heaven, here and beyond, the garden is the space of an ambiguous expectation, of a fiction where pagan shadows move—motionless—in the heart or on the limit of the realm of virtue. "Elysium" is a Greek noun, a fictive event, the advent of a Greek Parousia into the interstices left by the great Christian paradigms. I said it was "woman's place": Note the slippage. "Having admired the effect of the most respectable mother's vigilance and care in the order of her house, I saw something of her recreation in a withdrawn place where she took her favorite stroll, and which she called her Elysium."

An orchard, a *verger*: irresistible value of the signifier at this point. Hence the standing cypress, TREE, in my garden enclosed in tufts of bushes, opens the empty space of the scene: *O Hortus conclusus*, place of the Virgin [*Vierge*]. Presence, slippage of the missing *word*: *Vierge*, *verge* [penis], *verger*, in the suspended time of a beat, a scansion, the time of a breath, where the garden can then write its *jouissance*, "after supper" when "the extreme heat makes the inside and the outside almost equally unbearable." The place of the penetrated and forbidden woman. A woman closes and opens herself like space, and the text writes itself as a marginal digression at the heart of the narrative, the story of a passion that is dying under the effect of the law.

For the orchard is at the center of the property. It is the "natural" substitute for the house and yet is inserted in a minuscule gap in relation to it. Such is the superfluous, and yet necessary, supplement, the house where the most respectable mother deploys the rigorous order of her virtue, her work of ordering; the garden that lies so close to the house is the gap of her *jouissance* in the place of her work, the law's work of conquest. It is the supplement of a fiction that, within the space of the property and the house, inscribes its place *with no outside*, that is, as a place that is not seen. Such is the obscurity, the hiddenness of the caress. There is an inside and an outside only for the theater of representation. The entire effect of the garden in the text is to nullify that opposition in order to institute its fiction, its utopia. The perilous moment is, as always, as it has been since the beginning, the crossing of the limit by means of which the categories of outside and inside are set up as unavoidable and absolute. How to avoid this sort of *mise en abyme* or this infinite regression from one outside to the next, where, indefinitely, at every movement, an inside, an exclusion, and an identity are reconstituted? Such is the infinite risk of the double instant of the present in which the leap beyond the limit comes about. Two moments in a single moment, an infinitesimal moment that I read once more as the inaugural gesture of utopia. In the first moment, the garden does not exist as a supplement to the house because it is not seen ("this place is so hidden by the covered walk that separates it from the house that one does not perceive it from any point"). The closed place *seen* from outside is nullified; the gaze cannot contemplate it. There is no viewpoint on the garden. Because it is not a spectacle, its existence is posited in the text only to be neutralized by the law of the limit, which does not allow one to posit an inside from the outside. The garden is not seen, that is its law: With regard to the garden, the gaze loses its sovereign potency to break and enter. The *verger* is virgin to the gaze, to the Cyclops eye, the petrifying eye of perspective, law, justice, God. It is virgin to the phallic eye, and its tufts on the boundary-line prohibit violent entry into the place. "The thick foliage that surrounds it does not allow the eye to penetrate it and it is always carefully locked up." This is the timeless present of the limit. "I had hardly gotten inside when the door behind me became concealed behind the alders and hazels, which left only two narrow passages on the sides, and I, turning around, no longer saw where I had entered. Seeing no door, I found myself there as if I had fallen from the clouds" (Rousseau, *La nouvelle Héloïse*, part 4, letter 11).

In the second moment, the present of an inside is refracted into the past times of the narrative being written. Once inside, there is no longer an outside, and, as a result, the inside is the world itself, an open, limitless presence. Every trace of the passage is effaced through the enchantment of absolute closure.

Nor is it perceived; the garden does not exist for the intrusive eye when I am outside, and it nullifies its "own" outside when I am inside. At this point, the narrative, the linear trajectory of signifiers in the text, is interrupted. This rupture or spacing is that of the limit, where what lies beyond and what lies within are confused. The door disappears in the shrubbery. There is no return.

Two moments, then: the timeless present of the limit, which excludes the closed place from represented existence, and the other timeless present of the inside, where the limit nullifies itself and where another space, a space of otherness, opens. This space or place is not seen but radiates outward as the stroll that brings it into existence progresses. There is, moreover, a third moment, an instant that conjoins the first two and separates them from each other, a present instant between two permanencies, that of forbidden representation and that of perpetually productive fiction. It is the sudden present of the leap, without memory or design, a leap that makes fiction possible only with the disappearance of representation. And, in that present instant of the leap beyond the limit (a fall more like it, a vertical leap), time is nullified. Hence the Platonic "suddenly," *exaiphnès*, which intervenes in the series of alternatives, *nùn*.

A few pages later, through the voice of Wolmar, Rousseau conceptualizes this "negation" of perspective and its two poles of the eye and the gaze, the viewpoint and the vanishing point, a negation that affects space and time simultaneously but in very different ways. It negates space by constituting the place of the garden with no imaginary outside, as a pure inside, beyond any spectacular distance, with no possible representation, becoming, at that point, a body-space, a sentient being and a sensation, a body not seen but touched, caressing and caressed: a folding or refolding of the possible world, as Merleau-Ponty would say. It negates time by suspending plans, the goal of the journey, not in favor of an impossible retreat but in favor of wandering, uncertainty, an endless haphazard displacement. This displacement extends and expands the present instant, the vacant present, in a duration without orientation and without measure:

> The direction [of its paths] will have something oddly vague about it, like an idle man who wanders as he strolls along. He will not take the trouble to seek out beautiful views in the distance. The taste for viewpoints and distances comes from the penchant of most men for being content only where they are not. They are always eager for what is far from them.... But the man I am speaking about—the man of taste who knows how to enjoy himself by himself—does not have that concern, and wherever he is well off, he is not concerned to be elsewhere. Here we have no view beyond the place, and we are very content not to have one. You might easily think that all the charms of nature are enclosed here and I should be very afraid that the slightest vista might take away much of the agreeableness of this stroll. (Rousseau, *La nouvelle Héloïse*, part 4, letter 11)

The fact that Rousseau's position in "u-topia" (in the sense I have sought to define the term here or elsewhere) is hardly tenable appears most obviously in a note Rousseau added to his personal copy (1756–7), in which he falls back into the vocabulary of representation and of spectacle, in a word, into the language of the imaginary object. The essential—"English," if you like—idea is to hide the vanishing point through the curve given the garden walks; thus, writes Rousseau, "you would gain the advantage so dear to landowners of imaginarily enlarging the place where you are; at the center of a series of paths radiating in all directions, even though the paths are quite short, you would believe you were lost in an immense park.... Everything that gives free rein to the imagination excites ideas and nourishes the mind." This surprising aesthetics of economic and legal "property" obtains its effects of beauty through the anamorphosis of geometrical representation, but on the sole condition that the calculated distortions are not apparent: According to William Temple, that is the *sharawadgi* effect in the Chinese system of representation.

To underscore the same hesitation in the disciple as in the master, I shall make a digression within my digression, to consider Paul's garden in Bernardin de Saint-Pierre's *Paul et Virginie*:

> At twelve, more robust and more intelligent than Europeans at fifteen, Paul had beautified what the black Domingue had only cultivated.... He had arranged vegetation in such a manner that one could enjoy their view in a *single glance*. In the middle of this basin he had planted grasses that remained quite low, then shrubs, then medium-sized trees, and finally large trees bordering *the circumference*; such that this vast enclosure seemed, from its *center*, to be an *amphitheater* of greenery, fruit, and flowers, enclosing potted plants, prairie selvedges, and fields of rice and wheat. But by *subjecting* the vegetation to his plan, he had not deviated from that of nature.... Every kind of vegetation was growing in its own location and every location received from its crop its natural ornament.

I confine myself to underlining the few terms in the text that belong to the lexicon of representation. But Bernardin de Saint-Pierre continues: "Despite the great irregularity of the terrain, all the plants were for the most part as accessible to the *touch* as to the view.... He had made good use of the roughest places and accorded, in a most harmonious and pleasant manner, the ease of the stroll with the asperity of the ground, and the domestic trees with the wild." In this way, the text of representation insists on the desire for the caress. The harmony between the unifying law of the viewpoint and the immediate instance or punctual intensity of touch is found ideally in the way the gaze is dispersed, in its discreet dissemination:

> One path led into a grove of wild trees, where, in the center sheltered from the winds, a domesticated tree loaded down with fruit was growing. On one side the crop; on the other the orchard. From one avenue the houses could

be seen; from the other, the inaccessible mountaintops. Under a copse thick with tatajuba interlaced with liana, no object could be seen, not even at high noon; on the tip of the large rock nearby that jutted out from the mountain, one could discover all the objects in the enclosure, with the sea in the distance, where a ship from Europe or one setting out would sometimes appear. (Rousseau, *La nouvelle Héloïse*, part 4, letter 11)

18 June. Now the motionless journey can begin: the stroll, through which the most distant and the most immediate places come together, only to nullify each other. "Julie, the end of the world lies at your doorstep." The desert isles of the South Seas, "O Tinian! O Juan Fernandez!" are inscribed in the fiction of the orchard, in this same orchard where childhood memories reappear in the distance, an "other" scene that is present here and now.

In a single *blow*, the totality of the natural world makes its appearance in the sensible world, as *coolness*. The tree is, first of all, a dark shadow; the lawn, greenery in motion; the flower, dispersion; water, a bird's call. The ancient topos of the garden and all its cultural sedimentations—its Greek scenography and the objects it displays to signal fleeting happiness—are displaced in an instant from the pastoral text to the sensible body. Transport or rapture, a metaphor that moves from literary topos to the sensible shock by a body. But the instant of sensation ("I was struck by an agreeable sensation of coolness") is replicated in the imaginary, in the ideal fiction of a place, the most wild, the most solitary place in nature, the fiction of an originary penetration, to be resolved finally in the representation of a fascinated gaze. Hence, in the same instant, the theater of the world has disappeared in favor of a shock of the senses *and* has reappeared in the place of the garden.

The garden appears "originally" as a miniaturized landscape resulting from a varied combination of a certain number of fixed elements (the tree, the spring, the grass, the woods with diverse species of trees, the ground cover of flowers), which produce effects on the senses and on the imagination: the coolness of shade, but also the awakening of desire and its fulfillment, the perpetual spring of a happy life, the denial of death. This set of qualities "functions" historically as a topics, a generative matrix; hence, the woods become the grove; the combination of tree, prairie, and stream becomes the *locus amoenus*; and so on.[2]

This locus is also a locus of writing: The immediacy of contact between sentient being and sensation is repeated and distended in the narrative, where the enunciating "I" seizes hold of himself within the unimpeachable distance of reflexivity, where sensation is instituted as signifying object. In the *supposed* orchard, Saint-Preux *believes* he sees the most wild, most solitary place of nature, before language and memories intervene. This double movement of reflection is marked by the modal verbs of appearance and simulation, but only so that it can be nullified. For if the orchard is only a "false" orchard, it is because, in the letter addressed to Milord Edouard, nature in its entirety has been enclosed within rigorous limits and yet still produces as immediate sensation the complexity, the infinite variety of its sensible substance. But Saint-Preux *believes* he sees the most solitary and wild place only because the immediacy of contact is concealed at the very moment it is written and asserted, becoming merely the simulation of a "desert." Thus, the letter itself becomes a garden and the text an orchard, since the moments of its enunciation reiterate the ancient paradox of the garden, its unsurpassable contradiction, where art and nature, artifice and truth, the imaginary and the real, representation and being, mimesis and the original all play hide and seek with one another. The logic of the garden and the loci of the text are those of the imaginary: a displacement of space from nature to a privileged locus where its infinite diversity, its inexhaustible profusion, and its production are condensed and summed up in a product, a representation, which is substituted for it and takes its place. The true lie of the garden, the deceitful truth of the text, of the letter: Literature tends the garden just as the garden textualizes the great book of the world.

In this instance, too, the disciple makes explicit, insistently and in profusion, the master's presupposition that the place of the garden is also a locus of writing:

> Nothing was more agreeable than the names given to most of the charming retreats in this labyrinth. This rock, ... from which I could be seen coming from far away, was called *the discovery of friendship*. In their games, Paul and Virginie had planted a bamboo tree in this place, at the top of which they raised a small white handkerchief to signal my arrival.... The idea occurred to me to engrave an inscription on the stalk of this reed. Whatever pleasure I have had in my journeys upon seeing a statue or monument from Antiquity, I have even more so in reading a well-turned inscription. It seems to me then that a human voice is coming out of the rock, is making itself heard across the centuries and, addressing man in the middle of deserts, it tells him he is not alone and that other men in the same places felt, thought, and suffered as he did. When this inscription is from some ancient nation that no longer survives, it carries our soul into the realm of infinity and gives it the feeling of its immortality, by showing that a thought has survived even the ruin of an empire. (Bernardin de Saint-Pierre, *Paul et Virginie*)

The garden proposes itself as a stroll, a revery, a motionless journey; nature is lodged in the hollow of the imaginary, and the imaginary sets forth nature itself, here and now, in its representation. This interchange is the space of the fiction of the orchard, where space and time intersect and exchange places, like Julie's and Saint-Preux's replies: "The end of the world is at your doorstep"—"Twenty more steps bring you quickly back to Clarens"; "It seemed to me I was the first mortal who had ever penetrated that desert"—"This is the same orchard where you used to take your walks in the past and where you and my cousin threw peaches at each other." Tinian and Juan Fernandez are twenty steps from Clarens; the orchard of the past, the place of playful fights and adolescent walks is today's Elysium, at the cost of a mere dozen days' work a year on the part of the gardener. Hence, the other and the selfsame exchange places; the space of this exchange is the garden, and its topical fiction is the written text.

19 June. Let us return to this last point to signal that the philosophical chiasmus between the selfsame and the other—the far and near in geography, the past and present in chronography—is brought about in a transformation of the text's form of expression. A written dialogue, that is, a live exchange between the protagonists, comes to replace a narrative written in the first person (the letter from Saint-Preux to Milord Edouard recounting, after the fact, the former's visit to the garden—in short, a slow, deferred, recounted exchange). This dialogue is no doubt written, but its deployment in the text stems not from the diegetic but from the mimetic. This substitution is accompanied by all the transformations inherent to this mode (those of person, verb tense, and so on). The narrative breaks off and dialogue is substituted. The textual locus of this change is marked, in the content of the letter, by an instant of silence in its writing, an instant of stupefaction brought about by what is sensible and what is imaginary in the garden, by the shock of the sensation of coolness, by the fiction of the most wild, the most solitary place in nature: "Surprised, overcome, transported by a spectacle which I had so little foreseen, I remained motionless for a moment." The representation, of course, articulates sensation and fiction: The garden, which did not offer itself as a spectacle, which could not be perceived from the outside, has become a spectacle within. But this spectacle is a capture, a trap, not for the gaze but for the body. ("And I, turning around, no longer saw where I had entered.") Here, the spectacle is less a theatrical representation, a staging or scenography destined to be read, than a *sensible/fictive effect*: the punctual instant whose immediate consequence is silence, the disappearance of speech. Even more important than the term "spectacle" is the phrase that qualifies it, "which I had so little foreseen." The effect trips him up, catching him in the pitfall of the present, the motionless movement of the fall: "I found myself there as if I had fallen from the clouds [*tombé des nues*]." That is, as if he had fallen from the sky into another land; but *tombé des nues* is also a cliché, a stereotyped expression of surprise. This surprise, this sudden chill, this moment of immobility is a transport, a rapture. The intense moment that trips him up occurs in place, as an intensive accumulation of sensations, a silence whose discursive expression lies in a minuscule gap, in the cry, "O Tinian! O Juan Fernandez!" the names of faraway places and journeys that are also sites from the past, a reverse nostalgia.

(Cf. part 4, letter 3: "I stayed for three months on a delightful deserted island, the sweet and touching image of the ancient beauty of nature, which seems to lie at the end of the world only to serve as a refuge for persecuted innocence and love. But the greedy European follows his uncivilized ways by preventing the peaceful Indian from living there and imposes justice while not living there himself. . . . I landed on a second, less known desert isle that was even more charming than the first and where the most cruel accident almost confined us forever. I was perhaps the only one whom this so-sweet exile did not terrify; am I not henceforth everywhere in exile?")

> Stumbling on melons, as I pass,
> Ensnared with flowers, I fall on grass
> Meanwhile the mind, from pleasure less,
> Withdraws into its happiness:
> The mind, that ocean where each kind
> Does straight its own resemblance find;
> Yet it creates, transcending these,
> Far other worlds, and other seas;
> Annihilating all that's made
> To a green thought in a green shade.
> —Andrew Marvell, "The Garden"

Between Saint-Preux's cry ("O Tinian! O Juan Fernandez!") and his dialogue with Julie, the double exclamation is explained: The most distant becomes the most immediate, a past even more remote than the journey of exile and nostalgia returns to the present. In the dialogic exchange, wild nature and the familiar past of childhood are metamorphosed into the physical immediacy of the garden. In truth, a double transformation comes about: The two deserted islands of the journey to the antipodes return as Elysium, and childhood games are evoked in the present space between death and life. And, in this, in a second reversal, Clarens, the property dedicated to the rational exploitation of nature, to productive and profitable work, finds in its quasi center and at its boundary, its fulfillment as *jouissance*. In the dialogue in which the exchange and the metamorphosis come about (a metamorphosis that is none other than a transport in place, a motionless genesis), the enigma of an inside with no outside is set forth, just as, in the name "Elysium," the mystery of an outside with no inside was suggested. This enigma is the garden: work forgotten, time nullified, a place that opens itself to *jouissance*, the moment, the stroll. This is revery and fiction, a supplement, the enigma of an *economy*.

20 June. Initial exclamations open the dialogue, and their vibrations and echoes travel underground, beneath the readable surface, to burst out at the end in the great chord of return, where happiness and despair combine, the happiness of having returned, but at a cost, namely, the despair of disappeared enchantment: "Farewell Tinian, farewell Juan Fernandez, farewell all enchantment!

In a moment you will have returned from the end of the world." Two utterances frame the dialogue: first, Saint-Preux's cry of involuntary enthusiasm upon finding on the Clarens property, in Julie's "Elysium," the foreignness of the South Sea desert isles; and second, the woman's final word that sings of return, effacing the journey. The long dialogue itself is the stasis of the most respectable mother's reasonable prose regarding work and art in the order of her home. Then, and only then, can the stroll through the garden begin and its fiction be constructed at this price. The apparent function of the economic discourse may be the following: The utopia of the garden and of *jouissance* here and now is possible, realizable, and wealth and money are not its necessary and sufficient conditions. Hence, the pleasure principle is—at minimal cost—submitted to the reality principle, and utopia is resorbed, for the time of a dialogue, into the economy of a well-conceived plan. Or perhaps it is the reverse, and perhaps that is the meaning of the enigma: that reality and calculations, work and its travails, the time of waiting and realization are all abolished, or rather, integrated, without effort and without obstacle, into *jouissance*. And, as a result, utopia returns, since, all things considered, the real or possible is only one of the dimensions of pleasure.

Here is the enigma of a libidinal economy whose key principle is uttered by Julie: "Nature made everything, but under my direction, and there is nothing there I did not order." This is woman's economy: The garden is her place in reserve. But we still need to understand how woman's direction and order is less a command, an imposition of a plan, a rigorous scheme with a natural substance, than a connivance, a complicity of nature with *Natura naturans*. The *Darstellung* of the garden, its microcosmic representation of the macrocosm, can be deployed and *displaced* only with the help of an initial *Vorstellung*, implicit from the beginning of the letter, but stated here for the first time after the prosaic and bourgeois question that the most respectable mother formulates: "What do you think it cost me to put [this orchard] in the state where you now find it?" And, immediately afterward, in an explanation of her success, which is precisely an explanation of the first person feminine's discourse on money, she posits the delegated power of the husband, the master, man: "For it is good to tell you [this is the answer to the riddle, before the formulation of the feminine economic principle] that I am the overseer, and my husband grants me the entire responsibility." This laissez-faire granted the wife, this blank check handed her, is neither the prolongation or extension of the husband's power nor a passive abandonment to the great productivity of nature, as Saint-Preux believes: "By my faith, it cost you nothing but negligence. . . . You closed the door and nature did all the rest by herself, and you would never have known how to do it as well as she." In uttering the principle of *her* economy, Julie reverses the Baconian axiom "One does not command nature except by obeying her," perhaps because, between nature and woman, a co-naturality is instituted that is more primitive than the *Vorstellung* of man, of the husband. One index of this complicity is the profound remark by Saint-Preux: "I don't understand how, with pains and money, one could *supplement time; trees....*" Neither outlay nor work can be substituted for the time of natural growth, whose symbol is the great stature, the vertical growth of the tree, a manifestation of duration in reserve, an accumulation that cannot be the result of speculation. The husband's response evokes an origin more primal than the initial *Vorstellung*, the virginal moment of a more primitive relation to the father, to the tree that was already there: "Julie began this long before her marriage and it was soon after her mother's death that she came with her father to seek solitude here." The secret of the enigma, of woman-nature as garden: the dead mother, the vanished father, the husband who, some days, has become a child again ("And from Wolmar himself, who deigned to be my yard boy at times"). The libidinal economy of the garden, of the wife-mother, is an economy without expenditure; it is nature as a whole *displaced* into her own place, *her*.

Julie's garden, then, is the inversion of the Baconian axiom "One does not command nature except by obeying her." Here is another aspect of *sharawadgi*, the problem of economy. It is not without interest that we reread the essay Bacon devoted to gardens. I will quote only the first paragraph. The essay opens with an epigraph that, from the outset, permits us to fix the distance between Rousseau's garden and the Chancellor's, a distance that is nothing less than that separating the garden of origin and the "transitional" garden of the limit. "God Almighty," Bacon writes, "first planted a Garden. And indeed it is the purest of human pleasures."[3] In this view, every garden is a reproduction of Eden. How so? By ordering the (cyclical) *time* of seasons and months into the general classifications of botany, Bacon, the human gardener, nullifies, or rather, neutralizes, the effects of genesis and destruction inherent in "natural" duration: In this way, he "realizes" the atemporality of the taxonomic model and projects its economy onto the garden, which, at the same time, becomes the perpetually green space, eternal spring, since every plant appears only in full flower, in the "springtime" proper to it. "I do hold it, in the royal ordering of gardens, there ought to be gardens for all the months in the year; in which severally things of beauty may be then in season. For December and January, and the latter part of November, you must take such things as are green all winter: holly; ivy; bays; juniper; cypress-trees; yew; pine-apple-trees; fir trees; rosemary; lavender; periwinkle."[4] And after the enumeration of the botanical chart month by month, Bacon concludes: "These particulars are for the climate of London; but my meaning is perceived, that you may have *ver perpetuum*, as the place affords."[5] Julie's "Elysium" has a completely different economy: It is not a reproduction of an Eden of classification, in which contraries exist harmoniously "outside time"; it is, rather, the repetition or reconstitution of the natural and familiar environment in the domain of agriculture to create the *jouissance* effect.

"But Julie, who until then had held me back, told me in letting me go on ahead: 'Advance and you will understand.'" The narrative-descriptive stroll is interrupted for an instant, the time of a dialogue, and can then resume, unveiling the secrets of metamorphosis in the development of the fiction. The secret of woman's or the mother's garden is to be *the parasite of the tree*. That is the unique event of discovery in the long, sweet flow of imperfect tenses, in the revery-stroll during which the garden opens its topical fiction to duration.

21 June. Nature is displaced in the closed place of the garden. This is, no doubt, one of the components of the "economic enigma" of Elysium, but it also entails more serious consequences: What Saint-Preux finds in his revery-stroll, what Rousseau elaborates in his description-digression, is not a summary or compendium of nature in the garden, the universal botanical taxonomy deployed in the space of the world and the cyclical time of days, seasons, and climates, reunited and exhibited in a determinate place and time and offered to the scientific gaze. No. What he strolls through in ecstasy enigmatically forms not a metaphor for the macrocosm but a metamorphosis of the childhood orchard. Here, in a "region separated from the universe," is the natural environment of the Clarens property. The closest, the nearest, the most familiar, the best known thing is explored along his walk: "the plants of the region," not exotic plants from India. In other words, the garden's extreme difference is nothing but a certain return of the same in this place on the property: for ground cover, wild thyme, domestic thyme, balsam, marjoram; for shrubs, roses, raspberry, red currants, lilacs, hazel, elderberry, broom, clover; for the copse, wandering Jew, Virginia creeper, hop, bindweed, clematis, honeysuckle, jasmin. Hence, the Genevan herbarium Rousseau leafed through in his mind finds its topical space in the fiction, its place in Julie's garden. In this projection of the book, the botanical examples leave the pages where they had been dried to return to the earth from which they were drawn. The flowers and plant-signs find in fiction the opportunity to return to their referents: a botanical gesture, a reverse herborization of which we find other examples in Rousseau's novel, for example, in the letters to the "dear cousin," Mme Delessert. Julie's garden is the place of a fictive botany, the topos for a pseudotheory. The fictional process of "botanical science" is a certain return of the same in the garden's extreme difference. "Theory," science, and knowledge are instituted or constituted, only to be dissolved in a sensible *effect*, in pleasure. The entire description of the garden in the revery-stroll could be read as the deployment in the fiction of the sense shock, the sensation of coolness experienced by Saint-Preux, who seemed to have fallen from the clouds into "Elysium": "dark shade, animated, lively greenery, scattered flowers on every side, babbling streams, and the song of a thousand birds." The garden, Rousseau writes, is no more than a transporting of the primitive shock, the agreeable sensation, to the imagination. In this sense, the garden is not the topos of universal nature in the space of a particular culture but the displacement of that topos and, more precisely, the return of the always-already known to the place of its sensible effect. By "fictive botanical pseudotheory," I mean an almost immediate knowledge that gives pleasure. In *La nouvelle Héloïse*, Rousseau needs the fictive topos of the garden to produce this return, whereas in the *Rêveries*, this means disappears, and the stroll in memory and in the spaces linked to it are enough to make of nature a true garden: "And while I did not find the exotic plants and products of India, I did find those of the region arranged and brought together in such a way as to produce the most cheery and agreeable effect." Such is the garden's difference, in its repetition and within its limits, from the selfsame that lies outside: The most familiar knowledge is proposed only to produce a pleasurable effect. "One only works, one only knows, in order to enjoy": a bodily pleasure, a simple sensation of coolness, the pleasure of breathing during the suffocating heat of one hot summer afternoon.

Let me add a short semantic note on the distribution of verb tenses throughout the stroll through Julie's garden. There are two initial occurrences of the preterit, the time of past events, in the narrative memoir: first, during the stroll, and second, in the discovery of the pleasurable effect. The first preterit indicates duration in the past: "I began to move [je me mis à parcourir] through this metamorphosed orchard in ecstasy." The second marks the advent of the revery-fiction, framing the discovery that the garden's difference is none other than the repetition of the same in pleasure. "I did find [je trouvai] [the plants] of the region arranged and brought together in such a way as to produce the most cheery and agreeable effect." There follows a long series of descriptive imperfect tenses to establish the background, the decor, or rather, the display, the echo of the effect: "A thousand flowers were shining [On voyait briller] there.... From time to time I would discover [je rencontrais].... I would see [je voyais] here and there without order or symmetry.... I would follow [je suivais] the tortuous pathways.... It was as if the garlands were thrown [semblaient jetées] negligently." Then the second discovery, the second narrative event intervenes. This incident in the itinerary no longer concerns the cover, the ground, or the scene of the place, but the tree, which points as it were to the kernel of the initial sensation: "Only then did I discover, not without surprise, that the thick green shade that imposed itself from so far off was formed only by these creeping and parasitical plants that, guided along the trees, surrounded their tops with the thickest foliage and their base with shadow and coolness." Here we have the retrospective discovery of a cause whose effects had already been described in the metaphors of the garland and drapery. "I even observed that by means of a rather simple industry they had made several of these plants take root on the trunks of the trees in such a way that they extended even further but had less distance to travel."

The creeping plant is the parasite of the tree just as the garden is the parasite of the property and letter 11 is the parasite of the novel about Saint-Preux and Julie. There is a marginality at every level, even at the level of my own discourse, my own reading in relation to Rousseau's text. And, yet, I have the feeling, like Saint-Preux and Rousseau, that something important and central is at play in this marginality: *jouissance* as the removal of the guilt linked to work and, conversely, the universally guilty pleasure that is justified in the garden because it has no other end but itself. In a word, what is at issue is once more the garden's femininity. Perhaps this is its most extreme difference, the very sense of the return of the same in the pleasurable effect, since "only in this place had the useful been sacrificed to the agreeable." To *eat* an unappetizing piece of fruit in this "artificial desert" has no other function than to produce the pleasure of surprise, "of seeking and choosing."

> Luxurious man, to bring his vice in use
> Did after him the world seduce;
> And from the fields and flowers and plants allure
> Where Nature was most plain and pure
> He first enclosed within the garden's square
> A dead and standing pool of air:
> And a more luscious earth from them did knead,
> Which stupefied them while it fed.
> The pink grew then as double as his mind;
> The nutriment did change the kind.
> With strange perfumes he did the roses taint:
> And flowers themselves were taught to paint.
>
> Another world was searched, through oceans new,
> To find the *Marvel of Peru*.
> And yet these rarities might be allowed,
> To Man, that sovereign thing and proud,
> Had he not dealt between the bark and tree,
> Forbidden mixtures there to see.
> No plant now knew the stock from which it came;
> The grafts upon the wild the tame,
> That the uncertain and adult'rate fruit
> Might put the palate in dispute
> This green seraglio has its eunuchs too,
> Lest any tyrant him outdo;
> And in the cherry he does Nature vex,
> To procreate without a sex.
> —Andrew Marvell, "The Mower Against Gardens"

To trace the value of Saint-Preux's discovery, which provides him the key to the economic enigma of "Elysium" as a libidinal economy, we need only bring together a few scattered texts from Rousseau: an anthology, a botanical bouquet, in short, a garden of texts. From the *Dictionnaire de botanique*, we glean: "parasites: plants that are born and grow on other plants and are nourished on their substance. The cuscuta, mistletoe, and several types of moss and lichen are parasitical plants"; "graft: an operation by which one *forces* [my emphasis] the sap of one tree to pass through the vascular system of another; as a result, since the vascular systems of these two plants do not have the same shape and dimensions and are not placed exactly facing one another, the sap, in being divided, is forced to become more refined, which then produces better and tastier fruit.... The term 'graft' is given to the portion that is united and the *subject* [my emphasis] of the tree to which it is joined." Consider, as well, this passage from letter 7, written to Mme Delessert:

> My dear friend, one must not give to botany an importance it does not have; it is a study of pure curiosity that has no more real usefulness than what a thinking and feeling being can draw from the observation of nature and the wonders of the universe. Man has denatured many things to convert them better to his use, and in that there is no reason for blame; but it is no less true that he has often disfigured them and that when he believes he is truly studying nature by examining the works his own hands have fashioned, he errs. This error occurs particularly in civil society and also in gardens. These double flowers we admire in flower beds are monsters stripped of the ability to produce their own kind, an ability that nature has bestowed on all organic beings. Fruit trees are in almost the same situation on account of the graft.

Setting aside the double flower, the artificial "asexual" flower created for the benefit of cultural ostentation, we simply note that the graft of the fruit tree is nothing other than a useful teratology that diverts botany into horticulture. This diversion is termed the "transformation of nature into culture," which is constantly coming about on the Clarens property. In opposition to the Clarens graft, the parasitism of creeping plants in Julie's garden is a kind of natural perversion within culture itself—this desert *is* artificial—not in the interest of a knowledge of nature, as in the letter to Mme Delessert, but for mere sensation, the pleasure of coolness. That pleasure is prolonged and replicated in the pleasure drawn from the discovery of a cultivated fruit that has been turned away from its utilitarian function, diverted toward nature without, however, becoming wild again. "If you think how in the heart of a wood we are sometimes charmed to see a wild fruit and even to refresh ourselves with it [note that the pleasure of the wild fruit lies first in being seen, discovered, and, by way of supplement, in being 'pleasant to eat'], you will understand the pleasure to be found in this artificial desert of excellent ripe fruits [cultural fruits one might say] even though sparse and unappetizing [two traits of their natural, wild 'referent'] which also offers [as a supplement to the discovering and gathering] the pleasure of seeking and choosing."

22 June. The displacement of nature in the garden by means of parasites is replicated in a displacement of its contrary—agriculture—in the same place. Nature and culture are conjoined into a complex "semanteme" where, far from being nullified, each is transformed into the other. The garden is thus the art of metamorphosis: The necessary disfiguration of nature by social man is brought about in the interest of his passions (the double flowers of prestige) or his use (the grafts of fruit trees); "cultural monstrosity" is changed into a natural perversion whose only finality is not to have a finality. Or perhaps it is to give a finality to work, order, and the calculations of culture, namely, the finality of pleasure.

The grafted tree is called a "subject," the parasited tree is substance and support. As we have seen, the tree is certainly one of the necessary objects in the construction of the topos; in addition, in Julie's garden, it is the sign of the dead father beyond the marital relationship. The tree is a reminder of the law, even though this law of the father, of the husband, permits the daughter and spouse to have power—her own power—in this place, through an act of unqualified delegation. In that respect, it is time in reserve, the accumulation of duration, the continued presence of the family line and of alliance, the subject of the "grafting," which, as the *Dictionnaire de botanique* tells us, consists in "inserting the eye or bud of a healthy tree branch into the bark of another with the necessary precautions and in the favorable season in such a way that the bud receives the sap from the second tree and is nourished from it as it would have been from the branch from which it was detached." In the same way, the daughter passes from the father to the husband and becomes a wife: The graft is a botanical metaphor for society, for the diverting of filiation into an alliance, through which the social cell is constituted around the prohibition of incest. Such is Clarens and its trees, before the metamorphosis into the orchard. The parasite is a displaced metamorphosis of the graft: The parasitical plant is born and grows on another plant and is nourished on its substance. Such is the garden in relation to the property: "Only in this place had the useful been sacrificed to the agreeable; on the rest of the property we have taken such care in the plans and the trees that even after removing this orchard the fruit harvest is no less abundant than before." Such is Julie and her garden, with Wolmar as her yard boy: She is metamorphosed and displaced; she is neither daughter, nor mother, nor spouse, but, rather, a woman bringing about in this place, selectively, the perversion of natural and social law in the interest of her own recreation.

The same gap that affects the grafted tree and its parasite is also at work in the third element in the topos of the garden: water, as spring and as stream; the spray of water, standing vertical like a tree, the tree of the father, which the husband conserves out of respect. "But with what *pleasure* we come every day to see this water run through the orchard. It never goes near the garden [the other garden, not Julie's, but the one that prolongs the space of the house], for I direct the same water there by other routes." The same difference in the return of the same is reinforced by the homonymy of the two "gardens," since it is the same water that plays in one garden for others and that snakes its way into the other garden, for Julie, into her own garden. The ostentatious, prestigious water (like the "show" of the double flowers in their beds), which stands motionless as a spurt of water, to be seen and admired, is diverted in almost imperceptible dribbles and great running streams onto the pure, speckled gravel, into peaceful canals and bubbling springs, true aquatic parasites of the "cultural" fountain. The same economy of pleasure that, "by means of a rather simple industry," had made creeping plants take root in tree trunks to surround the treetops with the thickest foliage also perverts the water from the flower beds and from the public fountain into an indefinitely prolonged variety of circuits, detours, and falls.

Now reread the pages devoted to the birds in the garden, to the "false aviary," and detect once again the repetition of the same process of simultaneous parasitism of nature and culture with, at this point, the inversion, or perversion, of the relation between man and animal. "'I see you want guests and not prisoners,' said Saint-Preux. 'What do you mean by guests?' replied Julie. 'It is we who are their guests. They are the masters here and we pay tribute to them to suffer us sometimes.'"

24 June. Before the comparative discourse on aesthetics is set in place, a final metamorphosis comes about, and, with it, the creation of the fictive topos of the garden is complete. "Are you still at the edge of the world? No, I am completely outside the world and you have, in effect, transported me to Elysium." Make no mistake (as M. de Wolmar did, but in a different way) about Saint-Preux's reply and, in particular, about Julie's *out-of-the-world* garden. At the end of the stroll undertaken by the lover, the husband, and the wife, at the moment when the garden is being enclosed in the text of the letter (the digression or description) addressed to Milord Edouard, all the themes that had constituted the prelude return again. The last metamorphosis is this: The garden is nowhere—*utopia*. The first exchange, which is also the first slip away from everything that has been considered or written to this point, is the metaphor of "Elysium," the metaphor of transcendence within the name of the place, but also the transport, the *translatio*, of senses and fiction in the stroll, which has brought together lawn and flower, tree and parasite, water and stream, bird and song. "'The pompous name she gave to this orchard,' said M. de Wolmar, "'deserves to be made fun of.'" With the garden's name "in excess," the husband discovers a potency in the signifying power he delegated to the wife, a potency that overtakes him, but only in language. Julie's garden is only the *play* of a name, a play on words, just as Saint-Preux seems only to have been playing on words in his reply. Even better, the garden itself is only child's play, an infantile game. Suddenly, the feminine potency expressed in the garden is brought back within the limits of mere conjugal reason: The garden's excess is, one might say, an excess "on this side," a regression of the "mother" into the playful inanity of childhood. Nevertheless, even this excess is dangerous, for this regression to child's play is a risk that order and the project of understanding cannot take. Hence the husband's insistence: This excess is a supplement, a supplement that fills the inexplicable void left by the duties and cares of wife and mother, which nevertheless require her full attention. The garden cannot and must not be her passion. The lover agrees with the husband but displaces his moralizing observation ("I know, I am quite sure," says Saint-Preux); nevertheless, the excess on this side, the supplementary and superfluous regression, in a word, the play on the name and on woman's activity, becomes a supplement of pleasure that supplements men's work. Once again, this libidinal economy is not added to the political economy of Clarens and its master but substitutes for it in an imperceptible subversion, brought about with the help of a simple coordinating conjunction. "I know, I am quite sure *and* child's play *pleases* me more in this respect than men's work" [emphasis mine].

This substitution and subversion are enigmatically inscribed in Julie's garden, in the sense that they are apparently not inscribed, are not written, and this paradox points out the mysterious out-of-this-world in which the garden situates its place: no place. How can a radical difference from the selfsame come about without leaving a trace? How can the selfsame return as the absolutely different without this return and this repetition being inscribed as work? That is the lover's paradox; he, in turn, repeats his own difference and his own return within the conjugal couple. "There is nevertheless one thing here that I cannot understand. That is, a place so different from what it was cannot have become what it is but through cultivation and care; nevertheless, I do not see the slightest trace of cultivation anywhere.... The gardener's hand does not show itself.... I perceive no human footsteps." This is the final metamorphosis of the place in its fiction: The garden has become a desert isle. ("O Tinian! O Juan Fernandez! The end of the world is at your doorstep, Julie.") But it has returned only to curl up in the hollow of Clarens, as out-of-this-world, an idea that is realized, or rather, a reality that is metamorphosed into fiction. "Nothing belies the idea of a desert isle that came to me as I entered."

No doubt, the husband will rationalize the fiction before the lover shows his astonishment and the wife makes her reply. The garden is a lie, a "mischievous prank," because nature is reduced to imitating the height of artifice: In this inverted mimesis, the traces of culture have been carefully effaced, grass has hidden the vestiges of work, and the irregularities of nature are merely the pretenses of art. The husband's discourse makes explicit, in the textual space of closure, the constitutive work of representation that is its own negation. In this way, he resolves the paradox of a product without production, or rather, of a product that is only a product through the effacement or obliteration of its production. In this way, through the negation of the horticultural enunciation, the garden becomes a desert isle, but only in representation; in this way, Tinian and Juan Fernandez can return to Clarens, but only as imaginary objects; in this way, nature in Julie's garden is the result of work that negates work, the negation of negation, negativity. This is the aesthetic dialectic of representation. Utopia is certainly the garden, but only as an alibi, the alibi of original happiness. Nevertheless, as Rousseau writes a few pages later in a marginal note regarding the husband's observations on botany: "The wise Wolmar had not looked closely. He who knew so well how to observe men, was he such a poor observer of nature?" Just as, for Rousseau, botany is fictional science, pseudotheory (not a false theory, but a knowledge whose finality is neither external—horticulture or pharmacopoeia—nor internal—aestheticism, curiosity—but that finds in the very acquisition of knowledge a wish fulfillment, a supplemental benefit of pleasure, which substitutes for knowledge itself), for woman, the garden is a fictive representation.

And the fictive, utopian gesture is underscored at one point in Wolmar's discourse, a topological point, or rather, a topological line, of *jouissance* as the alibi of happiness, by means of mimesis. It is a question of the limit and, in particular, the edge of the topos or place. "These two sides were closed off by walls. These walls were hidden not by espaliers but by thick brush, which leads one to take the boundary of the place for the beginnings of a wood." Here, the height of the mimetic lie, submitted to the law of truth-value, conceals in its very unveiling its other, its falseness, an other that is not truth but fiction. It does not matter in the least that all this is played out in appearances, disguises, and masks. On the contrary perhaps. Here, as in other places, the wise Wolmar had not looked closely. What is essential is the undecidable at play on this line, even though it is pure appearance, or because it is appearance: The play of the transitional, of uncertainty, which, far from being childish, is *true* child's play, the uncertainty about the limit on the frame of representation, since the limit, the edge, is *also* its beginning. The garden is enclosed but its end is also the beginning of its opposite: the open space, limitlessness, the woods. The fictive topos of the garden, in fact, is elaborated along this line; it is constituted by this rough edge. Thus, it is the island in the world, outside the world, closed off by open space, opened by its enclosure, nowhere—utopia.

Within a moment, however, the return of the other-of-the-same comes about since this line, this play of the transitional, is also an instant, the now of fiction that is both conjunction and disjunction, place and separation. It is the limit between the past and the future, a temporal moment outside time, just as the garden at the end of the world, the desert isle, was also Julie's garden in Clarens, transporting the lover out of the world.

When Saint-Preux expresses his astonishment at Wolmar's dialectical aesthetics ("I found it rather bizarre that so much trouble had been taken to hide the trouble that had been taken; wouldn't it have been better not to take any in the first place?"), Julie responds with fiction, *jouissance*, a certain relation between the work of reason and the spontaneity of nature. "Despite everything you've been told, you judge the work by the effect and in that you are wrong. All that you see before you are wild and robust plants, which one need only put into the ground for them to come up by themselves." Saint-Preux's astonishment, the result of the denegation that constitutes representation (Wolmar), is a false inference, itself stemming from an act of understanding based on reflection. By inferring a determinate quantity of work from the use-effect and consumption-effect of the garden—from a stroll around it—Saint-Preux's discourse (the lover's discourse), coincides with Wolmar's (the husband's discourse), that is, with political economy. This is Wolmar's error (despite everything you might have heard), Saint-Preux's error, and the error of political economy itself. In the economy of *jouissance*, the productive cause, work, is not commensurable with the effect. In this, we are thinking "at the limit," since, as solitary walkers through the garden in our reading of Saint-Preux's letter to Milord Edouard, we stroll along the limit itself as transitional space. We could say with Julie that there is only *a single effect called jouissance*.

As for the ultimate productive cause, *Natura naturans* itself, it appears solely in its transcendence, exclusive of any representation or spectacle. It manifests itself where the eye cannot see, it exhibits itself in the pure and simple absence of the intrusive gaze. At the beginning of the fiction-stroll, Julie's garden was an inside with no outside; once it had been penetrated through a fall from on high, it was only a sensation of coolness, a pleasure in breathing. Many years later, the *Rêveries du promeneur solitaire* are to be written for no one, for the simple and painful *jouissance* of Jean-Jacques Rousseau: "I have no other garden but the meadows and woods. As long as I have the strength to take my walks there, I will find pleasure in living; it is a pleasure that men shall not take away from me." Julie's garden is nothing other than the fiction of a productive cause, of the spontaneity of *Natura naturans* in its *jouissance* effect, a fiction whose components are violence and illusion.

There is, then, a complete and simultaneous metamorphosis of nature and culture: The orchard from childhood has become the child's play of the garden, where productive nature plays in turn, at the risk of the violence of fiction, the space of a habitation, the place of the *jouissance* effect: woman's place.

One final word: There is, it is true, another place in Julie's garden, its double as it were, unspeakable, a deserted place that is the reverse of the desert isle, a place left to waste, censored from all memory, a gap separated from this central margin of "Elysium" in Clarens. But it is because that place exists in the doubling of edges and limits, in the interminable repetition of differences that insist in the identical space of the property, that the garden here and now acquires its potency of symbolic intensity. It is because of that place that the utopian miracle—the necessary supplement of pleasure in work—can be fulfilled here and now. And, in the end, it is because of it that the *jouissance* effect acquires instantaneously, intensely, all its violence. This place is the grove of the "inoculation of love."

> I interrupted my letter to go take a stroll in the copses that are close to our house. O my dear friend! I took you with me or rather I carried you in my bosom. I chose the places we were to pass through together. I marked the sanctuaries worthy of sheltering us; our hearts were full in advance in these delicious retreats; they added to the pleasure we were tasting in being together, they received in turn a new price from the fact that two true lovers passed through them; and I was astonished not to have noted by myself the beauties I found there with you. Among these natural groves that this charming place forms, there is one more charming than the others, in which I am happier and where, for this reason, I destine a little surprise for my friend. Let it never be said that he will always have deference and I never generosity. . . . For the rest, out of fear that your lively imagination may become too forward, I must warn you that we will not go into this grove without the *inseparable cousin*. (Rousseau, *La nouvelle Héloïse*, part 1, letter 13)

And the response:

> . . . We stroll through the garden, we dine quietly, you secretly pass me your letter. . . . The sun begins to go down, the three of us flee the last of its rays into the woods. And my peaceful simplicity was not even imagining a state sweeter than my own. As we came near the grove, I perceived, not without a secret emotion, the signs you made to each other, your mutual smiles, and the color of your cheeks taking on a new hue. (Rousseau, *La nouvelle Héloïse*, part 1, letter 14)

A flash of happiness, a single instant of pure difference: "I am no longer the same and no longer see you the same. . . . I feel you and touch you, endlessly joined to my bosom as you were for an instant."

To return to "Elysium": "'I have only a single reproach to make to your Elysium, but it will seem serious to you: that is that it is a superfluous amusement. . . . What's the use of making a new place to stroll about in when you have such charming and neglected groves on the other side of the house?' 'That's true . . . but I like it better here.'" At that point the husband, the master of the property, intervenes and traces the rigorous caesura of respect, virtue, and reason: "Since her marriage, my wife has never set foot in the groves you speak of. I know the reason even though she has always kept it from me. You who are not unaware of it, learn to respect the place where you are; it is planted by the hands of virtue."

Parodic envoi: *You who build gardens, do not make parks or green spaces: make margins. Do not make playing fields and games; make places for* jouissance, *make closures that are not beginnings; do not make imaginary objects; make fictions. Do not make representations, make voids, gaps; make neuters.*

8

A Society of Machines

My purpose here is to analyze a comparison that appears in chapter 10 of part 1 of the *Logique de Port-Royal*: This comparison introduces a society of automated statues as an example of the obscure and confused ideas that can be drawn from morality. Its aim is to show that the ambitious man's ideal of the self, his idol, is, in truth, nothing but a phantom, a fantastic aggregate of representations and signs. In considering this comparison regarding the idea of the self, I shall first show how the Port-Royal moralist displaces an essential motif from Cartesian philosophy. Second, I shall focus on the value that science and philosophy place on the image of a society of automatons. And, finally, I shall indicate the imaginary and ideological implications of this model for the functioning of exchanges in language and social relations and, more generally, in the political and libidinal economy.

Chapter 10 of part 1 was an addition to the second edition of the *Logique* (1664), and, along with several other additions, it reinforces the part played by moral and psychological considerations in the analysis of the great operations of the mind. But the addition of chapter 10 is located in the interval between the definition of the clarity and distinction—or the obscurity and confusion—of ideas and the examination of the powers of opacity and confusion exercised by signs, as if by their nature, in the world of representation. It is supported by examples from both physics and physiology. The comparison to a society of automated machines caps off the textual construction of the confused and obscure representation of self, which is advanced in order to better prescribe the ethical and religious imperatives of clarification. This comparison marks out a certain trajectory. It begins in chapter 10 with the clear representation of self as a thinking entity and ends in chapter 11 with an equivocal linguistic sign, the word "soul." "Soul" has two incompatible meanings: First, it designates the cause of animal behavior; and second, it connotes what makes human thought possible. And, yet, in moving from the clear thought produced by a self to the sign that, in expressing this thought, renders it opaque, we find that an entirely different representation of the self has taken shape. In this view, representations and signs are combined to form a specular monster, a specter or phantom of love; but it is only the moralist's feint, his fiction of a republic of automatons that can reveal this monster.

To prepare the way for our consideration of the comparison, let me make two remarks about chapter 9, which is devoted to clear and distinct ideas versus obscure and confused ideas. First, the logicians of Port-Royal repeat the Cartesian strategy of the methodological fiction, but they set aside its application to the idea of self as a thinking entity. According to Descartes, it is impossible to pretend that the self as a thinking entity *is* not, inasmuch as it thinks. Similarly, even though it is possible to pretend we have no body and no face, it is not possible that the representation we have of these things is anything but clear and distinct. The fiction of the automaton as a theoretical object, as both real artifact and epistemological model, is made possible only through the impossibility of feigning obscurity and confusion in our representations of extension and figure. Second, and as a result, the logicians, like Descartes, model the nervous system on a mechanical engine, a machine that would explain analogically, clearly and distinctly, the illusion of a severed member, for example. In this way, it is possible to undo the error of judgment constitutive of the confused idea—for example, pain—and thus bring it back to its own clarity and distinction—for only the soul feels pain. It is in the example of the severed member that another model, the mirror, appears in the *Logique*; this simple optical machine has a different status, however, since, far from explaining the illusion, it confines itself to illustrating by analogy the illusion itself. Fiction or illusion? What does the feint we are to encounter in chapter 10 consist in, since its aim is to show illusion in a negative light by using machines to account for that illusion, even though the machines are analogues of the illusion itself? It may just be that this ambiguity is the result of the entirely different representation of the self encountered in this chapter.

In the field of morality, in fact, what is at stake is not knowledge but rather "the conduct of one's life, the regulation of one's actions, the act of making oneself eternally happy or unhappy." Yet, foremost among the infinity of confused and obscure ideas of things good and bad, the moralist encounters the self-representation of a self. For representation produces these ideas and is produced by them. But this self-representation is no longer a thinking entity; it is, rather, an object of love. Whereas the methodological or epistemological feint was impossible in the case of the very clear idea of a *cogito-res cogitans*, this feint is necessary in the case of the very confused idea of the representation of self as lovable. The fiction produced is no longer the rhetorical trope of a critique of speculative knowledge: It is a figure of self-love. Although, theoretically, it is impossible to fictionalize a representation of oneself as an object of thought, it is practically necessary to fictionalize a representation of oneself as an object of love. As long as and inasmuch as I think, it is impossible to feign not being what I am. In order to love myself and in view of loving myself, it is necessary that I not be what I am. Beginning with "the corruption of sin that separated him from God, in whom alone man could find his true happiness, and to whom alone, as a result, he ought to have attached the idea of happiness," man instead attaches this idea to an infinity of things, and, rushing to find the felicity he had lost, he invests them with his love. Similarly, he has lost his true greatness and excellence through sin and "thus he is constrained, in order to love himself, to represent himself to himself as other than what he is." When one moves from the speculative to the ethical dimension, a substitution occurs in the model of representation: Instead of a methodological fiction, a model that simulates the impossibility of a thinking entity's negation in representation, we are presented with an ontogenetic mechanism, the necessary construction, in representation, of the negation of self as desire for self. This representation has all the characteristics of a dissimulating, imperative, even imperious fiction of an ideal self, an idol, a composite phantom of the self as other, in which representations and signs, having no other homogeneity than that of figures or lures for the self's desires, become indistinguishable from one another.

That is why, to respond to the necessity of the alienating fiction offered by self-love, love for a self that is other, the moralist deploys the strategy of a practical fiction, the very fiction that seemed impossible for the representation of self as *res cogitans*.

> To show that it is this phantom [the ideal self] they are seeking and adore, one need only consider that, if there were only one man in the world who thought; if all the rest of those having human shape were but automated statues; if, in addition, this single reasonable man knew perfectly well that all these statues that resembled him externally were entirely deprived of reason and thought, he would nevertheless learn the secret of moving them by some spring and extracting from them all the services we extract from men. (*Logique de Port-Royal*, chapter 10)

There, then, is the moralist's fiction: On the one hand, a man who is alone in the world and who thinks, in whom the metaphysical solipsism of the cogito is "realized"; an "I" that, because he is thought, is a unique thinking entity; a man who is one and unique; a man who, even though he is pure thought, has a body—since all the others resemble him externally—but a body that is not mentioned, that is transparent as it were. On the one hand, then, we have a thinking soul in a body that has been denied, and, on the other, we have all the rest, that is, nothing but bodies, machines without reason or thought; but bodies with a shape that is no different from the body of the first or that resembles it so closely that everything seems to occur as if they were the same. While the body of the first being is denied in its external shape, all the other bodies have a kind of absent reason, in this relation of perfect resemblance. A singular Leviathan is thus constructed who articulates a *social body* conceived (fictively) as a system of machines—a machine of machines with a principle of government, a soul of reason and knowledge, that is, with a single and unique engineer. For this Leviathan, the original principles of sovereignty and civil society are not the passion for glory and the fear of death but merely the total rationality of technical productivity.

The engineer's rational knowledge, which defines him in his entirety, is twofold. The engineer knows two secrets about the machines, and each of these secrets is, in turn, double. First, he knows that the statues resemble him externally, and he also knows they are deprived of reason and thought; while they are the same as he in their shape, they are entirely different in the matter of thinking. Hence the ambivalence of the automated machine, which, as we know, has fascinated the Western imaginary of the double, from Daedalus to Freud. In our text, this ambivalence is plotted figuratively at the point where technical reason and the denied body are articulated with the mechanical social body and its human shape. Second, the engineer knows how to move the machines with springs, he knows the secret of the automatons' technical and mechanical functioning; he also knows how to extract all the services from them that we extract from men—he knows the secret of their teleological economic functioning. In this dual knowledge of a secret that is itself dual, one secret concerns the essence of the machine, the other its function. In terms of essence, the machine is a radically "other" mechanism hidden under a shape that is externally "identical," that manifests its otherness by disguising it. In terms of function, the machine's apparent movements are made "servile" to an economy whose finality is man (the engineer in the parable, "we" in the text). I have developed elsewhere the ideological implications and the utopian anticipations of this "image" of individual—that is, capitalist and bourgeois—rationality. The engineer in a society of man-machines can be seen to represent the manual laborer in the factory, the worker in the modern plant, as much as the robot in postmodern science fiction.

At present, I would like to take the text in another direction:

> We can certainly believe that he would sometimes amuse himself with the diverse movements he would impress upon them; but he would certainly never invest his pleasure and his glory in the outward respect he would have them show him. He would never be flattered by their bows and in fact he would tire of them as quickly as one tires of marionettes; such that he would ordinarily be satisfied with extracting services from them that are necessary to him without worrying about amassing a larger number than those needed for his use. (*Logique de Port-Royal*, chapter 10)

Imperceptibly, the moralist's model hesitates at this point, though not, of course, in its conceptual armature. Taking up the great Augustinian distinction between *uti* and *frui* developed in *De doctrina christiana* (4.4), among other places, the moralist contrasts the rational engineer who *uses* things (the necessary services provided by the machines) to ambitious and vain men who enjoy them [*jouissent d'eux*] and thus reverse the true order according to which one enjoys only God and uses things only as means toward this enjoyment [*jouissance*]. But, on the borderline between *uti* and *frui*, between movements useful for the production of necessary services and movements in the interest of the passion for mastery, glory, and pleasure, there is an uncertain, indecisive zone, which, owing to that uncertainty, is all the richer in its imaginary and ideological implications for the Cartesian machine. For we can suppose that, at times, the solitary engineer's technical reason would go astray, would be led to amusements, but only in the movements of his machines. We might even suppose that, to invert the famous Bergsonian formula, the movements of automatons are amusing only when the living is plastered onto the mechanical, that is, when the mechanism "misses." But although we can suppose a momentary amusement, we must *certainly* think "he would ... never invest his pleasure and his glory in the outward respect he would have them show him." Thus, whether it is a question of pure movements or of those outward signs of respect the automatons make, the reasonable engineer is always the *primum movens*. No doubt, he tires as easily of them as we tire of marionettes; no doubt, he tires all the faster since he himself is pulling the strings; but it is certainly he who gives them impetus, if only for a moment. The question is, therefore, Why does the reasonable engineer, why does technical reason, divert the regulated sequence of useful movements that produce services toward this type of amusing movements, these diversions? Why, in conformity with his desire, have the automated statues become marionettes for a moment? This is a strange moment in the functioning of the model, both an exemplary epideixis and an explanatory apodeixis of the society of automatons, this moment when the machines are set in motion by the reasonable engineer, not to produce *services* but to produce *signs*. Could there be something like a fundamental "desire" for signs that would constitute one of reason's drives?

In truth, the term "sign" probably overstates the matter: It would be better to speak of "signifiers," since, strictly speaking, these "signs" of the automated statues have no meaning. We could, in fact, wonder how the reasonable and solitary engineer, considering certain movements that he sometimes impresses on his automatons, *knows* they are bows or signs of respect and not simple movements, "lapses" in utilitarian movements. Must we suppose a prior state of human society, a "society" *like* real society, of which the engineer surrounded by automatons would be the sole survivor? He is alone, but his memory has accumulated not only services but signs, the treasury of a social language that he draws on to make the automatons play at speech. This hypothesis would require as its corollary a shift homologous to the shift from the state of nature to the state of civil society, in this case, the shift from a political Leviathan to an industrial Leviathan. The model with its "misses" functions in anticipation, as a utopian fiction. The other hypothesis, which may not exclude the first, would be to consider—following the text's own invitation—these signifying movements as possessing only a ludic value, in which the engineer's labor finds "re-creation," in the two senses of the term. It is recreation, first, in the sense of a game with no useful goal but with an aesthetic finality. As social signifiers outside any real society, they acquire their signified, "outward respect," only in their use, in the reflection of the one who produced them (re-creation in the second sense).

In any case, in the moralist's model, the *social* machine of machines is not qualified to produce signs. It produces only useful goods. It is men lost in concupiscence who produce these signs they enjoy. Mechanical signifiers, bows, greetings, and prostration refer immediately to signifieds of passion: fear, respect, admiration. These social signs, this gesturality of the body, these expressions of the passions of the soul, are the real object of man's love and the source of his *jouissance*, because they form his ideal self. The model, the moralist's feint of a society of automatons in the service of technical reason, allowed him to show that beyond the political economy, beyond utility, beyond even the instrumentality of social relations, a field of social symbolics opens where signs are consumed in passionate relations of *jouissance* between subjects, between selves.

To which I add a methodological remark: The model constructed by the moralist, through its very functioning as fiction or figure, produces a surplus value in relation to the objectives of the demonstration for which it was fabricated. In other words, there is an intentionality in the functioning of the model itself that exceeds the intention of its constructor. The moralist's model is a "practico-theoretical" model in the two senses this term had in the seventeenth century, in Furetière, for example: that which allows man to make things beyond his own strength and that which moves by itself through art. It is an epidictic and an apodictic model, a thought machine that, functioning all by itself through its art of narration, produces meaning above and beyond the theoretical and practical thoughts of the subject who constructed it. To summarize: What is revealed to us, in the model of the automated statues forming a mechanical social body for a single reasonable engineer, is the opposition between the utilitarian machine that produces services and useful goods (both real society as a political economy and its constructed model) and this same real society as the symbolic producer and "gratuitous" reproducer of signs of *jouissance*. This model appears only as a symptom in the moralist's methodological and practical fiction.

As a methodological fiction, the logician/moralist's model is the displacement of a great Cartesian philosopheme: The moralist fictively projects the metaphysical *res cogitans* onto the empirical (albeit imaginary) solitude of a single man thinking in the midst of automatons that are at his service. At the center of his analysis of the piece of wax in the second of his *Meditations*, Descartes had had a strange experience concerning automatons. Leaning from his window, he *saw* fake men covered with hats and coats, men who were moving only because of springs, but he *had judged* they were real men: This "real" experience posed the problem of the *theoretical locus* of true knowledge. Conversely, the moralist *had seen* real men act, desire, and speak, but, for a moment, he fictively considered them fakes to better show what real men look for and love; this "fictive" model poses the problem of the *practical space* of upright actions. Through his example, Descartes discovered that what was *said* to be known by *sight* was *in truth judged* and known as real by the mind's inspection. Through his model, in contrast, the moralist discovered that what was *said* to be exchanged or demanded out of necessity and need was, in fact, *also* desired for symbolic *jouissance* and consumption. This displacement comes about through the change in the level of analysis, from the metaphysical and philosophical to the political and sociological, and also through the change in field, from speculative theory to practical ethics. It is, in fact, the Cartesian cogito that the moralist's model stages, but only for a social and political theater.

The reference to Descartes is therefore essential but displaced, and it is with Descartes that we will once more take up the key problem posed by both the moralist's model and the displacement it brings about, namely, that of the distinction between the automaton and man. In reference to man, Descartes uses the same methodological and epistemological strategy that he had used in reference to the world: the theoretical fiction of a hypothetical creature created by God, a human body without a reasonable soul, but a creature who possessed the lightless fire of blood in his heart, as a principle for his functioning. This fiction allows him to rediscover all the functions of the real body, that is, "all those that can be in us without our reasonable soul contributing to them." Descartes adds: "[That] will not seem at all strange to those who know about automatons or moving machines." From there, the Cartesian argument develops in the following manner: Although it is impossible to distinguish between a machine and a "true" animal, it is always possible to distinguish between a machine that resembles our bodies and imitates our actions and a "true" man; the moralist had supposed this problem solved *ex hypothesi* in his practical fiction. There are two criteria for making this distinction: The first is that of linguistic creativity, and the second, which is, in fact, only a generalization of the first, is that of man's universal adaptability. It is possible for a speaking machine (or a speaking animal, like the magpie or parrot) to proffer words, or even to proffer them on the occasion of corporeal actions that cause changes in his organs; nevertheless, the machine is incapable of arranging signs or words in different ways to declare a thought, or to attest to it, or to respond to the meaning of what is said in its presence. But we should not confuse words and natural or passionate movements, Descartes adds in his famous letter of November 1646 to the Marquis of Newcastle: "These words or these signs must not be linked to any passion so that we may exclude the cry and all that can be taught to animals through artifice." The magpie that says "hello" to his mistress is not speaking. Through training, it has come about that the prolation of this word has become the movement of one of its passions, the hope for something to eat. The parrot's words or the reasonable behavior of the ape is only the movement of fear or hope *without any thought*. It is in this sense that Descartes's theoretical model is the implicit complement of the moralist's practical fiction. We might, in fact, suppose that the society of automatons is made up of speaking machines. We might then suppose that the engineer, reasonable though he is, might sometimes amuse himself with the various movements of verbal prolation that he had impressed upon his statues, but he would grow tired of them because he would quickly conclude they lacked the value of conversation. As a result of our hypothesis, a displacement comes about in the Cartesian model of the speaking automaton, from the cognitive/theoretical field to the practical/ethical and sociopolitical field. The speaking machine reproduces the signs of language, not to communicate, but for the amusement of its master. We can even suppose it was taught to speak solely for that purpose: The language of the parrot-machine is thus a set of mimetic signs of man's language, which, in imitation, draws on their "meaning" as instruments of an aesthetic pleasure. But, at Port-Royal, human discourse in its indefinite creativity is considered bad when it ceases to be utilitarian in its use and finality, that is, when it ceases to be the transparent instrument for the communication of ideas or the exchange of representations. Man must use language and not enjoy it. He begins to enjoy it when the instrument-sign, rather than being transparent to the idea it represents, turns opaque and substitutes for it: Ceasing to be a machine/tool, it becomes a body of flesh and blood, a passionate body, an eloquent body, a poetic body, a body of aesthetic *jouissance*. In a sense, this is what the speaking machine becomes when it adorns itself with the parrot's multicolor plumes or the actor's golden garments and mask. Must we then believe, as Perrault wrote (granted, more than thirty years after the *Logique de Port-Royal*), "that in certain moments, the most perfect mind can love even marionettes without shame.... That even the most sane reason often tires of keeping watch for so long ... [and] takes pleasure in dozing"?

SELECT BIBLIOGRAPHY

Augustine, Saint. *De doctrina christiana*. Oxford: Clarendon Press, 1995.
Baltrusaitis, Jurgis. *Anamorphoses ou perspectives curieuses*. Paris: O. Perrin, 1955.
Beaune, Jean-Claude. *L'automate et ses mobiles*. Paris: Flammarion, 1980.
Boas, George. "Happy Beast in French Thought of the Seventeenth Century." In *Contributions to the History of Primitivism*. New York: Octagon Books, 1966.
Canguilhem, Georges. *La connaissance de la vie*. Paris: J. Vrin, 1965.
Cureau de la Chambre, Marin. *Les caractères des passions*. London: Thomas Newcomb, 1654. Reprint, 1662.

Descartes, René. *Oeuvres*. Ed. Charles Adam and Paul Tannery. Paris: J. Vrin, 1974–89. Vols. 4, 10, 11.
Gaffarel, Jacques. *Curiosités inouïes*. . . . Paris: n.p., 1629.
Gunderson, R. "Descartes, La Mettrie, Language and Machines." *Philosophy* 39 (1964).
Hobbes, Thomas. *Leviathan*. 1651. Reprint, London: Lindsay, 1962.
Kirknen, M. "Les origines de la conception moderne de l'homme machine." In *Annales Academiae Scientiarum Finnicae*. Helsinki, 1961.
La Mettrie, J.-O. *L'homme machine*. 1747. Critical edition by A. Vartanian. Princeton, NJ: Princeton University Press, 1960.
Logique de Port-Royal. 1662. Reprint, Paris: E. Belin, 1878.
Nicole, Pierre. *Essais de morale*. 1723–5. Reprint Geneva: Slatkine Reprints, 1971.
Poisson, Nicolas. *Commentaires sur la méthode de René Descartes*. Paris, 1670.
Rosenfield, Leonora Cohen. *From Beast-Machine to Man Machine*. New York: Oxford University Press, 1941.

9

Reveries: Utopian Practice and Fiction

> We can live only in the ajar, on the hermetic line between shadow and light. But we are irresistibly thrown forward. Every fiber of our bodies lends a hand and is giddy at that impulse.
> Poetry is both speech and silent provocation, desperate with our demanding being for the coming of a reality without compare. Incorruptible. Not imperishable, no, for it is in danger from all.
> —René Char, *La parole en archipel*

In a sense, the text I am about to present is a commentary on this passage from Ernst Bloch's *The Principle of Hope*:

> What, until now, has become real is both traversed by the constant *plus ultra* of essential possibility and illuminated at its advance. This border of light, a light coming from the horizon, shining ahead, which was also reflected in the most abstract forms in almost all social utopias, now appears, if we transpose it . . . to the aesthetic plane, as a symbol that conforms to the object of nature. . . .
> The content of symbols is only the possibility—everywhere realized in the form of indication—of a nonalienated identity of existence and essence in nature; that is why symbols are affected, touched, and remain in depth. They are veiled, they signify what concerns them by means of a particularly intense pathos of "meaning" because their content is not a possibility realized to a greater or lesser degree, but precisely a possibility realized in themselves in the form of indication. And it follows that . . . if this content is found at this point in "meaning," in the "cipher," it is because the content of the symbol is more central, thus less apt to be manifested than the content of ideals.

But precisely because this essence is found in the realized possibility only in the form of indication and cannot yet be found anywhere else, the symbolic is still veiled not only in its expression, but, in the case of all authentic symbols, in its content itself. For the authentic symbolic content is itself still at a distance from its full manifestation; that is why it is also a cipher at the level of what is objectively real; it is precisely in the light of a real possibility that this notation of a real kernel that has fallen due is produced in the concept of the symbolic.

The symbolic communicates with its expression solely by means of its objectively real content. It differentiates the particular symbols from objectively real material, which their particular contents, each time different in their manner of being veiled and identical, reflect as veiled and identical. It is only this reflection of a real cipher, a real symbol, that communicates to symbols their character of authenticity, the convergence of meaning that is joined to the reality of that meaning in certain objects of the external world existing in a peculiarly latent manner.

Poetry is opening: the world itself is full of real ciphers and real symbols, full of *signatura rerum*, in the sense of things that have a central meaning.

A commentary, but only in a sense, since the text I am about to present *will forget* the quotation from which it ought to have drawn support, in order to offer itself as a reading of and meditation on the fifth revery of Rousseau's *Rêveries du promeneur solitaire*. But we shall see, I hope, that the forgetting of Ernst Bloch's text *eats at* this text, its movements and its halts, at its reading of Rousseau as Rousseau writes himself and rewrites himself to bring into being what is at issue in Bloch—fiction, utopian practice.

"The man who meditates is a depraved animal." And yet, I propose to meditate: a text to be read, a text to be written. Such is our destiny as men devoted to signs, books, writing, from and toward our Greek and Jewish horizon. It is a meditation, however, that always twists about, turns back on itself, thinks what it negates through its exertions and what negates it if it finds its way: our universal animality, the happy silence of the brute. In this, we assume our destiny as sick animals. One of the symptoms of that depravation is the desire for utopia: The spirit of utopia is the necessity of depravation if we are to catch a glimpse of happiness.

REMINDER IN THE FORM OF SELF-QUOTATION: ELEMENTS OF A THEORETICAL REFLECTION ON UTOPIAN PRACTICE

At a first, conceptual level, utopian discourse is the ground zero of the dialectical synthesis of opposites. It is located in the gap between opposites, and, in this sense, it is the discursive expression of the "neuter," neither one nor the other. Hence, it occupies the empty place of the resolution of a contradiction. At the time, I wrote "the historically empty place of the historical resolution of a contradiction." If today I erase the term "history" from the initial hypotheses of my argument, it is because history—memory, which is history—and a certain philosophy of history are called into question by this utopia itself. Utopia cannot play the role of synthesis—not even an absent synthesis, not even at ground zero.

At a second—"schematic" or imaginary—level, utopian discourse is a discourse that functions like a "schema" of the imagination, like a figure in discourse. It stages or presents an imaginary resolution of contradictions: It is the simulacrum of a synthesis. This is another displacement in relation to what I wrote earlier: a figure *in* discourse, not a figure *of* discourse. It is not a matter of describing a narrative rhetoric or an image embedded in that rhetoric, such as a description that interrupts its course. It is even less a matter of the imaginary: Rather, in using the term "schema," I designate the inscription in discourse of a symbolic matrix through which discourse communicates with its other and, to a certain degree, is nullified by that other. The practice of fiction, if you like, or of real possibilities, as Bloch says, "a real kernel that has fallen due ... [in] the concept of the symbolic."

At a third, aesthetic level, the schema, or the utopian signifying practice, engenders spaces in the uniqueness of the symbolic object it produces: a plurality of "places," the plural organization of spatiality, spaces whose noncongruence needs to be examined. Here, again, is a new question, which, surprisingly, was forgotten in my earlier work. This forgetting is a manifestation of theoretical speculation's power to repress its very object, that which it aims to raise to the level of the concept. That new question is that of happiness. Hence, we need to say that the spaces the schema produces in utopian discourse designate the place for a historically unthinkable concept, and that unthought of history refers no less clearly, in an obviousness that is blinding, to the permanence of desire, to the quest for a straight out, "wordless" *jouissance*, for happiness. Hence, space drifts toward time—the memory of a lost object, the expectation of an advent or return—"place-moments" where happiness is indicated. Once again, to return to Bloch: "[Symbols] signify what concerns them by means of a particularly intense pathos of 'meaning' because their content is ... a possibility realized in themselves in the form of indication."

But another displacement will have an even more serious effect on these theoretical propositions. Their presentation in *systematic levels* will drift—and precisely in reference to Rousseau—toward a problematic whose unlocatable point of articulation is the utopian element of any thinking *outside* the law and order of discourses, the blinding and blind place that is nevertheless *in* the discourse in which this problematic is addressed. That is, it drifts toward a textual network of problems whose nodal point is in a state of constant displacement, as in the fabric of thoughts *woven* into a dream in the Goethean image Freud evokes, in which "threads slip invisible and every stroke links them by the thousand."

I. Axes-Trajectories:
A Problematic Network in View of Meditation

A general study of the Rousseauist utopia would travel the length of both the synchronic and the diachronic axes of his discourse in order to fix the point of articulation between the two, the place of the utopian figure that is concealed and revealed as incoherence or contradiction. We will not take that journey here. But we need to orient ourselves in relation to it, to suggest this massive problematic (synchrony/diachrony) only to install ourselves in its center *and* move toward its outer limits.

On the diachronic axis, the question raised is the relation between utopia and history. If utopia has something to do with happiness and if history is, by all appearances and in its very actuality, the deployment of unhappiness in society, or even *as* society, then the question of utopia is that of the origin and the end of human society, of culture in general. How to move from origin to genesis, and from genesis to end? A negative question: How to account for the unhappiness of historical man? Utopia is the very possibility of raising that question. As the philosophy of origin and end, utopia defines the very possibility of a questioning of the historical present, even as it makes a historical derivation of history from the origin impossible. The utopia of an originary state of nature is thus a transcendental ideality, a condition of possibility, not for the reality of history, but for its critical evaluation. That is the question posed by Rousseau's *Discourse on the Origin of Inequality*: Neither pure reality nor mere image, it situates itself in the place between representing the origin of history as utopia and positing the utopian question as foundation for the evaluation of history. The diachronic axis of Rousseauist discourse defines the function of utopia in historical reflection.

The synchronic axis, in contrast, develops the relation between utopia and political theory. Here, again, the problem concerns the foundation of civil society, a problem posed in the realm of truth. What are the conditions of possibility for civil society in general? Theoretical question: What is the fundamental structure that defines the social body? Practical question: What is the form of society that can best "realize" that fundamental question? Utopia is the *value* of political theory, what it *ought to be* [*son devoir-être*]. It explores the distinction between circumstance and law, the *de facto* and the *de jure*, which come together only in the actual practice of law. But if that is so, what is the place of the *quid juris*? What is the space of political theory since recourse to earlier worlds is explicitly ruled out, and with it, any form of unhappy theoretical consciousness? What is the place of the transcendental if it is not transcendence? How to conceive of a real structural possibility? How is conceiving of that question even possible? Such is the "abstract" utopia of the contract, which plots the true utopian question, namely, the status—difficult to imagine—of the gap between law and circumstance.

The foundation can never resemble what it founds; and it is not enough to say of the foundation that, well, that's another story: it is not only another story, another history, but also another geography, though not another world. (Gilles Deleuze, *Logique du sens*)

When we attempt to raise the question of the articulation between the synchronic and the diachronic axis, we discover how the blind point located on each of the problematic axes is projected outward. One question, raised at a literal level in Rousseau's discourse, is the relation between the *Discourse on the Origin of Inequality* and the *Social Contract*, a relation that is none other than that between the (ideal) origin and the (practical) structure of historical societies, or between the critical function of utopia and its theoretical value. It is the problem of the origin and the foundation, whose corollary is the problematic relation between historical temporality and the structural space of the social body, a relation that could be framed in the form of a chiasmus: What is the time of the fundamental structure? What is the space, the geography, of the originary?

On this point, I recall the injunction utopia carries with it: the injunction for happiness, which the preceding reflections repressed. I now seize upon that forgetting as the symptom of a desire in these very reflections. The space in which the theoretical model is elaborated has as its counterpart the timeless present of structural coexistence among the elements of the totality of the theoretical social body. The origin, an "ideal" past with a critical function in the present, deploys the geography of the state of nature in a time prior to time. Historical time is supported by that other time but also negates it: This denegation is the sign of desire in theory, the sign of desire in history. Structure—the theory and practice of theory—is the theoretical form of desire. Genesis—critical ideality and evaluation of the present—is its historical form. In nullifying time in the timeless structure of the model, the theorist of society *indicates* his desire for its fulfillment and, as he signifies it, that desire disappears. In positing the origin as the phantasmic ideality of which history and civilization are the progressive negation, in that gap between positing and negating, the historian *indicates* that desire as fulfilled; as a result, the desire disappears in the critique of the historical present of the society within which the historian signifies it. In both cases, the theorist or historian finds *jouissance* in the imaginary fulfillment of desire—in the founding model of the pact or in the description of the originary state of human society.

Now it happens that Rousseau—we need to ask why—wrote the practical fiction of utopia, the symptoms of his madness, symbolic signs, in a discourse other than that of theory or history, as the radical inscription of his desire as theorist and historian. What the *Discourse on the Origin of Inequality* plots as the ideal past of society and the origin of the historical present, what the *Social Contract* indicates as the timeless center of the space of political theory, the

Rêveries (or *La nouvelle Héloïse*) deploy fictively as moments and places of *jouissance* in which utopia is produced indissolubly as the real test of desire and (once more paraphrasing Bloch) as the *symbolic* object where it is fulfilled as a form of indication: The fifth *promenade* of the *Rêveries* stakes out, in its signs and in the time and space of the world and the text, this recognition of utopian practice and fiction.

UTOPIAN LESSON

Let me introduce a few notions at this point in my discourse to prepare for what follows. How to conceive of and express both the utopia of Rousseau's text and the *jouissance* it provides? Not the pleasure, but the happiness of the symbolic text, index of the no-place place, the place of happiness. Utopia, we said, in its most radical form is the neuter, neither one nor the other of the oppositions by means of which meaning is instituted and sense is transformed. The neuter circulates and is transmitted in the systems of exchange between one and the other, whether that entails the self and the other, the subject and the object, or the past and the future. But it is also, and for that very reason, *jouissance*. The neuter is the place—difficult to imagine—of an intensity that is its own opposite, the intensification of desire called *jouissance*. The neutralization of the signifying oppositions in representational structures suspends the systems of communication in *the intensification of a contract* in which the receiver and the sender nullify each other: the notion of the *immediate*. The neutralization of the signifying oppositions in perceptive structures suspends the spatial limits of the body and the world in *the intensification of a surface* in which subject and object nullify each other: the notion of *rhythm*. The neutralization of the signifying oppositions in temporal structures suspends the articulating breaks of duration in *the intensification of a permanence* in which past, present, and future nullify one another: the notion of *instant*.

How does the symbolic object—the text—indicate this intensification? Reread Bloch once more: "[Symbols] signify what concerns them *by means of a particularly intense pathos of 'meaning'* because their content is not a possibility realized to a greater or lesser degree, but precisely a *possibility realized in themselves in the form of indication.*"

NULLITY AND BRUTISHNESS

One last stop on my way to the stroll, a famous passage from the *Discourse on the Origin of Inequality*:

> Let not then my readers imagine that I dare flatter myself with having seen what I think is so difficult to discover. I have opened some arguments; I have risked some conjectures; but not so much from any hopes of being able to solve the question, as with a view of throwing upon it some light, and giving a true statement of it.... For it is no such easy task to distinguish

between what is natural and what is artificial in the present condition of man, and to make oneself well acquainted with a state which perhaps never existed, which does not now and will probably never exist, and of which, notwithstanding, it is absolutely necessary to have just notions to judge properly of our present state.[1]

With Rousseau, we are at the limit of the conceivable: We ask a question for which we have no answer. We do not know the authentic nature of man because as men of the present, we have definitively left immediacy, we no longer exist in ourselves. And, yet, nothing matters to us more than knowing that very nature, because it is the foundation, both constitutive and regulative, of our being and of our discourse on society and on man. The nature of man as it exists today is not the state of nature, and yet it is inseparable from it, a combination of the originary and the artificial. How to analyze that composition if we do not have the notion of what nature is? What does existing in conformity with the originary mean? In the nature of man as it exists today, there is an originary part, nature, and an artificial part, the product of culture. This "poetic" element is both the negation of *physis*—man, the cultural being, negates the nature that he is—and its fulfillment—man, the natural being, is perfectible, and, once triggered, the mechanism of history necessarily assures the deployment of that perfectibility.

Hence this idea that the originary in the nature of man as he exists today is both a remainder—that which is not artificial, that which is not cultural—and a structure in itself, a state. In short, nature is both the foundation and an element of what is founded by the foundation. What is this foundation and its mode of being? This question and the way it is framed is of decisive importance, since it engages the very possibility of culture and of its critical evaluation. The foundation's mode of being is signified by the mode of the question of the foundation, and, at the same time, the possibility of history is signaled in the possibility of its evaluation. And that mode is double: temporal and negative. The originary is temporal: It is not before or beyond time; it is neither an *origin* or a *Parousia*. It has the form of time and is its synthesis: present, past, future. An originary very close to what Husserl calls the "Living Present." It is the temporal transcendental of time. But how to conceive of a synthesis of time that is not outside time? An operation of synthesis that does not transcend the elements that it synthesizes? A transcendental "consciousness" that is both in time and the deployment of time?

The other mode of the question of the foundation is negation. The originary does not exist, never existed, will never exist. The temporal—omnitemporal—being of the originary is a nothingness, and yet it is posited as a structure, a condition of possibility for our present and its evaluation. This transcendental synthesis of time is fundamentally negative. But it is a self-determining, self-qualifying negation. The state of nature, writes Rousseau, no longer exists. The present negation of the originary is relative to a past in which the originary existed. But this past, in turn, is said to have never existed. The present negation is relative to an absence: an absence, however, that is not its negation. We are not dealing with a negation of negation or a temporal dialectic of the foundation. Rousseau adds "perhaps," *peut-être*. We need to give this term all its force: Not only does the originary have a "speculative" existence on the borderline of nonexistence, but, in addition and above all, the mode of this originary negativity is a may-be, a possibility of being. A power to be, a may-be that exists as past absence and as future void. In other words, the originary as transcendental is a synthesis of time and history—the foundation as the possibility of humanity in its historical reality and as condition of possibility for any discourse on that reality—but a negative synthesis: The very operation of the synthesis is an archigap and not a hyperpresence. But that absence, that negation, that void is the very negation of the present, and this according to its threefold determination: as possibility, as a "must be," and as a negative discourse that, in evaluating current reality, negates it. Such is the work of the foundation—originary oblivion, utopian fiction, and nonimagination of the origin.

What, then, is this originary negation, this lack? It seems, in fact, that Rousseau approaches it through its opposite, self-presence, total and immediate adhesion; the hypersubject whose world is the continuation of a self radiating outward toward things, an expansive sphere of being, the fullness of primitive identification, the *representation* of *jouissance* and of originary happiness. But, in the moment of description, the discourse that produces being in the element of language also effaces it in the play of negations, effaces it while asserting it; it nullifies the representation it gives of it. We find in Rousseau's *Essay on the Origin of Languages* the unprecedented formula that sums up this movement of the language of the originary, the *verbal expression* of the foundation: "Consciousness is thus nil.... [Man] is *nil*, he is *brute*." Being, as originary innocence, state of nature, origin and foundation, the condition of possibility for history, culture, and critical discourse, comes into language as nullity—as brutishness. This negative anthropology—in the way one speaks of a "negative theology"—sets in place what I have called the neuter. It signifies the foundation, the originary in a discourse structured by a series of negative disjunctions: It allows us to conceive of the foundation in saying what it is not. It thus indicates what it is:

> Whoever expresses himself in language, through that very expression, denies himself *jouissance* [*Celui qui dit, par son dit, s'interdit la jouissance*] and correlatively, whoever achieves *jouissance*, makes every letter—every possible verbal expression—vanish in the absolute of the nullification he celebrates. (Serge Leclaire)

But that is not a mere language effect, a nullification effect of what language would, in other respects, posit, an effect that it would be possible to promptly forget in order to assert the discourse of presence and Being. The originary's mode of being is available through the mode of the question about the being of the originary. The question *about* being is the question *of* being, which the being of the originary addresses to language: The neuter, originary difference, is simultaneously a no-place place and the place of happiness—in short, utopia.

Seeking—poetry, thought—is related to the unknown as unknown. This relation discovers the unknown, but in a discovery that leaves it covered; in this relation, there is a presence of the unknown. The unknown in that presence is made present, but always as unknown. This relation of presence must leave intact—untouched—what it bears, must leave undisclosed what it covers. It will not be a relation of unveiling. The unknown will be not revealed, but indicated. (Maurice Blanchot)

II. Stroll, Revery

I interrupt my discourse at this point

> when the cowbells keep tinkling from
> the slopes of the mountain valley
> where the herds wander slowly....
>   The poetic character of thinking is
>   still veiled over
>   Where it shows itself, it is for a
>   long time like the utopism of
>   a half-poetic intellect.
>   But poetry that thinks is in truth
>   the topology of Being
>   This topology tells Being the
>   whereabouts of its actual
>   presence.
> —Martin Heidegger, "The Thinker as Poet," question 3

no doubt because it can no longer be altogether discourse, even though I am still in language. I write a text with enough holes in it that the essential of the revery passes through its lacuna as it is read; commentary as dream. Understand that these syntactical lapses of discourse are to writing what moments of revery are to reading, moments when the eyes leave the lines and signs, and when thought drifts off; but I sometimes write this drifting as digressions, memories, free associations. A collage made of as many voids as solid forms, in the margin of the text, which is both a metaphor—in memory— of the utopian place-moment and a symbolic object that indicates the possibility realized by its content. How does one write an indication, both its gesture and the obviousness of the being it produces as appearance? Yes, this text, or, at the very least, a part of this text, is in the place of the differences of the utopian neuter. In their place, substituting for them, but also situated in this place and this text that comments on it but that hopes, inversely, to be nullified in placing itself there: notes on reading.

THE ISLAND: HAPPINESS

> Of all the places I have lived (and there have been some charming ones) none has made me so truly happy and has left me with such sweet homesickness than the Island of Saint-Pierre in the middle of Lake Bienne. (Rousseau, fifth revery)

The island of Saint-Pierre in the middle of Lake Bienne is a place to live *and* it is the place of thought and poetry as dwelling, a sojourn in the proximity of being that is always recognized as a welcome in the deferred action of memory; sweet homesickness, tenderness, nostalgia. Happiness, the lost object, makes a—lost—return in the retention of memory, present memory. To call it "representation" would be to short-circuit the long, peaceful phrasing of memory, where other memories are implicitly lodged—parenthesis. Nostalgia is made up of loss as the return of the lost, the pain of absence in the pleasure of return: homesickness.

And this place is an island like all utopias, a land surrounded by water, circumscribed by it: a land enclosed by openness or an opening in space as circumscription of the place.

> This little island, called the Island de la Motte in Neuchâtel, is quite unknown, even in Switzerland. No traveler that I know of has mentioned it. (Rousseau, fifth revery)

The island has several names, and yet the traveler does not name it. It is named only by those who live on it and by those in its proximity, but in various ways. Hesitation about the name, hesitation about being: It is absent from the map or travel narrative. It is without a "verifiable," known name, whose referent could be tested. It is nowhere else in the reality of geography and history, its place is a memory of happiness: utopia/eutopia.

> Nevertheless it is very agreeable and peculiarly situated for the happiness of a man who loves to be circumscribed; for even though I am perhaps the only one in the world whose destiny has made it law, I cannot believe I am the only one who has such a natural taste, even though until now I have not found it in anyone else. (Rousseau, fifth revery)

The absence of the island is its peculiar situation. It is situated as absence, and that is what makes it unique. There is no other like it in the real world. It is not an element in the class "island." The place of thought as a sojourn in the proximity of Being, its habitation, is unique. This place is, in its singular circumscription, one man's taste for happiness.

"Happiness is a permanent state that does not seem to be made for man here on earth" (Rousseau, fifth revery). Notice the "seem." That is the illusion: Happiness is made, here on earth, not for man, but for *a* man; not an individual, a serial, distributive individuality (bourgeois individuality), but a destiny. A natural, historical, metaphysical singularity defined as the point of intersection between a destiny and a desire: on the one hand, destiny, the law; on the other, a natural taste, desire.

Happiness is circumscribing oneself, but circumscribing oneself as an island, on the island: the enclosed (destiny, the island, land) out in the open (desire, the lake, water). That singularity of existence is a symbol of desire. It produces a sign, but toward what? It indicates, but what?

The whole is more than the sum of its parts, and yet, it is only that.

It is more, and yet, it is nothing else. In fact, it is this "more" only if it is nothing else.

The *tao*: "Do not seek to determine it, you will not find it outside beings." (Chuang-tzu, 22)

Discourse: (1) Happiness—or the feeling of happiness?—is a present past. We have here a first and decisive wound (the sense of our question): The wound (of happiness) is a deferred action—the inscription of an origin in the existent—but an inscription written *hic et nunc*, written and read. Wound, scar: the elegiac feeling of nostalgia. (2) Happiness is a permanent state: a permanently present past. That is the transit, the temporal metaphor (the shift from the present perfect at the beginning of the paragraph to the present tense at the end), a singular transit in which time is nullified. The "homeland" toward which I return is already there. I am the sign of its presence. The homeland is the opening of desire, of which I am the sign, of which I can only be the indication, because I am also under the dominion of the law and historical destiny: "I" am circumscribed. And, yet, I love to circumscribe *myself*: reconciliation in rejection. (3) The text that I read, that I conceive, the text I am reading and writing today is the sign *of* this sign, the echo of its silence in writing. I rewrite the inscription, I destroy it, I trace it once more. But the intensity of the text I am reading neutralizes the "of" (sign *of* this sign). In its turn, it indicates permanence. Such is its desire.

THE LETTER INDICATES

The second paragraph sets out, in the present, the originary sign (the inscription—the character, the letter) in the element of language. It is not a narrative but the representation of the gap between the happy moment of the present past and the permanent presence of the state of happiness. This gap is the letter, the text: a representation that is much more than an image. It is an indication, an index of the "homeland." We need to draw—trace—the representative and constitutive letter.

Hence, the formula of the letter: wild/cultivated; presence/nostalgia; nature/culture; contemplative/traveler; rest/displacement.

> This beautiful pond, which is almost round, encloses two small islands in its middle, one inhabited and cultivated ... the other, which is smaller, deserted and lying fallow. The smaller island will be destroyed in the end by the transportation of land constantly being taken from it to repair the damage that the waves and storms have done to the larger one. That is how the substance of the weak is always used for the profit of the powerful. (Rousseau, fifth revery)

Hence, in the utopian place, another letter, another constitutive representation is inscribed. "The geographical referent," which exists nowhere but in (present past/permanent present) happiness, is itself double: The center of the circle repeats the duality of oppositions between the circle and its outside. There are two islands, one cultural, the other natural. The interior welcomes into itself the opposition between the interior and the exterior. The meaning of the sign is inscribed in the sign, and the inscription of duality is that of an opposition of forces: powerful and weak, substance and profit. What is the effect of that dominating force on the sign? To place it in a state of disappearance. Such is the lesson the discourse draws from it: The *substance* of nature is exploited to *profit* culture.

But the future (the ought-to-be as annihilation) is also inscribed as a present in the sign of the lake-island, in or between the present past and the permanent presence.

Here is my lesson in turn: Death is in desire itself, a sign is in the sign, destruction is installed within Eros. More precisely, the representation of Eros bears a mortal inscription. In the sojourn in the proximity of Being, in the dwelling of thought, nothingness is at work.

But that wound within the wound forms a scar in its turn; the letter is a wound and a scar, the regenerative power of utopia. In fact, the text effaces that duality. Only *the* island is mentioned, and the other island is only the colony of the homeland. "[The mind] is prey to the homeland. The mind loves the colony and valiant oblivion" (Rousseau, fifth revery). The other island, the wild one, is the other of the (cultural) island. *Pensée sauvage*, superfluous complement, necessary supplement.

For the island is also natural society or cultural nature: the social analogy of nature. (Compare, for example, the texts from *La nouvelle Héloïse*, especially letter 7 of part 5.) That society is the paraphrase of Pascal's *pensée*: Culture, second nature; nature, first culture. The end, the center, the house in the center of the island, is the synthesis of the origin, the completely positive totalization of the gap in which we have always seen utopia and which is only its trace. If not, utopia is only the teleological representation of a regression, of a "retrogression" or a fixation that Rousseau rejects, but which is a symptom. "There is, I feel, an age at which the individual man would like to stop: you will seek the age at which you would like your species to have stopped.... Perhaps you would like to be able to go backwards. And this feeling must serve to praise your earliest ancestors, to criticize your contemporaries, and to frighten those who will have the misfortune of living after you."

> It is on this island that I took refuge after the stoning of Motiers.... In the foreboding that troubled me, I wished they would make this sanctuary my perpetual prison, confine me for all my life and, in taking from me any power and hope of leaving it, forbid me any communication with terra firma, such that, knowing nothing of what was happening in the world, I would have forgotten its existence and they would have forgotten mine as well.

In that natural society, as the center of the center, stands the one I have named "sign," the one who makes signs, Jean-Jacques (but that is only a name signifying that indication).

This index-sign has a surprising structure: Let us suppose it is the relation of two *relata*, a signifier and a signified. What is remarkable is that the two terms do not cohere in any way: The signified is the law, destiny; the signifier is desire. The singularity of the law of destiny stands in opposition to the universality of desire. And, yet, they are identified in the singular unity of the sign: a signifier marked by the imprint of the law—Jean-Jacques's desire. "I wished they would make this sanctuary my perpetual prison." In the openness of desire, the prison is a sanctuary, a life sentence, definitive circumscription. Or, to put it differently: The identification, in the sign, between signifier and signified, which are nonetheless opposites, is nothing other than the signifier, the letter of desire that constitutes and represents it. That identification is the motionless fixed point of a double negation: The absolute obstacle of the law of destiny totally nullifies the power of desire to spread out and wander, or rather, it nullifies any fulfillment of desire, nullifies even its possibility of fulfillment. But, in an instant (as in the social pact), the totality is reversed into nothingness. If the obstacle nullifies the self, the self nullifies the obstacle in turn, not by transforming it, but simply because the obstacle no longer exists for an "I" the obstacle has nullified. The obstacle is *forgotten* as the "I" is forgotten. (Compare the psychodynamic model, the psychological "fiction" of force and obstacle, elaborated in the first dialogue of *Rousseau juge de Jean-Jacques*.)[2] The structure of the neuter appears at this point: neither "I" nor the world, such is Jean-Jacques's situation on the no-place–island. The absolute opposition between the signifier (desire) and the signified (law) *and* the absolute identity of one and the other signify the simultaneous nullification of desire and of the law: neuter. I say that this nullification, this neuter, is desire itself—*le fond*.

> Where is *le fond*? Is it absence? No. The break, the slit, the stroke of opening makes absence irrupt—just as the cry does not take shape against the

background [*fond*] of silence, but on the contrary makes it irrupt as silence....

[The unconscious] is always about the subject as the indeterminate. (Jacques Lacan, *Séminaire*, 28)

They let me spend little more than two months on that island, but I would have spent two years, two centuries, all eternity, without being bored for a moment.... I count those two months as the happiest time of my life, so happy that it would have sufficed for all my existence without for a single instant letting the desire for any other state arise in my soul. (Rousseau, fifth revery)

Once more, the text deploys its antidialectical dialectic in the dimension of time, following the same motionless movement. In fact, that dimension is implicit in the earlier analysis (opposition-identity-neutrality) since those three movements are superimposed and intersect in logical instantaneity. The moment of sojourn on the island (two months) stands in opposition to the "eternity" of dwelling in desire, but is identified with that eternity. The instant is sufficient unto itself. Which could *also* be expressed this way: It nullifies every other instant. It does not let it arise. Instant means desire, not desire *for*, since then it would be only desire for the other, as the aim of fulfillment and the deployment of temporality by desire itself. Here, then, there is neither time nor eternity, here there is only the structure of the neuter, that is, the instant, that is, desire: Such is the "temporal" structure of utopia constitutive of the utopian text and whose representation it desperately seeks to give. Which could *also* be expressed this way: intensity of *jouissance*—"desire-instant," that is, happiness-*jouissance*, intensification of a point on the temporal line.

THE BOOK—THE FLOWER

What, then, was this happiness and what did its *jouissance* consist in?...
Precious *idleness* was the first and foremost of these *jouissances* that I wanted to savor in all its sweetness....
One of my very great delights was above all to leave all my books packed up and to have no writing desk. (Rousseau, fifth revery)

What is the indicating sign's role in terms of happiness? What is the place of the neuter? What is the intense point of *jouissance*? Note the idea of happiness as pure reserve, as nonexpenditure.

Jouissance of the absolute reserve.

Littré defines "*réserve*" as "economy in view of expenditure." The reserve is understood in terms of the finality of expenditure. Such is the cycle of productive and reproductive exchange. The pure reserve is the counterpart of pure expenditure; both are total, gratuitous, endless. In a certain way, the pure reserve, like the pure expenditure, is total consumption, inasmuch as it breaks the circuit of exchange, the reciprocal finality of gift and return gift. Just as, a moment earlier, the opposition between law and desire, prison and sanctuary, was transformed into an identity in the field of desire, here the opposition between expenditure and reserve, between settling in permanently and departing immediately, whirls *immediately* into identity. The reserve is a potentiality of exchange, but the pure reserve is the reserve of that very potentiality. And it alone is capable of providing total *jouissance*. Settling in is not settling in: Settling in would mean writing, reading, opening the book, opening boxes of books, completing the library, in short, the time of communication and exchange. Not settling in is also circumscribed by rules: Don't unpack anything, "leave all my books packed ... have no writing desk," images of the circumscription of the field and of closure, or perhaps it would be better to say nonopening. "The circumscription of the field by rules is less a closure than a sweeping away of the field, its reversal." To make the enclosure a nonplace: "Living in the place where I intended to end my days as if I were at an inn that I would have to leave the next day."

Consider the following passage by J.-F. Lyotard on the *coïtus reservatus*, and read it against the passage on masturbation and love from Rousseau's *Confessions*, with its signal phrase, "it was impossible to make with impunity the short trip that separated me from her":

> It is the act that determines in itself its intensity beyond measure. One enters into undecidable, incomparable singularity. The rule is no longer a line drawn around the field that encloses what must be done and excludes what must not be done. Rather, in turning about on itself in an oscillating rotation, it puts what is happening beyond reach and beyond memory; *it now serves only to engender, through the impossibility of situating the act in relation to it, this nonplace or this inconceivable place that is precisely the passing of intensity. A line engendering an evanescent region where emotion flares up.* (my emphasis)

Jouissance in the place of the neuter or the neutralizing identification of pure expenditure and pure reserve.

> In the place of those sorry papers and books, I would fill my room with flowers and hay; for at the time I was in my first botanical fervor.... (Rousseau, fifth revery)

Opposition between the book and the flower, work and amusement. In this botanizing, "the mind has no other duty than to make itself the transparent means through which a fragment of reality is replicated without alteration."[3] The assertion of the identical, the taste for the botanical finds in the plant from the herbarium a commemorative sign of a happy past event, "a mediation that intervenes to establish the immediate presence of the memory ... a mediation that consists in awakening sense experience in its integrity."[4] The room full of flowers, the herbarium-dwelling, is a reserve for the immediate past, a memory, but a memory Jean-Jacques inhabits, a reserve of happy plenitude, the condensation of botanical walks into a circumscribed place that, in its spatial reality, is a memory that lodges the subject and a duplication of the island of happiness in its representation. It is the botanical map of the island that Rousseau undertakes to chart, its (botanical) description, without residue or lack: "I undertook ... to describe all the plants of the island without omitting a single one.... I did not want to leave a tuft of grass, an atom of vegetation that was not amply described" (Rousseau, fifth revery). The writing of a natural, unfolded, transparent, open text, a mimetic representation of natural reality. "To that effect, I had *divided* [the island] into little squares with the intention of going over them one after the other in every season." But it is not a matter of knowledge but, rather, of *jouissance*: Leave the surprise of happiness intact. "Nothing is more exceptional than the delight, the ecstasy I felt with each observation." The letter of desire, both constitutive and representative, here becomes a text, but a double text, in which it is possible to read *jouissance* between the lines, between the "volumes": the book of knowledge, the library of culture enclosed in boxes, unread, held in reserve, in an infinite reserve through endless economy; and the book of nature, the memory-dwelling of open botany, in which nature is read and represented in its text, infinitely expended in a pure gratuitousness, in a consumption without finality, in an endless finality, a natural art. A double text that inscribes the gap between the gratuitousness of pure reserve and that of pure expenditure in the narrative of memory; a gap or undecidability, an oscillating line that opens the text I am reading, its narrative, to the utopian space, "this nonplace or this inconceivable place," an intensification of a moment-place: *jouissance*.

DRIFTING

> When everyone was still at the table, I would slip away and jump into a boat by myself and would steer it to the middle of the lake when the water was calm, and there, lying in the boat, my eyes turned toward the sky, I would let myself go and would drift slowly with the water.... Other times ... I would amuse myself by hugging the verdant banks of the island.... But one of my most frequent navigations was to go from the large to the small island, to debark there and spend the afternoon, sometimes on very circumscribed walks and sometimes by taking my place at the summit of a sandy hillock covered with grass. (Rousseau, fifth revery)

In the place of the center, journeys mark out the totality of space and unite it with time through the scansion of strolls. But, at the same time, there is an experience of nullity, the experience of the "plural" neuter. On the one hand, drifting; on the other, the stroll. The dominance of drifting: The stroll is the pole in relation to which drifting is marked off or is marked by its very absence of mark. Drifting on the water is the journey of continuous time-space.

It is the nonarticulation of a line without end (without goal or terminus): pure movement itself. He does not look at the bank, he does not *measure* the path taken by the reference points on the bank. His movement is not relative but absolute. The bank is to drifting what attachment is to detachment: *rivel dérive*.

A passive synthesis of time and space? The only external reference is the sky, a deep, continuous space, an unmarked, unarticulated permanence, a nonreference. Space is the sky, time is drifting: time-space. Time is not a succession of moments or instants but a single in-difference we could also call presence without difference, that is, space, the neuter of time. The continuity of the drifting movement is the continuity of limitless space, and, thus, the limitlessness of time. Hence this equation: Motionless time = movement = rest = present space: movement = rest = instant = duration.

The body plays dead: It is not only a body lying in the boat but a body "laid out," a dead body, eyes open in the death barge, which does not cross the Styx guided by Charon toward the other bank, but drifts, merely passing. He does not sleep—to sleep, to dream. But he has the posture of one sleeping, and also the ritual posture of death: Life moves—no, that is too strong—drifts toward the instant of death, a slow movement toward the identification of opposites, life and death, neither life nor death, life's mimicry of death and vice versa. A life more "profound" than life, if you like.

In the experience of the neuter, I see the experience of the originary, which is not only the passive synthesis of time, in a fundamental sense, experience, but a passive synthesis of time and space in which the oppositions that articulate the world in thought and make it conceivable are nullified. The limitlessness of life is death, a fundamentally inconceivable thought that is here called revery and which I call utopia: a thought unnamed by that name. It is not the absence of object; but the synthesis of the object by thought and language no longer comes about. Thought persists in this failure to come about (recall the state that no longer exists, that perhaps never existed, that will never exist). I am on the near side of language and thought, object and subject, in that motionless region, the place that has no duration, where binary oppositions—time-space, instant-duration, body-world, thought-being—become indistinguishable and nullify each other: Utopia-Eutopia. It lies on the near side of what are called "the pleasures of life," but whose pleasures are perhaps reflections in language and in objects, in a consciousness that reflects itself or conceives of itself. And yet that state is expressed, *written*. Yet another paraphrase of Bloch: a slow extraction in the text I am writing of the content, the real possibilities, which the symbol signifies by realizing them in the form of indication. I write what Rousseau writes: the pathos of "signification," the slow constitution of the symbolic object.

DIGRESSION IN THE FORM OF ALLEGORY

> The founding celebration of a colony of rabbits from the large island on the small island: the founding of utopia. (Rousseau, fifth revery)

The founding celebration is the ritual reiteration of the social pact, no longer as a transcendental, theoretical model but as an experience of the pact itself in the immediacy of reciprocal exchange. But in the anecdote, Rousseau deletes the two moments of utopian ecstasy. This is a significant cut, an "allegorical" indication of the way the two "place-moments"—the originary and the foundation of any possible society—communicate with each other. A relation is established between the subject of the revery and the subject of the pact: The same instant may be at stake. At the very least, the utopian point of articulation between what I have called the two problematic axes is indicated and dissimulated. In that cut, there is a double gap. First, it is not the little society of the large island that renews its founding pact in a celebration. Rather, that society spreads out and founds a colony. A Greek image: "It is prey to the homeland. The mind loves the colony and valiant oblivion" (Rousseau, fifth revery). Second, the small colony of which Rousseau is the lawmaker is a colony of animals, rabbits. Let us dream this text or let the text dream: The allegory is both the analogical image of distancing (the colony) proper to the proximity of the origin (the fatherland) but also the psychical and ontological regression toward the originary; the nil is the brute. Nature as originary state thus returns in the narrative both as allegory and as reality. The originary thus lies in the distance between allegory and reality: Allegory veils reality through its meaning, but reality disguises the meaning of the allegory. The digression is a symbolic cipher of the sign, which signals the utopian place.

RHYTHMS

> When evening approached, I would descend the island's peaks and go sit happily on the lakeshore in some hidden sanctuary. There the sound of waves.... (Rousseau, fifth revery)

First Refrain. Scansion of time, beacons of space: the alternation between moving (taking strolls) and standing still, stases in closed or open places, hovels, terraces, hiding places, and hillocks, a slow tension of ebb and flow ("sometimes ... sometimes") toward their neuter identification in the place, the instant of happiness. Here, in the text, the summit—a zenith at the crepuscule of time, at the edge of space.

First, there is the moment of inscription of the no-place place: *ou-topos*. In *space*, a descent from a high place (the peak) toward a low place (the lakeshore), which is an edge, the place of a central limit between the closed form of the island and the openness of water. In this place of the limit, there is once more the circularity of a closed, indeterminate place, "some hidden sanctuary," an unlocatable refuge of peace on the boundary line between the outside and the inside. In *time*, a duration, the approach of evening, the beginning of the end, which is also a coming, that of night, which catches one by surprise; a limit that lasts, an interval of time *between* two moments of cosmic movement. Let the text dream of this crepuscular moment, this flight of the Hegelian owl, the totalization of Being in the deferred action of philosophical thought. In this case, what is at issue is not taking flight or flying over this place of the limit but, rather, retreating into the hidden sanctuary, opening the originary to the body. Ears and eyes are caught in a trap—"entwined"—in what appears on this edge. A single sound without difference, in unison, prior even to melody, but a sound of a phenomenal multiplicity; a single profound substance that sparkles in the glow of appearances. The Being-appearance of the world leads the soul to the motionless point of rest. I am the sound of the waves, the agitation of the water; hence, I am nullified without "internal" agitation, in silence; hence I am *fixed* and open, deep in revery: im-mediation, direct contact with a double surface and, at the same instant, depth. The soul has become the body of the world, recreated, the substance of Being. Or, rather, the substance of the world is perceived in my body, in the soul; the world immerses the soul in a delicious revery—*jouissance*.

A depravation, a meditation, in view of innocence. First, the agitation of water fixes the senses, relaxes the organs that naturally transmit the agitation of the world to the soul and fill them with that agitation. But here, everything is reversed into its opposite: The agitation of the water not only immobilizes the sense but excludes all agitation from the soul. The movement of the world is *immediately* reversed into its opposite, the soul's repose. The paradox signals an identity: The multiplicity of the appearances of Being is the repose of Being in its manifestation; water is the symbol of Being, which reveals itself in appearance, from which it withdraws, into which it withdraws. The mode of its manifestation is the retreat into multiplicity: neuter-plural. Second, the surface of the soul *is* its depth, immediately so: In becoming the sound of waves and the agitation of water, in drifting on the agitated surface of the water with ears and eyes, the soul sinks into *its* depth, which is revery, where time is gathered together into a motionless duration. The imperceptible movement of the time of the world, by means of which night follows evening, becomes the instant of the night's surprise, its sudden arrival.

The ebb and flow of that water, its sound.... (Rousseau, fifth revery)

Second Refrain. Meditate on Being as rhythm, on the body of the world as scansion, while repeating: The soul is the substance of the world, which is perceived in my body as rhythm; then meditate on that substitution of the rhythm of Being for the internal movements of the soul, that neutralization of the boundary line between the outside and the inside. Finally, attempt to think what is not thought or is not conceivable without fainting, the feeling of existing as happiness. But do not follow that order, reverse it, leave the essential point for the end: What does it mean that the rhythm of Being replaces the internal movements of the soul in its depth? Being is substituted for it, but it also serves as a supplement for that nullification of the soul in revery. The movement of being as rhythm replicates the revery as agitation of the soul and substitutes for it. In a word, revery is only the rhythm of Being.

The fabric of the world folding about the body: That is the pure and *adequate* feeling of existing, and it is happiness. Above all, do not make the effort to think, do not add thought, the supplement of reflection, to the coming of Being as rhythm. Just as pleasure could be defined as absence of pain, happiness could be defined negatively: absence of thought. *To feel oneself existing*: The most difficult is also the most simple. *To let Being be* in the body, such is the other, positive definition of happiness. But pay attention to the reflexive in "feel *oneself* existing": Wouldn't that amount to a first and primitive reflection? Already a thought? Rousseau says: "The rhythm of the water is enough to make me feel my existence." *I* do not feel *myself* existing, it is rather the rhythm of being that comes to me as a feeling of existing. And that is a very different thing. It is not a subject that reflects its existence in the sentiment it has of it, but a "there is"; "no void, no stop in the teeming tissue, no vertigo. THERE IS." An internal Ek-thesis of Being (not ec-stasy of the self in Being).

> From time to time some fragile and short-lived reflection arose concerning the instability of the things of this world, of which the surface of the waters offered me the image: but soon these slight impressions were effaced.... (Rousseau, fifth revery)

A break at this point, or rather, something like a tremor of reflection, of "philosophy," on the smooth surface (ob-livio) of originary forgetting. The temptation arises to "read" the world as meaning rather than letting Being be, as rhythm of the body and happiness. This is the supplement of meaning that is added to it, that substitutes for letting it be: Read on the surface of the agitated waters the instability of the things of this world, make of the world a sign, a significant sign, substitute meaning for the power of indication. To make of the world a sign, whose signifier would be inscribed on the surface of the lake's deep waters, a page to be read, whose letters, whose words, would be the waves and whose signified—in the reflection of the signifier—would be the instability of the things of this world. But the "letting be" of Being effaces the letters on the page; it leaves the surface of the water to its agitation of waves. The world as book to be read is effaced.

> In the uniformity of the continuous movement that rocked me and that, with no active cooperation of my soul, did not cease to attach me.... (Rousseau, fifth revery)

A nullification of the signifier (the agitated surface of the waters) and of the signified (the instability of the things of this world) in the continuous-uniform flow that nevertheless rocks and attaches: Here is the summit, the high moment. Let it vibrate in my reading, while I provide, in support, the article by Emile Benveniste on rhythm. According to Democritus, quoted by Aristotle in his *Metaphysics*, things *differ* by means of their *rythmos*. Hence, A differs from N: Although identical as λ, they are different inasmuch as the third leg is inside the A and outside the N. The rhythm concerns the letter of writing, its configuration (schema), its inscription: Displace one leg from the inside to the outside, and the song of the vowel becomes the silence of the consonant; displace it from the outside to the inside, and the consonant speaks. Hence, the waves inscribe on the surface of the agitated water identical and different letters. The water of the lake is the surface of a page where completely identical and completely different letters are inscribed only to be effaced and then inscribed once more. It is not a matter of reading them, of deciphering them, since they change continually. One must let the play of their difference be, in this place where they nullify each other.

> Nature acts by progress, *itus* and *reditus*. Aa. It passes and returns, then goes further, then two times less, then more than ever, etc.
> The flow of the sea occurs in that way, the sun seems to work that way. aAaaAaaA. (Pascal)

Nonetheless, the "formation (*th*)*mos* indicates not the fulfillment of the notion, but the particular modality of its fulfillment as it presents itself before the eyes. As a result, *schema* is defined as fixed form, realized or posited in some sense as an object. *Rythmos* designates the form [*schema*] the instant it is assumed by what is moving, mobile, fluid . . . a 'fluidness,' the pattern of a fluid element" (Benveniste), an act of arranging that is made and unmade.

May I add that the rhythm of Being is the *instant* of a form that is made and unmade *in another form*: a state, but a state of change;   the *figure* of a present, a past-future that is its antisynthesis as it were. The figure of a dehiscence of the present that is made (the protension of a past) and unmade (the retention of a future) through an inversion of the passive synthesis of time;   the *scansion* (rocking and fixing) of desire. An attachment that rocks, a rocking that is attached. Desire manifests itself only in the beat of the rocking motion, in the fixed nature of the rhythm, the pulsing of the impulse.

The rhythm of Being envelops a difference or a negation with a very particular status. It does not introduce a temporal-historical dialectic or the distance of an absence: Difference is Being itself as the mode of its coming into being (and not its becoming), a utopian neuter. And now, as a reminder, here is the utopian representation, as they say.

Plato submitted corporeal *rythmos* to the law of number, determined it by measurement—*metron*—subjected it to an order. The contradiction in Rousseau, who speaks simultaneously of continuous noise and of interval, of a uniformity of movement and of waves, of rocking and attachment, far from being a mere descriptive incoherence, refers to something prior to the oppositions, in this case, something related to the senses, a descent or regression into the depths of the body-world (a depth that is pure surface, the surface of the agitated water) but whose historical (or historial, as Heidegger would say) dimension Benveniste discreetly marks—originary forgetting. Utopian representation *always* brings about the same subjection of the flow to measurement, of desire to law, in view both of showing it and fulfilling it, whether that measurement is of space or of time, in view of occupying the open space of the neuter by imagining a different—visible and expressible—world.

The rhythm of Being is still—and here we are getting even closer to the originary—the nullification of the signified of the law, the law of true and ultimate meaning (hence, the instability of the things of this world) in the signifier, the movement of the water. But the signifier itself is nullified in the instant, the figure, in scansion, since the rhythm of Being is the very identity of difference, the pulsing of the impulse, the intensification of an intensity. The name of that intensification, today devalued, is happiness.

MEDITATION AND BREAK

There are three possible directions I might take in the meditation on Rousseau's text but which I suspend in the text I am writing today: The first would move toward the present and the way it bursts forth as "making" and "unmaking," the relation between the instant and the figure; the second, toward the flow and its pulsing, the relation between the continuous, the repetitious, and permanence; and the third, toward the text as an object where we read—and where we write while reading—this indication (this "sign-making" of the sign) in ourselves, in our bodies, of the unconscious and its here and now. The body of the text, the body of the symbolic object called "text" is the pulsing in the poem of the pulsing of the flow; it is the bursting out of the present in the figure it traces. The body of the text is the figure inscribed in the text and a symbol of the unconscious. The pulsing of the libidinal body inscribes marks in the text and not in what the text is speaking about. It speaks only of *that* without saying so; intensity and utopian *jouissance*-happiness of the text, which we must, at all cost, keep in mind when faced with the various forms of "utopian happiness" of which certain texts speak and whose image they meticulously describe for us.

Utopian practice (fiction) lies in that: In the poetic inscription of the instant, of its figure, of the pulsing in the flow of the text, an inscription that makes of it a complete object that we enter, that we rewrite on ourselves through our entry.

Interruption: The Symbolic Object—The Text

By way, not of conclusion but of interruption in this text, I shall enter Rousseau's meditation-revery, the discourse of thought, for a moment. In the text of revery I read, that entry is marked by the shift to the present. Rousseau reclaims, through "philosophical" discourse and language, the symbolic object constituted by the narrative of the "ek-thesis" of the world in the body; he gives the originary the form of a concept. Hence, the shift is made from fiction (utopian practice) to its representation, its contemplative *theoria* in discourse. The theory of utopia is the end of utopia. Symbolic "sign-making" becomes a sign, that is, representation. What brings about this move is memory as the presence of past happiness in the mode of representation.

At this point, we must be attentive to a kind of doubling of memory. The symbolic object I have just read and written is, of course, only memory in its very inscription on the page. But that memory nullifies clock time, neutralizes *chronos*, not in order to situate me in the past, make me present to my past, but, rather, to interrupt the linearity of time, its continuity, with the other of time-space, the instant. In the instant, in the distinction between the present and the past as such, that is, of time in general as the capitalization of duration, the symbolic object can very well appear as a memory, as a very precious part of that capital of remembered time in its continuity. (The continuous "line" of time, far from being the dissolution of time-capital, is the continuous summoning of successive presents as time, in and through memory.) But, in thus constituting itself, by that very act, the instant is also forgetting, a lacuna in that remembered continuity, since it interrupts it and nullifies it in itself, opening it to its other, the moment-place of happiness: originary forgetting, a forgetting that is the originary itself, that is, the work of forgetting the origin in the a priori form of sense experience, time.

> As a result of certain psycho-analytic discoveries, we are to-day in a position to embark on a discussion of the Kantian theorem that time and space are necessary forms of thought. We have learnt that unconscious mental processes are in themselves "timeless." This means in the first place that they are not ordered temporally, that time does not change them in any way and that the idea of time cannot be applied to them. These are the negative characteristics which can only be clearly understood if a comparison is made with *conscious* mental processes. (Freud, *Beyond the Pleasure Principle*)

The symbolic object, which is properly the inscription of the utopian place-instant in the text, is both memory and forgetting. The text's functioning as symbolic object is to be conceived as the difference between memory and forgetting. "Difference is in-difference to the order of temporality" (Lyotard). "In themselves," writes Freud, "the unconscious processes are unknowable and even *incapable of existing.*" That is the issue in the fifth revery: the originary, the state of nature as it is posited in the *Discourse on the Origin of Inequality*. "It is no such easy task... to make oneself well acquainted with a state which perhaps never existed, which does not now and will probably never exist."

Rousseau's meditation transfers what is outside time, or better, what is repressed forever, into memory—that is, into the oppositions of discursive thought. In the symbolic object, in the possible-real world of the poem, the difference between memory and forgetting accedes to the "reality" of the text. In that, memory is the gesture of giving the unknowable and nonexistent originary the form of thought. But—and we need to pursue thought to that point—that also means that memory both indicates and conceals the other of memory—the motionless movement of the neuter, utopian practice, fiction—by signifying it in discourse.

Nevertheless, we must tarry within the discourse of thought and memory, within the representations of utopia. We must not set them aside, as if everything were over, with an "appeal to the late hour and the agreed-upon signal." We need to tarry not because this discourse, these representations, are the truth of the symbolic object, the lifting of the veil, the breaking of the seal, the dissipation of the "particularly intense pathos of [their] meanings" in the pure light of the concept, but simply because it *could* well be that the discourse of thought and utopian representations also indicate the impulse of some *possibility* of the symbolic body of the text, impulses and possibilities that might remain latent in the reinscription, the rewriting, the reading.

Such was the task I set for myself and that I leave interrupted: to rewrite today the text of the discourse of thought, not as the truth of the narrative we have just read, but by bringing back, returning the concepts to the state of real possibilities of the symbolic object, the state of fictions of the narrative of Rousseau's strolls and drifting on or around the island that is nowhere named, almost unknown, the island in Lake Bienne. One final paraphrase: "Assimilate all the objects of thought to fictions and, finding yourself *finally* led back by degrees to yourself and to what surrounds you, to the body-world, *be incapable of marking the point of separation between fictions and realities*." Such would be the path, the leap, toward the practice of utopia.

Part Two

♦

CROSSINGS

10

Rue Traversière, nos. 45–47

In crossing the northeast corner of the twelfth arrondissement on its way to the riverbank, about halfway along its course, Rue Traversière encounters the great intersection of Avenue Daumesnil before pursuing its oblique path. It celebrates that encounter—its seems to me—with a triumphal arch or a monumental gate that, for me, irresistibly evokes those magnificent gates built by Louis the Great in the Saint-Martin and Saint-Denis districts. But the association is ridiculous and my imagination quickly tumbles from absolute monarchy to bourgeois capitalism, from the seventeenth to the nineteenth century. For the monumental gate the street crosses is only one of the arches that was left open in the enormous embankment of the old Bastille railroad, which went as far as the mayor's office in the arrondissement and even beyond. The new Bastille opera led to the disappearance of the train station, long put to other uses; its site—a piece of architecture made of iron and glass—had welcomed salons and congresses. It deserves a passing thought since, on a hot July afternoon, M. Bouvard and M. Pécuchet met in front of it. The archway of the embankment, or what is left of it today, is occupied by garages, used-car or auto-parts shops, and a few short-lived dance or drama schools. The street that, since 1672, has done nothing but pass did not receive even the most modest dedication from the king, who, from far away and high above, was contemporary to its opening. In truth, how could a mere arcade have deserved it? It was by building the Bastille railroad that the triumphant bourgeoisie of the last century offered the street an incongruous triumphal arch, at the risk of an encounter between the railway and the street. The street does not know what to do with it, except to cross it and go on its pitiful way. The walls of stone, black with urban dust, are covered with crazy scrawls, palimpsests of graffiti, most often obscene; in my view, they can be read as the fall of the sublime Latin inscriptions of the Saint-Martin and Saint-Denis gates into the ignoble and grotesque. But a "cross" memory is probably needed to bring about that strange transformation from the seventeenth to the nineteenth century.

Politics and Seduction

11

The Right Choice as Remainder

Let us begin, then, with the fable of La Fontaine (book 3, 1), "Le meunier, son fils et l'âne" [The miller, his son, and the ass], and with its prologue first of all:

> The invention of the arts is a right of the first-born, and thus we owe the apologue to the ancient Greeks. But a field cannot be harvested so well that latecomers find nothing more to glean. The land of fiction is full of deserted fields, and our authors make daily discoveries there. Here, then, is a well-turned tale once told to Racan by Malherbe.
>
> Those rivals of Horace and heirs to his lyre, the disciples of Apollo—our masters, in short—met one day all alone, without witnesses. They wished to confide all their thoughts and their cares to each other. Racan said, "Pray tell me, you who must know about life, since you have passed through its every stage, and nothing must escape you at your advanced age, what shall I resolve to do? For the time has come to give it some thought. You know my wealth, my talent, my birth: should I settle down in the provinces, join the army, or take on duties at court? There is bitter and sweet in all things of this world. War has its pleasures, marriage its distress. If I followed my taste, I would know where to head, but there's my family, the court, the people to satisfy."

The problem posed by Racan to Malherbe, meeting one day all alone and without witnesses, is that of a choice of existence, of a right decision at the right moment: "What shall I resolve to do? For the time has come to give it some thought." It is the problem of the act in that redoubtable instant before the act. The facts are precisely determined: "You know my wealth, my talent, my birth." The choices are precisely and clearly defined, three in number: "Should I settle down in the provinces, join the army, or take on duties at court?"

Three exclusive possibilities, doubly exclusive, since articulating these three amounts to immediately *excluding* an infinity of others that *remain* undetermined, outside the space of the case at hand. Or better, the gesture through which the provinces, the army, and the court become possible choices is nothing other than the gesture of setting aside all the others. Problems or systems are always constructed in this way: To define a field of thought or action is to trace a boundary, to close one set and enclose oneself within it. But, in addition, the three choices are *mutually* exclusive, an "either . . . or." In Hjelmslev's words, we are dealing with a *system* and not a *process* (a "both . . . and"); we are dealing not with the narrative of transformative actions but with the rational calculation of the action to be taken. And its moment must be understood as atemporal, timeless: a system, a calculation, reasoning without internal remainder *because* it is a system, a calculation, reasoning. Therefore, Racan cannot *at the same time* get married, go to court, and go to war; nor can he do them *in succession*. The story of his life, his history, will enfold—after the fact—in *a single one* of these places: the provinces, the court, the army. It *will be* said of him, once the narrative is completed and the story ended, either, "He was a good husband," or "fine courtier," or "valorous captain."

Let us complicate the model, less in play—but there is also play involved—than out of concern for rigor and exactitude. It is a matter of acting and choosing and deciding, a matter of plans, reasons and motives, intentions and inclinations. Let us thus introduce into the system, the calculation, the strategy, two new facts that were, in fact, implicitly included from the beginning: the subject and others. Into the closed field of possibilities, into the table that charts them, let us introduce the self's desires and those of others.

If I followed my taste, I would know where to head, but there's my family, the court, the people to satisfy.

Let us understand Racan's discourse: One of the two factors, other people's desires, is known, explicit. Papa and mama want him to settle down; the king wants him in court; the people want his protection. But what does Racan want? He knows but does not say. That is the unknown quantity. This is odd, since Racan speaks at length and has no secrets from Malherbe: "They wished to confide all their thoughts and their cares." But is it pertinent to speak of his desire since Racan must *also* satisfy the opposing desires of others? Confrontation of desires: the family, the king, the people want something; Racan too wants something, but he *also* wants to satisfy the exclusive desires of the others. Desire against desires, but also desire for desires. Racan reasons, or rather, suggests this reasoning to his rival on the Parnassus: Either my desire carries me toward *one* of the three articulated possibilities, or it aims for a fourth possibility *not programmed into the table*. In the first case, in realizing my desire, I would fail to satisfy two of the other three, since the three possibilities cannot be realized together, in a process; in the second case, should I happen to write light verse, for example, then family, king, and people will all be unhappy.

If Malherbe were to enter into the play, the calculation, the system, he would no doubt object: There are only three possibilities, not four. You are going beyond the limits of the program. You are dreaming, not calculating.

And Racan would have responded to this hypothetical objection: That is true, but I have to choose, and somewhere, within or outside the system, there will always be a lack of satisfaction. In rational calculation, there will *always* be a remainder within or outside the limits it sets up in order to operate: In representation, there is a remainder of desire, whether mine or someone else's. Let us calculate: The right choice results from subtracting all the possibilities from the total of desires; it is a remainder equal to zero, which is, nevertheless, *both* lacking and in excess.

"Satisfy everyone!" Listen to this story before I respond.

As the good Norman he is, Malherbe does not give the solution to the problem. Instead, he projects the model onto a narrative, projects the synchronic field of possibilities onto the diachrony of events, the "either . . . or" system onto the "both . . . and" process. An old problem, an old escape. In divine understanding, in the world of pure ideas, in the system, all possibilities, even total opposites, happily coexist: the idea of "big" and the idea of "little," of "heat" and of "cold," and so forth.

And what is authorized by the eternity of possibilities is realized by the time of world history or human history: *Little* fish *will grow big*, and the cold of winter will follow the heat of summer. Racan goes to war, comes back glorious, goes to court at the Louvre, receives a good pension, marries in the country, and writes his rhymes in peace. The order hardly matters, for, at the end of the story, all desires *will have been* satisfied, his own and those of others. He and they will only have had to *wait*: the reality principle. Desires are fulfilled only at that price. The narrative, a pure projection of the model, models time, shapes it. The remainder, which appears at the end of the narrative exemplification, is no longer what it was just before, namely, desire in representation: It is *reality*, the duration that defers satisfaction. But, *in the end*, in the final accounting at the end of the story, when the narrative has once more become a table or chart, once the "realized" elements have been added up and all the "expectations" subtracted, the temporal remainder of reality will have been resorbed into the completed totalization of desires, now transformed into realities. The power of the narrative makes the remainder disappear: If we can just wait for the story to end, if we can just wait for death, there will be no remainders in the story. Scraps at the very most. "To philosophize is to learn to die" (Montaigne).

And yet, the apologue has a few surprises in store for us:

At this point, Malherbe said, "Satisfy everyone! Listen to this story before I respond. I read somewhere that a miller and his son, the one an old man, the other a child, though not a tiny one, but a boy of fifteen if memory serves, went to sell their ass at the fair one day. And so it would be fresher and fetch a better price, they tied its feet and hung it up just so.

Then this man and his son carried him like a chandelier: Poor souls, idiots, ignorant louts. The first one to see them burst out laughing. "What kind of a farce are those two playing? The biggest ass of the three is not the one you might think." At these words, the miller realized his ignorance. He put his beast on its feet and made it walk along. The ass, which had a taste for the other means of travel, complained in its own tongue. The miller paid him no mind. He had his son climb on, and followed behind.

By chance three good merchants happened by and were displeased by the sight. The oldest cried as loud as he could to the boy: "Oh, you there, get down! Don't let anyone accuse you of being the young man who leads a lackey in grizzled beard. You're the one to follow, the old man should ride."

"Gentlemen," said the miller, "we must make you happy." The child got on his feet, the old man on the beast. Then three girls passed and one cried out: "It's a terrible shame to see that young son hobble along while that simpleton, seated like some bishop, plays the fool on his ass and thinks he's quite wise."

"I'm nobody's fool at my age," said the miller. "On your way, my girl, and heed me well." But after many jeers thrown one after another, the man thought he was in the wrong, and put his son up front.

In another thirty paces, yet a third band found something more to say. "Those folks are mad, the donkey's on its last legs, he'll die under them. What then! Burden that poor beast like that! Have they no pity for their old servant? No doubt at the fair they'll be selling its hide."

"Parbleu," said the miller, "you're mad in the head if you think you can satisfy everyone and his pa. But let's try in any case and see if we can manage to do so." They both dismount. The ass, lolling about, goes ahead of them. Another soul meets them and says: "Is it the fashion for an ass to do as he pleases while the miller is inconvenienced? Of the ass and the master, which one is supposed to get worn out? I advise those fools to have it enshrined. They're wearing out their shoes and conserving their ass. Nicolas, turn around, for when he sees Jeanne, he gets on his beast, and the song tells us so. Fine trio of asses!"

The miller then spoke: "I'm an ass, it is true, I agree, I confess it; but from now on, whether I'm blamed or praised, whether they say something or nothing at all, I'll do as I please." He did so, and did it well.

The apologue is the journey of a miller and his son to the fair. And their ass.

That is the problem: the third term, the ass that is in excess, the inconvenient third term, since the couple wants to get rid of it. Or, rather, sell it. The nuance is important: At stake is not the elimination of waste but the economy of an exchange. At the end, at the fair, the third term in excess will have become calf, cow, pig, or brood.

The problem is certainly that of the third term, but it is *displaced*. It is not posited, as it was in the prologue of the fable, as a choice of existence, an end to deliberation, action; it is not posited as the fulfillment of the poet's desire or that of his father, his king, or his fellow citizens. The setting is not the fair, the place of productive "marketability," or the mill, the place for consumption or work, but rather the gap between, the trip, the journey. This is the first surprise the story has in store for us. In that intermediate space where the ass no longer carries sacks of flour and is not yet a commodity and object of exchange, the question is the following: How to behave toward the third term in this space between without function or end, in this moment between use and exchange, outside the program? For the ass necessarily loses its program, as the miller and his son lose theirs. This moment is nonetheless inevitable if the couple wishes to sell the third. Here, then, is a temporal and local "remainder" that slyly affects the ass and his pair of masters, unassimilable and ineluctable, between practice and use on the one hand, calculation and exchange on the other. The journey from the mill to the fair is both the experience by which the couple learn about that remainder and the construction of a gratuitous, insignificant, and ineluctable combinatorial table of all the possibilities of a relation between a couple and a third term.

In these two features, we recognize a theoretical-practical fiction: "The land of fiction [*feinte*] is full of deserted fields, and our authors make daily discoveries there" (La Fontaine). It is a feint, a fiction, because it is full of deserted fields that make possible the construction of heuristic models and exhaustive paradigms, the realized simulacra of simulations of strategic calculation. But simultaneously, simulacra, models, and paradigms are elaborated in the faults, the fissures of an economy, in the frayed spots of a network. A system of permutations installs itself in the blank spot of a program; a tactic emerges as the remainder of the strategy, both its lack and its excess. The journey from the mill to the fair is a narrative lesson on the remainder, we said, a lesson learned, in fact, not by the couple, but by the father, the old master, for whom wisdom comes late in life—but not too late—over and above his adventures, in excess of them. And that wisdom—the second surprise—will not be what we believe it to be. First episode: "At these words, the miller realized his ignorance." He knows that he knows nothing: He is a kind of Socrates covered with flour. Second episode: Thanks to the three good merchants, he recognizes his status, his authority as father. Third episode: He denies what is said to him by the three girls, but he acts on what he denies. The old story of the discourse of the willful subject: "On your way, my girl, and heed me well." But he "thought he was in the wrong, and put his son up front." Fourth episode: He discovers the theoretical solution, the solution of the supplement to the totality. "You're mad in the head if you think you can satisfy everyone and his pa." But from the outset, he challenges it as madness and impossibility. And, as a result, the solution is countermanded by an opposite practice: "But let's try in any case and see if we can manage to do so." And, finally, the fifth episode: He discovers his wisdom. But this wisdom is without rule or maxim, without theory or calculation, practical wisdom or desire. Its art—which lies entirely in its execution—is not given, except inasmuch as it entails doing things well, having the right attitude.

The journey by the miller, his son, and the ass is also a set of permutations, namely, those of a couple, a third term, and a simple relation between them: carrying. What are the possible permutations between the members of the couple, and between them and the third term? Such would be the necessary and sufficient conditions for a rational calculation with, at their end, the solution to the problem raised between the mill and the fair, between use and exchange, consumption and sale. A strange problem in truth: Why this question of "carrying"? We said it was gratuitous, insignificant, but that is not certain. "Hauling" or, in contrast, "fetching," is the economic value of the ass.[1] He is led from the mill to the fair. In moving between the two places, he already *no longer* hauls grain and flour (as in the past) but he does *not yet* "fetch" money (as he will in the future). What is at issue in this act of "carrying" during the journey? In this present time between the "already no longer" and the "not yet"? This present time is a *remainder*, which, during the course of the journey, through retrospection and anticipation, will be divided into a series of permutations of "carrying" between the couple and the third term, a carrying *already* divided between "hauling," a prior economic function, and "fetching," the future function. The present is a vacation or vacant space, a time of lack and latency, of gap and excess. It is the time of the remainder.

Let us, then, calculate the possible combinations. First episode: Both of them are carrying the third. Last episode: Neither one nor the other is carrying the third. The complex and the neuter. In the fourth episode, a transformation to the passive voice: Both are carried by the third, that is, the complex in the passive voice. Neither one nor the other is carried by the third: This neuter case in the passive voice is linked to the neuter in the active voice (neither one nor the other carries the third, that is, the last episode). In other words, the neuter is neither passive nor active, and, yet, in the two neuter combinations, the "carrying" relation insists and persists even though it is not manifested or realized. Here again is a remainder. There are, in addition, two cases of disjunction in the couple: In the second episode, one is carried by the third, but not the other; and in the third episode, the other is carried by the third, but not the first. Is the combinatorial table now complete? No, since there *remain* two possibilities that the narrative does not present: Either one or the other carries the third. This would amount to two transformations of the passive disjunctive into the active voice. Why are these possibilities not realized? Because they are physically impossible: Neither the miller nor his boy could carry the ass by himself, whereas the ass can carry both of them on his back, just as both of them together could carry it on their backs. The animal is the strongest and the heaviest. An ass is equal to two men. The third term has power over the couple. Actively and passively. I am carried by one and the other, thinks the third. Hence his satisfaction: "The ass... had a taste for the other means of travel." And he is strong enough to carry them both.

Let us classify the missing combinations, those that remain:

1) A remainder by *insistence*, the neuter remainder: Neither one nor the other is carried by the third. The paradox of an action (to carry or be carried) that does not act. Here is the pure act in language, in the infinitive.
2) A double lacking or absent remainder by *resistance*, the resistance of things to human action, the limit of strength and power, circumstantial necessity: Neither one nor the other carries the third. Here is the real, outside language.

Now the combinatorial table, constructed in the remainder of the present, in its empty space, is complete—without (*possible*) remainder.

The journey of the couple, father and son, is the calculation of possible combinations and their realization. But, on the journey from the mill to the fair, each combination has a double and contradictory characteristic, since it both *follows* another and is *independent* of all the others. It is as if each action, each of the miller's "solutions," were in a certain way determined by those that preceded it. No solution is repeated; each choice made contributes toward exhausting the totality of possible outcomes; that totality, in some sense, regulates from outside the actions as they occur in succession. But each combination is simply contiguous to that which precedes it, and the couple's aim in carrying out each action is to give each passerby encountered in succession the satisfaction he or she desires, the maximum satisfaction. Each, that is, except the first. For the first has a reason and an end defined by the actors themselves, by the miller and his son who are going to sell their ass at the fair: "And so it would be fresher and fetch a better price, they tied its feet and hung it up just so. Then this man and his son carried him like a chandelier." The carrying is determined by the future "fetching," by economic calculation, and the empty space of the journey is nullified in anticipation.

But this mode of "carrying" is transgressive of the "hauling," the animal's usefulness in the past: The ass hauls, it is not carried. And it is that transgression of the pack animal's use by the economic calculation, the transgression of the "hauling" by the "fetching," which sets off the series of narrative sequences, the interventions by the others and the constitution of the combinatorial table. "The first one to see them burst out laughing. 'What kind of a farce are those two playing?'"

From then on, in each case, with each outcome successively produced, the miller and his son start from zero once more. In contrast, the combinatorial table, the set of combinations, presents all the cases together, *tota simul*, in a single stroke and at the same time, since the issue is to satisfy everyone. The result of the table should be optimal satisfaction, the choice that is the least unsatisfying for everyone in relation to all the possible combinations. Such is the other surprise the apologue holds in store for us: It offers us the set of combinations (the description of all the cases) and the narrative as a set of combinations, in the form of a table. The text of the fable is situated *between* narrative and description: It is their remainder, which we shall call humor, where the synchronic or achronic reduction of time is manifested through strategic calculation, through the anticipatory representation of the totality of the story and the elimination of the unexpected, but also through the projection of that totality onto the time of realization and action, onto the delays and differences of the narrative. And the table comes undone. The calculation is weakened until the final about-turn by the miller at the last instant of the narrative, and the story—unforeseen and unforeseeable—which, far from being a circular return to the first instant, is rather the remainder both of the narrative and of the table and of all the remainders that insist, persist, or resist in both.

What brings about the transformation in the narrative and also the construction of the combinatorial table is the *discourse of others*. The *remark* is essential for two reasons. First, because the others in succession do not act, do not realize. They say what *ought* to be done, what *ought* to be realized; and their acts of language provoke a change in the relation of the couple to the third term—the father and son to the ass—regarding the relation of carrying. And it is they—the father, the son, and the ass, that is—who act, who realize. Second, because the satisfaction in each encounter is the satisfaction of the other. In each case and in succession, the miller brings about the satisfaction of the other and makes it his own. Thus, the remark is essential for two reasons: It posits the relation between saying and doing (and the possible remainder in excess or default, of doing over saying or of saying over doing); and it posits that relation not only as dialogical (the one, the other, I-thou) but also as a confrontation of desires. The others *speak* in order to express their desire; the self *does* what he can to *fulfill it*. But there will always be a remainder of the other's desire over and above its fulfillment by the self. In other words, each case is, in succession, a dialogical event of the discourse of desire and of the action that realizes it; and the totality of the cases in the table, *tota simul*, is a totalizing dialectic of dialogues of desire and of action, which consists in subtracting the remainders. The question is, then, Will there be a remainder in this subtraction of remainders? Will there be a remainder between the initial calculation of the *relation* between the ass and the fair, made by the miller when he leaves the mill, and the final act of reversal, both correct solution and pure expression of his desire?

First episode, the complex in the active voice: "The biggest ass of the three is not the one you might think." Last episode, the neuter: "Fine trio of asses!" In both cases, an other is speaking in mockery, ironically. From the first to the final case, there is the same assimilation of man to beast through the metaphorical value of the ass. But, in the first case, there is a reversal in order: The biggest ass is not the ass but the father or the son, one or the other. The ass is less of an ass than the human couple. In the last case, there is an identification of the ordered elements: The father, the son, and the ass are all asses, a "fine trio of asses." In the first case, the reversal of order between the ass and the man is the exact description of the real inversion: The function of the ass is to carry, and the human couple is carrying the ass. In the last case, the ass, which is made for carrying, is not carrying either one: The ass is no longer an ass because the couple is not being carried. In the discourse of the passersby, there is an ironic move from the neuter to the complex: All three are asses. The ass, an animal of metaphor (of transport); man, a metaphor of the ass realized and expressed in the first episode and expressed in the last through the immediate transformation of the neuter into the complex.

The three intermediate transformations between the two extremes come about—let us note—by threes: three merchants, three girls, a third group thirty paces off from which *one man* separates himself to present the discourse of norms and values. Two plus one against one over two: value and authority of age (second case); value and prestige of youth (third case); value (in the dual—economic and moral—sense) of the beast (fourth case). One is carried (but not the other) by the third party: The discourse responds by excluding the other and not the first. The other (but not the first) is carried by the third term: The discourse responds by making the reverse exclusion. This follows the logical principle of *tertium non datum*, the exclusion of the third term. But the third term is not the third; the ass is not the one you might think. The excluded third term is the first or the second, but not the third: dialectic. Subsequently, there is a synthesis: The first and the second are carried by the third. This passive synthesis is the reverse instance of the initial active synthesis, in which the first and the second carried the third. In the discourse uttered by the last agent of transformation, there is an instantaneous permutation of the neuter into the complex, of triple negation into identity: "fine trio of asses." In a word, the set of combinations and their permutations is a dialectical philosophy of history. But the ultimate identity, the absolute spirit in which all of history is summed up and completed, is, in fact, its reversal. The synthesis of the identical is the identification whereby all men are asses, the penumbra where all asses are gray. But then, the irony of the other will be transformed into the humor of the individual.

The last individual encountered (fifth episode) posits the untransgressible norm of the social and political order, which the miller and his son had initially transgressed both out of calculation and out of ignorance. There are millers and there are asses; there are masters and there are slaves; there are men who are carried and asses who carry them. In carrying the ass, father and son had reversed the order; in not being carried by the ass, they also reverse it, but in a different way. In the first case, they reverse it by inverting or perverting the order. The prescribed order is father, son, ass; for them, it is ass, father, son. They put the cart before the horse. In the last case, they reverse the order by contradicting its hierarchy: They act as if there is no order; they declare as much by their behavior. The result is anarchy: There is neither master nor slave, neither god nor king nor subject—the neuter. The arguments rush forward in the discourse of the passersby. The argument of religion: "I advise those folks to have it enshrined." Of economy: "They're wearing out their shoes and conserving their ass." Of *doxa*: "Nicolas, turn around, for when he sees Jeanne, he gets on his beast, and the song tells us so."[2]

Conclusion: You act as if you were saying, "there is neither master nor slave, you masters." I say, "Fine trio of asses; all three, asses." I call this conclusion that transforms the neuter into the complex "the metabole of communal irony," the about-turn of the neuter, the about-turn of anarchistic revolution in a massive identification with the lowest of the low: Neither master nor slave = all slaves, all beasts. An originary indifferentiation, a mere ironic stroke.

There is also a humorous about-turn of the ironic about-turn: This is the rejoinder, the retaliation of the miller. The father, the master, speaks, he takes the initiative, and yet his tactic is defensive. He repeats what the other—the individual, the undefined *doxa*—says, but *differently*. He exempts himself from the trio, positing himself as *singular* in the unique singularity of his madness: "I'm an ass, it is true, I agree, I confess it." The cogito of the dumb beast. A unique instant that marks a new departure in time: "But from now on. . . ." Beginning here and now, I am forever a singular soul, a unique soul, one of a kind. Separated from any relation of order or hierarchy instituted by blame or praise, from any point relative to the other in general, to the indefinite "they," to their rumor or silence. "But from now on, whether I'm blamed or praised, whether they say something or nothing at all, I'll do as I please." An irruption of the force of the singular will, a flash of the possible in the power of the neuter, a fulguration of the unique: I will do what I will. Romanticism and anarchistic pathos? Messianism, eschatology, utopia? Master, alone and without a slave? No. Humor.

The narrator (the voice of Malherbe to Racan in the narrative of La Fontaine) notes: "He did so, and did it well." What does he do? What is his program? All the instances of the relation of carrying between a miller, his son, and their ass have been considered and realized. The strategic calculation is complete.

114 / CROSSINGS

The field of possibilities has been run through and exhausted. What can he do? What, then, is the proper act, the right choice? *Nothing* that has been foreseen, calculated, programmed, nothing that stems from the totality of theoretically defined possibilities in the praxeological models. This inconsistency is, if you like, stupidity or madness. There is no order, no law of totality, or, rather, there is one, but it is as if the totality of possibilities foreseen and realized had, in addition, as a supplement, a remainder, an ultimate possibility it does not comprehend. An extraordinary, impossible possibility that, once realized, is still the only right action, the opportunity. Desire, taste, inclination, will—*outside the program*: the sole right choice. The wisdom of the old man is acquired in the end. It is, in the end, very dumb: "I'm an ass, it is true. . . ." Or, conversely, it is as if each realized—and ruled out—possibility in the journey and in the table suddenly moved into the remainder column, ceased to be a variable in the calculation, a parameter of the model, a part of the paradigm, a sequence in the narrative, a consequence of the program. The maximum satisfaction of everyone else, in turn, or the optimal satisfaction of all the others, becomes, on the theoretical plane, a fictive possibility of the self, the miller, and, on the practical plane, an instantaneous and total fulfillment of his desire. What possibility? What fulfillment? How do you expect me, the storyteller, to tell you? It is enough that *it is his own*. The opportunity is nothing stemming from the totality of the possibilities of other people or from the events of the discourse of other people. It is an impossible possibility, or each articulated possibility, or all possibilities already realized: the other of the totality of others, the other of the events of others. *Here is the remainder*, the opportunity the miller seizes upon once all the possibilities of the situation have been realized, once all the possibilities have been fulfilled in succession. Its sign is the instantaneous about-turn of the irony of others into a singular humor: "'I'm an ass, it is true, I agree, I confess it; but from now on, whether I'm blamed or praised, whether they say something or nothing at all, I'll do as I please.' He did so, and did it well."

The right choice is to be seized upon as it happens; it is a possibility beyond or prior to possibilities, an impossible possibility or any one at all of the possibilities and its realization. What is it?

> As for you, follow Mars or love or the prince. Go, come, run, stay in the provinces. Take a wife, go to the abbey, accept a job, choose government: People will talk about it, have no doubt.

12

♦

The Liar

I shall not undertake *a* reading of Corneille's *Le menteur* [The liar] here: Such an undertaking would go beyond the limits of this essay. But, in addition to this reason of circumstance, there is another, fundamental reason: To my thinking, a reading of *Le menteur* is quite simply—to paraphrase a witticism by Pascal regarding the Cartesian automaton—pointless, uncertain, painful, and, perhaps, ridiculous. This is not because there might be several possible and equally valuable readings for this play, but, rather, because one would have to read the *plural* itself in all its forms and on all the planes where we propose to articulate meaning: not polysemy, as the semiologists would say, but proliferating or, rather, unstable or metastable meanings. In *Le menteur*, it is as if the theme or content of the play, exhibited in its name, were reacting against all attempts to situate a coherent meaning; as if Corneille were obeying, in its conception and invention, a regime of "exchange," a law of mobility and alteration, a principle of uncertainty, a rule of variation, and all in the most precise writing possible, the most rigorous design, the tightest plot, in a dramatic performance governed by the most implacable dynamic of hearts, bodies, events, and social institutions.

Change, variation, mobility, and uncertainty are underscored by Corneille himself in his letter of dedication: "I present you with a theatrical play in a style so far from my last that it will be difficult to believe they both came from the same hand during the same winter." The preceding play was *La mort de Pompée* [The death of Pompeii], a tragedy, and it is likely that it was performed with *Le menteur* in Marais in 1644. *La mort de Pompée*, as Corneille also wrote to his unknown correspondent (Monsieur, the king's brother?), rediscovered the power of verse in *Cinna* beyond the tenderness and sweetness of *Polyeucte*; *Le menteur*, in contrast, satisfied "the mood of the French [who] like change and asked [him] for something more lively that would serve merely to entertain them" (Corneille, letter of dedication to *Le menteur*). It was thus in response to a desire for change that he not only moved from one dramatic genre to another, from tragedy to comedy, but more subtly (and with more mastery, as well), to a play *about* moving and mobility. For *Le menteur* exhibits the metastable effects of lovers' lies in hearts and bodies, in a play that is itself movement, change, a "comic" variation on its own "tragic" variety, *La mort de Pompée*, where the effects of the instability of (Machiavellian) politics in nations and courts are represented—and with what force!

Hence, *Le menteur* and *La mort de Pompée* represent two varieties, two genres, two variations on the same "theme," that of *variation*, which also *varies* in the two plays, as it should. It *varies* incessantly in its names: deception, disappointment, secrecy, coup d'état, confusion, artifice, detour, double-dealing, breach of faith, treason, chance, exchange, flattery, feint, seduction, ruse, tale, trap, color, grimace, fard, inconstancy, gaping, extravagance, fiction, revery, caprice, dream, appearance, false brilliance, dupery, look, outside, semblance, ingenuity . . . in short, lies.

Corneille himself establishes the structural rule for this variation between *La mort de Pompée* and *Le menteur* in the "realm" of versification and the "effect" of the subject, in manner and matter, form and content: "In the first [*Pompée*], I wanted to test what the majesty of reasoning and the force of verse stripped of all pleasure could do; in this one [*Le menteur*], I wanted to test what the subject of pleasure stripped of the force of verse could be."

This principle of uncertainty, this realm of exchange, and this rule of variation also produce their effects in the sources of the play and in the manner of treating them (and, in a way that is less anecdotal than you might at first think). In 1644, Corneille expressed his immense admiration for *La verdad sospechosa* by the "infamous Lope de Vega," the guide he had followed "for fear of getting lost in the detours of the many intrigues of our Liar," acknowledging in *L'examen* (1660) that its true author was Don Juan Ruiz de Alarcón. No doubt, he "borrowed many things from that admirable original," but only to immediately "take the subjects from their own country" and "dress them in the French manner." No doubt, he constantly imitated, but he also effaced the resemblances in the thoughts and terms that expressed them. Finally, he justified "the extraordinary respect" he had for this Spanish poem by means of two epigrams taken from Constantijn Huyghens, which reconcile "the grace of poetry with the highest political posts and the most noble functions of the statesman," epigrams from which the reader cannot fail to extract these two lines: "In short, he [Corneille] is a poet: by double-dealing, ruse, fable, and lie, theater delivers itself [or seeks revenge, *scena vindicavit se sibi*]." In this epigram, the political intrigues of *La mort de Pompée* and the romantic intrigues of *Le menteur* find, in their very variation, the ambiguous rule of their unity, namely, theatricality itself (that of political will and of love's desire), the infinite reflexivity of the illusion of reality and the reality of illusion, feint, and fiction.

To which we would have to add (and we will never exhaust the historical and aesthetic circumstances of the play as they are revealed in the published texts that frame them) that *Le menteur* had a sequel a year later, entitled *La suite du menteur* [The liar, continued], which was a new and remarkable variation on the first play. This variation is internal in terms of genre—it, too, is a comedy—and sequential in plot—we rediscover Dorante, Cliton, and Philiste, and the first scene tells us what has occurred in the two years separating the events of the two plays. Finally, and above all, there is a variation in the theme itself: The lying lover has become the lying man of quality. And, whereas the fictions of the first play led the liar to a place this side of true and false, through the mobility of bodies and the exchange of their signs, the deceptions of the liar in the second play exalt him beyond good and evil, in the recognition of what is valorous in each.

There is no reading of *Le menteur*, then, that is not led into the mad saraband of variation, into the plural play of manner, into the vertigo of the *mise en abyme* of the theatrical stage, through the speeches and behaviors the stage presents and encloses. What are the means of this dance? What are the markers of this game? What reference points can we cling to in the motionless fall provoked by the "lies" or "reveries" of our irresistible liar in love?

The first of these means, through which we immediately recognize the dramatist and the force of the comic poem, is also one of the most commonplace methods, the *quiproquo*, the mistake that, as the dictionary says, consists in taking one person (or thing) for another, in this case, Clarice for Lucrèce. We can easily imagine the effects of such an exchange of love's desire. But this method becomes less commonplace, more refined, when this *quiproquo* develops into arabesques, with more and more subtle detours of these fictions called lies.

But what is the meaning of that *quiproquo*, "Clarice for Lucrèce"? Its meaning is too obvious, too clear in appearance. Listen to Corneille as he evokes Lope de Vega, or rather, Ruiz de Alarcón:

> Dorante loves Clarice throughout the whole play and marries Lucrèce at the end.... The Spanish author thus puts him on the wrong scent as punishment for his lying and forces him to marry Lucrèce, whom he does not love.... For myself, I found that way of ending the play a bit harsh, and thought that a wedding that was less coercive would be more to the taste of our audience. That is why I was obliged to have him develop an attraction for Lucrèce in act 5.

But where do the "wrong scent" and the punishment, the seemly [*bienséants*] effects of the *quiproquo*, come from? How, in fact, is it possible to take Clarice for Lucrèce? The answer is very simple: If, as the *Grammaire de Port-Royal* writes, "a proper name such as 'Socrates' is the name befitting a certain philosopher named Socrates (just as 'Paris' is the name befitting a city named Paris)," it appears that, at the beginning of the play called *Le menteur*, a series of names and, first of all, those of "Clarice" and "Lucrèce," do not fit the two young women who bear them. Let us go even further: For Corneille, proper names "in general," those already mentioned and others, occupy all possible positions in relation to persons, individuals, and perhaps, even more precisely, in relation to faces, voices, and bodies, occupy all possible positions, that is, *except* the position that corresponds to the "true" or "grammatical" definition of "proper name." According to that definition, proper names are suited to the things they designate *because* those things are called by such names. By a kind of reverse Cratylism, all the lies and all the lover Dorante's feints are traversed by the exacerbated quest—in faces, voices, bodies, and signs—that will allow Dorante to name them by their true names.

But the faces, voices, and bodies also do not remain inert objects waiting to be passively read, scrutinized, interpreted—in truth, to be named. They are animated by the specific gaps, displacements, and false appearances constituting them; they slip or skid under their names. Hence, Dorante's desire on arriving in Paris from Poitiers is to *make himself loved*, that is, *to make a face for himself according to the fashion* (1.10). Whereas in the provinces, even "a fool passes muster [*passe à la montre*]" (1.66), that is, "has enough of a way about him to be received by company" (Furetière), in Paris

> one is not dazzled by false brilliance / And the many well-bred men who live there together / Mean that one is not welcome / Unless one resembles them. (ll.67–70)

Dorante, then, presumes the ambiguous adequacy of being and appearance (Is being only appearance? Does appearance reveal being?), presumes the dubious propriety of words and things, names and bodies. Cliton, his valet, replies with the principle of uncertainty, the law of mobility, the rule of exchange:

> Paris is a vast place full of merchants of all kinds, / The effect does not always correspond to the appearance, / One can be duped there as much as anywhere in France / . . . In the confusion that this great world brings, / There come from all places people of every sort / . . . Since it is difficult to find one's way around, / Everyone puts up a front. (ll.72–4, 77–8, 80–1)

If, in Paris, every "body" can make a name for itself (a pseudonym) at will, every "body" can also conceal its name. As the characters come on stage, *the order of bodies* corresponds to *the order of names*. That is, Clarice's body, "*stumbling as if allowing herself to fall*" [my emphasis] and Dorante's body—he extends his hand, touches, takes her hand, but is unable to touch and capture her heart—correspond to a double *faux pas* in naming, a double skidding. On the one hand, Dorante fills his name to the brim, or rather, makes a name for himself through the fiction of his Germany campaigns ("My name in our successes was touted rather high / And made quite a noise, not unjustly" [ll.172–3]); on the other, Cliton lets the name "Lucrèce" slip onto the body of Clarice owing to the coachman's words, which are transmitted like the word of an oracle ("The coachman's language has done its duty. / 'The lovelier of the two,' he says, 'is my mistress. / She lives at the plaza and her name is Lucrèce'" [ll.196–8]).

The mistaking of names, as Corneille wrote in *L'examen* (1660), comes to a head in scene 4 of act 1 (but does not reach its denouement until the next to last scene in act 5), through Dorante's repetition of the coachman's act of naming, a repetition, however, that displaces it, transforming it into an ontological assertion: "The lovelier of the two is my mistress ... *her name is Lucrèce*" becomes "the woman who spoke to me, who was able to captivate me, / *That is Lucrèce, that is she, without a doubt: / Her beauty assures me of it, and my heart tells me so*" (ll.202–4). Cliton echoes this remark, evoking the other, silent woman, whose body, let us note, did not pretend to fall a moment before:

> It is she most assuredly who is called Lucrèce; / Seek another name for the object that wounds you, / That is not her own; she who has not said a word, / Sir, is the lovelier of the two, or I am but a fool. (ll.221–4)

Throughout the entire play, from the first to the next to last scene, this uncertain play of names that fit or do not fit the bodies that bear them—a play or lapse in the interstices into which an objective lie insinuates itself—functions as the comic and psychological equivalent of the tragic, transcendent, metaphysical, or political destiny of *La mort de Pompée*. It is as if, through this gap between names and bodies, some sort of irresistible draft of cold air were being created, the air of voices, discourses, fictions, imaginary representations of language that fill the intolerable void.

Hence we find the rightly famous tales in *Le menteur* such as, in act 1, the meal on the water and, to a lesser degree, Dorante's wars in Germany; and, in act 2, the lover's surprise in Poitiers in the chamber of his beloved. We would need only to analyze closely the discursive and psychological "triggers" of these "stories," the stimuli for the liar's narrative drive, to perceive how they occupy and fill the interval between the proper names and the bodies these names fit. Despite the dramatic intensity of their content and the stirring force of their narration, or perhaps because of them, they tend to be immobilized into "tableaux vivants," as if their narrator were merely describing a work by Carracci or a painting from the Fontainebleau school, or even a genre scene or a bawdy print of a Fragonard canvas. There are probably no features more remarkable than the power of these "ekphraseis" that, escaping the liar's will and intentions from the outset, suture the voids and faults of the correspondence between language and the real, and reveal *jouissance* in the imaginary of a phantasmic aggression of bodies. When Cliton declares: "These pure fictions are very natural to you," Dorante responds:

> I like to brave storytellers that way, / And as soon as I see someone imagining / That what he wishes to tell me is anything astonishing / I'll serve him up an *imaginary story* on the spot / *which will astonish him and force him to*

be quiet. / If you could know what pleasure one has then / In turning their stories back against their own bodies. (ll.361–8, my emphasis)

One of the instruments of the play, another of its markers or reference points, in the vertigo of the feint, is the window. This is, in fact, a privileged place on the borderline, which, even as it distances the lovers, even as it forbids bodies to touch and recognize each other in an embrace of singular bodies, also authorizes communication and exchange through the gaze, and, especially, through breath, voice. Of the six occurrences of *fenêtre* [window] in *Le menteur* at the end of the line, that is, in the position of establishing the rhyme or providing it, the word rhymes four times with *connaître* [know] or *reconnaître* [recognize] (ll.389– 90, 918–9, 1721–2, 1761–2), once with *paraître* [appear] (ll.453–4), and once with *faire naître* [give birth] (ll.918–9). Yet, as Cliton tells Dorante in *La suite du menteur*, "Those windows have always brought you bad luck." The window, far from being that instrument or, at the very least, that transitional place of knowledge and recognition, even of birth, far from being the threshold of the appearance of a being, always turns out to be the frame for a disappointment, a failure. Not a lack or defect, but an exchange: The voice heard at the window does not come from the "right mouth"; the name proffered or given there is emitted from a body or attached to a body other than the body proper to it. Yes, windows always bring bad luck or lies to Dorante: They always reflect back his own fictions, his own unrecognized illusions, his own mistakes, as if the window were mere surface, as if it enclosed him in a mirror. "In the past, at the window, you took Clarice for Lucrèce," continues Cliton: That is, he took a body for a name, expecting to attribute that name to *another* body. And yet, that other body is the truth of the name in the institution of language and in that of marriage.

Descartes (and this is less odd than it appears) might very well have suggested to Corneille the metaphysical schema for the disappointing setup inherent in the window separating names and bodies. Descartes's *Meditations* were published in Paris in 1641 and in Amsterdam in 1642, precisely at the moment when the poet was writing *La mort de Pompée* and its variation, *Le menteur*. In the second Meditation, Descartes has just begun the famous analysis of the piece of wax, discovering that this body can be conceived only through understanding, through the mind. He continues:

> For although, *without speaking*, I consider all this in my own mind, yet *words stop me, and I am almost led into error by the terms of ordinary language*. For we say we see the same wax if it is put before us, and not that we judge it to be the same, because it has the *same* colour and shape: whence I would almost conclude that one knows the wax by the eyesight, and not by the intuition of the mind alone. *If I chance to look out of a window on to men passing in the street, I do not fail to say, on seeing them, that I see men,* just as I say that I see the wax; and yet, what do I see from this window, other

than hats and cloaks, which can cover ghosts or dummies who move only by means of springs? But I judge them to be really men, and thus I understand, by the sole power of judgement which resides in my mind, what I believed I saw with my eyes.[1]

Dorante and Clarice, Lucrèce and Cliton, will never attain the serenity of the philosopher, even after the proper names have rejoined their proper bodies, since it is always possible to ask if the sudden slippage of Dorante's desire (in scene 4 of act 5), from Clarice (under the name "Lucrèce") to Lucrèce (under the name "Clarice"), does not bring about the division of desire, not as Dorante says, between two bodies, but between a name of love, "Lucrèce," and a desired body, Clarice:

> I've just seen that charming object pass / But her companion, or may I die! is very pleasing / ... For my first love, my soul is a bit troubled: / My heart between the two is almost divided / And *she* would have it were it not already committed. (ll.1619–20, 1622–24)

To my thinking, this division of desire between the name of one and the body of the other keeps the gap open at the very heart of the appropriateness of names and bodies in their mutual appropriation during the last two scenes of act 5. And it is that scission alone that can account for the strange beginning of *La suite du menteur*, which links it to the first play: Dorante's flight to Italy, to Rome, the day of his wedding to Lucrèce, with her dowry; the subsequent remarriage of the "poor abandoned girl" to Dorante's father (l.60) whom "in a little less than two months [she] put in his coffin" (l.69).

A dozen years later, Pascal undertook this radical questioning of identity, or rather, undertook to show how the lover's desire for the other "eats away" at self-identity, a theme that may be the guiding thread in the "plural variations" of Corneille's play. In a famous *pensée*, Pascal writes, "What is the self?" a question Lucrèce implicitly asks Clarice, and that Clarice implicitly asks Lucrèce, speaking of themselves, but speaking "in truth" of Dorante, the liar with whom they are inexorably linked in the vertiginous play of bodies and names. "I don't know where I am," says Lucrèce to Clarice (l.1685); "I no longer know myself, where I am as well," echoes Clarice to Lucrèce (l.1716); "Lucrèce, listen to one word." Dorante to Cliton: "Lucrèce! what is she saying?" (l.1717) and yet, "Tonight, I thought I recognized her at her voice" (l.1721), Cliton to Dorante: "Clarice, in her name, spoke at the window" (l.1722). This work of identification occurs along three poles, in a reciprocal displacement through a window frame.

Reread Pascal in conclusion:

> What is the self? A man goes to the window to see the people passing by; if I pass by, can I say he went there to see me? No, for he is not thinking of me in particular. But what about a person who loves someone for the sake of her beauty; does he love *her*? ... And if someone loves me for my judgement

or my memory, do they love me? *me*, myself? . . . Where then is this self, if it is neither in the body nor the soul? And how can one love the body or the soul except for the sake of such qualities, which are not what makes up the self, since they are perishable? Would we love the substance of a person's soul, in the abstract, whatever qualities might be in it? That is not possible, and it would be wrong. Therefore we never love anyone, but only qualities.[2]

13

Gyges

Operating (or reading) instructions for what follows.
1) Reread Herodotus, *Histories* 1.7–14.
2) Read the story I draw from it as an exercise—in the form of commentary—in seductive discourse.
3) Ask whether I have truly understood it by rereading the story of Gyges, King Candaules, and his wife, which Herodotus tells us.
4) Once this is done, reread Plato's *Republic* 3.349b ff. and Charles Perrault's fable "Peau d'Ane."

The little story I am about to tell you—a little story that is also a big story of empires and myths—will be about gazes. Seductive gazes, but also the seduction of gazes. The very possibility of an inversion that makes sense, of a reversal of the expression and of what it signifies beyond the play on words, points to what is at stake in this essay by underscoring the instability of the two notions it considers. It will thus be about a kind of gaze, the gaze that seduces. But, it will be just as much about the very process of the gaze, of any gaze that might be a gaze of seduction. In this process, the reader will perceive what is lacking in the two notions, since, in this case, the genus and the species are coextensive, and something like the logical order of sense and sign is compromised thereby. For it is a question of the gaze and a question of seduction. Is it possible to conceive of the two terms as they are presented in language and experience, to confer a *status* on each of them? Is it possible to produce an object of experience or to construct a conceivable concept of "gaze" or of "seduction"? No. There is neither object nor concept since, in experience and in speculation, an object "gaze" and a concept "seduction" escape production or construction. To stabilize or objectify them, they must be conceived as a relation, but beginning from the poles that relation links: Hence, the gaze is the path between an eye (the subject of the gaze) and an object (its aim as visible thing); and seduction is the trajectory, whose modalities one would have to specify, between a seducing subject and a seduced object, the path of a transformation between an active and a passive term. But how is it possible to conceive of the *relata* beginning from the *relatio* rather than the reverse? How is it possible to conceive of a *relatio* that is both constitutive and regulative? A *relatio* that brings into existence the poles it links, a *ratio* or a challenge where nothing exists except in the challenge thus issued? As, for example, God in Pascal's wager, where the gambler exists as a believer only in the challenge he issues to a god he does not believe in, and where God exists only as the stakes of that challenge.

The little story I am going to tell will also be about power, political power, and, very precisely, about a change in power that is linked to an exchange of gazes. In the story, the representative of political power has decided, in a moment of vertigo and fascination, to risk—through a gaze—the law of which he is both the product and the depositary. As he does so, the old order of power collapses and is dissipated, and a new power, instituted in death, finds its origin (or absence of origin), its foundation (or absence of foundation) only in the double violence or the double power of the gaze of seduction and the seduction of the gaze. The story may lead to a reflection that surpasses everything in political science. And, in this story, the moment of seduction is at work both suddenly and permanently on the system of representation and its law.

First Moment

In book 1 of his *Histories*, Herodotus tells us of an abrupt and violent shift in royal power in Lydia, a shift from the Heraclids to the Mermnadae, a break of great moment since it encapsulates all the conflict between the Greeks and the barbarians. Candaules was the king of Lydia, a happy king, powerful and rich and madly in love with his wife, who he thought was the most beautiful woman on earth. He had "in his bodyguard a fellow he particularly liked whose name was Gyges, son of Dascylus[.] Candaules not only discussed his most important business with him, but even used to make him listen to eulogies of his wife's beauties [*to eidos tès gunaikos*]."[1] A little while after his marriage, Candaules ("who was doomed to a bad end," adds Herodotus) spoke these words to Gyges: "It appears you don't believe me when I tell you how lovely my wife is. Well, a man always believes his eyes better than his ears; so do as I tell you—contrive to see her naked."[2] This is the first moment of seduction between the king and his confidant, between the master and the slave, where the king or master risks his mastery in a challenge issued to the confidant. He risks it not in a fight to the death between two desires, a fight whose guiding force would be the desire for the desire of the other, and where the entire dialectic of the story would find its origin, but rather in a discourse, a discourse of persuasion: "It appears you don't believe me when I tell you how lovely my wife is." The king puts into play the power, the effectiveness of the royal word; the word risked is the word that brings a belief into existence in the man to whom it is addressed. The king's discourse does not bring the queen's beauty—invisible to all—into existence, does not make it visible. Language expresses the thing, but the thing itself remains at a distance, in the infinite distance of negation inherent to any language. In language, a particular sense-reality (*that thing*) vanishes, only to be better sublated into the universality of the concept. In speaking, Candaules sets in play the performative nature of his own word: He does things with words, he persuades, that is, he makes visible. But, in the very moment of this challenge, when the king takes the risk of doing things with words, what is at stake in this game is to bring the queen's beauty into existence. That beauty exists only at this moment and for a moment, in the discourse of the king, when the king risks his discourse by challenging his servant to "see." "Contrive to see her naked." And we understand, by the same token, why Herodotus begins his *Histories* with this story, not only because it is the first phase of a grandiose conflict, but also because it is emblematic of any story, of history itself, which entails not saying what has been said but telling what has been seen. Hence, the power of the historian's narrative rests on the strange symbiosis of simulation and seduction, since it is always *as if* he had seen what he could not see, *as if* he offered, in the present, the necessary absence in the past of the thing itself. "If it were possible to be present to all the events oneself, that would be by far the best form of knowledge," writes Ephorus of Cyme in the fourth century before the Common Era. Marcel Détienne comments on the ancient requirement for historical autopsy by evoking the historian's desire for a knowledge founded on a direct view of human things and actions, but he underscores the fact that this desire is always and forever frustrated or, at the least, feeds on its own frustration, since the historian can only confess, with every line of his narrative, "his exile in the present" and the immense absence that envelops the past he is recounting in its unreality.

We need to go further, no doubt: In the narration of history, and perhaps in any narration, there is only a simulation of reality, since even if the historian writes that he has seen what he is recounting, for the reader or listener of his narrative, everything takes place *as if* that act, that monument contemplated in the past, were again present in the discourse or in the text, *as if* that past, surging up anew from death, from its burial place, were presented to view in the imaginary of the reading or the listening. In effect, Candaules tells Gyges, I am not persuading you when I speak of what I see and what you cannot see (the beauty, *to eidos*, of my wife)—therefore, contrive to see her naked. In a single stroke, these words convert the simulation of the narrative (narrated in the powerful words of the king) into the seduction of a gaze upon the beauty of a body that he challenges his listener and confidant to cast. And, in telling us this story in the first pages of his *Histories*, Herodotus also sets in play his own undertaking and that of any historian. Hence, the strange seduction of that moment in the text, on me as a reader, to which I surrender by rewriting it in my way. This moment is suddenly effaced a few pages later when Herodotus confides to us that he saw Gyges' wine bowls of gold and silver, the documents, or monuments, of this disappeared past, deposited in the treasury of the Corinthians at Delphi. Seduction is reconverted into simulation: In that way, the historian's narrative has some relationship to the king's discourse. It repeats that discourse to its own account, but only to nullify the risk that Candaules ran one day, the risk of death; in this way, the historian's narrative in its (simulated) power of making visible has some relationship to the discourse of the master, the discourse of power.

Second Moment

"Contrive to see her naked." Thereupon, Gyges strongly protested.

> "Master," he said, "what an improper suggestion! Do you tell me to look at the queen when she has no clothes on? No, no: 'off with her skirt, off with her decency [*aidôs*]'—you know what they say of women. Let us learn from experience. Right and wrong were distinguished long ago—and I'll tell you one thing that is right: a man should look only on his own. I do not doubt that your wife is the most beautiful of women; so for goodness' sake do not ask me to behave like a criminal.[3]

A duel of words is thus engaged between the master and the slave, the king and his subject. Gyges seeks to escape the challenge, reject the provocation: the reaction of a circumspect courtier, the contemporary translator notes, of someone who would mistrust the perfidious fantasies a suspicious despot might have. Perhaps. But these remarks themselves lead us into the cruel and rarefied space of seduction, into the order of arbitrary obligation, where death is always at stake somewhere. What, then, is Gyges' response to the challenge issued? His parry is twofold, from below and from above, if I may say so. In the first place, it is a parry from below, since he casts away the king's provocative discourse as unhealthy and perverse. In giving such an order, the master no longer speaks as a master but as a sick man. (In the same way, Khrushchev explained Stalinism as the pathological excrescence of madness characteristic of the individual Stalin.) First tactical defense: The royal order is reduced to perverse singularity. This points out the proximity of seduction to perversity, and the distance that separates them. The seductive challenge is always perversity, but its perversity is the name given it by the one to whom the challenge is addressed, the one involved in the mortal risk of the duel that any gesture of seduction opens. The response to the challenge is to cling to the norm, the law, the abstract generality of the commandment, by calling seduction by the name of subversion or transgression. Hence, seduction transgresses the norm and, in doing so, negatively recognizes that its power is well founded. Everyone is to be subject to the law, to generality—even the king, even the master. Submission constitutes all people as universal autonomous and reasonable subjects; otherwise, the prince is a despot and the citizen a fool. But we cannot help but notice that here, this position is not at all speculative. It is only a response to the seductive challenge, a parry of the first thrust, the provocation. It is the tactical gesture of the slave challenged by the master, in the duel to which the master commits him. It takes on meaning inasmuch as its (speculative, theoretical, and practical) meaning collapses. That is why Gyges expounds the master's perversity only in generalities. Two maxims: off with her skirt, off with her decency [*aidôs*]; and, look only on your own. Conclusion: Your discourse as king is a powerful discourse; in telling me the queen is the most beautiful of women, you make me believe it, and I tell you I believe you and that you are telling the truth. And let us just leave it at that. You are master, even of truth, of the law and by the law.

Where, then, is that law in which, according to Gyges, the master is himself caught? It lies simultaneously in two places that are completely heterogeneous in appearance but that, in this case, are closely tied to each other: the feminine and the gaze. Playing on words in his turn, Gyges posits the first precept of the law: *Eidos* is *aidôs*. The beauty of the feminine body is its modesty, its honor, its decency; more precisely, the *visible* form of woman must be *hidden* to be beautiful. As a result, seeing the queen's form—seeing her naked—is seeing what must not be seen, at the risk of reversing, for the time of a gaze, honor into shame and beauty into ugliness. The feminine—a fortiori when it concerns a queen—is the fascinating, sacred place of the contradiction of the law, of the visible [*eidos*] (which is not visible in the excellence of its beauty [*aretè*] unless it remains unseen), and of the gaze (which is accomplished only by lowering one's eyes). Recall Plato's *Protagoras*, where the *aidôs* and the *dikè*, honor and justice, are the two essential political virtues, given by Zeus "to *all mankind*, to be the principles of organization of cities and the bonds of friendship."[4] We then perceive the force of the slave's retort to the master's challenge: It reveals to the prince the law that grounds political power, reveals it in the very place of the feminine that the master sets into play, in the place where the prince posits his own word as the stakes. But it also uncovers, in the same place and with the second maxim, the fact that the law is also the foundation of truth, which the royal discourse brings into being in pronouncing it.

Second maxim of the law: Let everyone look only on his own. If truth is the unveiling of the hidden [*alètheia*] (another contradiction of the law), this unveiling of the female body can only come about hidden; by definition, it can only be a veiling, whether it concerns the king or the subject, the master or the slave. In other words, the truth, the law of truth, whose place is the feminine, cannot be made public or shared: It is literally incommunicable because its unveiling remains, and must remain, hidden away in the privacy of everyone's property in order for political society to exist and the community to be founded. In short, the law of truth and of power, the law of the power of truth and of the truth of power, where truth founds its power and power its truth, that law is feminine: Its place is the feminine, and its force of law lies in the very contradiction between the gaze and the visible. There is a gaze that must not see what it wishes to look at; there is a visibility that must not be seen; there is a truth whose unveiling must remain veiled in order for there to be gazes that see, visibilities that are seen, truths that are shared and communicable, in order for there to be a powerful royal word that brings things into being by saying what it says. Gyges responds to the challenge of his master's seduction by articulating the feminine law of any representation and any truth, by formulating the contradiction between the gaze and the visible, the contradiction in which any representation finds its foundation and any political power its essential seat, the contradiction that is power, representation, truth.

But, I repeat, that response is not speculative; it is not thesis or theory. It is a tactic, a retort, a counterthrust in the duel or challenge initiated by the royal provocation. Far from encompassing the seductive discourse of the prince in a system that transcends it and in which it is grounded, far from positing this discourse as a "failure," an "infelicity," a perverse singularity in the functioning of the system, that parry does the opposite at the moment of seduction: The system of representation and its law are caught within the duel that Candaules and his confidant engage in; they become challenges that Gyges issues to Candaules. In effect, he says, you challenged me to see the queen naked. In pronouncing the law where your power is grounded, I challenge you in turn. A double "reversion" of the law: first, in the king's provocative discourse, where the sovereign, performative word is offered as the stakes in the seductive game; and, second, in Gyges' challenge, his retort, where, stripping bare the contradiction that gives to the system of representation the force of law, the slave challenges the law where the power of the master is grounded. It is easy to see, in fact, that the law Gyges articulates in his two maxims infinitely transcends the power of the prince, however legitimate. It is not Candaules who decreed that *eidos* is *aidôs*, or that everyone should look only on his own: "Let us learn from experience. Right and wrong were distinguished long ago." The law is transcendent in relation to the king, even as it grounds his power, even as it gives sense and power to his word as command. The king, however, does not transgress the law since what he commands Gyges, "contrive to see her naked," has no other meaning than to fulfill, to bring into existence, the absolute beauty of the queen by making public the truth of his word at the price of a gaze on the visible [*eidos*] that must not and cannot be seen. He puts it in play in the game of provocation that his challenge abruptly opens. For his part, Gyges, reminding the master of the law of his power in order to respond to his challenge, also does not posit that law in its sovereign transcendence. He includes it in the game that has been initiated. It is the weapon of his own challenge: "Contrive to see her naked"—"No bet." There is neither king nor subject, neither master nor slave; nor is there something between the two, in a dialectic of the relation of mastery. Rather, there is only the pure constitutive and regulative dual relation of two partners in a situation of reciprocal challenge.

Third Moment

To Gyges' counterthrust, Candaules responds in turn: "'There is nothing to be afraid of,' he said. 'Either from me or my wife.'" He denies the mortal danger of the game to which both are committed. The lightness of tone is proportionate to the degree of risk and the importance of the stakes. "I'll manage [*archèn egô mèchanèsomai*] so that she doesn't even know that you have seen her. Look: I will hide you behind the open door of our bedroom. . . . Near the door there's a chair—she will put her clothes on it as she takes them off, one by one. You will be able to watch her with perfect ease. Then, as she's walking away from the chair towards the bed with her back to you, slip away through the door—and mind she doesn't catch you."[5] What does this ruse, this machination of the king consist in? An absolute, total ruse, says Candaules to Gyges. This underscores the fact that the ruse plays on the essential, that is, on the formulation by Gyges of the law of the system of representation and of its two maxims; better yet, the essential of the ruse consists in playing on the double contradiction that the enunciation of the law by the confidant sets forth, even as it implicitly refers to the dynamic principle that gives the law the *force* of law. But, at the same time, we note that Candaules situates his reply not on the plane of generalities where Gyges had placed his own ("you know what they say of women"—"right and wrong were distinguished long ago"—"a man should look only on his own"), but, rather, in the field of the particular and the local. His ruse is total but it only has value for one place, one space, one moment, which is unique and specifically determined: the conjugal bedroom, the chair near the door, and so on. Yet, although the ruse is unique, a calculation for this one time only, and in circumstances that are themselves unique, it is operative and effective only when inserted into a ritual, played out in the repetitive, temporal framework that the rules of this ritual guarantee, rules that, though not institutional, religious, social, or political, are nonetheless constraining. It is the queen's nightly ritual of going to bed: "She will put her clothes on [the chair] as she takes them off, one by one. . . . Then, as she's walking away from the chair towards the bed with her back to you . . ." This set of habits is constraining and arbitrary. Its explicit intentions, rules, and finality (to get undressed in order to go to bed and sleep beside the king) are deflected toward a completely different objective in and by the royal ruse: The queen undresses every evening before going to bed, but this undressing becomes a "striptease" offered by the king to his confidant. "You will be able to watch her [*theèsasthai*] with perfect ease [*kat'èsuchièn pollèn*]." The king's total and particular machination, whose effectiveness stems from the royal bedtime ritual, plays on this ritual by instantly turning it into another ritual on this particular occasion, into the queen's "striptease," an erotic and no longer practical or technical ritual, but one that is such only to Gyges' forbidden gaze as he hides behind the door.

Such is the third moment in the duel of mutual seduction, in the alternating challenges in which the master and slave are engaged. Something like a pact now links the two partners; the ruse that one orchestrates and proposes to the other appears when the ritual played out between the queen and the king is diverted into another, into one between the queen and Gyges. Without changing the content or the rules, the first becomes the opportunity (the favorable moment) for the second. The trick the king plays in his reply to Gyges, in the discourse of ruse—the stage director's trick, which he asks Gyges to interpret in the bedroom-turned-stage-and-spectacle through his presence—also has the remarkable characteristic of making the protagonist of the play disappear. The duel remains a duel, but it now unfolds between the queen and the servant. The master stroke calculated by Candaules the stage director has the result of effacing Candaules from the stage, rubbing him out in the penumbra of the bedroom, burying him deep in the conjugal bed. His triumph is his death. In seduction, there are always two actors, never three.

The ruse is total, we said, in that it puts into play *as ruse* the essentiality of the essential, the contradiction of the law, the blind spot of the system of representation. It puts it in play by playing (in the sense a gambler plays a card or a chess player a pawn) the contradiction, but also by playing around with it, trivializing it. We said that the contradiction that guarantees the force of law of the system of representation is that of a gaze that does not see and a visibility that is not seen. The contradiction would be unsustainable if the constatives that articulate it were not transformed into prescriptives that order it: The gaze *must not* see (a forbidden gaze); the visible *must not be* seen (a forbidden visibility); the unveiling of truth *must remain* veiled. Such is the law, such is representation, such is the social and political contract. Candaules's ruse plays the law, representation, the contract; it plays the essential. How? By transforming the contradictory essence into appearance. Looking without seeing becomes (with the help of a door) looking without being seen. The visibility that is not seen becomes a visibility invisibly seen, a visibility that does not see it is visible. Appearance. In effect, the law that "your gaze must not see," which grounds the contract (let everyone look only on his own), is converted into the rule, "your gaze, which will see (what it must not see), will be invisible to the visible (which must not be seen), which will not see that it is seen." The pact between the partners in the game is sealed with this rule: "Only you and I will know that you looked at what was mine and that I let you look." And that is how the king plays with the law. The law ceases to have the force of general law in the master's discourse of ruse; it becomes, through the machination he sets in place, the key to the dual manipulation of appearances into which he has led the slave. Granted, you'll say, but the king is a traitor to the law, and the confidant is cheating on the order of representation. That, we respond, is an illusion of perspective. Treason and cheating characterize them only for *a third party* (you, me, the reader of Herodotus) who is situated in the order of law and representation. It cannot be so for either the king or Gyges, since both have played the law and representation in the duel of challenges and provocations in which they are engaged and in which they find themselves caught, risking death. Once the mechanism, the machine of the machination of the game, has been constructed, all that remains is for the scene of seduction to be played out. There is neither treason nor cheating, for each one plays his part: "Gyges, since he was unable to avoid it, consented."[6]

FOURTH MOMENT

When bedtime came Candaules brought him to the room. Presently the queen arrived, and Gyges watched her walk in and put her clothes on the chair. Then, just as she had turned her back and was going to bed, he slipped softly out of the room. But the queen saw him. At once she realized what her husband had done. But she did not betray the shame she felt by screaming, or even let it appear that she noticed anything. Instead she silently resolved to have her revenge. For with the Lydians, as with most barbarian races, it is thought highly indecent even for a man to be seen naked.[7]

Fourth moment of the scene of seduction: The feminine, up to this point a place in the discourses of challenge between the master and the slave, becomes woman (the queen, the mistress). She comes on stage to play her role in the play of gazes. Gyges changes his partner and his position: not the king but the queen; not discourse, but gazes. The reversion of the law is complete. In the reply to his master, Gyges, provoked by the challenge of Candaules, has made the feminine the very place of the law. This time, with the mechanism in place, the woman becomes the agent [*actant*] of his about-turn. She is no longer the stakes of the king's discourse, which, with the feminine, risks the performative power of his word. She is no longer the generalizing topos of the confidant's discourse, which found an escape to the master's challenge by uncovering the very place of the law that—in its contradiction—grounded power. Yet, that very escape led the king's partner into the duel of words, led him all the more necessarily to begin the about-turn in the manipulation of appearances. In a word, and quite simply, she is no longer the field of a duel in discourse. The feminine-become-woman is henceforth—without discourse, without words—the mute agent of the relation of seduction. The woman plays her role according to the rules of a game she knows—the evening ritual of undressing—and of a game she does not know—the erotic "striptease"— exactly according to the mechanism on the stage, set up between the master and the slave. She is in her place, he in his, and, nevertheless, she seduces because she is never where anyone (the king, Gyges) thinks she is, nor even where she thinks she is. She is not where she thinks she is—in the royal bedroom, undressing and placing her clothing on a chair by the door as she does every night before getting into bed next to her royal spouse. Rather, she is on an erotic stage and in the erotic scene in which the prince is the stage director and the confidant the spectator, to the sole end that the first rediscovers, but in a forbidden and silent gaze, the immediate power, the instantaneous force of his word. And, here as well, and for the time of a glance, the wife is also not where she is thought to be by the two partners of the discursive game. She is not a simple visibility invisibly seen by a gaze that should not have seen her. Because, for an instant, the time of an instant, the visible [*eidos*], by definition, the real or potential object of the gaze, *sees* [*epora*], according to Herodotus: She sees what happens all of a sudden, but sees with an impassive eye. The visible sees no objects, only a gaze, that is, she sees what, by definition, is the invisible itself: Not only because it is not possible to see the immaterial trajectory between an eye and its object but also because *that particular gaze must not see*, especially (for an entirely empirical reason) when she walks toward the bed and turns her back—that part of her body that she herself does not see—to the man hidden behind the door. A pure moment of seduction: The feminine, that seeing visibility for the time of an instant, is the invisible gaze that sees the other's gaze, at a moment when that gaze does not think it is seen and when no one else thinks it is. But, in the same instant, the definitive reversion of the law of representation is accomplished. Although the woman, suddenly sighted, sees what occurs, sees the invisible gaze that sees her, she sees it with an impassive eye: She does not cry out in shame [*aischunè*], in which case the honor of her beauty [the *aidôs* of her *eidos*] would collapse. She conceals herself from the law of the Lydians and the barbarians (which Herodotus recalls to us in a parenthetical statement) not through forgetfulness or transgression but in playing against the one—Gyges—who invisibly sees her the same trick that Candaules had played against him. She conceals herself from the law like Candaules, like Gyges, by converting it into appearance: She *pretends* not to see that she is seen, she pretends to be the visibility that is not seen and which, for that very reason, must not be seen. She pretends to look without seeing. Her behavior articulates the law, but as a pure appearance, and its reversion is complete: Not only has the woman entered the game of seduction—provocations, challenges, thrusts, retorts, raising the stakes—but, in an instant, she brings it to an end by impassively manipulating appearances, not in discourse, but in acts. Henceforth Gyges, without knowing it, without wishing it, is her partner, without her knowing or wishing it either. To the king's manipulative machination of appearances in the seductive discourse addressed to the confidant, there corresponds the queen's machination, which manipulates appearances in the absolute seductive discourse: pretending not to see the invisible gaze that sees her in her naked visibility. One can even ask whether, in this semblance, there does not finally come into being, in a dazzling flash of a gaze cast and captured, what was at stake in the master's seductive challenge to the slave from the beginning of that story: the absolute beauty of the woman, the impassive lure of seduction.

Fifth Moment

But, in the early morning, everything changes; or rather, everything is repeated:

> She sent for Gyges.... There was nothing unusual in his being asked to attend upon the queen; so Gyges answered the summons without any suspicion that she knew what had occurred on the previous night. "Gyges," she said, as soon as he presented himself, "there are two courses open to you, and you may take your choice between them. Kill Candaules and seize the throne, with me as your wife; or die yourself on the spot, so that never again may your blind obedience to the king tempt you to see what you have no right to see [what is consecrated by usage, *ta nomizomena*]."[8]

Everything has changed: Substituted for the silent impassivity of the gaze, which saw the invisible (the other forbidden gaze), is the cold determination of the discourse of the double injunction, both exclusive and necessary: "Kill or be killed." The choice is impossible to escape.

(What a mistake to think, as the translator seems to suggest, that the queen and Gyges could be a pair of lovers plotting both the overthrow of a king and the elimination of a husband; what a mistake to reduce the seductive challenge to a psychology of love and to its consequence, a dramatic news item. It is not a matter of love but of seduction; it is not a question of the fusion of bodies and hearts in the happiness of impassioned rapture, but a matter of agonistic seduction, the ineluctably constraining traps opened by the distance between gazes and the violence of confrontational discourses.)

Everything has changed, then, and yet everything is repeated, with merely a substitution of partners. For the queen's discourse at the end of the narrative is strangely symmetrical and opposite to the king's discourse, which introduced the narrative. The king had set in play the performative power of the royal word by challenging Gyges to see what he was forbidden to see and, simultaneously, to bring into existence the absolute beauty of the queen and conquer to his advantage the power of immediate and absolute persuasion outside discourse, the persuasion of the gaze: Either you see what is forbidden and you immediately believe what I have always told you, that the queen is the most beautiful of all women, or you conceal yourself from the effective power of my word and whatever you allege, you disobey. Gyges consented to see the visible that should have remained invisible, but the visible, sighted for an instant, saw that it was seen. The *eidos-aidôs*, hidden beauty and secret honor, collapsed in silent shame [*aischunè*]. After the seductive gazes, the discourse of seduction returns. Its provocation is the following: Look no longer on what it is forbidden to see, but rather *blind the gaze of the third party cast upon the forbidden, on what must remain invisible, whatever the person, the individuality, of the third party might be.* "Let everyone look only on his own." There cannot be three of us who have seen: the king who offered the sight, the confidant who saw, and the queen who saw and was seen. Death must strike down one of the three: either the master who set up the machine of the invisible gaze, or the slave who was that gaze, or the mistress who saw it.

(This last hypothesis, however, that of a suicide by the queen in the manner of Lucretia, a way of effacing her shame through her own death, is not evoked in Herodotus's narrative, no doubt for the same reasons that make Gyges choose to save his own life. The queen and Gyges both know that the other knows; only the king, who knows that Gyges knows, does not know that the queen knows. In truth, in detailing the hypotheses, we are led to believe that Gyges would have been executed had he remained invisible to the queen.)

There is thus one gaze too many. *One must close another's eyes so that one can close one's eyes to the moment of the reversion of the law.* The queen, as we have noted, does not put herself in play, just as Gyges, a moment later, chooses not to put himself in play. But if the king's death is decided upon, it is perhaps, no doubt, because in the earlier moment, the king had already been effaced, had himself already closed his eyes. That amounts to saying that the secret must be kept and that it can be kept only in the dual pact. Shared by three, it is necessarily public. "Let everyone look only on his own."

Here, then, is the tragic dilemma in which Gyges finds himself, tragic because it is absolutely constraining and already resolved. Either put to death the one who *offered* the sight that must not be seen and receive the *offering* of power, the queen and royalty; or put to death the one who saw because he accepted the *offering* of the gaze on what was forbidden by the law. In both cases, the law is restored but displaced, eaten away from the inside by the permanent threat of seduction. Were Gyges to die, his disappearance, his absence would be secretly at the foundation of the king's erotic and political power: The contradiction internal to the law of representation would no longer give law its force; rather, his dissimulated death, the past trace of the gaze of seduction, would provide that force, and would continually threaten the law. That is Freud's hypothesis in *Moses and Monotheism*, the Jewish solution. With Candaules dead, the secret of his death remains. (Does not Herodotus tell us that the Lydians took the murder of Candaules very hard and were prepared to fight against Gyges until the response of the oracle?) It is upon that secret that the power of Gyges, king of the Mermnadae dynasty, is founded. But there again, death and seduction mysteriously continue their threatening work in the royal line issued from the new sovereign. Does not the oracle of Apollo, in designating Gyges, add that the Heraclids would take their vengeance on the fourth descendant of Gyges? But, notes Herodotus, "neither the Lydians nor their kings paid any attention, until it was actually fulfilled."[9] This is the Greek solution, the destiny of seduction, discontinuity and return, the differences of opportunity and necessary repetition.

Sixth Moment

Major conclusion: Gyges attempted to persuade Candaules to renounce his challenge by retorting with the enunciation of the law, but he did not succeed because his reply itself was caught in the field of the duel of provocation. In the same way, he now attempts to persuade the queen to nullify the mortal dilemma in which she traps him but fails because, though he does not know it himself, though she does not want it on her side, the necessarily constraining seductive pact was sealed between them at the instant when he saw the visible that should have remained invisible (her *eidos-aidôs*) and when she saw the invisible and forbidden gaze. Then "he soon saw that he really was faced with the alternatives, either of murdering his master, or of being murdered himself. He made his choice—to live."[10] He then raised this question: "Tell me . . . since you drive me against my will to kill the king"—for that is the pact that ties one to the other beyond or before their own wills and desires as autonomous and responsible subjects—"how shall we set on him?" She responds: "We will attack him when he is asleep . . . and on the very spot where he showed me to you naked."[11] The same scene is repeated, therefore, and the scene of seduction becomes the scene of death. Gyges is hidden behind the bedroom door when night falls. Instead of the gaze, he wields a dagger (undoubtedly, the same thing in this case), but instead of the woman's gaze that sees the gaze that invisibly sees her, he finds the closed eyes of the sleeping Candaules.

Thus Gyges usurped the throne and married the queen. This is the Gyges whom Archilochus of Paros mentions as a contemporary in his Satires.[12]

Seduction of the gaze, the gaze of seduction: The invisible gaze that sees what must not be seen, the secret beauty of the woman, the honor and virtue of the social and political contract, is nothing more than the invisible and necessary death carried out against the man who, putting in play the power of his effective word to publicly bring into existence that beauty and overturning the law of representation, offered for view what should have remained invisible and unknown in order for that law, and with it his own power, to be exercised.

Minor conclusion: these few verses from the fable by Perrault entitled "Peau d'Ane":

> It is said that in working too much in haste,
> There fell from her finger and into the paste,
> By accident, one of her rings of great price;
> But those who relate the end of the tale
> Assure us she purposely put it in there;
> And I, to be frank, quite simply believe it
> For I'm certain the Prince, who appeared at her door
> And looked through the keyhole,
> And saw her, was seen in turn by her:
> For in this a woman is so quick
> And her eye so adept
> That one cannot see her a moment
> Without her knowing the deed.

14

The Sublime, the Obscene

THE SUBLIME

One scene sums up, or rather, condenses, all the signs and insignia of political power at its highest degree of potency: the king contemplating his own portrait. The scene reveals to its stage director the imaginary nature of all power, in the very desire for the absolute, a desire consubstantial with that power. In recognizing the icon of the monarch he wants to be, the king recognizes himself, identifies himself with his portrait. The hidden, reverse side of that contemplation is the disappearance of the model. The prince, of course, does not pass through the mirror of Narcissus. He simply imitates his portrait, just as the portrait imitates the king. King of representation and representation of the king—a mutual mimesis in which we can read the fundamental figure of all power and all representation, but in which each is subordinated to the other, belongs to the other, appropriates the other in an exact reversibility. The representation of the king is both the exact designation of his power and its most efficient means; but, in its reversal, "king of representation," an ironic distance opens, dividing representation and power into two unequal parts. Part of the brute power, the immediate violence that orients all power as its origin, its foundation, and its last resort is lost in theatricality, where it is nevertheless fulfilled and legitimated. Representation of the king, King of representation: on the one hand, a mere image; on the other, a role. In that reversion, a "real" individual disappears; in that disappearance, the "king" acquires a capital, a capital letter, and becomes the King. His name—semantically—has not changed, but through the representation of his image, the initial letter of his name is heightened and exalted. An excess is introduced into the signifier that begins the common noun (but an excess that does not transcend its meaning or its limit), making it a proper name to signify his uniqueness, to mark a symbolic supplement fit for only one: through representation, the height of power; through power, the fullness of representation. An exchange in which they fulfill each other, an equivalency in which they legitimate each other, but also, the excess of a double challenge, a game of bidding wars, not through a transgression of limits, but through the very process that fills the place, the role, the image, the name, beyond the limit, but without ever overflowing. In short, a fullness: to be precise, the sublimity of power and representation.

The body of the king is his portrait; the portrait of the King is the King—in an impressive obviousness: It is the King, first, through the accumulation of royal signs that produce his identity, his being, his presence, not those of an individual but those of his office, his function, his role. There is not a single element of the portrait that is not a symbolic ornament or a historical document, from the great dais with the scarlet canopy, the gold in the crimson carpet, from the gilded throne with blue velvet in a *fleur de lys* pattern, the royal blue mantle with gold scepter, from the great ritual wig to the sword of Charlemagne, from the collar of the order of the Holy Spirit with its lace ruffle to the white shoes with red heels. . . . Even the light and shadow playing on the metal, the precious stones, the marble, and the fabrics contribute to defining this place and its figures in the divine *numen* that envelops the royal body, covering his face with a mysterious sublimity.

The King is standing. But has he risen from his throne? Did he step down a step from the platform that holds the seat of majesty? In truth, he is neither at rest nor in motion in this swarming arrangement of signs borne by a body-mannequin. The King is standing, fixed in the pose, pausing for the pose: his left hand posed on his hip, the crook of his arm in the fold of the lining of the great velvet and ermine mantle; his right hand on the scepter planted on the stool; his two legs sheathed in white silk; his figure suspended in a motionless dance that fashions a kind of corporeal ideality in an instant, an infinite duration brought together in a dense moment. "The King." The Prince's portrait on display is an apostrophe, the naming of a name, an iconic *epideixis* outside time, outside aspect, outside modality, the pure, timeless, permanent present of the presence—in representation. Present, *prae-sens*: not being there or being in front of, but being ahead of, in a state of imminence and suspense, in an excess of presence, but within the limits of representation. That presence saturates the representational arrangement of the portrait, completes it, but without compromising its hierarchy or its economy, the profuse expenditure it presents to the view and the inexhaustible reserve from which it draws. The King in the portrait of his sublimity is looking, but he is not contemplating his subject, who is crushed by the gravity of the office, nor even the model of the king in its perfect figure. The King is not looking at anything. Just as the pose is the fullness of a state of being and of movement, the King's gaze is the ultimate excess; the extreme passion of the face nullifies any determinate passion in the imminence of presence.

The sublimity of royal representation, between a leg and a gaze, between the ostentation of a body of love and that of a face of power, is a vertiginous space between love and the law, where aesthetic representation and political power mutually reinforce each other and bring about the irresistible effects of the seductive persuasion and listless majesty of the self/state.

> His sleep, even while he was enjoying such health, was always agitated and uneasy, a bit more than usual; he spoke often in his sleep and even got out of bed, which was to me a convincing indication of some overheated bile and of the effect of the great affairs he decided during the day, the images of which passed through his head again during the night and awakened the actions of the soul during the body's rest.... We must add the heat of his loins as a disposition of the subject very likely to be set off at the slightest opportunity... overheated face, heavy head, and indifference of the entire body, sorrow and melancholy without reason, accidents... caused by the little rest he allows himself, staying up too late and not sleeping enough for a man whose mind works as much as his does.[1]

THE OBSCENE

The King: You're making too much of it, you're going too far, and at the same time the spectacle you offer to persuade me or make me believe the scene you're playing for me, to seduce me, withdraws imperceptibly, but enough to place it at a new distance: it is now too far away for me to cross the ramp in my imagination, the ramp that separates me as a spectator, seated in my armchair on the ritual platform, from you, the too eager actor at its foot, too far away for me to enter your game, to coincide with your character, to invest your mannequin body with my fears and hopes, my desires and hatred, to identify with you, recognizing myself on that stage. The irony is that, instead of the flash of conviction, the thrill of complicity (and I know you're seeking the signs of such things on my face), there is a retreat into apathy, withdrawal; a blank neutrality, sometimes even a half-smile.

I see through your game, I see you coming. You have not found the right distance—not too far, too high, too low, too close—the right distance that would have allowed you to play it just right, to measure your gestures, to find the proper voice, use the inflections to good effect; the exact distance where excesses cancel out lacks, where the "too much" nullifies the "not enough," and the perfect figure takes shape. Because you make too much of it, you suddenly take your distance, withdraw to another stage, and yet, at the same time, I am close enough to touch you. I discern the sweat on your forehead, the saliva on the corners of your lips, even the beating of a little muscle in your eyelid, the trembling of your hands, the way you rub your index finger and thumb together. These accidents, these tiny events of your body and face that lie beyond the power of even your most attentive will, tell me in an instant more than the well-turned sentences of your speech, the accent of truth, of sincerity, that animates your voice. In an instant, my ear is too close to your mouth, as if I had extended it to hear a secret you whispered to me alone in the crowd of courtiers, and I no longer hear what you are telling me but only the way you catch your breath, the hard breathing in the words you pronounce. And they erase the words for me. And I now listen only to the mechanics of your speech, and behind it the sneezes, belches, spitting, wheezing. You make too much of it; you go too far, you no longer persuade me, no longer seduce me. Instead of the pleasure of recognizing myself and dissolving into the portrait of myself that you hold up with consummate art, I withdraw, ironic, from your game, because "I see you coming." I withdraw to the impassive neutrality the prince has to maintain when he is addressed. But that neutrality often dissimulates the delicious desire to believe he is, in fact, the one depicted in the portrait created by the discourse of praise, leading him to fall into the nets of beautiful language, where he thinks the truth of his power, or the greatness of the state it incarnates, is constructed. Yet here I am alone, abandoned to myself and at the same time fascinated by your body, your face, your voice. I am infinitely distant from you as you speak ceremoniously: etiquette places you in the exact position required by the hierarchy, the precise distance from my chair. Yet at the same time I am so close to you that in the ballet of your body and your words, I now see only the drop of sweat that drips from your wig onto your forehead, the saliva on your lips which the face powder does not absorb; I now hear only the wheezing of your lungs as you speak; I now smell only the slightly rancid odor of your ancient flesh, which the perfume no longer succeeds in covering. Yet I myself instituted the choreography of that ballet, because I knew, even though I had never been taught, that the omnipotence of the state was first of all this constraining and absurd game. Fascination: I see through your game, but cannot see clearly the favor you wish to obtain or the pension you'll manage to wrench from me with that very calculated praise you address to me; I cannot see clearly the cabal, even though I know you're becoming its spokesperson, or the malevolent insinuations, even though you allow me to decipher the intention; I cannot even see clearly the secret I was not supposed to know and that you madly betray—how could you be so careless in a discourse of this kind when I know in advance the elements and compliments that necessarily compose it? What I see in your game is not its strategy, not the staging I myself set up, the tactics you decided blow by blow in the close mesh of the ceremonial discourse where you wish to trap me. I see rather what underlies the game, which is suddenly exhibited: your flesh on your body, the skeleton of the mannequin who wears your suits, ribbons, and brocade, suddenly so visible that it fascinates my myopic gaze. You make too much of it, without wanting to, I'm sure, since you know very well that flattery can turn into its opposite, and you are too old a courtier not to know the indivisible point of inversion that no discourse of praise, no compliment, can cross without being rendered impotent or ridiculous. You go too far, and I'm sure it's not your discourse that leads you beyond your intentions, since you say nothing I don't already know. Could it be my doing, then, as I listen to you with the majesty that the entire court and all my people recognized in me, despite my size? Could I, seated in my chair, motionless, be withdrawing into the infinite ironic distance of my dignity? Could I be rushing too close to you in an instant, despite the nausea I feel from seeing too much, hearing too much, of that obscenity in your flesh, your face, your voice, your gestures. That fascination or that rushing forward is a strange discomfort, and I let nothing of it show on the outside. Yet it infects me to the point that I no longer feel anything but this solemn shell through which I show myself to the court. No, I do not even feel, I am empty, all sensibility, all life has withdrawn in the brief instant when I see you, hear you—too much. It's as if I were now only a surface with no inside, the exact measure of the platitudes in your attitude and in the praises you discharge in front of me. I also know that, in the eyes of the world (the best judge of these things, nonetheless), that seamless surface is called depth, the depth where the world believes the monarch's coups d'état are meditated upon and dissimulated. You make too much of it, you go too far, and yet you are playing your role perfectly in the great political representation. You and I are only cogs in that machine—I don't hide it from myself, I'm only a cog, but an essential one, since all the others interlock their movements with mine—the great representation machine I found ready to receive me when I took the throne, and that you found when you came to court. You play your role and I play mine, and the representation endlessly unfolds in its pomp, regulated by the hierarchy of its planes, the order of etiquette, down to the abysses of my divine wisdom and power whose secret it represents by concealing it, and even I do not know the bottom of it. And yet you make too much of it. And I am too close to you, fascinated by that drop of sweat that runs from your forehead to your cheek. I too make too much of it, like you, I see too well—I now see nothing but that drop of sweat and I have become that surface just as you are now only a machine with springs and whistles, belching, spitting, sweating, coughing, an absurd display. And the beautiful representation of the power of the state is instantaneously set off kilter, flattened. I suddenly have the feeling that everything is in suspense in a moment that stretches out continuously, interminably, like that day at the siege of Namur when a bomb fell into the trench. That minute was a century of silence, and in that silence of things and men I felt once and for all what it is to be King, the impossibility of death for we who are of another nature, our Sublimity, the fullness of the royal representation, in that inexpressible moment when all eyes were fixed on me, waiting for the explosion. And I, impassive, as if I were leading the parade. And an idea came to be, when I returned from the campaign to the entertainments at

Versailles, to set off the fireworks machines on the last night, the machines that had until that time been invisible, that had produced the fireworks, and to illuminate for a short moment, through the very destruction of the light displays, the gardens, ponds, palace, court, taking the celebration, the representation, to new heights, in a great consuming explosion. It was, I think today, as if the Namur bomb had waited several weeks for the spectacle of my triumph, had suspended the time of men in order to explode to my glory. That drop of sweat that is running down your cheek when you move to proffer my praise also suspends time, but in a very different way from the Dutch bomb: not in the exaltation of my divine body but in an irresistible fatigue, the threat of the unknown, obscenity, death. That's why I don't begrudge you, because in truth neither you nor I know what is taking place at this moment. The spectacle where you represent yourself in order to praise me has vanished into an indiscernible point at infinity, leaving you alone to gesticulate your ridiculous words like some great sea larva foaming on the sand of a beach from which the sea has withdrawn. And I, suddenly myopic, entranced by that drop of sweat that keeps running down your cheek, an absurdity, where everything falls apart by simple juxtaposition. The visible, which becomes visible only by drawing support from the invisible shadow of things that reveal themselves to the light, suddenly vanishes, not because it gets very dark but because there is no longer anything to see; not because the stage is empty of its actors (one assumes they are still backstage or lost among the flies above the stage); not because the curtain has fallen on the play at its denouement (one imagines the mysterious half-light of the boards, which the specters of heroes haunt during the day, reappearing there in the splendor of their representation the next night). There is nothing more to see because everything is in view, so much in view that I could never get to the end of telling you what I see in what you show me, which is usually enveloped in a word. So much in view that everything, and to the same degree, and without differences, is present in an abstract and threatening imminence that is blinding. Strange discomfort, this change that infects the world, things, men, words—in my palace, my court, my throne, in the place of representation, in the center of the state where I place myself and where I find my ordered omnipotence. What a strange discomfort, this too-close presence of a body in precise detail, each detail of which imposes itself absolutely, beside all the others, fixing my gaze to the point that it is effaced in amazement. For an instant, I no longer know who is seeing the drop of sweat that flows motionless, minuscule, down the cheek. That drop has become an eye without sight, but it still captures me. I imagine Medusa like that (her story was told to me): wide open eyes, multiple eyes on the serpents of her hair, and when she surges up at the detour in the path, suddenly the world and its landscape, the rocks in the desert erected into statues, the sky—everything—flees in an instant, far away, too far away, and the traveler's gaze becomes motionless, rolls back in his head, repulsed by those eyes that do not look, by the breathing of the open mouth, voiceless, and the hanging, red tongue. Fascinated by the drop of sweat, by that eye, by Medusa, I think of La Beauvais, the chambermaid of the Queen Mother, that one-eyed creature who taught me how to sleep with women; her skirts lifted, legs hanging, spread open over the edge of the bed, her sex open, and on top of the crumpled taffeta, her eye fixed on me, the half toothless mouth of her engaging grin. I recently reread a few pages of the health journal my doctor, Fagon, compiled in secret. He explains the strange discomfort this way: vapors rising from the spleen, carrying with them melancholy and sorrow. But what is the good of knowing since he can't cure me? Moreover, displayed on the page were the arteries, the heart, and the lungs, the agitation of spirits in the eye, their spinning to the principle of the nerves: in reading, I was looking at my own body, its parts shown line after line, set out in the even light of the medical words, and the thick night of the organs, of fluids and humors, of bile and liquids, dissipated. I no longer had any insides; I rediscovered in the excrement the peas and artichokes prepared for me during Lent, and in the urine, the sour foam of champagne, which I like to drink chilled despite the doctors' opposition.

This flat body dispersed on the page into spirits, ducts, pipes, liquids and serous fluids, bones and pustules made me dizzy, suffocated me and made my head spin, the very things it was supposed to explain. In the same way, the drop of sweat that runs down your cheek fascinates me.

For that obscene anxiety to end I need only turn my eyes by a few inches to contemplate, above the head that is beginning to make the ceremonial movement of the bow, the royal representation of Myself, the great portrait of the King that I had placed facing my throne, the sublimity of my divine body in the stiff pose in which my office is concentrated, and in the impassive gaze the portrait casts.

Your last compliment is stifled by your wig as you bow before me. I am certainly what you said I am: King, the greatest who was ever on earth, lovable in peace and terrible in war. In the end, comparable only to himself. The representation ends and immediately deploys another of its figures. I cast my eyes over everything, the master's eyes: everything is in its place, on stage, in order.

15

The Caesura of the Royal Body

Under the Sign of the Cross

From December 1869 to December 1885, that is, for sixteen years, the first intimate journal of Louis II of Bavaria numbers thirty-three folios, two or three per year on the average. May and June 1886 barely make up five pages: The second and last journal of the king ends with a postscript written 7 June. He died tragically on the thirteenth, before reaching his forty-first birthday, which he had fixed as the last possible deadline for his spiritual reformation. This arithmetic and Louis's intimate journals themselves reveal from the outset a growing scarcity of discourse, an impoverishment of writing, the lacunar or torn fabric of a singular existence in its inscription on the page. Two enormous and sumptuous albums contain them, as if the splendor of the container signified the inestimable price, the incomparable value of the gaps, the exceptional quality of the blanks and silences of an exhausted content.

Intimate journals? We might wonder about that expression, in his case, if it is supposed to designate a transcription of events in the life and thoughts of an individual, someone caught up in the daily, or almost daily, scansion of clock time and whose aim is contemporaneity, the instantaneity of the conjunction between an existence and its writing, though the writer is never able to attain it. As a result, the intimate journal is never a narrative; what gets written in a journal are incidents, accidents, events, opportunities, chance happenings, encounters, in short, raw material deposited as soon as it appears, or almost, before any narrative structure can give it the coherence of a form. Even when thoughts and reflections, or narratives themselves, are found there, they are still only fragments of that raw material. Hence the effect of authenticity and sincerity that each dispersed transcription carries within it, an authenticity reinforced by the articulations of the "objective" chronicle, the inscription of dates, which give to the registering of events the validity, albeit fictive, of a photograph, precisely what Roland Barthes called the *punctum*, not of detail, but of intensity: "It is Time, the wrenching grandiloquence of the poem ('so it was'), its pure representation."[1]

Louis II of Bavaria's intimate journals? Yes, in a sense, in that the notations are fragmented, dispersed. But they are intimate journals at their limit, and for two reasons: first, because of the depletion of incidents, the poverty of "events," the impoverishment of accidents and opportunities both in "objective" time and in the written record of royal existence; second, because of the astonishing redundancy of the text, the obstinate, obsessional repetition of a few utterances, oaths, invocations, supplications, promises. These are performative utterances, for the most part, events of thought and will, of feeling and affectivity that escape clock time, the time of writing. In addition, the very act of writing them down is an integral part of their content, their enunciative "force." Because of their very repetition, these utterances require our attention, require an attention devoted to discerning the differences among them. The "rarity" of the king of Bavaria's intimate journals functions as a notice or warning to the reader: Unlike many intimate journals, they discourage the indiscreet gaze and disappoint the reader's voyeurism. That may be how Louis II succeeded in being as isolated in writing of his existence as he was (or sought to be) solitary in his existence itself. Hence, he keeps his secret.

The first folio of the first journal may offer one of the keys to a reading. It opens with a ritual invocation to the Trinity, "In the name of the Father, and of the Son, and of the Holy Ghost." In the Catholic liturgy, the utterance of those words, of the three divine names, is accompanied by the sign of the cross, a gesture by the orant's right hand, which touches, in turn, four parts of his own body, the head (the Father), the heart (the Son), the left shoulder, and then the right shoulder (the Holy Ghost—Amen). The words of invocation, "In the name of ...," are inscribed, albeit through a gesture without trace, on the body, enveloping it in a sign. This sign, written by the spoken word, signaling a few of the body's places, which makes it a crucified body, that of its redeemer, a divine body that—however automatic the ritual has become or even *because* it is automatic—is superimposed onto the body of the individual in prayer, transforming it symbolically into the very substance of the divine body. In raising the earthly body to its death on the wood of the cross, the divine body brings about the earthly body's death to the world, to sin, to evil, that is, it makes true life real or present: all through a simple sign, a simple gesture of the hand made upon oneself, reflexively, *on the body itself,* a gesture accompanying the enunciation of the three names of God.

What happens, then, when that inscription of the divine body on a human body is itself written on the page? Does not the page itself, the mere support of signs, become body in turn, the skin of a body, both symbolic and present, where the words and sentences to be engraved do nothing more than repeat the divine enveloping, the trinitary superimposition that the initial formula of invocation fulfills in its performance? That repetition is articulated by the first sentence: "I find myself under the sign of the cross (the day of redemption of Our Lord)." It is articulated in the reflexivity of "I" and "myself," which places it—the expression is noteworthy—*under a sign*, that of the cross, as the substance that this formless sign hangs over, and, even more perhaps, as the servant bent under the law, the Law that is written and inscribed *on* him by that sign. The key to reading the journals, which I announced a moment ago—one key, at least—is linked to that constellation of terms that literally encircles the "I" of the king—writing of himself—with another Trinity: the body of God, "my" body, the "Law" in its sign, Father, Son, and Holy Ghost, which, no less literally, divide the self into four parts, quarter the self the king reflects or attempts to reflect by writing *under* the sign of *their* cross. From the first to the last folio, these journals could be read as the monotonous refractions of that cross into the diversity of its figures.

The Trinity, in the opening invocation, is itself repeated, not only in the first sentence, "I find myself under the sign of the cross," but also, by a kind of *mise en abyme*, in what follows: "I find myself under the sign of the cross . . . under the sign of the sun . . . and of the moon." That cosmology of cross, sun, and moon is less strange, esoteric, and personal than it might appear, since the sun and moon constitute an iconographical theme in many crucifixions. Moreover, Louis makes explicit the connotations of these three thematic elements by initiating three series of figures, three series of refractions of meaning: the cross or redemption of Our Lord, the sun "*nec pluribus impar*," and the moon "Orient! resurrection by the grace of the magical horn of Oberon."

The sun, *nec pluribus impar*: the Sun King (Louis XIV, king of France and of Navarre), one of the essential characters in the journals, is superimposed on the iconographical sun of the redemptive crucifixion. The legend, or, as it was called in the seventeenth century, the "soul" of his motto, "*nec pluribus impar*," defines both the sun/star and the Sun King. Hence this first chain: cross ---> image of crucifixion ---> sun ---> Sun King ---> "*nec pluribus impar*" (which, word for word, means "not to several unequal").

On the other side of the transverse arm of the redemptive cross, there is the sign (or image) of the moon (or of its crescent), which is immediately associated with the Orient, for obvious reasons. This word "Orient" and its meaning refer to the resurrection, but it is noteworthy that, while redemption stems from the Catholic (Christian) cross, oriental resurrection comes about only by grace of the "magical horn of Oberon." The king of elves in Scandinavian mythology, transfigured by Shakespeare (but even more by the poem by Wieland and the opera by Weber), Oberon danced with his wife, Titania, at the origin, at night, by moonlight, only to hide in a tree trunk as soon as day made its appearance, and he possessed a magical horn that made all those who heard it begin to dance. In his last opera, Weber, repeating a method he had already used in *Freischütz* and *Euryanthe*, makes three notes on this horn form a fascinating leitmotif from the outset. On one hand, then, the engraving of the classical, royal motto; on the other, the enchanted breath of romantic opera; on one hand, writing; on the other, voice; on one hand, the politico-theological; on the other, the mythological and aesthetic.

THE IMPOSSIBLE RECONCILIATION OF TWO BODIES

At that point, the self appears in the writing on the page, a self whose emergence we witness in the reflection of the "I" under the sign of trinitary Law; it appears in an imprecatory, negative-optative formula, in a curse, as the object of condemnation by the Law, a condemnation that is nevertheless suspended in the repetition of a single necessary sin, an identical fatal fall: "Might I / and my ideals be cursed were I to fall again." This sin is that of the physical, individual body, subject to the passions of the flesh, and, in the end, to death ("Only psychic / love is allowed, sensual love in contrast is cursed. I solemnly hurl / anathema at it"). And it is this body that the divine body crucifies with the sign of the cross—under the signs of the Law—only to redeem it: cross, sun, moon. It is in this way that the quartering—the interminable, monotonous quartering—of Louis begins....

"Thanks to God, / it is no longer possible [to fall again] for I am protected by the sacred will of God, the sublime word of the King." The trinitary Law that condemns is, in its very condemnation, protection. But that sacred will of God is replicated, or rather, figured and expressed, in the sublime word of the king, *which Louis II of Bavaria is also*. It is his sublime word written on this day in December 1869, in the first folio of his journal: "In the Name of the Father, of the Son, and of the Holy Ghost." It inscribes the divine body on the natural, sensual body of the king, pronounces the imprecation, hurls the anathema.... This sublime word becomes, in the concluding paragraph of the folio, a sacred will ("absolute obedience to the King and to his sacred Will") simply through the exchange of attributions with God.

We are well acquainted, particularly since the work of Ernst Kantorowicz and, before him, of Marc Bloch,[2] with the doctrine on which the great absolute monarchies founded the legitimation of their force after the Empire, and through which the canonist jurists raised the secular state to the sphere of mystery. This doctrine distinguishes, *in the oneness of the royal person*, the *persona personalis* of the mortal king from his *persona idealis* (the *regia dignitas*, the *regia majestas*), which never dies: two bodies—one natural, mortal, similar to that of other men; the other, political, through which the king is incorporated into his subjects and they into him, a motionless, impassive, immortal body, whose symbol is the phoenix.

The drama of Louis II of Bavaria, revealed on the first page of the first journal, is that, *far from experiencing the conjunction in his person of the two bodies of the prince, far from "realizing" that unity, Louis experienced their scission.* The body of majesty condemns and protects (protects by condemning and condemns by protecting) the natural body; the sublime word, the sacred will of the king, is banished from the subject, even while it remains the prince's word and will; it is externalized, even as it is inscribed on his skin and in his body as Law; it transcends him as divine will, even as it comes so close to him that it almost brushes against him. Louis lives in that separation, in that spaceless distance; he writes his journal in that unique gap, blank, or void, up to the very brink of death. The king speaks to the King, the King he is as well: "*You come close as a messenger of God*, I follow you respectfully *from afar*, and *you leave* for countries where your star shines eternally." Or perhaps this "Angel King" is someone else, someone whose name shares its initial letter with the Latin, French, and Spanish words for king ("Rex," "Roy," "Rey"); someone named Richard, a name the god of opera and of Wagnerian music shares with the riding master, the lover.

The journals are thus filled with figures of impossible mediation, of fatally forbidden reconciliation between the two bodies of the king, the divine body and the natural body. This articulation, which the absolute monarch realizes in his very person, and whose model is provided by the Church in the sacrament of the Eucharist,[3] cannot be carried out, perhaps because Louis has entirely displaced it. For the great English or French monarchs, for James I or Louis XIV, the relation of identification moved from nature to divinity, from the physical to the politico-theological, through an assumption of the individual into the royal office, of the "private" body into the "mystic" body of the state. The young prince lived this unity romantically, in alienation, not only because the union of two bodies was, during the age of constitutional and parliamentary monarchies in the second half of the nineteenth century, a vestige of the obscurantist magic of the past, but also, and above all, because, for him—and this is what his dramatic displacement consists in—the divine body of the king has become a body of love and the natural body of the king, a body of desire, even though the former can never be fulfilled or transformed into the latter. More precisely, for Louis, the King's divine body of love is identified with his body of desire, and, at the same time, that relation of identification can only be experienced as lack; it cannot assert itself except in the reiterated, interminable, empty space of the spaceless gap we spoke of a moment ago.

In fact, the political theology of the two bodies of the king had long been threatened by that displacement. To take only one example, the famous portrait of Louis XIV by Rigaud, which dates from the early years of the eighteenth century, exhibits the old king's magnificent ballet dancer's legs sheathed in white silk, paralyzed by gout and overwhelmed by military, political, and dynastic reversals; it exhibits, in short, that "other" body of love *in* the very ostentation of the body of his office and majesty, offering it to the desire of the declining monarch, well before making it an erotic object for his people.[4] But that was only an image, a representation, in a word, the portrait of the king, the final incarnation of the theological and political doctrine of the two bodies, in which it was fulfilled and came to an end: the king's divine body of love as the profane body of Louis's desire, love as desire, that is, as forever unattainable.

Hence the figures of mediation that, from the two poles of the divine and the human, the king and the creature, attempt impossibly to fill the—nonexistent, neuter—distance that separates and unites them. The divine sphere thus emits the names of the Trinity, of God, and of the Redeemer: the Angel (folios 1, 2, and 17), the dove (14, 15, and 22), the holy chrism (14 and 15), the olive branch at the end of the Flood and the Covenant (15), the star of the three Magi (1 and 17), the Grail (22), the Holy House of Loreto (24), the Holy Sepulchre (22 and 24), the crucifixion (26 and 32), the cross (26 and 28), Saint George (29), the Holy Virgin and the Baby Jesus (second journal, folios 2, 3, and 4). In these mentions, the same figures return again and again; but, at certain times, some become more insistent (for example, the Virgin and the Baby Jesus in the last months of Louis's existence) while others disappear (the Angel) and still others suddenly appear, only once, linked, no doubt, to an incident or accident, which they transfigure and encrypt (the Grail, the Holy House of Loreto, the olive branch).

THE NAME OF LOUIS AND THE LILY

The royal sphere is almost congruent to this divine sphere: This near identity reveals, in a stunning manner, the politico-theological reference we already mentioned. This identification of the two realms, like that which grounds and encompasses it, is concentrated in a few privileged figures, surrounded by the halo of others that are more episodic or less precise, others that constitute its aura, the radiating rays of their influence on Louis's thought, will, and imagination. A moment ago, we alluded to the magical powers of homonymy: Now it appears that the "royal sphere" is altogether directed by the force of identification inherent in the identity of the name *Louis*. From Saint Louis to Louis XVI, and including Louis XIV and Louis XV, "Louis" reverberates throughout the intimate journals, on almost every page, and Louis II of Bavaria is, in some sense, the last feeble echo of that name. "Saint Louis IX" (1:19, 31 and 2:2, 4) anchors the royal sphere in the divine sphere, and the noble king Louis XVI, whose blood was shed on 21 January 1793, is joined to the figure of Jesus, staining the royal mantle purple. This bestows the crown of martyrdom on the Monarch's immortal body and the halo of saintliness on the decapitated head (1:8, 11, 16, 21, 24, and 27; 2:2). Louis II of Bavaria is accompanied in this last adventure of absolute monarchy by his feminine double, Marie Antoinette (1:12, 26, 28, and 32). At the origin and at the end, though in very different manners, the name "Louis" finds a way to posit a sacred royal body.

Moreover, "Louis XIV" shines in the center of the series in all his glory, as much by his name and title as by his nickname, the "great King" (1:2, 8, 12, 19, 25, 31, 32; and 2:1, 2, 3, 4, 5). And I do not think I am overinterpreting the text in reading his name, on the first page of the first journal as we have noted, every time that, in the solemn form of a transcendental injunction of the Law, King Louis II of Bavaria offers his natural body (of desire) to the sacred order of the absolute will of the King. Folio 1:3 is noteworthy from this point of view:

> BY ORDER OF THE KING ... no return here, in any case / absolutely not before 10 February, and then always more rarely, / always, always more rarely—No question here of / "For such is our pleasure"—But it is / It is now a question of a law to be strictly observed and / "All justice emanates from the King" / if the King so wishes, so wishes the Law [*Si veut le Roi, veut la Loi*].—/One faith, one law, one King [*Une foi, une loi, un Roy*] ... (Louis)

And beneath...

> You protect / me in my distress / And I faithfully observe your Law.

Or in folio 14:

> The Lord shall anoint you with his strength / The true king, he who dwells in thy heart / shall rise up bearing the crown of his ancestors / and the purple of divine blood / and this king in truth will not die!!! (LOUIS)

At the end of folio 15, which immediately follows, the "King" (also the Great King, Louis the Great, identified with the immortal body of King Louis II of Bavaria) addresses Louis, the body of unstable desire, the passive and passionate pathetic body, and subjugates him to the law:

> You yourself will soon be another man / for before your head has been anointed with that oil [the sacred oil of coronation] / know that the spirit has forbidden me the King from saluting you.

Among the other monarchical figures that surround the name of Louis, we need to evoke, in addition to Charles 1 (1:16, 24 and 2:3) and Philip V of Spain (1:29), in addition to characters from the King's readings (from Diane of Poitiers or Marie de Médicis to Jean Bart, Mazarin, and Mme de Pompadour), one very remarkable name, which plays on the double register of language and image, with all the symbolic, political, and religious connotations attached to it, but also with all the effects of sensation, sensuality, and affect it bears. This is the lily, the royal flower, which might very well play the role of the articulating figure that transforms Louis's body of desire into the King's body of love. At the same time, it makes the second incline toward the first, spreading over the surface of the body as if to soften the rigors of the Law. The lily is thus, simultaneously, the Law of the body of love and the natural body's loving desire for the Law. It appears in one form or another in the first journal with a frequency that is almost equal to the occurrences of "Louis XIV," the "great King" (1:5, 6 [several times], 7, 11, 13, 14, 20, 25, 26, and 28).

Its first emergence on page 5 is symptomatic:

21 June oath in memory / of the vow uttered in Pagodenburg/ 21 April. / In memory of the allegorical destruction/ of Evil.

(Note the expression of an almost sacramental idea of the effectiveness *ex opere operato* of allegory.)

Soon, I shall be a spirit, / *the purity of ether* [Louis's emphasis] envelops me, 777 / sworn I repeat it and cling to it, as true / as I am the *King* [the king's emphasis], never again before 21 September. / *And then to attempt something else*, for the third time if / that succeeds, remember 9 May 3 times 3!—Feb.-April-June-Sept./ Perfume of Lilies! Royal pleasure . . . / This oath has the force of law and its success owing to: / By order of the King.

This last expression, in French, is underscored and decorated with two arabesque flourishes, one of whose loops encircles a monogram surrounded by rays, and below it, "DPLR," accompanied by another monogram on both the left and the right, which one can read both as "DPLR" ("*de par le Roi*," by order of the King) or as "LR," that is, both "*Le Roy*" [The King] and "Louis Roy" [King Louis] or even "Louis-Richard." Having *allegorically* destroyed evil (through what *past* allegory?), the "I" is perceived *in the future* as evaporating into a spiritual breath, vaporizing into pure "ether" once the *present* oaths have paraded by under the injunction of "*Roi = La Loi*" [King = The Law (" . . . as true as I am the *King* . . . —this oath has the force of law"). As the oath passes, in this narrow space, the lilies, their perfume, and their purity appear, allegorizing the spiritual ether of the "I," but in and through the symbol of the French Monarch: "Perfume of lilies! Royal pleasure."

In other words, the *Loi = Roi* equation invades the "I=ether," the pneumatic "I" as a sweet odor, a "spiritual" perfume, and Louis's body of desire is fulfilled in pleasure—"royal pleasure"—in the love of the Law, in the King's body of Love. This pleasure taken in the perfume of the monarchical lilies is a king's pleasure, that of Louis's natural body of desire, that of Louis II's divine body of Love, and that of Louis XIV, the great King, the Law. This oath, which thus has the force of law in the royal pleasure of love and in the desire vaporized into the pleasure of love for the "*Roi = la Loi*," bumps into and telescopes the performative mode of the discourse of the senses and of feelings, the performatives of promising and ordering, instructing and prescribing. It is that operation of conjunction, in and through a "mystic" odor, that is rewritten in the monograms we see on the page, which blur into the ambiguities we have mentioned. The monogram has come to dwell in the spaceless distance, into the nonexistent gap between the two bodies of the "King." The monogram is a single, unique letter (mono-gram): At the same time, it is two or three or four letters, perhaps more, superimposed on one another, written on one another, taking possession of the letter by hiding it under or in itself. Kant used the term "monogram" in an attempt to approach the mystery of the transcendental imagination and its productive schema. This monogram is both written and drawn, it displays while dissimulating, keeps a secret in the very act of exposing it. Louis transforms it into a sun, the sun of the King, the Great Sun King with the rays of his irresistibly effective influence, the fragrant rays-effluvia of the royal and sacred lilies.

It is a drawing of this emblematic lily—which looks like an engraving—that opens the next folio: The flower has disappeared, there remains only the sign or the seal, the inscription or the mark, motionless, the mark or stain of condemnation. "*De par le Roy*," writes Louis, in French, and underneath it, "7 August night *last* fall 14 August." The term the king underscores articulates the two dates, 7 August and 14 August, making the date of the fall undecidable between them.... But it is also "*by the grace of* that fall" that there can be "*expiation*" (my emphasis), expiation of the condemnation reiterated by "*le Roi = la Loi*," but experienced as a pleasure, if not a *jouissance*. On the following line, the lily reappears with its perfume "by the grace of the lively / and reinvigorating perfume / of the royal Lily." Is it the perfume of the lily that brings about this expiation? What a "royal pleasure"!

Nevertheless, the parallelism of the graphic formulas ("by the grace of that fall ... by the grace of the lively / and reinvigorating perfume / of the royal Lily") leads in another direction, in the equivalence between the perfume of the lily and sin. The folio continues with a postscript to the entry dated 3 August, hence, before one of the possible dates of the last fall on 7 August (though a 4, written at the end of the line, could be added to the 3 to arrive at 7): "In the name and on the order of the / royal and sacred / Lilies." Here, the flower with the "lively / and reinvigorating perfume," the flower of the pleasure of expiation and /or of "sin," disappears to make way for the Lily, the emblem, the engraving, the seal of the royal Law, written this time in a ritual, legal formula that transcribes into language the drawing that began the page. The page ends with the writing and inscription of that tension and conjunction between the perfumed flower and the engraved emblem. "Never again August or September or October / Today Lilies—A kiss on the lips of King Schachen / the last": and underneath, a signature in Spanish, "Yo El Rey" (but in the flourishes of "Rey" can be discerned another, illegible name). This signature is supported by the drawing of a sun and its rays, which refers to Louis XIV, evoked a few lines earlier—"Solemn oath before the portrait of the Great

King"—and finally by the flamboyant engraving of the royal emblem, the lily surrounded by a nimbus of dazzling rays that come to efface the "Louis XIV sun." Subsequently, when the figure of the lily returns in the first journal, the perfume has disappeared, and with it, the flower of purity and pleasure. It is the *sign* of the royal lily, the symbolic mark that has no other function than to attest to and guarantee the oath that subjugates Louis to the Law.

The figures emitted from the profane sphere of the natural body are, of course, much more rare inasmuch as that body, in the writing that transmits it on the pages of the journal, can only be the object and the patient of the operations endlessly reiterated by the King and his figures. But that passivity itself reveals the passion that moves it, the violence of which interminably requires the divine body to set to work and ground its power. All the notations that traditionally belong to the "genre" of the personal—if not the intimate—journal stem from that sphere, however: walks, visits to the royal castles, encounters, incidents, the minutiae of profane life, all the traces in writing of Louis's movement in empirical space and time, places and dates that are both the traces of the princely domain, the circle of the "court" and those familiar and intimate with it, and the traces of his "private" body. Hence, for example, in folio 1:6, "for three months abstaining from all excitation," or "a kiss on the lips of the King / Schachen / the last"; or, in folio 1:7, "celebrations, theaters, walks, the presence of the / prince heir to Prussia very troublesome and disagreeable! / ... Hours of happiness, garden, sitting in the grotto / faithful / unto death"; or folio 1:9: "Saturday 28 July 1874 Fernstein / Rain for 6 hours"; or folio 1:8: "3 February—hands down / *not one more time*" (underscored in the text).

Nonetheless, as these excerpts suggest and as a total reading would allow us to generalize, rare are the notations on the "profane life" of Louis's sensible body that escape the power of performative, imperative, prescriptive, injunctive, promissory, et cetera, utterances. And, even when one notation evokes an event of that life, accepts its happiness, it is still caught in the injunctions of the oath of love, or more discreetly, but more sensually perhaps, in the present instructions of memory, in anniversaries, for example, in folio 1:9:

On 6 March 1872 / Just 2 months before / the 5th anniversary of that 6 May 1867 / blessed day when we saw each other for the first time, to never again be separated or leave each other, until death. Written in the Indian hut.

It is as if Louis's singular, physical, empirical body could not express itself and its life in a constative mode or in the narrative mode of history, as if it were, in some sense, endlessly traversed by prohibitions, overwhelmed by orders and prescriptions, articulated to the point of disarticulation by commitments, promises, supplications.

Royal Canopy

In the text itself, there is an interesting figure for this phenomenon, interesting because it stems from the profane sphere even as it marks the boundary line to and the contact zone with the divine or royal sphere, that nonexistent or neuter space *between*, a space that Louis of Bavaria seemed to occupy throughout his lifetime. We see it appear in folio 1:3 in all its ambiguity of desire *and* pleasure, of "here" and "there," of reality and dream, without either of these polarities receiving a precise ethical attribution:

> Far from the Royal canopy / Transported forever toward the / mat of a dreamland in the Orient, / but no return here, in any case / absolutely not before 10 February and then ever more rarely, / ever, ever more rarely . . . . No question here of / for such is our pleasure—but it is.

This passage opens a boundary only to negate it: "Far from the Royal canopy [*ciel de lit*]." The *ciel*, in this case, is not heaven or sky, not the open space of a transport toward the ideal, but, rather, a canopy covering the King's bed. It is thus beyond that *ciel* (the royal canopy) that the king wishes to flee, into the *ciel*, the heaven, of a dream, but a dream that is still a bed, a "mat" without a *ciel*, a canopy. It is an oriental mat, as in the loves of Oberon and Titania, of Huon de Bordeaux and Amanda: The Orient is a lunar, but not at all nocturnal, space (see folio 1:2), the moonlit space of the resurrection by the grace of the magical horn of Weber's opera (folio 1:1). It is a mat of pleasure where "desires are fulfilled in an exquisite plenitude" (folio 1:2); but, above all, not *here*, absolutely not before 10 February, and then, ever more rarely. And we will never know whether it is the return here under the royal canopy that requires the ever more complete reduction of the fulfillment of desire.

That figure of the limit, or boundary line, is imaginarily marked not only by the *ciel between* the royal bed and the oriental mat but also graphically, with the blank that ends the line of writing: "Ever, ever more rarely . . . . No question here of [blank to the end of the line]." "For such is our pleasure."

Here, the blank may be that of an unwritten word, which cannot be written because it would reawaken desire. "For such is our pleasure" would then be the ritual formulation of royal will. Or it may be that, through the sudden and violent return of the pen to the beginning of the line, Louis is forbidding himself to fulfill his desires in the royal pleasure of the love bed. The formula of the Law performed on the human body of desire could also very well be the utterance of a henceforth forbidden access to the divine body of love, a way of crossing out that "possible" identification, with a blank: between the two, the (royal) canopy.

In folio 1:7, we rediscover the same figure of the royal bed, but involved in a different associative series: There, again, the bed is linked to the limit, to its prohibitions and to its transgressions, but in different modes.

The first at ten-thirty finally saw again the friend / the adored friend after a long time of separation! / Heavenly accolades.— / Hours of happiness, garden, seated in the grotto, faithful / unto death.—In thought oath / before the railing of the future bed / of the royal Lily.

The royal canopy has become the railing of a bed to come: It is no longer a matter of fleeing that canopy toward the mat of pleasure under the oriental sky, of accepting—in the very experience of happiness, seated in the *grotto* with the beloved friend—the visitation of a thought, of an oath sworn before the railing, that is, on the borderline of a place of the King, untransgressible, where it is not his natural body, that of desire and passion, lying on the bed, but the pure emblem of his body of majesty, of the divine body of the absolute Monarch, the Great King, the royal Lily. The bed of the royal Lily with its railing, where the oath is taken, has become the bed of the "*Roi = la Loi*," of the pure divine body of Love, uncrossable, in the grotto of happiness and heavenly accolades with the beloved friend! Hence, immediately afterward, the order that the "I" gives to the self, "*Let that sink in but good*" [*Pénètre-toi bien de ceci*] (royal emphasis) with its deictic replicated by a demonstrative pronoun. And no one will ever decide whether that pronoun refers or shows, refers to the utterance of the royal Lily lying in the bed beyond the railing of the oath, or shows the thing that can receive no name.

Double and final appearance of the bed, of its railing and canopy, in folio 1:14, where the figure of the profane life and the natural body of desire have been definitively transformed and move to another sphere, the royal or divine sphere of the body of love, of the Law. The page opens with the evocation of the royal bed as a place forever preserved: "Behind the inviolate railing, forever uncrossable, / which surrounds the royal bed." It is in this place, beyond the borderline, that Louis writes this in particular:

> In the course of the year that has just begun, as much as / it can be done, resist all temptations with / the most extreme vigilance; never give in to them to the extent that is possible either in acts or / in words, or even in thoughts. And in that / way purify myself ever more of all the filth / that is attached alas! to human nature, / and in that way make me ever more worthy of the crown God entrusted to me.

Louis attempts to become Louis II of Bavaria by situating the writing of the sensible, natural, desiring body, that of the forbidden body, in the very site of the royal bed. And, at that point, as if to signify in language itself the transcendent instance of the royal Law in that place, as if to transform the bed where the king sleeps into a bed of justice, Louis shifts into French and Latin:

> Slept in the King's chamber, in the baluster, / sacred and uncrossable, kneeling on the platform, head / protected by the dais of the Royal bed / *Nec cessabo nec errabo.* God will help me.

The place of the solemn oath, the chamber, the bed: But the railing [*balustrade*] has become a baluster [*balustre*] and the canopy a dais, signs and figures of the sacred boundaries that isolate it and protect it against evil and filth. It is from the canopy, from the dais, that, in the following lines, the dove of the Holy Ghost descends from heaven to bring him the holy chrism and the king's sacred unction.

To conclude, a note on the second journal. On page 1 (written in French) of this journal that has only five folios, God and the Great King, that is, Louis XIV, are posited as the guarantors of Louis's spiritual ascension, his assumption to the divine, royal sphere, as royal divine force and sanctification, both against the sensible individual body

> so that I may vanquish evil / dominate the senses, that not a single / time may it be a question in this book, / of a renewed fall (the last in the year / of the fortieth. / Given to Hohenschwan / Gan Louis / 19 January / 1886.)

And then, Louis adds, "*before the King's portrait* . . . ." That may be the most striking characteristic of this last text by Louis II of Bavaria, this presence of the King in his representation as a portrait. The royal figures that, until now, had been written in the journal, made their presence known in their names, either by the force of homonymy with Louis of Bavaria (the Louis, kings of France, from Saint Louis to Louis XVI) or by their historical and ideological "value" (Charles I by association with Louis XVI, both martyrs of the absolute monarchy, and Philip V through his filiation with Louis XIV and his presence on the throne of Spain). All these figures, all these Louis introduced into the text by their names, were manifested as a (sublime, secret) *word* and as *will*, which the ritual formulas accompanying the royal decisions in France linked to each other in the order and prescription of the Law. In only two places did Louis the Great, the Sun King, appear as a portrait, in folios 1:6 (1871) and 1:32 (1885), as the guarantor of an oath whose solemnity Louis underscores by pronouncing it before the royal image. In the few pages of the second journal, *the King is first of all his portrait*, the portrait of Louis XIV (2:1, 2, and 3) or the image of Saint Louis (2:2 and 4 [twice]). Even more remarkable, the divine sphere is itself represented in the text by its images, those, in particular, of the Holy Virgin and the Baby Jesus (2:2, 3, 4 . . .). It is only on the last page, a few days before his tragic end, that the Great King returns to his name.

In that insistent presence of the portrait of the King, I, for my part, see only the beginning of the definitive effacement of Louis into the divine and royal Law. At the end of the existence of the sensible body of the prince, even in remaining what it is, even in requiring his sensible annihilation, the Law offers itself to him as the *image* of the body of Love: the imaginary of a representation where his desire had been caught from the beginning and where it was exhausted until the end, even unto death.

Chance and Secrecy

16

Simonides' Memory Lapse

Narratives of origin often have this remarkable virtue: They bring together all or most of the elements that history, after a few uncertain steps, then makes every effort to compose, combine, displace, or even efface (to better accentuate them by their very absence), becoming, along the way, better documented and better supported by texts and images.

This reflection leads me to the subject of the theaters of memory. What I have called the "narrative of origin" offers to view, and from the beginning—provided we are attentive and respectful, provided we refuse to summarize, that is, to forget, provided we refuse to extract what appears important and significant today—a complete set of figures and motifs, themes and relations, whose coherence is outlined or inscribed in the luminous mists to our east, on the horizon of our past and our beginnings. In short, the narrative of origin provides a "turnkey" memory for any meditative reflection that agrees to read it seriously—and not as a fable for children—to listen to the reverberations of its harmonics. The narrative of origin is thus a theater of memory or, more precisely, a part of the repertoire of the theaters of memory, a play that no actor has to learn, that no stage director has to direct, a play that needs no spectator since it is known from the beginning, played and interpreted from the beginning, unbeknownst even to its actors, stage directors, and spectators. This is also true, through a new twist, of a legend—on the borderline between history and myth—of a certain fable, rather, which, one day in Greece, inaugurated the history of memory for what it is fitting to call the thinking of the West, prepared forever(?) the stage for this theater of histories *en abyme*, the theater of the memory of memory.

This narrative combines gods and men, the eulogy and the ceremonial meal, architecture and death. Let us lend an ear: At a banquet offered by Scopas, a nobleman of Thessaly, the poet Simonides of Ceos sang a poem in honor of his host but inserted into it lines praising Castor and Pollux. Scopas told the poet he would pay only half the price agreed upon and that the divine twins to whom part of the poem had been devoted would have to pay the rest. Shortly thereafter, Simonides was informed that two young men were asking for him at the main door of the house. He left the banquet, arrived at the door, and found no one there. But, during his brief absence, the roof of the room collapsed, crushing Scopas and his guests under the debris. The bodies were so unrecognizable that the relatives who came to pick them up could not identify them. Simonides did them a last service by recalling where they had been seated around the banquet table. Hence, the dead could be buried under their names. Of course, the two invisible young men at the door were the two gods come to pay the price of the poem by saving the poet's life. But it was also as a result of this that Simonides discovered the art of memory. By remembering the place settings, he was able to identify the bodies of the guests: It is thus order that can best guide and enlighten memory. And Cicero, from whom we take the narrative of this history, concludes with this "moral":

> By those, therefore, who would improve this part of the understanding, certain places must be fixed upon, and that of the things which they desire to keep in memory, images must be conceived in the mind, and ranged, as it were, in those places; thus the order of places would preserve the order of things, and the images of the things would denote the things themselves; so that we should use the places as waxen tablets, and the images as letters.[1]

It might just be, however, that Cicero was a bit too hasty in his assessment: Perhaps he distracted our attention from the narrative of Simonides, its events, incidents, and accidents, toward what appears henceforth as a theory, if not of memory, then at least of the artificial mechanisms that allow us to exploit all the power of that natural faculty. Of course, the elements he extracted from the narrative were elaborated into arts of memory throughout history: places as image reservoirs, images as representations of things, things as memories, the arrangement of places standing in for the order of things, and images standing in for the things themselves. But we can only wonder about the effectiveness of this constructed mechanism that, in the end, replicates the very mechanism nature bestowed on man. The comparison that assimilates memory to writing—which has been constantly reiterated up to the modern age[2]—no doubt answers that question: Like the wax tablet, which conserves on its surface the letters (syllables, words) that the scribe traces on it—letters that become available to him as soon as he looks at the tablet—places are the empty volumes (reservoirs) that the images chosen by the man of memory (the orator) fills, and are also available to him when required.

It is easy to see, however, that the vehicle of the comparison is not strictly isomorphic with the tenor, and, as a result, that the response the image on the wax tablet provides to our question is merely partial. In fact, the third dimension, depth, is missing: The wax tablet is a surface. And Cicero considers the written signs as if they were immediately words, and as if the words were the images themselves. The "theater" of memory, in contrast, is a composition of volumes—places—and, paradoxically, the relations that the images deposited there maintain with the things that they represent displace the conventional, abstract, and necessary relations that characterize alphabetical writing, transforming them into relations of visibility and contingency.[3] In any case, the theater of memory requires a third dimension in order to be realized, just as it demands a third term (the image) to function. Hence our question once more: What good is that complex construction, that erudite artifice that "adds to" the mechanism of memory and its operations, that "improves on" it? Our question is, no doubt, badly phrased, or rather, it does not seem to be pertinent to the object to which it refers. It inquires into its economy in the name of profitability. The system proposed by Cicero seems to "consume" excessively, to spend too much for what it allows in the way of production. Yet, it may be that the theater of memory, under the cover of mnemonics, has no other end than to represent memory, or to attempt to occupy its field, in order to master its alarming power and ward off its redoubtable fascination, a fascination, or vertigo, provoked by the unfathomable depths that the mind "contains" and into which it might fall or become lost—as in a foreign land.

With the comparison to writing and the wax tablet, then, Cicero was a bit hasty, yet he was still going after the essential. The narrative of origin regarding Simonides can tell us a bit more, provided we agree to listen, to hear as in a dream: In that way, we may have a chance to enter the theater of a memory more ancient than our very first memory, an opportunity—once cannot hurt—to tumble deliciously into the depths that, unbeknownst to us, we "contain." Simonides,[4] the story tells us, was thus invited to Crannon in Thessaly, to the home of Scopas, a rich and noble man.[5] But he was not there as an ordinary guest, even less, as a special guest. He had been paid, or was to be paid, for singing the praises of his host.[6] Just as we can suppose that Scopas's cook created rare and special dishes and selected fine wines in honor of his master, Simonides, a word chef, was supposed to compose—for a fee—clever songs, to choose resonant words for the lord of the manor. And what is a eulogy if not the construction of a monument of memory, the *kleos* that, through the poet's words, assures its subject and his acts an immortal memory, in the family and in the commonwealth?[7] Simonides was invited—contracted—to be the architect of that monument, to erect, precisely, the language "tomb" of Scopas, which is better assured of permanence through the infinite repetition of the inspired words, than is the edifice of marble on the boundary of the property or the stela raised in effigy. The banquet, the convivial ceremony of a group of aristocrats brought together to honor one of their own, was not only the privileged "place" and "moment" for erecting the poetic monument; it already constituted its seat and foundation. It entailed the inscription of the words of praise in the hearts and minds of the community of the powerful; it was an initial memory in words and rhythms, of one of their own. And Simonides recites his poem in praise of Scopas, a long poem, which he sings from memory, line after line, stanza after stanza, mastering, with all the poet's techniques, the long and paradoxical difficulty of *a living word that repeats, that invents as it reproduces*.[8] One memory is exchanged for another, the poet's memory, of which he is both the author and the simple instrument (for the muse who inspires him, whom he summons at the beginning of his song, is none other than the daughter of Mnemosyne, the goddess of Memory),[9] and the lord's memory, which is constituted as a permanent celebration through the poem. Hence the contract that sanctions it: not only a meal, wine and meat, at the banquet, but also money, a fee. The words are exchanged for coins just as the memory of the poet is exchanged for that of the hero.[10]

And, yet, I cannot help but think that there was an accident at the banquet of Scopas, a first accident, well before the one that dramatically interrupted it. I cannot help but think that Simonides, singing the glory of Scopas, had, in the middle of the recitation, a *memory lapse*: How else to explain the "digression," the eulogy of Castor and Pollux? If only the twins had figured among the mythical ancestors of Scopas! He had a memory lapse, therefore, but the poet's mnemonics were infallible on that occasion: In the empty *place* of silence, Simonides plugged in a long fragment on the two gods—one of those fragments that, once transcribed, was considered by scholars to be a late interpolation. Perhaps none of the guests noticed this supplement filling in the blank of a missing word, perhaps no one saw that a near fall had been transformed into an *excursus*.[11] The words resonated like the striking of bronze, and the rhythms of the song excited a great swell of anger and pride in the best hearts. Except for Scopas, who felt "swindled." ... It was not really a question of money, but of the monument, if you will. How can one imagine a tomb of honor, a monument of glory erected for the aristocratic self (comparable to no other), which would be merely the lean-to attached to the temple of Castor and Pollux? Especially since the accident of memory, concealed by Simonides in the eulogy to the two gods, could not be uncovered again. Men of the future would go on repeating the praise of the divine brothers and, only as an appendix, that of Scopas. The only way—rather ridiculous, we have to admit—that Scopas finds to correct the mistake is economical. He gives as good as he gets: "Here is half your salary; let the twins pay the rest and we'll be set." Money has no odor; it has even less memory. It is not a token, a mark, a symbol. It is a general, abstract measure of equivalence, and the rule of equivalence or of value is conventional: In short, it is a blank operation.

History does not say whether Simonides disputed Scopas's mercantile proposition, only that someone came to the poet and told him that two young men were asking for him at the door of the house. Without allegorizing unduly, I think we have to understand that, by the grace of the gods, Simonides leaves the spaces of memory—but not its places. He leaves them, in truth, so that he can transform them into places. He leaves not only the banquet room and the palace of the noble from Thessaly, but also the space of the poem, the *kleos*, the monument of words and its damaged repetition. He leaves his poet's memory, his memory as son of the muses, "grandson" of Mnemosyne, just as he leaves the memory of Scopas and his peers, the lords of Thessaly, called as he is by an anonymous word (that of a slave, a servant) to go meet... no one. The two young men had vanished in an instant: "displaced" discourse, subjectless words, lack of object. Hence, the narrative stages or figures the poet's memory lapse: Well, there is nothing more to say about Scopas—quick, "Castor and Pollux" in his place, but off the subject. Out, poet! To meet gods? No, no one.

The whole of the narrative, its thread up to this point, is, let us acknowledge, a marvelous theatricalization of memory and its various incarnations. In truth, men spend their time leaving their memories through the radical accident of death. This exit lasts a little longer or not quite so long according to the case. There are some successes, some failures, but sooner or later, success and failure are effaced. It is precisely that exit—even in slow motion—that Scopas wanted to ward off with Simonides' poem and with money. The fact that we are writing about it today, after so many others before us, might be the proof of his success, except that the story being told here is precisely, completely, a narrative or fable destined to place before our eyes the hidden art of memory in the depths of the soul (as Kant said of the imagination). But is it possible to "leave" one's own memory, as Simonides left the home of his host, in any way other than figurally? The opposition is interesting: Men *forget one another* by the very destiny of their perishable humanity, by the fatality of their ephemeral being, in death. Yet no one can escape the terrible law of his own permanence, his identity as memory: No one gets a new skin. The skin is, from the beginning, a surface of inscription where the letters of each time come to be written, indelible, or, rather, since there is really no skin and no surface (as we suggested with this story), everyone is condemned to wander in memory, and each trajectory traces the outline that encloses an identity, a memory "proper," in the other, collective memory, where each temporal being, because it is such, is in transit.[12]

The narrative of origin points in that direction with extreme precision: *Outside*, then, at the door, there is no one; but, during this time, *inside*, the ceiling of the dining room (and, for good measure, Scopas's home as a whole) collapses, burying in the rubble the lord and his fellow banqueters. Imagine Simonides turning around as everything crashed down, contemplating the ruin: Here, then, is the tomb of Scopas; here is his monument realized *in situ*. For the edifice of words and memory that the poet had imperfectly *erected* over and around the hole in *his* memory, and that he alone conserved in his poet's memory, was replaced—through chance, destiny, the gods (who would have thought that the Tyndaridae had so much power?), each or all together—by the collapse of a home, the rubble of ruins, another "tomb" in the form of a bottomless hole, a hole of memory. A trace, if you like, or a vestige, granted, but signless, nameless.... And that is how Scopas and the elite lords of Thessaly might have definitively left the memory of men, under the ruins of a palace, if Simonides had not had a memory lapse, had not sung of Castor and Pollux, had not left to meet two young men, finding in their place the blank of a lack. Memory is representable only against the background of an originary forgetting or, rather, of a forgetting that is the origin.

It seems to me, then, that the accident of the collapse is, figurally speaking, an essential moment in the staging of memory in the theater of memory. A little later, Simonides exploits that accident with the relatives of the victims— and here, again, I cannot help but think that he received a fee from them that was a hundred times that of the contract with Scopas. This essential moment, in fact, establishes not only memory's close affinity to architecture—that is, to the art of a man's home in space—but also, and perhaps especially, the timeless, structural equivalence between construction and destruction, composition and annihilation, erection and collapse.[13] The narrative of origin says so in its way: The monument of language raised to the glory of Scopas in the banquet room of his palace is in a relation of equivalence with the architectural ruin that crumbled to Scopas's misfortune, burying him in the central site of his home. The theater of memory that the narrative relates through its figures— characters, actors, incidents, and accidents—is none other than that affinity between an art of space and memory, an equivalence that reveals the astonishing power of memory to convert time into space and the frightening violence with which it conserves death in presence.

At the beginning of this chapter, I signaled, in passing, the figure of the narrative that gives meaning to the collapse, namely, the ceremonial meal for the lords, the banquet, and, to be precise, the table and guests it brings together. It is through that figure that the time-space of memory in general becomes the places of that particular memory; it is through the banquet that present, conserved death becomes signs, names. At the banquet of Scopas, it was not only, or even primarily, a question of being fed, of satisfying hunger and thirst, but also, and especially, of speaking and listening, of welcoming the words of the song along with the dishes, of listening to the poet singing the glory of the master of the house, after the meat had been consumed and the wines tasted but before the arrival of the dancing girls and flutists. This ceremonial meal conformed to certain norms, entailed several episodes in succession, followed certain hierarchical rules regarding the placement of the guests present. Perhaps every "true" meal is a powerful memory mechanism, the regulated, normed conjunction of two axes: the temporal axis of succession, which entails the substance of the ceremonial meal's content, food and words; and the spatial axis of position, which entails the articulation of the meal's forms and agents, the speaking and eating subjects. Perhaps every "true" meal, as a mechanism of memory, is, by that very fact, structured like architecture, that is, like the art that transforms the spaces of being into places inhabitable by men.

Meals, architecture, and memory: In these three areas, which overlap and encompass one another in the narrative of origin we are discussing, the time of succession is joined to, or rather, converted into, the order of places, place settings. Or vice versa.[14] In reading the story, we may suppose that the families of the dead did not ask Simonides about the menu for the banquet, the wine list, the speeches and ideas of the guests, or even about the poem sung by the poet. Rather, they asked him for signs, they demanded names to identify the piles of crushed bones and flesh, names by which they could recognize what has no name in any language. And Simonides went over the banquet table in his mind, in memory's imagination, went around the places and gave to each seat a sign, that is, he gave to each unrecognizable body a name that identified him. But, in doing so, who cannot notice that Simonides was once more constructing the monument of Scopas, but this time not as *kleos*, as poem, as monument of language, but as ruins or tomb, with a list of names its only epitaph?

Not only did our poet—who was a bit of a sophist around the edges—get money for that substitution (or, at least, I suppose he did), he also transformed the accident into the occasion for a more lasting benefit. According to Cicero, he made a practical model out of the chance event, the indecipherable sign of the gods; from the destruction of the palace and the crushing of the guests around the banquet table, he deduced the rules of an exercise and the principles of an art. The home had collapsed on the "tomb" of honor he had erected in language to the glory of Scopas, had thus annihilated it from collective memory. But no matter; the clever poet constructed a memory mechanism that reproduced, intentionally this time, and in the form of programmed operations, the events of the catastrophe. In the rubble of the palace, a table plan—that is, the order of the seats that the guests of Scopas had occupied— was discovered. Simonides' method found the principle of its development in those ruins. He constructed a structure and defined a principle of— "empty"— arrangement. In his imagination, he composed an architecture, a system of places, beginning with a plan that constituted the stable and motionless order of the representations of things, things that the places enclosed because he had set them there beforehand (just as Scopas had placed his guests in the places that the ceremonial etiquette of the banquet reserved for them). He then went over these places in his mind, one after the other, and extracted images from them (just as the bloody and unrecognizable bodies, the unfortunate guests, had been extracted from the rubble) and produced from them the terms of language corresponding to the things represented, following the very syntax of their placement (just as he named with their proper names the human debris demanded by the families). Simonides' art of memory thus reproduced, if not the event of his poem, at least the disposition of the meal, the order of the ceremony, the architecture of the dining room, and the structure of the home, but by reversing the accidents that had struck them into voluntary opportunities.

In other words, whereas the first sequence of the narrative of origin represented, in the play of its narrative figures, memory in general, memory in space and time, a memory *beyond mastery* with its lapses, abysses, incidents, and incarnations, Simonides' ultimate model represented that representation but plugged up its holes and filled in its abysses, to make a *constructed* order from its indecipherable order, which was hidden behind the decrees of chance and of the divine. In short, he *mastered* the functioning of memory. Through that architect's mastery of the places of memory, through that capacity to invent images, the poet or sophist believed he was making us forget the other architecture, as vertiginous as a Piranesi prison, namely, the prison of memory that, instead of *totalizing* knowledge and history as the art of memory claims to do, simply repeats ad infinitum its spacings and telescoping, its openings, porticos, thresholds, walls, blind alleys, and shafts. Rather than the collapse [*effondrement*] of the palace of Scopas, he established the *effondement*, or "efoundation"—to use Deleuze's expression—of the natural faculty of memory. Unless, of course, the first is merely the narrative figure of the second.

At a time when ancient culture was ending, Saint Augustine again spoke of that *effondrement-effondement* of memory in a kind of lyric hallucination.[15] And it may well be that, with book 10 of his *Confessions*,[16] the narrative of origin regarding the theater of memory, repeating itself in another mode, once more consecrates a loss, which Simonides' memory lapse had indicated modestly, humorously. In Augustine, this loss is the figure of an originary forgetting, an abyss of memory that man discovers in himself, as his being itself, and yet— strange paradox—as a place he wanders through endlessly, from room to room, from stairwell to stairwell, from floor to floor. All the arts of memory tried to ward off, capture, that memory lapse, that originary forgetting, for the benefit of all the arts and all the techniques of mastery, tried to master the *vis memoriae* that, through this lapse, through this forgetting, manifested itself as irresistible, inhuman transcendence.

> The next stage [in my ascent toward God] is memory, which is like a great field or a spacious palace, a storehouse for countless images of all kinds which are conveyed to it by the senses. In it are stored away all the thoughts by which we enlarge upon or diminish or modify in any way the perceptions at which we arrive through the senses, and it also contains anything else that has been entrusted to it for safe keeping, until such time as these things are swallowed up and buried in forgetfulness. When I use my memory, I ask it to produce whatever it is that I wish to remember. Some things it

produces immediately; some are forthcoming only after a delay, as though they were being brought out from some inner hiding place; others come spilling from the memory, thrusting themselves upon us when what we want is something quite different, as much as to say, "Perhaps we are what you want to remember?" These I brush aside from the picture which memory presents to me, allowing my mind to pick what it chooses, until finally that which I wish to see stands out clearly and emerges into sight from its hiding place.[17]

And then a stupor seizes Augustine's mind as he meditates on the edges of the abyss: "The power of the memory is prodigious, my God. It is a vast, immeasurable sanctuary. Who can plumb its depths? And yet it is a faculty of my soul. Although it is part of my nature, I cannot understand all that I am. This means, then, that the mind is too narrow to contain itself entirely. But where is that part of it which it does not itself contain?"[18]

It is in this *effondement* of memory in(to) itself, in what today is called the unconscious, that Augustine reads the presence, outside place, of his divine interlocutor: "See how I have explored the vast field of memory in search of you, O Lord! And I have not found you outside it. For I have discovered nothing about you except what I have remembered since the time when I first learned about you."[19] "But in which part of my memory are you present, O Lord? What cell have you constructed for yourself in my memory? What sanctuary have you built there for yourself? ... Why do I ask what place is set aside in my memory as your dwelling, as if there were distinctions of place in the memory?"[20] "Where else, then, did I find you, to learn of you, unless it was in yourself, above me? Whether we approach you or depart from you, you are not confined in any place. You are Truth, and you are everywhere present where all seek counsel of you."[21]

17

Falls, Encounters, and the *Premier Venu*

> A man engaged in collecting contributions would have gone to a certain place for the sake of getting the money, had he known; but he went there not for the sake of this, and it is by accident that he got the money when he went there; and this happened neither for the most part whenever he went there, nor of necessity. And the end, which is getting the money, is not a cause present in him, but it is something done by *choice* or by *thought*, and he is then said to have gone there by luck [*tuchè*] . . . .
> And the tripod which fell [on its feet] is a chance [*automaton*], for though its being on its feet is for the sake of being sat on, it did not fall for the sake of being sat on.
> —Aristotle, *Physics*, 2.6.196b.33–197a.2 and 197b.16–8

In *La vie de feu M. Pascal* [The life of the late Mr. Pascal], written by Pascal's sister, Mme Gilberte Périer, the attentive reader may note that the pious biographer uses two different terms to name an event (let us understand by "event" that which happens suddenly, unexpectedly, in the life whose narrative is recounted to us), two terms that punctuate that existence, divide it into two classes, two great opposed paradigms, two names: chance and opportunity. Here are two occurrences chosen from many others. The first: "*Once, by chance, when someone* struck an earthenware platter with a knife while at the table, he [Blaise] noticed that it made a great sound, but that, as soon as someone put his hand on top of it, it stopped. At the same time, he wished to know the cause, and that experiment led him to make many others with sounds. He noticed so many things that he wrote a treatise on them at the age of eleven, which was found to be well reasoned." And the second: "That occupation [the experiment on the vacuum] was the last in which he occupied his mind with the human sciences. . . . *Immediately afterward* and when he was not yet twenty-four years old, *the Providence of God provided an opportunity* that obliged him to read writings of piety, and *God enlightened him* in such a way by that holy reading that he understood perfectly that the Christian Religion obliges us to live only for God and to have no other object but him" (my emphasis).

The two narratives, excerpted from *La vie de feu M. Pascal*, where they appear a few pages apart, evoke two events with the same "structure." In both cases, "something" from the outside (?), unforeseeable, suddenly occurs. In both cases, this something is *a fall*: that of the knife on the earthenware plate, which the guest at Pascal's table dropped inadvertently, and that of Etienne Pascal, the father, on the ice in January 1646, a fall that dislocated his leg. The leg was then cared for by two Jansenist gentlemen who, during their visits, had the Pascal family, Blaise, in particular, read Jansen, Saint-Cyran, and Arnauld. A fall, an *accident* that turns out to be the first moment in a complex series of consecutive and deliberate actions, through which a *subject* may be said to constitute, show, assert, and demonstrate itself. If these two narratives still raise questions for us, it is because of their banality, and, beyond that, because of this point, place, and moment of articulation between the accident or event and the wills, intentions, and acts that follow it, a point I would be tempted to designate by the expression used by Duchamp, "*infra mince*." For, in fact, it very often happens that a knife falls inadvertently on an earthenware platter, but only once was a treatise on sounds written by a child of eleven. How many legs have been dislocated by falls on the ice? Yet it was only in January 1646 that the result was a passionate reading of Saint-Cyran, Jansen, and Arnauld. A *banal* event—a knife falling on a platter, a bourgeois man falling on ice—is resolved as briefly and abruptly as it happened into an *exception*. Nevertheless, the banal and its conversion into the exceptional, both at that instant and in the long term, are remarkable only because they are remarked upon, noted, told by the writer in the fervor of religious and familial piety. But it may just be that, in a new twist, that writing, the biography of Pascal by Gilberte, fulfills no other function, has no other finality than that of making someone (me, in particular) speak and write of that banality and its transformation into the unique. Could it be that the exceptional event is more banal than we think? Or that the banality of the accidents and events that make up everyday life is merely another way for the exceptional event to occur? And that event is so exceptional, so unique, so different from everything else, that it becomes imperceptible, hence indescribable, and, thus, only very rarely becomes a narrative or history, and, then, always in a peculiar manner.

Gilberte calls the first fall chance, and it occurs abruptly: a knife slips out of the hand holding it and strikes an earthenware platter, making a great sound. She calls the second fall—that of the father, Etienne, which she does not recount—an opportunity provided by God the Father. The knife falls on the earthenware platter by chance, but divine Providence makes Etienne fall on the ice, so that the opportunity to read will be given to him and his family. In the end, God occupies the same place in that occurrence as the young Blaise occupies in the other: It is, after all, the child of eleven who, taking notice of the acoustical effects caused by the falling knife, seeks to know their cause. At that point, the event is no longer a fortuitous accident happening "one day" as the Pascal family sits around the table. It is, rather, some other "thing" that manifests itself when, *for example*, any knife whatsoever strikes any earthenware platter (and not, be it understood, *the* knife that slipped out of the guest's hand on that day and *the* earthenware platter that happened to be there). The event, the sudden accident, and the no less sudden moment when Blaise took note of its effects, becomes an experiment at that instant and in an instant, the first in a long series of experiments in which the "cause" (the other "thing" both manifested and hidden by the accident itself), little by little takes shape, assumes an intelligible structure, becomes a mark, and is finally remarked upon in a treatise on sounds "which was found to be well reasoned."

As I said, what interests me is this moment of sudden attention to the event, an attention as sudden as the event itself, and in which, in an instant, the event diverges from the accidental to the structural, from the fortuitous to the intelligible, from a given of the instant to a construct over time. And it is in that divergence, on the spot, at that moment of the accident and the experiment, in that gap in the same place, at the same instant, that the subject of knowledge manifests itself and that *its* science is constituted. The child's age, eleven years old, adds nothing to the story except the fact that the exceptional individual was a genius; it adds merely a legendary connotation to the narrative. We need to bring the story and its narrative as close as possible to that gap between accident and experiment in order to read what I have called the conversion of banality into exceptionality. Yet, strangely, in the narrative, the event-accident does not conserve this character of plenitude that we recognized in it from the outset. More precisely, what Blaise takes note of is not the fall of the knife on the earthenware platter but the acoustical effect of that fall, which is immediately contemporaneous to it: "It made a great sound." Within the sudden occurrence of the accident, there is inscribed a kind of dehiscence between the fall and the sound that, at the same time, conceals the event from itself, since only its resonance is retained, maintained, conserved: The suddenness of the fall is prolonged in its sonority, the accident is forgotten and only its auditive form is retained by the subject. But the subject of knowledge, for the moment merely an attentive ear (an ear that retains and conserves as it takes note), is posited in the fortuitous event only as a mere echo, its persistent echo: an ear ringing from the reverberation.

And, suddenly, something disappears: "He noticed that it made a great sound, but that, as soon as someone put his hand on top of it, it stopped." Suddenly, silence. Here again, the gesture is banal: I imagine the clumsy guest at the Pascals' dinner table immediately putting his hand on the platter he had struck with his knife to stop the sound. I imagine the double silence, of the guests at the great sound made by the platter and of the platter on which the guest placed his hand. I also imagine Blaise's ear still ringing, even after the sound had vanished. Then the subject rushes into the gap, and the will to knowledge comes to dwell in that double, *almost* instantaneous hiatus of the accident, between fall and sound, sound and silence. He repeats the fall, even down to the noise that bursts forth, resonating like an echo; repeats it even in the silence of the written signs in which the accident is effaced and corrected. And, from that day forward, the accident becomes a first experiment, already a first proposition of science. But the accident is converted into a primitive theorem only after the fact, after the blow of the knife on the platter, not because the knife falls by accident but because that blow instantaneously splits the instant in two, into a great sound and a silence. And, between the two, a subject constitutes itself in order to retain, to take note of, both the sound and the silence, to recuperate them once more and again, until the echo resonates and dies away in the writing of a very well-reasoned treatise.

In the second incident, the reader may note, the narrator begins with a silence; her narrative opens with an event about which nothing is said, nothing, that is, but its name, opportunity. It is only because I am curious by nature that I learned—outside the narrative, outside the biography—about the accident of Etienne Pascal, the father, his fall on the ice, about the care by the two Jansenists, the books of piety they lent the Pascal family and that Blaise, in particular, read. At the end of the cascading series of events linked to the initial accident, to which the narrator gives the name "opportunity," a reading is said to have been obligatory. A light of the soul is born in that reading, a truth that obliges the one who welcomes it "to live only for God and to have no other object but him." Since truth lies at the end of a road leading through effects and circumstances, a truth that is obvious, necessary, and useful, a total truth that is itself terminal ("it ended all his research") and exclusive ("he renounced all other knowledge to apply himself to the unique thing called necessary by Jesus Christ"), we then understand why, due to the powerful effect of the deferred action of this terminus and this end, the narrator wished to skip any account of the initial event (the father's fall on the ice) and of its no less fortuitous consequences (the two gentlemen doctors who happened to be Jansenists, the books by Saint-Cyran, Jansen, and Arnauld). We understand why, in labelling the entire event with the term "opportunity," she wished to recognize in it a preexisting pattern or plan: a structure of intelligibility (the coherence of a system composed of the lasting consequences of the events), a transcendent intention aimed precisely at a determinate end, and a plan implying a selective choice of means, a plan that concerned her brother, Blaise Pascal.

In the first incident, the subject of knowledge constituted itself by rushing into the double breach of the fortuitous accident and by making itself the repeated echo of that accident, which it had, in some sense, "always already" converted into an experiment, before condensing it into the signs of the subject's scientific truth. In the second incident, that truth—which has become *the* truth—deposited in signs (the writings of piety) from the beginning, catches the subject in its net, makes it part of a close network, and constitutes it as a subject of belief. The proof of that belief, its peremptory demonstration, after the fact, is made in the series of events that follow from the initial event, events that unfold without a hitch until that end, and which now appear inexorable. But it is only that end, with the requirement for belief and the truth of belief, that makes the events a determinate series because the last sequence was absolutely determining. Thus, throughout her narrative, Gilberte Périer sets out transcendent actors or performative figures of belief, of the subject of belief, and of its conversion, to fill in the silences and blanks, the things she finds it ridiculous to say and, even more, to write. First, she sets out "the Providence of God," which produced the opportunity, produced the origin (the birth) through its action (of bringing forth). In its name (*providere*, to foresee), the Providence of God also designates everything to follow as a complete representation, a tableau (*providere*, to see before one, to have something before one's eyes). Second, the narrator sets out "God" himself as light, spiritual illumination. Reading is the instrument of that light: It is as if the writings of piety and their signs, arranged in the foreseen and exhibited tableau of Providence, had to receive a light which, in allowing them to be seen, gave them all their effectiveness.

But this illumination by God occurs only at the end of the narrative process. It is only after Pascal has abandoned profane scientific research, has renounced all knowledge other than the sole and unique necessary knowledge, that the "enlightened" Blaise perceives there was a trajectory, or even a path to follow, and that this trajectory began at its starting point, "the opportunity." Or, at the very least, this enlightenment is a central moment along the trajectory of the circumstances and effects of the accident. The injunction Gilberte Périer underscores both in the obligation to read (books of true piety) and in the obligation to lead a certain kind of life (to renounce profane curiosity) is here only the remarkable mark that what matters in this entire "adventure" is not knowledge but belief, not theory but practice, not speculative truths but a norm of existence. Nonetheless, the specific obligation to read and, especially, to live a certain way appears as such only at the end of the process or, at least, as the articulation between the first and the second obligation. In February 1646, during a harsh winter in Normandy, the father, Etienne, confined to bed with a dislocated leg, could do little more than read, and, among other things, he read the books of piety lent to him by his Jansenist "doctors." The head of the family and family members, Blaise, in particular, virtually needed to do so. This is a necessity and not an obligation. And it is the conversion of this necessity, after the fact, into an obligation, that provides the most striking proof of the religious conversion in the biographical narrative.

In the first incident, the *chance* of an *accidental* fall (that of a knife) *returns at the same instant* as a *scientific experiment* in acoustics; in this instant, the subject of knowledge constitutes itself catacoustically, as a producer of written signs (the treatise on sounds).

In the second incident, the *chance* of an *accidental* fall (that of the father) *returns soon afterward* as an *opportunity* of faith; the subject of belief is constituted in this return as the product of the written signs (the writings of piety). The subject is obligatorily engendered in Truth in keeping with the opportunity generated by the Eternal Father. But, in each case, as producer or as product, in the scientifically reasoned echo of a great sound, a treatise on sounds, or in the silence deserted by everything but God, who manifests himself only through the marks and signs of his passing, the subject comes into being or is born in an *encounter* with reality: chance as accident, accident as opportunity, a reality that, for an instant, bursts forth and then suddenly falls with all its weight, falls its entire length. But when science writes the theorem of that fall, when faith requires its ascetic practice, the reality is already past, and the subject is forever caught in the network of signs.

Chance, opportunity, an encounter:

> What is the self? A man goes to the window to see the people passing by; if I pass by, can I say he went there to see me? No, for he is not thinking of me in particular. But what about a person who loves someone for the sake of her beauty; does he love *her*? . . . And if someone loves me for my judgement or my memory, do they love me? *me*, myself? . . . Where then is this self, if it is neither in the body nor the soul? And how can one love the body or the soul except for the sake of such qualities, which are not what makes up the self, since they are perishable? Would we love the substance of a person's soul, in the abstract, whatever qualities might be in it? That is not possible, and it would be wrong. Therefore we never love anyone, but only qualities.[1]

It is no longer a question of the subject but of the self in the network of signs. Nonetheless, the narrative begins with an encounter or returns to an encounter. The question is not "Who am I?" but, rather, "What is the self?" Perhaps "I" ask the question to better know who I am who is asking the question. And from the outset, the reader may have noted that the question "I" ask (myself) has no meaning, or rather, that the "I" can only develop it beginning with an encounter and through a series of encounters, in order to return to the first encounter, and then only to assert peremptorily that it did not take place because it could not take place. In fact, it did take place, but I only learned of it by going over the entire cycle of encounters—it was only a missed encounter.

The way of positing the question of the self, the only way of positing it, or of leading the self to the question I posit, is by asking insistently not for love—all lovers in the world have said, say, and will say "I love you" to each other—but for its reason (this is, no doubt, one of the heart's reasons that reason does not know): the reason or the cause. The reason for what? The cause of what? Why? Because of what? But from one question to the next, the reader discovers that asking for the reason of the "thing" is the same as asking for the thing itself, and, in the meantime, the narrative has shifted from the interrogative "Can I say . . . ?" to the negative, in the form of a conclusion: "Therefore, we never love anyone." Not anyone? No one? That is, someone who *is* no one [*une* personne qui *est* personne], who is nothing but a *persona* (the resounding mask) of these qualities. And that may be the end of any encounter (in the two senses of the word "end"): to miss the unique, irreplaceable being and discover, in the end, the being as that which was missed. In the place of the being are its qualities, which remain behind, even though there was never a totality from which the qualities were subtracted, saved, in order to remain behind.

Chance, opportunity, an encounter: In the near agrammaticality of his position of enunciation, Pascal offers the encounter as something to be read and, almost, as something to be seen. There is, first of all, an indefinite "he," a man, the subject who "goes to the window to see the people passing by." He is an anonymous being, framed by the window, who looks, who frames himself in the window only to look. Second, there is the object, the passersby, both those who pass within his gaze and those who are merely passing through, for whom all being is in the passing, as Montaigne said. A double, indefinite "he": a man, a framed, motionless subject, who is only at his window in order to see; and the men who *are* not *there* [ne *sont* pas *là*], in the street, under the window open to the gaze, but who are *passing* [sont *passants*]. It is in this strange arrangement, which links a (phantasmic) gaze and the passersby who offer no focus for that gaze, it is in that very banal staging that the encounter takes place. But it takes place, and only place, in the writing that is made of it, or, to be even more precise, in the blank of a break where "a man," who places himself at the window, suddenly loses the *verb* that would determine him as a subject and through which he could posit himself as such. As a potential subject, in keeping with my reading, he remains at the state of the possible, a subject suspended, framed by his window in his desire to see the passersby. All of a sudden, he loses that capacity for determination, because "I" pass by. In fact, "I" do not really pass by. It could be that I pass by. On the one hand, then, there is a man who places himself at the window to see the passersby. But what does he do, what does he say, what does he think? No one will ever know. On the other hand, another possibility arises: "I" pass by. Among all the passersby who pass, who do nothing but pass, it could be there is an "I." It's almost certain, but not absolutely. Let's suppose an "I" passes by, this "I" that leads the man (who placed himself at the window to watch people passing by) to lose any access to his determination as a subject. And now the man also loses what he is, loses the quality of having placed himself at his window to *see* the passersby *pass*, since, if I pass by, I cannot even say that he placed himself there to see the passerby that I am pass by (if, in fact, I pass by and there's a very good chance that an "I" passes among all those who do nothing but pass).

Thus, there is every chance that there was an encounter (between a man who places himself at the window to see the passersby and an "I" who might have passed by), every chance, as well, that this possible or altogether probable encounter was a missed encounter, that this encounter did not take place except inasmuch as it was missed. A man at his window to see passersby will see a passerby pass by, will see someone pass, someone who does nothing but pass among all those who are passing, but he will never see this "I" passing by, should the "I" happen to pass, and whom, however, the man sees passing by. "Can I say he went there to see me?"

But how could there be an *encounter* if he placed himself at the window to see me? For then it would not have been an encounter but a plan, a design entailing expectation, hope, or fear. For there to be an encounter, he must not be thinking of me in particular, and moreover, no doubt, he must not recognize me. Hence this dialogue, which I imagine taking place the next day: "What! You passed by my window yesterday afternoon! But I placed myself at the window precisely to see the passersby.... We might have encountered each other." That's always the way we encounter each other, *by chance*, missing each other. And so it is with love: He discovers that he loved someone only for her beauty; he discovers he no longer loves her when smallpox has disfigured her. Banal anecdote: Where, then, are the great oaths, the passionate cries? He discovers why he loves her when he turns away from her. But it just might be that the thing *one* loves *me* for is also lost *by chance*, even though I myself am not lost, and one will discover, as the other did a moment ago, that *one* loved *me* for what I have lost.

In this way, the writing runs through all the grammatical positions of the enunciation of each encounter ("a man ... I," "he who ... someone," "one ... me") until the paradoxical exhaustion of the subject in the indefinite (one) and the exhaustion of the object in negation (no one), which opens the space between, the space of an exchange, a borrowing, a shift between "one" and "no one," a space that is being itself, that is, a network of qualities without substance. Hence, any encounter as lack is disguised as a passionate love that, in the end, heroically, is never more than a chance encounter, a fleeting love.

A chance encounter, a fleeting love, the *premier venu*.[2] "A man goes to the window ... if I pass by," *for him*, I am not the first one to pass. Others have passed by before me, and others will follow me. For him, I am merely anyone at all, one of the many who pass by under his window. As for myself—the palisade!—I am the first and the only one to pass by, for one reason or another, in view of some end or another, the first to pass by *as (my)self.* The others, to recall the Cartesian image, are for me no more than coats and hats. Solitary among a collectivity of automatons, because I am—for myself—the only one to have plans and memories, goals, a will, habits, knowledge: unique. Such is the *aporia* of solipsism: each one, an irreplaceable self, and all, a crowd of "anyones at all." How is it possible, then, to love one another (or oneself)?

Or more simply, how is it possible, just once, to encounter one another (or oneself)? "A man goes to the window to see the people passing by; if I pass by, can I say he went there to see me? No, for he is not thinking of me in particular": *For him*, I am anyone at all. He is the unique one, singled out by his window and his gaze and his plan; or, rather, in the syntactical break of the sentence I signaled above, in the "leap" from the gaze out the window to the discourse of the other that passes by, from the "he" to the "I," the second is singled out suddenly, in the midst of everyone and no one, but negatively: "Can I say he went there to see me? *No*, for he is not thinking of me in particular." It is no longer an encounter between the unique one who watches the passersby pass by, and the "anyones at all" who pass (and among them, me perhaps, if I pass by); rather, two unique beings—he at his window, I who pass and who wonder if he placed himself there to see me—confront each other and encounter each other and *miss* each other since, in truth, "no . . . he is not thinking of me in particular." The two unique beings miss each other in reality, but they encounter each other *by missing each other* in the text the "I" writes, and in which he *does* recount his encounter with that man who had placed himself at this window to see the passersby pass by. He recounts it because he saw that he was seen, but not as "me," only as one among everyone else, anyone at all. He recounts the encounter as a missed encounter: He might have been seen, re-cognized as (my)self. Hence the imagined dialogue above. What is admirable and altogether perspicacious in Pascal's *pensée* is that these embryos of narratives of encounters and of love are written and told through personification and figuration, through narrative actors occupying all the possible positions of enunciation. And it is only in that way, when the combinatorial table of discourse is realized on the narrative stage of the text, that the inexpressible reality can be outlined as banality, as missed encounter, as the figures of chance or "luck," as the term *tuchè* in Aristotle's *Physics* is translated.

The *premier venu*, the first to happen along, is not just anyone at all, and, yet, he is also not the first to come along among all those who come or will come. The expression is a "moneme," a noun that—strangely enough—can only be used with the definite article. Does one ever speak of *a premier venu?* If one were to do so, the noun would cease to be a true noun and would go back to being a composite expression where the adjective "*premier*" determines, singles out, the one who *came in the past,* and defines him as *unique* ("a first one, who came"). The *premier venu*, in fact, *was* the *only one* to come, the one who came before all the others, who preceded them forever, if only by a nose, to an encounter with another. "Out of despair, she married the *premier venu*," says the *doxa* of communal discourse, "and so settled down." The man who is today her spouse was the first of all the possible suitors who *might* have appeared at the moment when she was desperate. In truth, we see in this modest and vulgar example that there will never be other suitors: Curiously, the *premier venu*, without predecessor because he is the first, also has no successor, since he would then no longer be the "*premier venu*" but, rather, the "*premier choisi*," the first to be chosen, the elect in the series of those who came in succession and among whom he happened to be the first. And, from that point on, the series of suitors forms a set, a group of coexistents. Which means—to draw out the example—in this case, she did not, as one says, throw herself at the first, at the *premier venu*, but, rather, deferred her decision during all the time when new suitors appeared, until the moment when she chose as her spouse the first one who had presented himself. That différance (with an a), which transforms a series in time into a localized set, is also that which distinguishes the encounter from the deliberate decision, the calculated choice, the accomplished plan. In the end, the *premier venu* was the first to come, but if we may allow this paradox, that was because he was the only one; not because there were no others but because all the others came too late; not because they might have been running late, not because they might have hesitated or procrastinated, but, quite simply, because they did not know that the encounter was going to take place, because the very idea of the encounter had not crossed their minds, because they knew only after the fact, and then, perhaps, regretted it. Hence, this altogether increasingly strange notion: The *premier venu* is the one who was exactly on time for a meeting he knew nothing about, that is, to a meeting that the Other, the absolutely Other, had granted him in particular. But, you will say, to "follow" the example, then the Other, the absolutely Other, is that woman who, out of despair, settled down by marrying the *premier venu*. Yes, no doubt; she is precisely its figure, since the Other, the absolutely Other, by its very definition, can never show itself, can never appear here or there, now, or soon, or a while ago, except as a figure. What would the Other, the absolutely Other, be if one could say: "There it is: That's it, *itself*!"?

Nevertheless, as we have already underscored, the *premier venu*, even as a noun, a "moneme" stripped of any temporal mark, is also a composite expression, in which the past participle asserts its meaning: The *premier venu*, if I may say so, is already come. He is not coming, he is not to come, he is past, already. He is even the first to be past. The example we gave was significant: The *premier venu* installed himself in the narrative, in the little love story, from the outset, in the (distant) third person and the definitive past. In addition, if, from a certain point of view, all the others arrived late in relation to the *premier venu*, in relation to the encounter itself, at the present instant of the encounter, the *premier venu* is, one might say, too prompt, too on time, a bit early for the meeting. In this place and this moment of the meeting, *he is come*—already. Not that he has come again: The *premier venu* is without habits, without past, without memory. If he were coming back, he might not even know it. He came to this place and this time, *the first*, early, too early. If he had any memory, we might say he is waiting. Thus, when the encounter takes place, at the instant of the encounter, he passed, and it is because he *passed* that he encounters her, that he does not miss her like those who are to come—late—he misses her in a different way than they do, by insistence, in this place and this moment, by excess, as if he were watching for her; which he naturally does not do since he does not even know that he is already at the place of the meeting, at the time of the meeting, already passing. It is precisely when he meets her, she who is so deep into her despair that she draws from it a kind of indifference and almost a gaiety, like a mask on her face, it is precisely at the moment when he runs into her and passes by her that he was there as if to wait for her. It is in passing her that, at the same time, he passed the instant and the place of the meeting, that he was the first because he was already come, that he had to turn back and retrace his steps in order to truly encounter her. But then it was no longer an encounter but only a way of finding her again, of pursuing her.

We could also, if we wished, modify the example, the narrative utterance: "Out of despair, she married the *premier venu*." To avoid that *fall* into the grayness of everyday life, of the institution, which smells like cheap perfume, we might try to recount the encounter by itself, the encounter with the *premier venu*, the moment, the instant two passersby crossed. At that moment, there is always the flash of a look, "a brief, sharp flash that wounds," as Ernst Bloch writes. *Augenblick*, almost nothing. And, yet, for there to be an encounter, that flash must leave a trace in one party or in the other, or in both parties, but unbeknownst to either—a trace that is the wound Bloch speaks of—a reverberation like an echo, a trace, a wound; an echo that, each in its own way, according to the feelings of each party, designates the encounter as essentially missed. Hence, it will often happen that one of the two protagonists in the encounter—who, be it understood, only becomes an actor in that brief instant—turns around after passing the other. For what? I am asking you. To get a look at that faceless silhouette moving away from him with hurried steps, among the passersby? That would be quite ridiculous. I imagine that, for a moment, in the flash of a look, an unknown "possibility" fluttered, a possibility that, if it had developed over time in an existence, might perhaps have revealed a singular, unheard of, truth.

I also imagine that it is an instant of that nature that Massignon was evoking in Islamic thought, the irruption of divine causality in its present efficiency, "the blink of an eye, the laconic announcement of God's judicial decision, conferring on our nascent act its status [*hukm*], which will be proclaimed one day when we hear the Clamor of Justice (Q. 50,41)."[3] A unique, perfect instant then, adequate to itself, "the *Hour*, that of the Last Judgment, final summons of the status of all responsibilities undertaken": of all encounters, I will add, encounters that could only be missed. Truth, Justice, out to encounter the *premier venu*. He has caught a glimpse of her in the blink of an eye; he turns around as she passes; he is come now, for she carries away with her all the possible present; he has passed, simply marked by the indelible seal of the encounter that never takes place, the encounter that the *premier venu*, for one distinguished instant, most often forgets a few minutes later, a few meters down the road, but whose mark forever designates him as the one responsible.

That is also how I happen to read this *pensée*: "This is not the home of truth; it wanders unrecognized among men. God has covered it with a veil that keeps it from being recognized.... The place is open to blasphemy."[4]

18

The Secrets of Names and Bodies

We have read Balzac's tale (to use the fashionable expression),[1] entitled "Le chef-d'oeuvre inconnu" and have attentively consulted the introduction and the valuable notes by René Guise.

We were greeted by a marvelous surprise upon "reading" the dedication: "To a lord," followed by a regular seed bed of 135 periods distributed along five lines (seventeen per line), ending with a date, "1845." It is as if the typography were offering the contemporary reader what Poussin and Porbus saw in the Frenhofer painting when they entered his studio in early 1612: "A chaos of uncertain colors, tones, nuances, a kind of formless fog." "To a lord . . . 1845" would be the equivalent, in writing, of the "delicious" foot, the "living foot" before which "they remained petrified with admiration." I am not petrified, but I am amazed at that strange correspondence.

I have learned that the dedication (and the date) were introduced in 1846 to tome 14 of the Furne edition. I have also learned that its secret has not been fathomed. "There's a woman lurking behind all that!" cried Porbus, pointing out to Poussin the various layers of colors that the old painter had superimposed one after another, in the belief he was perfecting his painting. Who or what can be read between the lines of the 135 periods sprinkled at the beginning of this book? (Do you read something there? No—Do you? Nothing.) Who or what can be read between the title of the tale, "Le chef-d'oeuvre inconnu," and the first chapter title, "Gillette"? Who can read the unknown narrative of the "tale" between these lines of periods, this most primitive form of writing? "There is a story lurking behind it," but I could never point out the layers of colors, only the monotony of the aligned periods.[2]

"Gillette": I have learned that this name was substituted for another in that place, but also that it was displaced in 1847 to serve as the title for the tale as a whole.[3] Of this name, I retain only its movement to the margins of the book: an incitement to follow the displacements of names in the twenty-five pages of the narrative. It may just be that the novella was constructed exclusively from these displacements,[4] each occurrence of a name in the lines of the text being only a trace, a mark, a point in a series of trajectories that interweave to form, precisely, a text, and, in the end, a narrative. In that, we might discover again, in another form, the seed bed of periods with which the tale opened and which appear on its margin.

Gillette, a woman's name.... And here are the others: Marie de Médicis, St. Mary of Egypt, Catherine Lescault, Angélique, Beatrix. To which I add an "outline drawing of Mary," "inaccessible Venus," a "lovely Giorgion," "a young Georgian," and "a [nameless] woman, semi-nude." Such are the names of women, of paintings, of images: trajectories. There is a woman lurking behind it all: Gillette, perhaps, whose name provided the title of the work or the first chapter, just as that other name, "Catherine Lescault"—might it be hers as well?—serves as title for the second part. And, in that second part, at the end, Gillette tells her lover the final words, while Catherine disappears a second time, not under the paint amassed on the canvas but under the canvas of green serge with which her father, her lover, her God covers her. Gillette first appears at the turning point of the *narrative*, as a life model, surprised in a movement of love, before receiving from the mouth of her lover and her painter her name as a "real" painting, but one written in the text: "Near the one dark window of that room [here is the frame for this painting], he [Nicolas Poussin, painter and beholder] *saw* a young girl who, at the sound of the door, got up in a movement of love.[5]—'Go on, *Gillette*, we shall be rich and happy! There's gold in these paintbrushes!'"

> Gillette: In the feminine, one speaks of a "Reine Gillette," a Queen Gillette, when ridiculing a woman who is decked out, playing the great Lady even though she is of little consideration. (Furetière)
>
> Gillette, grisette: n., fem. Woman or young girl dressed in gray. Used with scorn for all women of low condition, no matter how they are dressed. People of quality often entertain themselves by frequenting *grisettes*. (Furetière)
>
> Gillette: Fem. of Gille, clown in the theater or at the fair, a silly and naive man, a coward who runs off at the slightest appearance of danger. *Faire gille*: to escape, run away, go bankrupt. Gille's costume is white, like Pierrot's. (Furetière)
>
> Gillette, the sister of Watteau's Gille: "He has lively eyes, a thin and sharp turned-up nose, small, curving mouth, pinched at the corners; irony and mockery seem to flutter about his lips and tickle them. This Gille is alive. It is truly the miracle of true presence. The man himself seems to be there. He listens, he hears, he waits, he is silent, he is about to move, his arms are about to become detached from that hat of soft, downy felt that caresses the eyes. The sky itself does not seem to be fixed and imprisoned in a canvas; it is not a background, it is air, the day hovers about there, the light palpitates."[6]

Gille, in whom Panofsky believes he can recognize the disguised self-portrait of its painter.[7]

Gillette, a model or a painting, a portrait come alive, a model become portrait. Has the living Gillette been transformed into a representation? That would truly be the miracle of real absence in a name—the reverse of the miracle noted by the Goncourts regarding her brother Gille in Watteau's painting. Gillette is the name of a character, but also the title of this *tableau vivant*, this living painting, which, at the center of the narrative, takes on life on the mysterious borderline that the art of painting, the art of portraiture, maintains with the life of bodies, this borderline where identities and identifications come together and fall apart. A journey: Marie de Médicis, the queen, and her painter Porbus; Porbus, "Henri IV's painter whom she abandoned for Rubens."[8]

St. Mary of Egypt, "a painting that, in this time of trouble and revolution had already become famous.... That lovely page represented a St. Mary of Egypt preparing to pay her boat passage. This masterpiece destined for Marie de Médicis was sold by her when she was poverty-stricken."[9] Two Maries, two women with the same first name, share the starting point for the story within the story: The widow, regent of the kingdom, and the holy prostitute headed toward Jerusalem and her conversion. St. Mary of Egypt sells her body to the boatman in order to cross the river, just as Marie de Médicis in exile sells the representation of St. Mary to confront misfortune: Two historical tableaux are exchanged here for yet another name (the same one, however), the name of the Virgin Mother of God, which they encode, repeating it twice, in reality and fiction.[10] Two women, an Italian and an Egyptian, meet in the painting; one as its recipient and owner, the other as its subject.

Three painters are brought together in front of the painting, but, for the moment, only one of them has been named: "Toward the end of the year 1612, on a cold December morning, a young man, very lightly dressed, was pacing in front of the door to a house situated on Rue des Grands-Augustins in Paris. In the end, he crossed the threshold of that door and asked if *Mr. François Porbus* was at home." Three painters: Mr. François Porbus; a young man, a "poor neophyte"; and an old man whom "the young man guessed" was "either the protector or the friend of the painter." But, in the narrative recounted to us, this old man is himself a *painting*. The young man examines him like a model to be painted: "There was something diabolical in that face and especially that *je ne sais quoi* that entices artists." The author, for his part, represents him to us as a canvas come alive: "You might have thought he was a Rembrandt canvas walking silently and without its frame in the black atmosphere that this great painter had appropriated for himself." Three painters in front of the painting of Mary (St. Mary of Egypt preparing to pay the boat passage), painted for Marie (de Médicis) by the *master* François Porbus. The first sells herself, the second sells the painting, and "the painting of Rembrandt," transformed into an anonymous old man, friend and protector of the master, proposes to buy. But what? Is he buying the painting, like Marie de Médicis, or the painted woman, like the boatman? "'Your saint pleases me,' said the old man to Porbus, 'and I would pay ten *écus* in gold above the price the queen offers; but compete with her on her own turf? . . . The devil you say!'—'You think it's all right?'—'Oof! Oof!' said the old man. 'Well, yes and no. *Your good lady is trussed up good all right* [*Ta bonne femme n'est pas mal troussée*], but there's no life in her.'"[11]

This is painters' jargon, but, as a matter of fact, St. Mary of Egypt, in offering herself in exchange for boat passage very precisely *trussed herself up* [*se trousse*]:[12]

> In the Eglise de la Jussienne there was a stained glass window remarkable for its naivety: St. Mary of Egypt was represented at the moment when, crossing a river and with no means for paying her passage, she offered to prostitute her body to whoever would pay; seated in the boat, she was lifting her robe to the knees. Under the stained glass window was the legend: "How the Saint offered her body to the boatman." . . . The stained glass window was judged indecent and was removed in 1660.[13]

Your good woman is trussed up good all right, but there's no life in her: You truss her up but she doesn't really truss herself up. . . . The subject of the painting is a scene of prostitution (St. Mary of Egypt preparing to pay for her passage); the painting is the object of prostitution (the old man outbids the queen to "buy himself" the saint); the painting is a gesture of prostitution, not trussing up the figure to sell it, but allowing the figure to truss herself up, display herself, elicit admiration, as a *living* prostitute to the gaze.

And, by this very gesture, the painting of a story—an episode from the legend of St. Mary of Egypt—becomes merely the portraiture of a model, the "singular" body of a woman to be auctioned off to the gaze: It will now be a question only of this body—her bosom, her shoulder, her hand, her hair, her blood, her skin, her eyes, her eyebrows. And, despite his remark, which evokes the episode of the saint and the boatman in the narrative of the *Acta Santorum* or in the stain glass window of la Jussienne,[14] the unknown young man nimbly copies only the Mary, in red pencil on a piece of paper. This portrait sketch requires a signature: "'Oh! Oh!' cried out the old man. 'Your name?'" The young man *does not name himself*; he *writes* "Nicolas Poussin." He has no identity but that of a sign inscribed at the bottom of a drawing, which he identifies as his own. He *enters* the drawing as *one of its parts* in representation.

In December 1612, Nicolas Poussin was quite probably in Paris. He came from Les Andelys where Quentin Varin, it seems, taught him to paint, while executing three altar paintings for the Eglise de Notre Dame du Grand Andely that same year: a *Martyrdom of St. Vincent*, a *Saint-Clair*, and a *Regina coeli*.[15]

It is this drawing, and the name of the future master painter that is a part of that drawing, which provokes the surprising apparition of a second painting, a complement, precisely, of the first. The singular old man tells Poussin: "But since you are worthy of the lesson and capable of understanding it, I shall let you see how few things are needed to *complete* this work. Give me all your attention, fix your eyes on me."

complement, n., that which completes a number, thing
complete, v., to make complete
complete, adj., lacking nothing

This minuscule complement, this practically nothing, or rather, "this nothing that is everything," "this last stroke of the paintbrush that counts" because it turns the painting to account, makes it a totality that is *lacking nothing*, affects only the figure of Mary's body metamorphosed into an "ardent Egyptian." Extracted from the history painting of the master Porbus, in an outline drawing signed "Nicolas Poussin," the holy prostitute, through the effect of that copy, steps out of the painting "alive," thanks to that ultimate complement, that last difference that makes all the difference, that nothing that expresses "life overflowing, that *je ne sais quoi* that may just be the soul and that floats like a cloud on the envelope." She steps out of the painting; she no longer belongs to the artifice and the artifacts of painting, or, more precisely, she leaves its surface by nullifying it as depth, a daemonic (or demoniacal) movement that leaves Poussin and Porbus "mute with admiration," stupefied by the apparition. But it is also in this place of the narrative that St. Mary of Egypt leaves the text, to be replaced by another woman's name. The old man says to the two painters: "That [Mary, completed by him] is not yet the equal of my Catherine Lescault, but one might well place a name at the bottom of such a work." What name? The name of the painter, the way Nicolas Poussin identified himself by placing his name at the bottom of the drawing of Mary, or the name of the figure, Catherine Lescault (*my* Catherine Lescault), the name of the "complete" figure of St. Mary of Egypt? No doubt both: "'Yes, I will sign it,' he added, rising to pick up a mirror and looking at the painting in it." The absent name of the demon old man substitutes for the name of Porbus and, in the mirror (a traditional mechanism for "control" or "surveillance" of the painting by its painter), Catherine Lescault serves as the *complete* reflection of St. Mary of Egypt. The singular old man was presented (or represented) in the first pages of the narrative as a Rembrandt figure stepping out of the painting's frame. The demon who makes painted figures step out of the space of representation preceded them in this perilous, mysterious process. Not that he refuses to explain himself; on the contrary. The demon is garrulous, but, although the "negative" conditions of his secret procedures are the object of his *discourse*, he can only *show* Porbus and Poussin, in the painting complement to Mary-as-painting, the excess, beyond the canvas, of Catherine Lescault.

For the reader, however, the displayed secret remains secret; the discourse can never express this supplement of life born from the complement of representation, except through oxymoron, "this nothing that is everything," or by hyperbole, where language confesses its impotence, "life overflowing, that *je ne sais quoi* that may just be the soul and that floats like a cloud on the envelope." For the reader, this supplement *in* the complement, this excess *in* representation, through which representation is nullified, finds its equivalent less in the signs of language than in the delay in *naming* the demon: deferred name, different name? Out of "a disturbing curiosity," Poussin approaches Porbus, "as if to ask the name of his host; but the painter placed a finger on his lips with a mysterious look." It is as if the enunciation of the name were to provide the key to the great, almost alchemical transmutation of representation into presence: "The young man, keenly interested, kept quiet, hoping that sooner or later some word would allow him to guess the name of his host."

Nonetheless, this name difference, the aim of which is to identify the "fullness" of representation, its difference or its internal excess, is marked out by another name and by two paintings: "'O Mabuse! O my master!' added this singular character, 'You are a thief, you carried off life with you.'"

> Mabuse or Gossaert (Gossart) Jan (Malbodius), born in Maubeuge in Hainaut c. 1480, died in Antwerp after 1534.

Why Mabuse? Why the appearance of this painter's name in the story? Why does it surge up at this place in the text? In his critique of the "good woman" by Porbus, the singular old man has already named, as a system of drawing, Holbein and Dürer, and as a system of color, Titian and Veronese. Titian and Dürer reappear once more to mark the painter's indecision: "If you did not feel strong enough to meld together two rival manners in the fire of your genius, you should have opted frankly for one or the other in order to obtain the unity that simulates one of the conditions of life."[16] Raphael, the king of art, comes next; for the old man, he seems to have seized "raw nature in its true spirit." Raphael covers with his divine name the third part of art, the intimate meaning that realizes the unity of the first two, color and drawing. Titian and Raphael reappear once more: They captured "the flower of life," "that *je ne sais quoi* that may just be the soul and that floats like a cloud on the envelope."[17] It is at that point that the name of Mabuse abruptly appears: "O Mabuse! O my master!"

Why Mabuse? There are at least three possible responses. The first stems from the history of art and styles. Gossart went to Italy, accompanying his patron Philip, Bastard of Burgundy, on a mission for Margaret of Austria in 1508. He returned in 1510. "He received an extremely keen impression from this, and a complete transformation took place in his talent. Until then, his compositions were of an austere placidity, cold- and stiff-looking, with fine, but sad and monotonous color. Under the influence of Italian masters, Mabuse adopted a bold, animated style on a grand scale, with warm colors; when he came back to his native land, he made a true artistic revolution." In his *Descrittone di tutti i Paesi Bassi* (1567), Guicciardini himself noted that "Giovanni di Maubeuge was the first Netherlander to bring from Italy the art of painting history and poesy with nude figures."[18] Mabuse: the trajectory, the round trip, of Flemish drawing and Italian color.[19]

The second response stems from his works, in which we discover a number of paintings with two figures, a nude man and woman, life-size, most often in an architectural setting: Adam and Eve, Neptune and Amphitrite, Mars and Venus, et cetera.[20] It is precisely this problem and this subject that Frenhofer treats in his debate with Porbus, as if Balzac had split this subject type in two, between Mabuse and Frenhofer, assigning Mabuse the male figure, Frenhofer the female. It is significant that, a few lines later, he attributes only an Adam to Gossart and the studies on the female nude, Eve, to his only student, the singular old man. Scission of works, scission of names. Mabuse and Frenhofer: How to name the difference between Adam and Eve, Flanders and Italy, drawing and color?

The third response stems directly from the name "Mabuse." "O my master! You are a thief, you carried off life with you. . . ." You *abuse* and you *abuse* me [*m'abuse*]: a play on names or a play on words. To be precise, it is an *abuse* of the name Mabuse, used to signify the "ontological" abuse evoked by Balzac a few pages later: "The contempt the old man pretended to express for the most beautiful efforts in art, its richness, its manners. . . . The painting that had been secret for so long, that work of patience, of genius no doubt, if we are to believe the portrait of the virgin that the young Poussin had so openly admired and that, still beautiful, even next to the Mabuse *Adam*, bore witness to the imperial talent of one of the princes of art. Everything in this old man went beyond the limits of human nature."

> abuse: n. (1) wrong use, wrong employ; (2) excess, overabundance
> abuse: v. (1) to use wrongly; (2) to use excessively; (3) to deceive, present under false pretenses

"What the rich imagination of Nicolas Poussin grasped clearly and perceptibly upon seeing this supernatural being was a complex image of artistic Nature, that mad nature to which so many gifts are entrusted and that too often *abuses* them. . . . For the enthusiast Poussin, this old man had become, through an abrupt transformation, art itself." Mabuse is the name for the abuse of art in the deferred name of the old man, his pupil.

Chains of names thus trace filiations, genealogies of painters. The discourse of the singular old man has uncovered two fathers, Titian and Raphael, behind François Porbus; and the master was unable to choose between them. And, ahead of Poussin, anticipating him, a future master: François Porbus? That is not certain.[21] The old man names his own master: Mabuse, but he is a master of lack, a father of death. "You carried off life with you." A family line is extinguished: "Only Mabuse possessed the secret of giving life to figures. Mabuse had but one pupil, and that is myself. I never had any, and I am old!" This is an ambiguous position for the old man in relation to his master and in relation to Poussin. Mabuse carried off life but, though it is never said explicitly, Mabuse gave life (not the secret of life) to his sole pupil, who then carried it off once more. Nonetheless, the neophyte can guess the rest, can guess the secret, the nothing that is everything; he catches a glimpse of the supplement, the excess in the complement. Three names, then, signify three relations between life and death. "Mabuse," "X" (the as yet unnamed old man), and "Poussin": life stolen away by death, death-life, and death stolen away by life. In short, past, present, and future. Mabuse, we might say, is difference, but a negative, mortal difference, in the family line of Titian and Raphael, the masters, the kings of light and art. The impossible task for Porbus, indicated by "X," is to choose between Holbein and Titian, Dürer and Veronese, and to be both Titian *and* Raphael. Between the dilemma and the synthesis, there lies a name, the very name of that difference: Mabuse, who lends his name to "X" in anticipation. Death = life: He holds the secret, but he has no pupil. Did we not know that already? "X" is a Rembrandt figure who has stepped out of his frame and who walks silently in the black atmosphere.

Two paintings remain to be seen before we will learn the name of the old man: one by Mabuse, a painting cut off from its "other," and the other, under a well-known name, but a name that turns out to be a pseudonym.

"Young man," Porbus said, seeing him standing dumbfounded before a painting, "do not look too long at that canvas or you'll fall into despair. That is the *Adam* Mabuse made to get out of prison."

Thus, a painting has passed between Mabuse and the anonymous old man, a painting-origin that marks their filiation, a painting of the first man, "the only one . . . to come immediately from the hands of God," a painting of the first model, whose creator was not the painter but God. This new ambiguity, like that mentioned earlier, traces a secret equivalence: God, creator of Adam, and Mabuse, painter of Adam. But that equivalence is established only through the identity of a name: Adam, the first man; Adam, the title of the only painting left behind by Mabuse for his sole pupil, as the remains or trace of the life he carried off with him. Unlike Poussin and Porbus, the singular, anonymous old man is not dumbfounded before the canvas of his master. He is critical. He marks the difference that makes all the difference. It is not life, but "'there is life,' he said. 'My poor master surpassed himself; but there was still a little bit of truth missing in the background of the canvas.'" And, yet, "'this man is quite alive, he is getting up, coming toward us. But the air, the sky, the wind we breathe, see, and feel, are not there yet.'"

Nonetheless, in this missing or missed relation, the double gap—between Mabuse and his singular disciple, and between Adam the divine creation and Adam the painted creation—shows through. The relation between the figure who steps out of the painting and the "real" space that enters into it as atmosphere repeats another relation, that between Balzac and the fabricated origin of the Mabuse painting of Adam and Eve. Balzac suppressed the Eve figure, *covering it over* in the fictional signs of his writing, just as Catherine Lescault is later covered over by successive layers of paint. "The only man to come immediately from the hands of God must have had something divine about him, and that is lacking." God is missing from the painting of Mabuse, according to the old man; Adam is missing Eve, according to Balzac. God or woman: "life overflowing," excess or lack, the figure absent from the master's word. In that gap at the origin, the anonymous man's aim is to assume the name of God in the painted/living body of a woman: What other name, then, than that of mystery, in the unknown of the masterpiece? That is what Porbus's gesture imposing silence on Poussin suggests.

A second painting makes a pair with this last painting of the first man: "Poussin, seeing a magnificent portrait of a woman on the dark oak paneling, cried out: 'What a lovely Giorgion!'" In that other painting, Eve returns, but she immediately receives her name from the name of her painter, bestowed on her by the neophyte: Giorgion. "The Adam that Mabuse made to get out of prison"; "a lovely Giorgion." But "Giorgion" is a false name here: "'No!' responded the old man, 'what you see is one of my first scrawls.'" And we come full circle with the name of the unnameable, the name of the lack in any representation in paint: "'*Tudieu*, I am therefore at the home of the *god* [dieu] of painting,' said Poussin naively." Giorgion is a false title, a false name. It is a false attribution, a false identification, just as Adam was *both* the name of the first model *and* the title of the unique painting: The gap, the difference, is repeated, and only the name of God can name it.[22] And superimposed upon that name is the name of the "demon," which finally appears in the prosaic request addressed him by Porbus: "*Maître Frenhofer*... won't you have a bit of your good Rhine wine brought in for me?" The triangulation of names comes to an end: Titian, Raphael, and Mabuse, names of difference and impossible synthesis; Porbus, Poussin, and Frenhofer, names for the difference between the master, the neophyte, and the name of truth in painting. "I owe you the truth in painting and I will tell it to you": "I," the name of God, of the origin, of creation, the unknown name preexisting the unknown masterpiece.

And now, Gillette can be named as the last link in a long chain of names. Let us retrace that chain: Marie de Médicis, who buys and sells; St. Mary of Egypt, preparing to pay the boatman for her passage; a rough sketch of Mary made by the neophyte; the same Mary completed by the demon and substituted for its supplement, its excess, Catherine Lescault; and finally, a Giorgion that is not a Giorgion, that is not yet its name. Giorgion, Gillette: the false name of the creation and the name yet to come of the model. But the second name can be read in the first, even before we read in the name "Gillette" yet another name, Catherine Lescault, since the model will be transmuted into the painting of Catherine Lescault. In the metamorphosis of Mary into Catherine and of a finished history painting into an unknown portrait, the crux, the place of exchange, lies in the names Giorgion and Gillette. Between the two lie God or Frenhofer: unknown names.

From the *Grand dictionnaire Larousse* of the nineteenth century, we glean:

Joseph von Fraunhofer: Skillful German optician, curator of offices in optics and physics in Munich, born in Straubing, Bavaria, in 1787, died 1826.

The son of a poor glazier, who left him an orphan at twelve, he was apprenticed to a glass manufacturer, educated himself during the hours set aside for sleep, passionately devoted himself to the study of optics especially, and succeeded in buying a machine for grinding lenses.

To support himself when he left the glass manufacturer, he engraved visiting cards. He escaped safe and sound when the house he was living in collapsed into ruins, and became the object of interest of Maximilian Joseph, king of Bavaria, whose assistance allowed him to procure books to learn the elements of science. That was how he learned mathematics. At twenty, he entered the great establishment of instruments and mathematics created by MM. Reichenbach and Utzschneider. The rare intelligence demonstrated by Fraunhaufer, his skill both in executing and supervising work, earned him the privilege of being placed at the head of the optics section of that establishment, whose prosperity and reputation he greatly augmented and of which he later became the owner. Fraunhofer possessed vast knowledge in physics, mathematics, and astronomy; he was eager to make discoveries and expand the boundaries of science. He is known above all for the study he made of the spectrum rays of the sun. Fraunhofer is the inventor of a repeating filament micrometer, of a heliometer, and of an achromatic microscope. It is to Fraunhofer that we owe the perfection of the Dorpat telescope, described by Strune as the "giant refractor."

The advancements in optics credited to Fraunhofer earned him this epitaph, which was placed on his tomb: *Approximavit sidera* [he approached the stars]. Fraunhofer was a member of several scientific societies. He left behind various memoirs, which were inserted into Schumache's *Astronomische Nachrichten*. He was curator of the office of physics at the Academy of Munich, and was also associated with the Astronomical Institute of Edinburgh and the University of Erlangen. The king of Bavaria conferred the decoration of the order of Merit on him.

Fraunhofer, Frenhofer: two names that echo each other, with only the change from the diphthong "au" to the vowel "e" at their center. That difference changes the son of the poor glazier, fatherless at twelve, into the only son of a master who disappeared, carrying off the secret of life with him. Fraunhofer discovered mysterious arcana in science and in the techniques of optics; Frenhofer thought he had penetrated the same arcana in the art of painting. "He is known above all for the study he made of the spectrum rays of the sun." "'Perhaps it would be better,' said Frenhofer, 'to attack a figure in the middle, focusing first on the best-lit protrusions, and then go on to the darker portions. Isn't that how the sun, that divine painter of the universe, proceeds? ... Too much science, like too much ignorance, leads to negation. I have doubts about my work.'" We said that "God" and "Frenhofer" were both unknown names. Let us replace that sacrilegious and profanatory equivalence with this new triangulation:

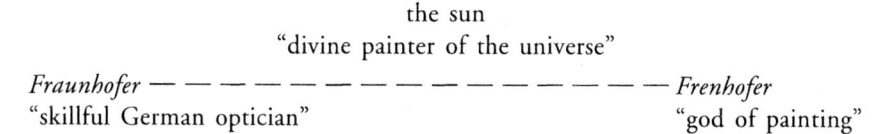

the sun
"divine painter of the universe"

Fraunhofer — — — — — — — — — — — — — *Frenhofer*
"skillful German optician"   "god of painting"

One "approached the stars" by scientifically analyzing their light; the other sought to identify with the sun by painting the forms in the way it illuminated them. Such is the secret difference that the unknown name, finally revealed, suggests in the space between *au* and *e*. Such is the terrible secret that Frenhofer lets slip when Porbus asks him to show him his work ("a beautiful sinner," Mary, in exchange for "a mistress," Catherine) in order to paint "some tall, wide, and deep painting where the figures would be life size."

Frenhofer's response is, I think, decisive, if we, in turn, are to appropriate the surprising "unknown" of the masterpiece, and here, again, the response bears with it, in the very words of Mabuse's pupil, a difference, a contradiction in which the mystique of painting and the madness of the painter find a place to lodge: "'Show my work!' cried the old man, beside himself. 'No, no, I must perfect it still. Yesterday, toward evening... I thought I had finished.'" To finish the work, to complete or fulfill it, would be to give life to the figure, autonomous life on the painted surface, a "power of reality" over the gaze, an effect of "presence." "Her eyes seemed moist to me, her flesh alive. The tresses of her hair fluttered. She was breathing!" Frenhofer might have added that, as in Mabuse's *Adam*, she was preparing to step out of the painting. In fact, he gives the precise reason for that effect: "I found the means of realizing [in the strong sense of making real] on a flat canvas the relief and roundness of nature." Success then, the work is finished: But between that evening and the next morning, night and day, candlelight and natural daylight, error creeps into the success itself. In order for the work to be a masterpiece and the painting life itself, it is not enough that the figure take on life with the relief of nature, that the figure seem about to leave the flat surface of the canvas. In addition, "the air, the sky, the wind we breathe," the light we see, the medium of all visibility, the sun, must also enter the painting.

The decisive moment lies in the relation between the painted figure and the ground upon which it appears and from which it detaches itself. "The line is the means by which man accounts for the effect of light on objects," and, we might add, by which he accounts for it on the canvas. But, in that case, the canvas remains a painting and a work of art, a representation. But, continues Frenhofer, "there are no lines in nature, where everything is full: it is by modeling that one draws; that is, one detaches things from their environment."[23] In the end, modeling, as a way of drawing, is sculpting with light and shadow, with values and intensities, the flat surface of the painting, in order to make, no longer a *representation*, but a *double*, a piece of nature that is its own simulacrum on the canvas. Not representation, but presence, and the part holds sway over the outlines. The outlines must no longer be true lines, circumscribing lines that define the figure exactly but also close it off, enclose it on the plane of representation: "I spread a cloud of warm, golden half tints over the outlines, so that it is no longer possible to put your finger precisely on the place where the outlines meet the ground."

Hence the tension or contradiction of a limit that is traced only to be blurred, of differences that cannot be distinguished. Frenhofer believes he can solve this problem by playing with the placement, the positioning of the beholder: "*Close up*, this painting is cloudy, lacking in precision, but *from two steps away*, everything firms up, stops, and detaches itself; the body turns, the forms become salient, one feels the air circulate around them." Nevertheless, that solution can only be provisional: "I am not yet satisfied, I have doubts." It is the work itself that must *realize* what is required, by positioning the eye in "real" space, but to do this, its painter must identify with the divine painter of the universe, the God-sun. "Perhaps it would be better . . . to attack a figure in the middle, focusing first on the best-lit protrusions, and then go on to the darker portions. Isn't that how the sun, that divine painter of the universe, proceeds?"

Of course, what Frenhofer is seeking is the *absolute trompe-l'oeil*; presence in representation; the *simulacrum* in painting. But the means for obtaining it nullifies it. In a strange about-turn, the painted canvas is not transmuted into a totality of presence, into a fragment of nature, into a piece of life indiscernible from nature and from life; rather, nature and life themselves become clouds of paint *on the painting, in its frame*, "a chaos of uncertain colors, tones, nuances." The "cloud of warm, golden half tints" spread by Frenhofer over the outlines "on the place where [they] meet the ground," progressively fills the entire painting as a "formless fog." Hence this paradox: *The absolute trompe-l'oeil, that is, the fullness of a representation where the figures in the space of the painting cease to figure, in order to literally make what they figure appear in the space of reality, is nothing other than a painter's and painting's abstraction, an "abstract painting," a painting that does cease to figure, but not by becoming real, by becoming nature, but merely by becoming a figureless painting.*[24] At the end of the story, Poussin says of the "so-called painting," "I see . . . only colors amassed in confusion and contained by a multitude of bizarre lines that form a wall of paint." A transcendent painting, as if painted by the sun.

If we may be allowed to combine fiction and history, Poussin remembered that strange encounter fifty years later when he gave his definition of painting: "It is an imitation made with lines and colors on some surface of everything under the sun." But only "under" the sun. It is on that "metaphysical" condition that "its end is its delectation."[25]

That paradox, that contradiction, and that deconstructive construction of the painting in the total *trompe-l'oeil*, are signified in the names "Gillette" and "Catherine Lescault," in the space between the body model and the body of paint.

The painting, the figure in the painting, is the body of the woman, of *a* woman who might be *woman*, beauty itself, real: "'Yes, my dear Porbus,' replied Frenhofer, 'until now I've not managed to meet an irreproachable woman, a body whose lines are of a perfect beauty and whose carnation. . . .'" In this case, the lack consists not so much in the fact that he has not encountered a certain body but in the fact that he has not been able to define the relation between the "carnation" and the "lines." "But where does she live . . . that inaccessible Venus of the ancients, so often sought, and of which we encounter barely a few dispersed beauties? Oh! To see for a moment, only once, complete divine nature. . . . Like Orpheus I shall descend into the hell of art to bring back life."

Mabuse is life stolen away by death, Frenhofer death stolen away by life: life as death, death as life. And the inaccessible Venus is Gillette, mistress of the young Poussin.

Gillette, a heavenly Venus—"the smile erring on the lips of Gillette adorned the attic and rivaled the effect of the sky"—is hired by her lover, her painter. And she agrees, out of total love for him, to be part of a transaction that is not without similarity to the subject of Porbus's painting, St. Mary of Egypt preparing to pay her boat passage, or to the order Marie de Médicis placed for this same painting, or to Frenhofer's bid. But this new exchange, even though it concerns bodies—natural and painted bodies, real and represented bodies— and even though its aim is fortune and glory ("'Go on, Gillette, we shall be rich and happy! There's gold in these paintbrushes!'"), is an exchange of gazes and of bodies offered for view. Gillette's body—the inaccessible Venus, perfect beauty—is presented for Frenhofer to view so that, in return, he can present the body of Catherine Lescault for Poussin to view. In that exchange and that gaze, Poussin is to become a "great man," a "great painter," Frenhofer's successor, his other, or rather, the same thing.

Gillette is thus the *perfect* model who, by posing for the *absolute* painter Frenhofer, becomes the *total* painting, the painting of Catherine, but a painting *to come*. And the transaction is to Poussin's advantage. The pose, or rather, the decision to pose, carries with it all of painting and all the painter's destiny: life become painting, the fullness of artistic representation.[26] And Gillette does not know how right she is when, "pulling Poussin by the sleeve of his worn-out pourpoint," she says: "I told you, Nick, that I would give my life for you; but I never promised that while I was alive I'd renounce my love." For to pose is to give one's life to the painting to be painted; it is a living death, which means renouncing the love of the painter out of love for painting.

Frenhofer faces the same horrible dilemma, but in reverse: While Poussin must present the living body of Gillette, have her pose, make her become a painting, Frenhofer must put the painted body of Catherine on view in order to bring her to life. Porbus posits the contract of exchange in complete lucidity:

"The young Poussin is loved by a woman whose incomparable beauty is without imperfection. But, my dear master, if he consents to lend her to you, it will at least be necessary to let us see your painting." "What!" cries Frenhofer, in pain. "Show my creature, my wife? Rip off the veil that chastely covers my happiness? But that would be a horrible prostitution!"

This remarkable "structural" proximity between Poussin and Frenhofer in relation to Gillette and Catherine leaves a trace in a name: "I told you, *Nick*, that I would give my life for you; but I never promised that while I was alive I'd renounce my love." Nick, the pet name, the nickname of the future great painter, bestowed on him by the young woman who is passionately in love with him. Granted. That "English" grapheme still elicits surprise in a novella that is situated in Paris at the beginning of the seventeenth century. Let us try to read some meaning into that insignificant variation. "In Flemish," writes Wachter, "*Nicker* is the devil. The name seems to be derived from the Saxon *Noec-an*, to cause to perish, to massacre, since the devil has been the killer of man since the origin." In his *History of English Poetry, Dissertation I*, Thomas Warton notes that "Nicka was the Gothic demon who inhabited the element of water, and who strangled persons that were drowning."[27] According to him, "Nick," joined to the epithet "old," became the name of the devil in Christian theology. In *Hudibras* (part 3, chapter 1), Butler credits Machiavelli with this nickname for the devil.

It is enough (quoth he) for once / and has repriev'd thy forfeit bones: / Nick Machiavel had ne'er a trick, / (though he gave his name to our Old Nick) / But was below the least of these, / That pass i' th' world for holiness.

But, if we may add to the learned commentary of Charles Richardson in tome 2 of his 1867 *Dictionary*, Butler is playing on another sense of "nick," which also means "trick" (probably from the French *nique*, itself from the German *nicken*, to wink the eye or nod the head). Robert Gordon Latham's 1870 edition of Samuel Johnson's *Dictionary of the English Language* gives the following two meanings to the noun: "(1) exact point of time at which there is necessity or convenience. (2) winning throw or trick, that is the one by which the adversary is nicked." The verb means: "(1) to hit, to touch luckily, to perform by some slight artifice used at the lucky moment. (2) to defeat, or to cozen as at dice, to disappoint by some trick." This last sense can also be found in French: "In the game of Krobs, to win with the first throw of the dice by getting the points called."

Nick, the devil, or *nick*, the good "throw," the decisive ruse that the demon might play to annihilate the adversary; *Nick*, an affectionate *nick*name for Nicolas Poussin. Balzac said of Frenhofer that "there was something diabolical in [his] face," and he himself gave the painter the supreme mission of stealing away God's secret. And, when he "completes" Porbus's Mary, "it seemed to the young Poussin that there was a demon in the body of this bizarre character." The demon passes from the body of Frenhofer to the name of Poussin at the decisive moment, the "nick" or "trick" of the exchange of the living body of the perfect model, Gillette, for the painted body of the total figure, Catherine Lescault. And Gillette articulates the diabolical pact of the exchange between life and death, love and art, with the pet name she gives her lover. At the starting point of the journey of names, St. Mary of Egypt was, in her legendary story, a prostitute become saint; at its end, Catherine Lescault is a "saint" become prostitute in her own painting. The "agent" of the transformation is Gillette, the inaccessible Venus, the perfect model, who moves from Poussin to Frenhofer, with Porbus playing the pimp: "'Have my Catherine bear the gaze of a man, a young man, a painter? No, no.'—'But isn't that a woman for a woman? Isn't Poussin giving you his mistress to look at?'" Frenhofer's final hesitation indicates the final difference between life and death, nature and art, to which the body of Gillette in its pose refers. "'My painting is finished,' said Frenhofer. 'Whoever sees it will think he perceives a woman lying on a bed of velvet, under curtains.[28] It will seem to you that you see Catherine's breast moving as she breathes. Nevertheless, I would like to be certain.'" Gillette, the perfect living model, is the definitive proof that Catherine is the *total* painting, both because she is *less perfect* in her perfection than the painted figure and because she is identical to it, just as perfect: Gillette-Catherine, Catherine-Gillette.

And here is the last stop in our journey of names: "Gillette was there in the naive and simple attitude of a young Georgian . . . presented by thieves to some slave merchant." Poussin is "busy contemplating once more the portrait he had earlier taken for a Giorgion." When Porbus and Poussin are finally admitted into the studio, after Gillette's pose, Frenhofer says, "'My work is perfect . . . and now I can show it with pride. Never will painter, brushes, colors, canvas, and light create a rival for Catherine Lescault.'" Poussin and

Porbus pause "first before a figure of a life size woman, semi-nude, seized with admiration for it." But that is not Catherine, merely "a ruined ... canvas used to *study* a pose." It is not yet Gillette become Catherine. And, at that moment, the old man allows them access to the absolute masterpiece: "You are before a woman and you seek a painting.... The air is so true that you can no longer distinguish it from the air that surrounds you. Where is art? Lost, disappeared! Before you is the very shape of a young girl." "'Do you perceive something there?' Poussin asked Porbus. 'No. Do you?' 'Nothing.'" Nothing—and there is Gillette, whom no one is looking at.

Catherine is Gillette, and the painting is life.

Gillette, a Georgian, a Giorgion, a semi-nude *woman*.... We witness the progressive extinction of names in phonic echoes, until they become anonymous, until they approach the unnameable: nothing.

Catherine Lescault has disappeared along with art. There remains only the wall of paint on one side, Gillette on the other.[29] In this neutralizing movement of exchange, there is a remainder, a *foot*, "but a delicious foot, a living foot. They remained petrified with admiration." The effect of that "fragment escaping ... from a slow and progressive destruction" is the petrification of the gaze. Catherine, having disappeared along with art, lets only her foot remain caught in the painting—an anonymous *foot*. It has lost the name of its body but has retained its life, a "mortal" life for whoever looks at it: It is Medusa, and I am surprised, indeed, petrified [*médusé*], to read the other name for Medusa in the false name of a painting by Frenhofer: G(i)org(i)on. Nothing, or rather, a foot: Gorgon.

Gillette, Georgian, Giorgion, Gorgon... such is the choice: Gillette ("Perish both art and all its secrets") or Gorgon, in the form of a living foot, itself trapped in the painting's wall of paint.

One last remark: One of the truths about the *trompe-l'oeil* (one of its stakes) in painted representations is that it can never appear except as a fragment, a part, with the effect of hyperpresence. But this fragment makes obvious the space of presentation for the painted representation, through the painting of a "thing" that, even as it remains "really" caught in the mechanics of representation, also appears to exceed it *fictively, in the real itself.* That painted thing, outside the painting as it were, seeks the beholder in the place of contemplation he occupies; it attacks him, through the very constraints of the mechanics of representation, in the place where the thing is inserted as a double, as mimetic excess, without ever contributing toward the order of resemblance. "Seeing" is reversed or poured back into a "being seen" by the thing itself, an impure mixture of anxiety and petrification: Gorgon.

19

The Logic of Secrecy

A secret—the etymological reference is, has been, and, no doubt, will be mulled over again and again—is something set apart (*se-cernere*), separated, reserved. Take any set of individuals (individuals who, in one way or another, make up *a* set: things, words or sentences, thoughts or discourses, beings), and take one element, no more, away from it. This setting apart is the primitive gesture of secrecy: sifting, straining, filtering, sorting; discerning, distinguishing; separating the wheat from the chaff, the nugget from the sand, the idea from the train of thought, genius from a group of mediocre minds. And, yet, if we examine ordinary language, it is easy to see that the operation of separation—whether technical, scientific, or poetic—seems to be, if not the opposite of the secret, then, at least, its disappearance, its resolution. It is when the wheat was mixed in with the chaff, the nugget with the sand, the idea with a train of thoughts, genius with mediocrity, that the wheat, nugget, idea, and genius were secrets. It was then that they were secreted away—in a mixture, in confusion, indistinction; unperceived, out of sight, singular, unique, in the midst of the others. But who knew it at the time, who saw it, who perceived it? The farmer, the prospector, the thinker? Not so. For it can happen that, with a paltry harvest, there is only chaff; in a poor lode, only sand; in a weak speech, only stray thoughts.... It is only once they have appeared, once they have been found, discovered, or revealed, that they are found, discovered, or revealed to be secrets, or rather, to have been secreted away in the mixture and the confusion. The secret: a deferred action of revelation.

That is the paradox: The secret does not constitute itself as such except through its disappearance; it is written only in the future perfect, or better, in the imperfect tense. Let us play the role of grammarian for a moment: I said the imperfect or the future perfect and not the simple past. The secret is not a past event from the past; there is no real story, no true account of the secret.

The secret is the present effect in the present of a past state—but its negative effect. When the narrative of a secret is written all the same—every narrative, perhaps, is the bringing to light of a secret, and, in that respect, it may just be that a *true* narrative has never been written—it will be *secretly* affected by all the modalities of the future perfect: No one knew at the time that Bonaparte was already Napoleon. Napoleon was Bonaparte's "ontological" secret, and, no doubt, Bonaparte himself did not really know it. It is the narrator who, in the brilliance of this real moment, writes: "Already Napoleon was showing through in Bonaparte." Bonaparte *will have* already been Napoleon—or might have been Napoleon, since who can know today in all certainty?—when he changed the position of a cannon battery at the siege of Toulon: already Austerlitz or Wagram. Bonaparte, the mask of an absent Napoleon; Toulon covers, "suppresses"—as they said in the seventeenth century—an imperial victory that had not yet taken place but which will have *already* been won when it does. Thus, Austerlitz will make us forget Toulon until the moment when the historian resuscitates the memory of the one as the schema or matrix for the narrative of the other, its—revealed—secret.

That amounts to saying that the secret seems quite unable to be—to be a thing, a being, a word, a thought, a discourse, a "what" set apart. It is only an appearance or an apparition, a light, incorporeal envelope that floats over things, beings, thoughts, discourses, once the characteristic operation has been carried out: the operation of characteristics—of science, of art, of technology, of thought—namely, discerning. *Dis-cernere, se-cernere.* The secret is an incorporeality, a simulacrum, a nothing. The Stoics understood this well. It is always *as if*— the formula for a fiction not only of thought but of being. It is always as if, through a more primitive gesture, the singular thing had been introduced into the set, mixed in with all the others, in order to be hidden there. By whom? God, nature, history, chance.... There are no lack of names to "cover" that operation of the secret: dissimulation of the unique by assimilation to all the others that are part of the set. By whom? God, nature, history, chance ... the clever genies of fiction, but good genies, genies of the true discovery, of the discovery of truth, reality, the wheat gathered up by the hand that sowed it, the nugget that shines at the bottom of the pan.... The secret is not a setting apart but an act of mixing together *in order to set apart.* The secret is a secret teleology of the simulacrum in the heart of any revelation.

Secrecy does not consist in holding back what is different, and only what is different, but rather in identifying it, in order to allow for its identification in the end. This play on words is a fiction indicated by language: Make the different identical and identify it as different. In this case, "and" means "in order to." The play on words plots the terrifying power of the gods who play with men, who play the game of the hidden-uncovered truth: the secrecy game.

Onward with our thought, our analysis, and try not be fooled. If a singular individual is thrust into a mass of similar entities from which he differs, if he is to be hidden there, then he must be (or must have originally been) distinguished from them. His singularity must have been marked by a singular difference. Thus, at the origin, in a primitive gesture (whose? God's, nature's, history's, chance's . . .), he must have been marked with a unique difference, extracted from the original chaos, the confusion of the continuous, must have had that primitive, first difference inscribed there. But—and conversely—in order for this singular individual to be introduced into the crowd of similar entities, in order for him to be hidden, he must have been similar to all the others that compose the set, in at least a few of his features. He must have been, in some way, the same as all the others, and the features that constituted his difference could not have totally nullified the fact that he belonged there. And this sameness must have been more primitive, in that chaos of sameness, than his most primitive difference.

The game can now begin, the secrecy game, the truth game: It consists in recognizing, in that individual similar to all, the feature that makes him singular—or in marking him with that feature—so that, in exhibiting those features that relate him or assimilate him to all, the secret that sets him apart will be forgotten, and, hence, he will remain hidden. But exhibiting the sameness of what is different—and there will always be, at least in the discourse of secrecy, in its fiction, a moment of display, even an ostentation of sameness, of the identical, a display of in-difference—showing it, in order to dissimulate what is different in this sameness, will always amount to indicating the difference of that sameness (upon the foundation of sameness). For why show he is the same if not to dissimulate that he is different and, by that very means, display the dissimulation and thus point out the difference? Such is the metaphysical revolving door of the secret: The gods might very well get caught up in their own game if all of metaphysics itself did not rest on the consistent fiction of the secret, its simulacrum, the secrecy effect. Unless, in a new twist, that metaphysics (of the origin preceding itself, of the hidden-uncovered truth) is not that of the simulacrum, of the effect, of fiction.

Such is the vertigo of the secret agent: He loses his head—or his life—because he has forgotten the secret of the farmer who divides up his crop, the prospector who sifts his sand, the thinker who discerns his thoughts. . . . That is his vertigo, or his game, since, in playing his difference as an identity, that identity will be marked as difference and that difference, in an upward spiral, will be marked once more as identity, which, once again, will be marked as difference, et cetera. The spy—and this is often a natural trait, a mark of vocation—is *just like everyone else*: office worker, engineer, hotel manager, musician, and so on. But he is always *too much* like everyone else, too similar, excessively paradigmatic in the group, class, or set into which he has been introduced, and it is that excess—"he tries too hard," as they say—that gives him away. Those who are the same will suspect he is singular because he resembles them to excess, or rather, because he shows them that he resembles them. Nonetheless, that singularity that tends toward identity will be his best means of defense: It is because his difference—his excess of resemblance—shows itself that he must not be different from the others. He is not shrewd enough, subtle enough, wily enough to be *merely* similar. But, precisely, they will hurl back at him: That is the height of dissimulation.

In fact, the secret agent does not play the secrecy game by himself. He is also played. By whom? we must once more ask. God, nature, history, chance ... in this case, the names for the politico-juridico-economico-military apparatus that appropriate the terrifying power of the gods only on the condition they forget—and they always forget, since they are profoundly stupid, and that stupidity is their very essence—that this power is a simulacrum, an effect. The gods, in contrast, conserved that memory, which was consubstantial to them, just as the others conserve their forgetfulness, their stupidity. When the gods pulled the strings of human marionettes, provoking wars and massacres, passions and ecstasies, disasters and suicides, they were not being serious. They did it at the end of a banquet, *for laughs*; not for wild laughs, but for laughs that burst forth in frank gaiety. Kings, strategists, and priests—the apparatus of power—call this gaiety tragedy in the theater of their world. Unlike the Olympians, these kings, strategists, or priests possess power and the terror emanating from it—the seriousness it requires, the respect that surrounds it, the astonished admiration it calls for—only at the cost of forgetting the fiction: That is their incommensurable stupidity. The secret agent, both the game piece they push around the chessboard of their strategies and the paradigm of their power, is the metaphysical symbol and the empirical product of that powerful stupidity. What are they playing, then, without knowing they are playing, without knowing what a game is, even though they call the calculations of their designs and the schemes of their projects games? What are they playing if not at *making themselves believe they have secrets*, as if secrets were things, the weapons and resources of power, which they fantasize as absolute; as if the secret were an absolute they could hold onto like a treasure—*arcana imperii*, said the emperor's canonists in the Middle Ages—whereas, in truth, the secret is only the effect of the operations by which they make themselves believe they have secrets, by which each one believes it, by which each constitutes himself into an absolute power through that very belief. The incredible, true story of the secret agent, where "truth is stranger than fiction," is merely an ornamental, aesthetic variation on the theme—*basso continuo*—of seriousness, of the serious stupidity of the apparatus of power. In the end, death is the product of that stupidity.

We are less concerned with asking how the secrecy game, the truth game, is played, than with paying more attention, as disabused spectators, to the players caught in the game being played between them. The secret, let us repeat, is not a thing or a being set apart, but the—negative—effect of a play of relations and interactions. It is probably less important to know what is being exchanged or set aside—if, in effect, the secret is an effect, a simulacrum—than to describe the rules the players observe, whatever they might be, the cheating they do to avoid them, their tactics of transgression, which, in one way or another, at one moment or another, still stem—though they do not know it while they are participating in the game—from the set of rules in which they are caught.

Let us consider a caricatural but revealing limiting case, the case where the secrecy game is played by an almost indefinite number of persons. This is known as *le secret de Polichinelle*,[1] understood in two senses. Everyone knows the secret except Polichinelle (the secret *from* Polichinelle), or only Polichinelle believes he knows the secret (Polichinelle's secret) when, in fact, everyone knows it: a false secret or, rather, the simulacrum of a secret. But, since every secret is itself a simulacrum, the *secret de Polichinelle*, the simulacrum of a simulacrum, is, in some sense, the fulfillment of the secret. The structure of the game and its dynamic as it is played is best perceived in that secret: Everyone is in on the secret *except one* who does not know it; or the reverse, which amounts to the same thing, only one is in on the secret *except for everybody else*, as it were— everybody else who knows it. For everyone to play the secrecy game, only one must be excluded, only one need be excluded; everyone but one shares it. In this structure of exception, this dynamic of exclusion, the paradox of the game reaches its perfection: One of the players does not participate *as a player*, precisely *so that* the game can take place. The secrecy game is the game of the included-excluded third term: Thus, the canonical number of players is three, and the topology of the secret is that of a triangle in which one of the points lies outside the field on which the figure is traced. This point is the missing but determined intersection of two sides; unless, of course, the notion of an excluded point on a figure was invented in order for the figure to be constructed in the first place.

(Digression: Could it be that legitimate perspective in painting, the secret of its mechanics of representation, the powerful, fictive effect of depth on a surface, is the exact projection of the triangular structure described above? For, in fact, the vanishing point in the network of lines is the simulacrum that brings about the point of intersection of the orthogonals on the picture plane, at the point at infinity, which, by definition, is outside that plane. At the same time, that point is one of the necessary and determined elements of the perspectivist construction. Pascal, who knew his way around the rhetoric, logic, and theology of the secret better than anyone, raised this question in one of his *pensées*, using the very model or fiction of perspective. "*Two infinites, mean . . .* It is like looking at pictures which are too near or too far away. There is just one indivisible point [the fiction or contradiction of a fragment of indivisible extension] which is the right place. Others are too near, too far, too high, or too low." In these four positions, the pictures are not correctly seen, that is, they do not fully bring about their fictive effect. What is the reason for this effect?

In the question that concludes the *pensée*, the secret of perspective is projected outside the field of painting: "In painting the rules of perspective decide it [*assigne*], but how will it be decided when it comes to truth and morality?")[2]

Three players, then, and the game begins. Imagine a completely banal story. *A* knows something about *B* that *B* does not know, something about himself, his life, an event from his past, about his origin, but something that—it is supposed—he would have a positive or negative interest in knowing. For example, knowing it would increase his potency, consolidate his power, overcome an obstacle, or simply give him knowledge. Or, conversely, not knowing it would produce the same effects. *A* knows something about *B*, something that, in any event, concerns him in some *essential* way: The shepherd's son is, in truth, the son of a king; the son of the king of Corinth is, in truth, the son of the king of Thebes; the man he encountered and killed at a fork in the road was not some stranger, but his father; the (widowed) queen he married as the reward for distinguished service rendered to his commonwealth—by answering a riddle posed by a monster at a border—that queen, that woman was his mother, and so on. *A* therefore knows all that about *B*, and *B* does not know, but *ought to* (*or ought not to*) know. Why? A plague, an epidemic, a scourge, is ravaging the commonwealth where he reigns as prince, and its cause is the patricide and the incest he committed without knowing it. He has an interest in knowing, an interest that is both positive and negative at the same time: He must know in order to save the kingdom; and when he knows, he will discover that he is twice a criminal. And the one is only possible through the other.

Is *B*'s story a secret simply because *A* knows its truth from a to z and because *B* does not know it (or believes it is other than it is) when, in fact, it concerns him not only because it is *his* story but also because he has an essential, vital interest in knowing it? No. In order for the secrecy game to begin, *A* must, in some way, transmit that story to an indifferent, disinterested third party (or one who, at the very least, does not have the same interest as *B* in knowing), and *B* must continue to be excluded from that story, his own story. The game now begins: *A* shares his knowledge of *B* with *C*, a knowledge that *B* ought to possess, that he would even like to acquire because his interest is at stake, and from which he remains separated for a moment. To repeat, using the Pascalian model, the model of perspective: *B* is at the vanishing point of the figure constructed between *A* and *C*, but, in this knowledge of his story, in this self-knowledge that escapes him, he is at the point of infinity, outside the field. Nevertheless, the lines, the vectors of the triangular figure ABC must all point toward B, its summit, must plot the point at infinity and determine it even as they exclude it from the figure. They must signify it without enunciating it, imply it without declaring it, mark it without indicating it: In a word (and it is Pascal's word) we need to understand in its legal sense, they must ascribe [*assigner*] it, but as a question, they must summon it as a suspended response. Thus, the plague is devastating the commonwealth, and its buboes, its purulent secretions, are "monstrous" to exactly the same degree as the monstrous knowledge they do not show.

It is therefore when A shares with C what B ought to know, a knowledge that assigns B the role of addressee, that the secret begins to be operative. This secret will find its full potency only when B, overwhelmed by the vertigo of a knowledge he does not know but that he suspects concerns him—for such is the power of fascination of the secrecy effect—begins to go over the signs and the marks that identify him as its receiver. The secret becomes fully operative when he begins to know what his history is and who he is—a man guilty of patricide and incest, a monster, in short—at the interminable moment when everything begins to be known: his birth, the shepherd, Corinth, the encounter on the road, the scuffle, the murder, the riddle, the marriage, and the royal dignity acquired in that way. The apocalypse of the secret will be at its height when everything is revealed to the light of day. The secret *is* blindingly obvious in a flash only when it *will have been* (secret). And it is unbearable: B gouges out his eyes. The secrecy game ends precisely at the moment when the player, excluded from the game so that the game can take place, has been reintegrated into it. Such is the paradox: The game ends when—finally—all the players are seated around the table, when the vanishing point and the point at infinity coincide in the completed painting. It is when there is no longer a secret that the secret—we might say—is at its height, at the height of its tragedy, and that the tragic destiny comes about. Let us name the players, the actors, now that we are at the end of this "premiere" that forever repeats the origin. A is destiny, the gods, the space where the secret is constituted in all its weight only in order to be set down as shared knowledge. C is Tiresias, the soothsayer, the blind seer. Have you not heard that a secret is too big to remain the secret of only one? Is not every secret too big to be kept? Is not every secret a secret only because it is too big to be kept? And, finally, B is the addressee at the vanishing point of his own story, at the point of infinity, outside the field: Oedipus.

Note that, in trying to define the structure of the secrecy game and the dynamic of how it is played, I imagined a narrative whose protagonists I concealed in anonymity—A, B, C—to give the game an exemplary character, a force that, if not demonstrative, is at least persuasive. I led you to believe, with a good chance of success, in the validity of a description, by allowing you to substitute names, indicators of singular individuals, for the abstract symbols of the letters, and, hence, to produce a story that is itself singular, your own story, which could verify my propositions, at least schematically. Every narrative, as we know since Aristotle, is singular, and the proper names of its actors are such powerful means for establishing the credibility of its singularity—and its reality—that the borderline between real and fictive is, at least for the time of the telling, neutralized, suspended. In writing *A* in the place of the gods, *B* and *C* in the place of Tiresias and Oedipus (and I could have substituted *X* for Corinth and *Y* for Thebes), even as I told stories of plague, incest, and patricide, I situated my imagined narrative in another world, a fictive world, one that is, however, very different from the fictive or real world that I have just evoked in specifying the narrative. The latter world is the—real or fictive—world of singular beings, while the former is the world of theoretical fictions, that is, the world of scenarios or general models. The generality of the model lies not only in its power to generate classes of narratives, multiple narratives, but also in the fact that these narratives do not take place in the real world or in a fictive world, in a story or novel or myth. But its power also lies in the fact that one of them could have taken place or might one day take place in a story, novel, or myth. And, as it happens, that very thing happened to me while I was writing this text and imagining that story: To be more precise, in wishing to imagine a (theoretically fictional) scenario that would describe the structure of the secrecy game and the dynamic of how it is played, that scenario engendered, on its own power—as if it were itself inhabited by a secret intentionality—the singular story of Oedipus. To give an exact account of things, I would have to say that it "turned" into the story of the unfortunate prince of Thebes, in the sense that milk "turns" sour or a sauce "turns" bad. From there, it is only a short step to the idea that any scenario constructed to describe the logical operation of the secret, the relations and interactions it produces, refers in its very generality to a singular story. Hence, any fictive, theoretical model of the secret would rest, in the last analysis, on this single narrative, which would therefore be, by rights (the right of the first-born), an originary narrative, the origin of all possible narratives (of secrets), a singular-general narrative, a narrative-model. And every model of the secret would reproduce the structure of that narrative and would repeat its dynamic in generating the class of singular narratives of secrets and, naturally, among them, the narrative-model of the set itself, the story of Oedipus. And, if every narrative, as we believed for a moment, is a narrative of secrecy and the story of its coming to light, then the narrative of Oedipus is the singular-general scenario-model of every narrative: past, present, or future. The narrative of history itself would be a repetition of it: Universal history [*Geschichte*] would be the pure and simple repetition of the singular myth that recounts the paradoxical logic of the secret.

    All these remarks, whose epistemologically adventurous character I readily acknowledge, were, at bottom, provoked by the substitution of symbols—letters—for proper names. But, if you agree to believe in this little event that affected the writing of this text, that is, if you believe that the imagined scenario-model was "unconsciously" transformed into the story of Oedipus, then you must concede that that substitution was not an authentic substitution. It is not that the letters of the model were substituted for the true names—for then I would have had to imagine and formulate the story purposely, and then substitute letters for the names. But, in fact, it happened the other way around. It was not a substitution but a slippage. The letters slid into names, as if I suddenly said to myself: "Why, that's the story of Oedipus I'm telling in this model I'm constructing." Or, to be even more precise, it is as if the substitution had taken place—primitively, originally—without my knowing it. Or as if, when "the gods," "Tiresias," and "Oedipus" appeared in the letters *A*, *B*, and *C*, they had, in fact, already been there. (It is for that very reason that you only half-believe me when I recount my "little event" in writing.) In other words, at a certain point, I felt I ought to add some precisions of an epistemological nature regarding the relations between the general scenario-model and the singular narrative used to describe the structure and the dynamic of the secret; and this matter of letters and names, as a theoretical accident, very precisely obeyed that structure and that dynamic of which it was one of the elements of description. The secrecy effect was at play—and with what force!—in certain parts or regions and relations of the model, whose aim it was to describe the functioning of that model.

Let us now apply these reflections to the particular case of the anonymous author, the individual who does not write his name on the title page of the book he wrote, who does not sign it. We may suppose that, out of mechanical, material necessity, every book was written by someone—*a someone*, so to speak—and that, out of legal or social obligation, that someone bears a name. As a result, the absence of the author's name or signature on the surface of the volume written, far from neutralizing the act of authority, the power of paternity at the origin or the end of the work, instead marks it, indicates it with an insistence that will not fail to provoke the question: Who wrote this book I am reading? What is the name of its author? And with that question, others arise: Why did he not name himself? What motivations and motives did he have for not signing? What interest does he have in hiding *himself*, in keeping his name secret? And, from this last question, we move inevitably to another. Not, what interest does he have in hiding *himself*, but, what does he have to hide? Or, more exactly, what has he, in particular, written in his book that forbids him or does not permit him to name himself, that is, to give the mark of acknowledgment (his name) that he is its author? And the reader, almost necessarily, will seek in a book that has no author's name the marks, signs, or indexes that demonstrate that absence. I say "demonstrate" because the lack of the name shows itself well enough by itself—in a sociohistorical context, at least, where the authors of books name themselves. Marks, signs, and indexes disseminated in the book "prove" anonymity while suggesting reasons and explanations for that actual absence. In this, the reader is another Oedipus. Oedipus commits himself to the tragic pursuit of signs that lead him to repeat his own narrative *in his own name*, as responsible for all names, that is, to make of it *his* story, to produce, from an "other" narrative and a narrative of another, his own narrative proper, his true and verified story. In the same way, the reader of the anonymous work will reread it, but through the marks, signs, and indexes that demonstrate its anonymity, will attempt—at the end of his trajectory—to show, if not the missing name (for one does not show a name but, rather, names it), at least what one could call its place, the place where it might be found, that is, the position of the author responsible for the book. One might think, however, that the reader differs from Oedipus inasmuch as, in this instance, the reader and the author are not identical. But in believing that, we may be falling prey to a referential illusion, we may be held and fascinated by the secrecy effect. For the Oedipus who enters Thebes as king is very different from the Oedipus who, guilty of incest and patricide, his eyes gouged out, leaves Thebes. Or, rather, it is perhaps at that instant that the first Oedipus is identical to the second, in the sense—a sense that is the whole secret of that story, its entire secrecy effect—that the first is now the second he had always been, and the second will have been the first that he was. Similarly, the reader of the anonymous book who rereads only in order to know the effaced name, only to recognize it by producing the demonstration, by indicating the place where it lies, also produces that author missing from his name. And, in producing it by his rereading, he, in some sense, becomes that author; at the very least, in reading the book in that strange way, not its text but the signs that lie beyond or prior to the text, he rewrites the book in the very place where someone—the author—wrote it, and, as it were, in the name missing from it. When the reader imagines he discovers *a* name—will it ever be certain that this name is *the* name?—this name does not so much name the real individual in flesh and blood, the one who wrote the book in person, as the place of the "author-of-the-book": not the real anthroponym but an imaginary toponym, the name of a place produced by the secrecy effect.

As we see by these few observations, the brief scenario of reading an anonymous book repeats, as we might have expected, the story of Oedipus and his secret: The same themes run through both, the secret of the origin and truth, which is also the secret truth of the origin as the secret origin of truth. Whatever the permutations of terms, of scenario into story, the logic of the secret is the logic of its effects: Or, to put it another way, these permutations, these plays on words, constitute the secrecy game itself, the secret as game, and the reason for its most powerful effects.

Part Three

◆

FICTIONS

20

Rue Traversière, no. 48

As strange as it might seem, it was his innocuous appearance that attracted my attention; or, rather, a certain air of anonymity in his demeanor, his clothing, his face, even his look. Not that everybody exhibits his name by some external trait that individualizes him as such and such: But it is very rare that, at the first glance, the virtuality of a name belonging to a man does not appear in two wrinkles on the forehead, in the curve of the eyebrows, the crease in a jacket collar, or the rhythm of a step. It is as if the passerby, so similar to all the others, were giving a sign that he wanted to be named by me. But there was nothing of that in him. He was not tall or short, fat or skinny, happy or sad. He was null or neuter down to the last detail of his demeanor, his clothes, his face, even his look. I caught sight of him from a distance, at the bus stop, coming out of that awful Burger King, which appeared a few years ago near the intersection of Rue du Faubourg-Saint-Antoine and Rue Traversière. He started down Rue Traversière at an even pace, neither quick nor slow. This instance of anonymity was so rare that I followed him, setting my pace to match his own, neither quick nor slow. He seemed to be strolling along a street that rarely attracts idlers, and that alone was enough to single him out among those who, in a hurry, took the street as a shortcut on their way to the Gare de Lyon, or those who, hesitating, turning back, sought out the address of an interior decorator or a paint salesman. The anonymous fellow accompanied the street in its pure crossing; he confined himself to a regular crossing movement, transparent, along the shortcut of Rue Traversière. If I dare use the expression, his body was at one with the street, an empty body of a discarded chrysalis, in keeping with the emptiness of a street that does nothing but pass. Then, all of a sudden, as if taking advantage of an instant of inattention on my part, he disappeared. No doubt, he went into a shop or one of these sad little houses that line the street at that location. Lifting my head, I caught sight of him as suddenly as he had disappeared, on the embankment of the railroad, on top of the arch the street crosses, among the brush and weeds that have invaded it for years. He was standing there, motionless, and, at that altitude and distance from the street, his anonymity took on a most enigmatic, mysterious singularity. As I turned around, to my surprise, I saw him again in front of me, walking at his own pace, neither quick nor slow, strolling with his hands in the pockets of his gray jacket. And yet I was certain of it, though I did not dare turn around to verify it, a double—his identical twin—was on top of the embankment, looking at him with his washed-out blue eyes, indifferent, as he once more walked along Rue Traversière, as if it were in his very nature to pass, as if he knew only crossing. At number 48, still at his even pace, he entered the church where Abbot Lenfant used to stage the operetta *Niquette et sa mère* at the beginning of the century. I followed him in. In the choir, seated on the straw-bottomed chairs that had replaced the old stalls, were other anonymous men in gray suits, with washed-out blue eyes—no doubt, the singers in a parish choir. They watched him approach a kneeling woman. He addressed her in a drone, neither loud nor soft, as if reciting a psalm: "Hail Mary...." I didn't catch the rest. The woman got up, frightened, knocking over her chair. I also hurriedly left this cross-place, this nest of archangels Gabriel waiting for the crossing that one of them had made nearly two thousand years before, and that each one, identical in their order, was making again in every *rue traversière* of every city of a certain size.

21

The Bamboo Pole

The object was made of a large bamboo stalk about a meter and a half or two meters long; the insides had been removed and it had been carefully closed at its base. The other end, bevelled and open, was placed under a stream of water whose flow varied naturally according to the time of day, the day of the week, and the season. The bamboo pole rested at a 45-degree angle, in the middle of a thin, transverse branch, no doubt another bamboo pole, itself supported by two vertical branches that forked at one end and were planted into the ground at the other. The base of the object rested on a reddish, porous rock, which was circular in shape and hollowed out in its center. The water that flowed into the bamboo pole slowly filled it, but when it reached a level slightly higher than the cross pole, it emptied into the stream's current in an instant, rocking and then falling back, striking one sharp blow on the rock at its base, making it reverberate. Sometimes, but not always, it bounced once, but the second blow was lighter and the sound more "flutelike" than the first. The time it took for the object to fill was more or less (but only more or less) the same each time, but, depending on the intensity of the stream and the size of the particular pole—we saw three or four different ones—the amount of time could vary greatly. The one in the hermit poet's retirement villa was located—like all those we saw, in fact—at the far end of the garden, at its selvedge, hardly discernible in the jumble of luxurious vegetation sustained by the sweet air and humidity of the place. You could sit on a stone bench on the other side of the stream, near the sand garden, and watch it, waiting in delight for the brief moment of the "catastrophe," for the impact (sometimes repeated) on the stone, and for the resounding blow that accompanied it.

Note that the reversal (the water pouring out into the stream) always occurred out of mechanical necessity. This necessity, however, allowed for tiny variations, which made you dizzy with expectancy and put your heart and thoughts on edge, especially in the late afternoon, when birds were quieter, and there was less noise all around. You would concentrate on watching that strange object, so strange and yet so simple, at the edge of the garden, near the stream, in the hermit poet's retirement villa. What held your attention, what attracted your thoughts, what fascinated you was not so much the mechanism of the rocking bamboo pole but, rather, this stream or ribbon of time, as thin, as clear, as empty as the stream of water coming from the pole, *cut off* at almost regular intervals by a resounding catastrophe, and inexorably *taken up again* in the expectation, without surprise, of the next time, which was almost the same: a ribbon of time unreeling around the drainage knots. Or perhaps it was a filling up, a fulfillment, a plenitude. Note that, in this case, these words are not "big" words, philosophical metaphors, but, rather, express or describe simple operations, whose end consisted entirely in coinciding, for an instant, with *its* end, its emptying, its emptiness. Or it was a vacuity, an "aperity" whose time, duration, nothingness—"not yet, not enough"—consisted entirely in slowly, peaceably, tragically, annihilating itself, that is, in filling itself up, fulfilling itself. Curiously, strangely, the expectation without surprise, all the time wasted and regained, took on value, acquired weight and density, found meaning only in the brief moment when the fullness was cut off, when it emptied itself, in one stroke. That is, it found meaning only in the short moment of suspense, the catastrophe, the resounding blow of the impact on the porous red stone, in which you could hear the silence, listen to the time—the rest of the time. History, this story, unreeled like the ribbon or stream of water—now lively, now lazy—that poured into the moss and lichen. In the end, the story is astonishingly empty of events to enliven its course: Even the variations in the flow of the water are too imperceptible, too irregular, too insignificant to provide the framework for a narrative. An empty story and, nevertheless, one that swells slowly, whose plot thickens lethargically, that becomes heavy, but without haste, in the expectation of the perfectly foreseeable unforeseen Event of reversal. A story in which the water that fills the bamboo pole is the emblem for this time accumulated not in memory or in memories (the story—let us repeat—is completely empty) but in simple duration, a process of growing old in its purest state, a process that does not alter a body or trouble a thought. Not simply accumulated time, time hoarded like the water that weighs heavier and heavier in the bamboo stalk and pushes more and more firmly on its stone base. This story is empty, emptied out, in keeping with the unique Event that necessarily occurs sooner or later, which is only a unique Event (and that is why I write it with a capital e) through the mechanical necessity of its future, through the weight of accumulated duration. And yet this empty duration weighs more and more heavy, and all this weight, because of its weight and its incessant increase, is consumed in an instant, and, in an instant, empties out and becomes lightness, is filled with emptiness—the drainage Event—to the point of becoming unstuck from its stone base. And it is, of course, *because it becomes unstuck*, because what was foundation and base suddenly becomes top and summit, because the heavy becomes light and the low high, that the bamboo pole suddenly returns to its former position, though not before making the stone sing, not before singing itself for a brief moment, with the help of this emptiness that fills it.

Note that, at this same moment, all oppositions meet, producing the reverse of their effects: The emptiness fills and the fullness is emptied out; the heavy lightens and the lightness weighs heavy, before everything again finds, with time and the stream of water that flows out of the bamboo pole, the peaceful but empty order of cause and effect. The instant of reversal, of upending and pouring out, thus deserves meditation; it deserves a thought that tarries on the Event of that story, if only because that is the only event in the story. But it is always too brief: You have hardly begun to think that it is all over already and the stream of time is once more emptying itself out. Thus, to think fully, one must await the return of the same event that, sooner or later, will not fail to reproduce itself, only to be once more disappointed in its flight, to seize only the minimal echo of the shock of the bamboo pole on the red and porous stone. They say that is how Ishikawa Jôzan died in 1672, in contemplation, at the far end of his garden on a stone bench, slowly drying up, day and night, under sun and rain; his servants, in the meantime, did not dare interrupt this meditation in front of the Sôzu, the rocking bamboo pole, which his steward had placed at the edge of his Shisendo property to scare off wild boar and deer. In truth, he did not die from a slow, progressive entry into the "nothingness" of things and beings. No, I believe he died because he waited too long, because he kept encountering the ever too brief but ever repeated catastrophic Event, which remained beyond reach for that reason. Does not the feast of the Joyful Reversal of Opposites, which some see as similar to our carnival, date from his death?

It seems that a very ancient manuscript tells the story of a people living on the circular bank of an immense lake, which was fed by a river flowing from an open breach in the chain of mountains that cut off the horizon. This river, according to ancient cosmology, had its source in heaven, as a gift from the gods. Following some crime or another or some mysterious degeneration, this people, who had attained an unimaginable degree of power and wealth, was swallowed up in a catastrophe, a flood come not from heaven but from the unfathomable depths of the lake. The assembly of Wise Poets and Secret Hermits had, in fact, noted that the level of the waters was rising imperceptibly but regularly over the centuries. But the king of kings, the princes, and the court did not listen to them. Moreover, and even worse, year after year and century after century, they falsified the statistical report by the High Council of Calm Earthly Waters. One night, when, because of the heat, the river from the sky was flowing from its opening only in a thin stream, when the waters of the lake were lapping with tiny waves at the top of the marble quays and onyx wharves, when a hermit poet was contemplating the stars in the black curve of the sky, suddenly (here we are giving a literal translation of the text, despite its incoherence) the lake emptied itself toward the sky, carrying with it the prideful city and its inhabitants. Only a few survived, including the hermit poet, the author of that history and that cosmology. He notes that, for an instant, he could see the sky at the bottom of the dried-up lake, and then, in a deafening sound, "louder than ten thousand claps of thunder," everything took its place again, except the people. He adds that, according to his calculations and those of the assembly of Wise Poets and Secret Hermits, a similar flood must occur every two thousand years. This last remark authorizes some speculations on the influence of Plato on this text.

Others have suggested that the rocking bamboo pole on the edge of the sacred property might be the emblem, the realization, or the miniaturized form of this end of the world. The forgetting of its "metaphysical" sense *would be consecrated* in a pragmatic little machine, a scarecrow for deer and wild boar. The point is well taken: Deer and boar disappeared ages ago, and yet the rocking bamboo pole continues to resonate on the edge of the stream, near the sand garden, in the villa of the hermit poet. Perhaps, in this last century of the millennium, it is time to express not what it reproduces—a catastrophe of origin—but what it announces: the disaster of the end.

22

"Hello, Who Is This?"

Language must be studied in all the variety of its functions.... To give an idea of its functions, we need to provide a succinct outline bearing on the constitutive factors of any linguistic process, of any verbal act of communication. The *sender* sends a *message* to the *receiver*. To be operative, the message first requires a *context* to which it refers ... a context that can be grasped by the receiver and that is either verbal or able to be verbalized; then, the message requires a *code*, common in toto or at least in part, to the sender and the receiver ...; finally, the message requires a contact, a physical channel and a psychological connection between the sender and the receiver, a contact that allows one to establish and maintain the communication.

... There are messages that serve essentially to establish, prolong, or interrupt the communication, to verify if the circuit is functioning.... This accentuation of the contact—the *phatic* function to use Malinowski's term—can give way to an exchange of ritualized formulas, even to entire dialogues whose sole object is to prolong the conversation.
—Roman Jakobson, *Essai de linguistique générale*

One of the many varieties of the dialogue situation presents itself under what may appear to be the most commonplace social conditions, but which is, in fact, one of the least common. B. Malinowski has pointed to it with the term *phatic communion*, calling it a psycho-social phenomenon that functions linguistically. He traced its configuration based on the role language plays in it. It is a process in which discourse, in the form of a dialogue, grounds an exchange between individuals.... A personal relation is created and maintained through a conventional form of enunciation that entails no object, no goal, no message: a pure enunciation of the agreed-upon words, repeated by each sender. The analysis of that form of linguistic exchange remains to be done.
—Emile Benveniste, *Problèmes de linguistique générale II*

An intermittent and regular ringing in the gray box, an electric flow, a signal. "Someone" is calling *me*; "someone" wants to speak to *me*. "Someone," that is, the Other, an infinity of subjects, the indefinite "he," the absent one, the nonperson. But, at the same time, the ringing signals that that "someone" wants to become "I," that the person of the absent one wants to manifest its presence through its voice. Telephone: "Tele" connotes that gap between "someone" and "I," the tension moving from "someone" to "I." The two are distinct in space or slightly different in time, but only in appearance. More essentially, this tension is the desire to move away from absence in favor of presence, from silence to voice; it is a desire for manifestation, for a subject position.

Hence the dizzying sensation, the fall even, when I pick up the receiver and my ear is met with silence. No one speaks: the chasm of pure desire, a present absence. I am dizzy and I fall into the emptiness of the Bakelite ear that should have spoken to my corporeal ear: I listen to *a* silence, to an ear that is speaking a silence. In picking up, I comply with "Someone"'s desire to speak. I am magnanimous, I bring the "I," the subject of speech, into being. That is why my dizziness upon hearing the transmitter's silence is both a fall into the other's desire (to speak to me) and a fall from mastery, a mastery that is suddenly—and for a long time—without object. At that instant, a vertiginous power is constituted on one end: I make the other ("someone") a subject ("I"), but this inchoative subject escapes my hold and withdraws into its silence and absence. Hence the fascinating desire of the other: a desire for speech of which I am the goal and which, suddenly and in my presence, is not fulfilled since it remains voiceless. And that is why, conjointly with the other ("someone"), who has withdrawn into the empty anonymity of his silence, I fall from my position of subject (of power), to which his silent call had allowed me access. "Someone" could become "I" only through *me*, only through my act of listening to his voice. Silence: As my voice resonates in the emptiness, I fall into the retreat of his desire. Such would be the pure phatic, the "apophatic phatic." The network is functioning, the line is busy, the circuit is not interrupted. But, at the two poles, there is a double retreat, a double negation, both vertiginous and fascinating.

Apophatic phatic: Such would be the communication of God and men, according to Pascal. A telephone rings continually—you would not seek me if you had not already found me—man picks up endlessly: "Hello, who's there?" Silence. *Deus absconditus*: The absolute desire to enter into communication with man can only be fulfilled by withdrawing "into that strange . . . secret place, impenetrable to men's sight." "Instead of complaining that God has hidden himself, you will give him thanks for revealing himself as much as he has, and you will thank him too for not revealing himself to wise men."[1]

Intermittent and regular ringing in the gray box, a signal. "Someone" wants to speak to me. I let it ring six, ten times, I do not pick up: Silence. A sudden, heavier silence envelops my immobility. I do not want to answer. I do not want to speak to "Someone," the other. A lapse: I will never know who called at that minute. Someone will forever remain the other, however much I try to verify, inquire, catch up with him later on. "Were you the one who called at 5:18 P.M. last Wednesday?" Even if it were you, at that instant you will never be anything but the other. An incompleteness was opened at that instant in my knowledge of a piece of information, the initial and originary information: not *what?* a message, *what "you" wanted to say to me,* but *who?* The message of an identification: *Who,* at that instant, was possessed with a desire for speech addressed to me? The power of that lapse lies in the fact that I leave you in anonymity, a "someone"; I reject you, efface you through the immobility of my hand. I leave you in the opacity of the gray box, in the remote distance of the place from which you are calling me. *Your* voice will never be anything but that ring repeated six or ten times. It will never be anything but the undefined voice of an infinity of subjects, belonging to no one: the ebb of desire in telespace. But, in that instant, the soliloquy of the master "I" is proffered, and it attempts to supplement its ignorance: "Someone" thinks I am not here, "he" represents me absent. I am not in the place and at the moment where the other's desire (to speak to me) places me. "I" represents himself as missing to "someone," whereas "I" is really where the other situates him. It is not a lie: I am here now but I do not want to be here, and, in truth, in not picking up the phone for the other ("someone"), I am not here, since the signal and the sign, the hand gesture that picks up and the first sound of my voice, would be my only presence for "him." Merely a fiction. I give myself a fictive nonbeing, or rather, a mixture of being and nonbeing. I *am* a figure of absence. If you call me, I drag you with me inexorably, into this world of fiction, since you will never accede to the "I" of "interlocution" that you desire to be now in calling me. You will remain the undefined other. Through my silence, I bring into being your representation of me as a fiction, whoever you are. And I lose the knowledge of your identity and make you lose your identity, the part that lies in your desire to speak: power of the subject, of the solitary master, at the price of his *own* absence. "Aphatic phatic."

Intermittent and regular ringing in the gray box. "Someone" is calling, "someone" wants to speak to me. I pick up. "Hello, yes, who is this?" The "communication" is established; before any message, before any information, even before the recognition of a voice or the utterance of a name, the exchange of two or three words makes the circuit "take." By the same token, I accept *the position* of receiver as I listen to a voice, at that *place* where the other (someone) positions me, at the end of a circuit that his call completed, at the end of a line. A fish caught on the hook. In saying, "Hello, yes, who is this?" I agree to the call, I fall into the place where I was placed and where the other (someone) who wants to speak to me situates me here and now. My position—I position myself as a receiver, I listen—suddenly comes to fill my place, that given to me in the alphabetical list of telephone customers, the place of my name among my numerous homonyms, defined more exactly by an address and an eight-digit number, seven digits of which I share with other names on that same list (I am identified by the eighth). This place can be replicated—it is the same and yet it is also different—in another, more intimate place, in a personal address book under the letter M, in the set no longer of telephone customers but of friends and relations, of the other who calls me, who wants to speak to me now, precisely. These places, identical in the end—in all cases, it is L. M., 62, Rue du Faubourg-St-Antoine 12e, 43 48.98.61—are also diverse, with the diversity of the sets to which they belong (the telephone book of Paris customers, the address book of Jules, of Amélie, of Arthur, the file of a secretary, the dossiers of an institution). That place—like the set of these places—mine (who else's?) is the terminal point for several (numerous or few, depending on the case) *potential* speech programs, both their goal ("to speak to . . .") and their object ("to speak to *me*"), which specifies this goal in a certain type of speech relation and in a certain type of interlocutor: me.

"Hello, yes, who is this?" In saying these few words, I realize the possibility of one of these programs, to the exclusion of all the others. (Or, rather, their near exclusion: If someone else calls me, wanting to speak to me at the precise moment when I pick up and say, "Hello, who is this?" he will hear the "busy" signal, that is, a description such as, "He's home, he's speaking to someone else, I'll call back later." A program with a deferred realization, which remains potential. Nonetheless, its potentiality is almost realized, but a bit later, in the near future. Or it is realized as a possibility: "If he had not been called right now by another, he would be speaking to *me*.") And, immediately, I occupy, I fill with my voice that place as a set of places, which is my own place in the various sets to which it belongs. I position myself as receiver of a particular allocution. But that self-positioning is, at the same time, the agreement to really occupy the place that was fixed for me in the network. I fill it, and I recognize that I am filling it as my own. In speaking, I occupy it and recognize that I occupy it. I speak. "I am on the line here and now, I am 43 48.98.61, I am this name and this address in the telephone book, in this address book." I am identified in time and space in a place and moment, a name, by the other who wants to speak to me and who finds me here and now because I am subjected to the network, the connections, the lines, in a point on a field of words in circulation, a point of a potential locution-interlocution. I am a telephonic subject and a subject of speech that installs itself only to posit itself phonically in the place and moment where "someone" places me; a "telephonic" cogito in the place of an emission of the voice (my own), summoned by a signal in a place assigned it in a system of sets of places, a system that is the inscribed form of "Someone," the other. In saying, "Hello, who is this?" responding or reacting by these words to the call signal, even before "someone" answers in turn (and usually, by uttering his name), by my acknowledged position in my place, I place "someone" in the position to become the "I," I provide him with the necessary condition (in the field of speech) to gain access to his situation as subject of speech. In other words, I comply with his desire to speak to me, I open the space of fulfillment to him, a fulfillment whose first act, whose first gesture, will consist in uttering his name, identifying himself first as a name, being recognized in and through his name as a desire to speak to me. A fulfillment of desire whose first gesture consists in being recognized by his name as a subject of that desire, but which is possible only because I am assigned a place by the other, only because I find myself subjected to that place, and necessarily so. The desire is fulfilled only on the condition that I fill the place with a voice, that I manifest myself there as a subject of speech. My power to bring the other into being as an "I" is, thus, only the exact counterpart of my subservience to the field of inscription of the other, as "other." The "cataphatic phatic," the double access to the status of subjects by both parties, at the cost of a double collapse into the pure relation between the two. The other desires my voice in order to be an "I," "*the* one" among the infinity of others; but I can be "I" only by being assigned a place in the system, in the sets of places, that is, in the other, "someone."

Military variant: "Hello, who is this?" becomes, according to regulation, "X, second class, to whom do I have the honor (of speaking)?" At the ring, once the receiver has been picked up, I respond to the other (1) by stating my rank or, rather, my absence of rank, (2) by uttering my name, (3) by uttering both as the designation of a "he." A triple point of reference that must immediately be given to the other, not, as at times, by indicating the number called or by "defining" my place in the network, but by indicating my hierarchical place in the military order and by giving the name that is found to occupy that place. Not only is "I" positioned as a receiver in the place where the other situates him; he is also required to give the explicit formula of acknowledgment of his relation of ordination in the institution to which he belongs. He offers himself to identification by the other in that order, under the law of that order, and in expectation of that order. The principle that grounds the law (but it is also the law that grounds the principle), a principle presupposed by the required formula, is that the place occupied by the receiver in the relation of order is always and absolutely *subordinate*; in other words, this place has only and can only have predecessors, not successors. "I" can be only an object or a patient of the absolute power of the other. Hence, the dispatching of the "I" who proffers the designation—his name itself is a designation—and through which he enunciates himself as "he," a "he" that is the exact reverse of the "he" in authority that every call presupposes in the hierarchical order. The signal is, by definition, posited as the mark of the call of majesty, and the designations that initiate communication define the subject by a "he" of servility. The formula that follows, where the "I" appears, confirms this definitive positioning, since "I" accedes to the status of subject, not as receiver of the message that will follow but first, and essentially, as the recipient of *the honor* of being spoken to by the other. The communication is established before any utterance as the acknowledgment by the receiving subject of the pure gratification of the other's speech. As a result, the message that is uttered will be an order or will necessarily presuppose the order.

If he utters his name and I do not recognize "him," do not identify him, if he names me with a name that is not my own, then it is a wrong number: "What number are you calling?" Double vacillation: "I" still occupies the place where "someone" wanted to speak to him, but, all of a sudden, "I" is only a name, a transparent film, an empty chrysalis floating in that place, a place too big for this too-light name. The place is still filled, there is a voice someone names, and yet there is too much emptiness under this name, around it. I occupy the place where someone wants to speak to me. "Someone" still accedes to the status of "I" through my voice, by stating his name, but this name, like the one he pronounces next (mine?) suddenly "says" nothing, means nothing to me. And, at the same moment and for a very brief instant, it happens that, in this name, I am another. Subtle temptation: I am taken for another, the object of a desire for speech that is enunciated; perhaps I can disguise myself for that other who is speaking to me, slide into that name that he uttered an instant ago and attempt to "invent" it and, with it, the circumstances of this desire to speak to me, its source, its motives and reasons. Perhaps I can be recognized as its subject and support, can learn the role appropriate to it by playing, reply after reply, the seductive game of an illegitimate appropriation, a usurpation: a "diaphatic phatic" fantasy, for an instant, two instances of speech that only play at coming together in a dialogue, but whose play, in subverting its rules, uncovers the law of the system of the sets of places, that of the network, the field of inscription to which I am subjected.

All these variations on the telephonic phatic (played out only from the viewpoint of the one receiving the call, the interruption of the signal in the silence of a home) suggest a constant motif in their discourse, a motif that accompanied the discourse and made it possible: that of obliteration, the obfuscation of the visibility involved in speaking and hearing. The other ("someone") announces his desire to speak to me only through an auditory signal, then through a voice, in a contact between the speaking ear—that of the receiver—and the listening ear—that of the body. When the reversal in the enunciation occurs, when the one spoken to becomes the speaker, moving from one structural position to the other, mouth and lips speak in contact with an instrumental ear, a mechanism that reproduces *here* the mechanism that is functioning *there*. But between here and there, between now and a moment ago, between the two ears that are speaking and the two ears that are listening, between the mouths and the ears that, whether of flesh or plastic, are nonetheless caught in the inveigling mechanisms, the mechanisms of transmission and reception, nothing else intervenes except a "line," an element of the network with its connections, its centers, and its junctions and, running through it in every direction, vibrations, energy flows, at almost infinite speed, "immediate" circuits. Hence the paradox of auditory or phonic immediacy realized by the most mediated of mechanisms: You who speak to me, I who speak to you, here and now, from mouth to ear, in the double presence of an exchange between speaking and listening, I am not in the place where I am speaking to you, and you are not in the place where you are speaking to me. This paradox results from the disembodied voices that I have named obliteration or obfuscation: the obliteration of bodies, the obfuscation of sight. The communication of both parties is blind. I do not see you, you whom I hear, and you do not see me, I who speak to you. Thus caught in the mechanism of speaking and listening, let us obey, you and I, the rules of the phatic rituals to establish (or maintain, or interrupt) the ritual communication, which we may play around with (I "pick up," you do not speak, I do not "pick up," you will speak to me later, I speak to you as someone I am not, or vice versa, and so forth) but which are necessary if we are to speak to each other. For the perception of bodies, faces, hands, and their signifying gestures, the phatic ritual substitutes the mechanics of language, within the mechanics of telecommunication. The network, a vast artificial body, a voice carrier, substitutes for bodies. This great, artificial body would be a mask, a "persona" (since, as we know, the mask "per-sonates" [*per-sonat*], makes the voice resonate as it carries it far [*tele*] into the theatrical spectacle), if an actor hid in his role by finding the figure for his identity in representation. But no one hides and no one shows himself, no one masks himself or uncovers himself. The network is no one [*personne*] because it is everyone, a simple field marked out by multiple mediate/immediate circuits. It is the other, in general, where persons take shape phonically and acoustically, become an "I" by observing the rules of the phatic rite of establishing communication.

And, among all the paradoxes of this story, the history of the term "phatic" is not the least significant. Roman Jakobson borrowed the term from Bronislaw Malinowski, giving as a first illustration of its *linguistic function* the example of the telephonic "hello." Yet, Malinowski invented the term to characterize a type of *discursive usage*, which created a social *communion* in and through the exchange of words, among the Melanesians, those Argonauts of the Western Pacific. Whereas, in Jakobson, it is a particular *function* of a model of communication, of the transmission of messages, in Malinowski, the "phatic" is a *discursive mode of action*, which institutes its own context of discourse and whose aim is to link interlocutors who are strangers to one another, strangers who are facing each other in silence, in a feeling of convivial sociability. We can take stock of the displacement involved through this remark by Malinowski, which I cite in conclusion: "To break the silence and commune through words is the first act that establishes ties of camaraderie which will be consummated only by breaking bread and communing in food."

23

The Angel of Virtuality

He had read the following in Saint Thomas Aquinas's *Summa theologica*, which made him dream of another kind of mental adventure:

> Since the angels are not bodies, nor have they bodies naturally united with them . . . it follows that they sometimes assume bodies. . . . By Divine power sensible bodies are so fashioned by angels as fittingly to represent intelligible properties of an angel. And this is what we mean by an angel assuming a body. . . . Although air as long as it is in a state of rarefaction has neither shape nor color, yet when condensed it can both be shaped and colored as appears in the clouds. Even so the angels assume bodies of air, condensing it by Divine power in so far as is needful for forming the assumed body.[1]

Since that time, he found himself saying: "Angels are species of clouds," but also, "Clouds are the genus of angels." It was through this double, and apparently reciprocal, proposition, through this linguistic sleight of hand, that he explained to himself the profound, esoteric wisdom of certain painters, who let him catch a glimpse of figures in the swellings and whorls of the clouds they painted in the background of their paintings, behind the large, sacred images that stood facing the faithful, images that looked the beholders straight in the eye with a severe, tender, or desperate look. No, these images in the clouds were not even figures, but merely cheeks, buttocks, breasts, bellies, luminous and soft folds of fat, but also blond curls, red lips, mouths half open in pink listlessness, potential flesh in its inchoative state, emerging from the cloud and immediately becoming indistinguishable from the specks of foam and vapor, which a source of light, come from who knows where, made iridescent with golden sparks. Unless, he thought suddenly, all these metamorphoses existed only in his gaze, and the emotion they provoked had no subject other than his own mind. "Some have maintained that the angels never assume bodies, but that all we read in Scripture of apparitions of angels happened in prophetic vision—that is, according to imagination."[2] But the Angelic Doctor responded that the angels who had appeared to Abraham had been seen by him, by his whole family, by Lot, and by the citizens of Sodom. In the same way, was not the angel that appeared to Tobias seen by all? It is true that Saint Thomas Aquinas was speaking of a written text and not of paintings on canvas. Strange oscillation, hesitation, uncertainty, undecidability: "There," on the painted canvas, in that ground of shadow and light where clouds take the form of bodies, where bodies vanish in an airy inconsistency; "Here," in his gaze, which put off abandoning itself to his desire, put off bringing these figures into being. These figures exist *in* the ground, which is precisely only the condition for the appearance and inscription of those other figures, those that assert themselves as presences, that appear as circumscribed forms. It is that hesitation he found in the passage from the *Summa theologica*, which he reread incessantly: "By Divine power sensible bodies are so fashioned [*fingunt*] by angels." Angels fictionalize bodies for themselves, bodies the human gaze can see, touch, and feel, but which are feigned or fictive bodies. And that feint, that fiction, is composed of an invisible element, which is only sensible in the puff of air that grazes the skin, stirs the curtains, swells the sails, pushes the clouds about in the sky.... The Clouds, the clouds, angelic creatures, no doubt, which conceal themselves from capture if not from sight ... sensible bodies that dissipate not in the evanescence of vapors, not in the iridescence of clouds, but in *representation*. By divine power, angels fashion themselves sensible bodies that represent their intelligible properties, body-signs in a word, bodies that have no other presence to the senses than their reference to sense, a sense or, rather, a plurality of senses (their intelligible properties), a potentiality of—intelligible—sense, and, nonetheless, one buried in the unfathomable immensities of celestial hierarchies. For how can one know the intelligible properties of the angels, as they surround the throne and sing in unison, except through the sensible bodies they fashion for themselves from the air, in the form and color of clouds.... And when, attentively, with all the power of his eyes, he contemplated the ground of luminous shadow and nocturnal brightness in a Virgin and Child by Raphael, as myriads of angels, cheeks, mouths, curls, dimpled arms, and chubby thighs came to life before his gaze, he wondered what intelligible properties the divine Raphael, completely permeated by grace, was proposing that he recognize, what all these bodies and faces in clouds might represent. Unless, he thought, all of a sudden, that was just it, *that* was the mysterious function of these angels in a state of suspended apparition: to provoke, in their turn, in his gaze and his mind, the fictions of properties that pure spirits possessed when, invisible, they besieged with their presence the One whom no one can see without dying. Thus, he attempted to imagine forms without matter, infinitely diverse forms, extremely quick and extremely slow movements without a body in motion, colors without a space or a place in which to extend their varieties, pure luminous intensities where hot and cold, dry and wet, dense and sparse coexisted, times that, though still time, consisted solely in an inexorable permanence. And, he thought, this time was made only of a myriad of simultaneous instants, present together in a mobile order in each of its parts, whose relations remained mysteriously unchanged since the instants were immediately compensated for in the positions between them. Was all that not what the exchange of clouds signified when he contemplated them in the sky, clouds or angels or the wind that pushed them about, made them appear and disappear in so many wrenching epiphanies, wrenching because they remained unperceived?

But what properties of intelligible things did the angel-clouds in Raphael's painting signal by their evanescent, sensible similitudes, when they smiled with all their carnal dimples as he looked at them? What mysterious affects, what secret passions, what unknown desires, did these pure incorporealities lead him to glimpse in that smile on their faces, on their bodies, on faces and bodies that slipped away into the golden shadow of the ground, only to be metamorphosed into another body, another face or cloud, a universal smile that belonged to no face in particular, to no mouth, cheek, lip, belly, or thigh? And he could not even say that the smile signified the simple blessedness of being, of persevering united in one's being, since all these angels, properly speaking, which he discerned in the luminous mists and clouds of the painting, *were* not, not yet, or already no longer, but were only in the process of fictionalizing themselves into an airy body by means of condensation, of fictionalizing themselves to the extent necessary to attract his gaze to their formal presence. Or they were in the process of dissipating their sensible assumption of body in a breath of the spirit that lay beyond reach, in order to inspire a way of thinking that was entirely detached from things, to lead it to inquire into the unknown properties of the intelligible substance.

They were smiling, it seemed to him, as they took on the childlike bodies of their cousins of Eros but also when they let their fictions vanish, impalpable. An immense, general indifference in being or not being: That is what the myriad smiles, the unstable, shimmering smiles might be suggesting. Not certain affects, passions, or desires, but the sole passion of indifference, that unperceived indifference to edges and intervals, the indifference that precedes beginnings and follows ends, because no one can ever know whether that thrust, that intention, that power, had being or disappearing as its aim: air, cloud, flesh of light, body, but the reverse as well, the return to pure mind. Indifference: the passion of potentiality, the affect of virtuality, the mark of a lack, the negative index, the hollow vestige of potency. An indifference to the direction of desire: The motion toward was a welcome and a retreat, a disappearance. In Pseudo-Dionysius the Areopagite's *Celestial Hierarchy*, he read that angels' eyes—those little whirlwinds that spiritual passions fashioned for themselves in their pneumatic faces—signified "their tendency to rise up in full brightness toward divine light, but only in the manner they received transcendent illumination, impassive, which is to say tenderly, with suppleness, without resistance, quickly and purely taking flight."

He also extracted from Saint Thomas Aquinas the two responses the saint gave to the objections raised about angels assuming "living" bodies. First, in reference to speech: "Speech is the function of a living subject, for it is produced by the voice, while the voice itself is a sound conveyed from the mouth."[3] In the voice, a resonant modulation in the oral cavity, he rediscovered the breath of the wind and the solidified air of which clouds were made, these clouds from which angels fashioned bodies for themselves. But that air had become a cry, and then speech, the prolation of sense, living expression. Was the body of the angel truly a living body, like those evoked by Saint Augustine in *De genesis ad literam* (3.10) in reference to Platonic demons? Were they animals of air because they had the nature of bodies of air? Do angels speak? Saint Thomas Aquinas answered him: "Properly speaking, the angels do not talk through their assumed bodies, yet there is a semblance of speech, in so far as they fashion sounds in the air like to human voices."[4] What mysterious, spiritual communications did these sounds represent, sounds so perfectly similar to human voices that those who knew divine wisdom could transcribe them into words and phrases intelligible to human beings? He wondered how pure, spiritual substances could communicate among themselves, whether the terms "communication," "sign," "code," and "syntax" still had any meaning. He imagined an immediate interpenetration, a transparent overlapping, transmission through permeation, like the trickle of ink on the blotter that becomes a black sun. But how is it possible to conceive of these enigmatic transmutations of speech in limitless, perceptible beings without borders, without transparence, without opacity? How to imagine bodies as porous envelopes? For angels can be distinguished from one another, angelic substance can be divided and multiplied into an incalculable number of spiritual individuals. (Were there not generations and hierarchies of angels? Seraphim, cherub, thrones, dominions, virtues, powers, principalities, archangels, and angels?) How to envision envelopes that, without resisting, filtering, or sifting, transmit knowledge from one to the other by the simple effusion of one into the other? And that knowledge is not articulated in words—nouns and verbs—or uttered in sentences and discourse; it is wind and light, instantaneously or almost instantaneously, displaced from the top of the hierarchy to the bottom, and from its unfathomable base to its inexpressible summit, "for you do not know from whence the wind comes or where it goes." "Angels need an assumed body not for themselves, but on our account, that by conversing familiarly with men they may give evidence of the intellectual companionship which men expect to have with them in the life to come."[5] He also wondered whether angels could have secrets from one another, whether a seraphic thought could remain enveloped in a spiritual mist that would make it incommunicable to the nearby cherub, or whether two dominions, for example, through that porous exchange of diaphanous surfaces he had managed to imagine as their mode of conversation, could make a thought known between them without all the dominions—to take only the celestial powers of the same rank—immediately having knowledge of it. It could well be, he thought with some satisfaction, that given this *lack of secrecy*, one of these mysterious, intelligible properties of pure mind could be recognized by a human mind, so burdened by corporeal matter. This was the first true thought he had had about angelic properties—all the others he had merely imagined—and it concerned a lack. Angels do not have secrets from one another. But perhaps the simple fact of having a secret or of communicating it to another—necessarily excluding a third party from that communication—was a defect or imperfection. Thus, in thinking of spiritual substances, he had to get it into his head that they could have no private being, that they were without interior and exterior and that the only means of conceiving of their limits—since, again, they could be distinguished from one another—was to imagine porous membranes and transparent envelopes, with communication taking place between them by transfusion, without intermediary or duration, in an instant that was only suspended time. He was amazed that the language of angels, which men hear and understand, was only the sonorous echo of puffs of air that the pure spirits incessantly emitted in inaudible unison, or rays of light that blazed in eternal dazzlement, as a double tribute to divinity.

The day will undoubtedly come, he thought, when angels will be so numerous, so present among us, so accustomed to the heaviness of our bodies and to their obscurities, or, in contrast, when we will be so accustomed to that innumerable presence among us, when our flesh, its membranes and its skin, our homes and walls, our dwellings and their borders, will have become so light, so porous, so evanescent that a general translucidity has become the angelic space of universal community. Was it not for that reason, he asked, that the angels formed cloud bodies, reflecting on their white and gray screens the forms, colors, and—why not?—the words of men; white and gray translucid screens that are both mouths and ears, mouths emitting a breath that inscribes—by what enigmatic operations?—traces of sounds that are altogether similar to the human voices and words in the ear, on the grayish-white eardrum that hears them in that silent form. . . . Yes, perhaps it was to make us understand our universal destiny of annihilation, in a resonant cavity and on a vibrating membrane, to make us understand the finality of abnegation promised us. And so the words disappeared into a mouth-ear where all hesitations, misunderstandings, *quiproquos*, stammering, where all the time of coding, decoding, and counting up, were erased, suppressed, effaced, or telescoped, not into a single name or formula—a small form that, in itself, delivers the inexpressible, unfathomable, invisible secret of the universe, of worlds and societies—but into a breath, a puff of air, a sound that, this time, this one time, this last time, no longer resembles—no, not at all—human voices.

From one mouth to the other: He noticed—and in his passionate interest for things relating to speech he could only be surprised by this—that in three lines, Saint Thomas Aquinas provided a solution to the question of the language of angels, but that, in contrast, their food merited a much longer exposition. "Now when angels appeared in their assumed bodies they ate, and Abraham offered them food" under the oak on the plain of Mamre, at the entrance to the tent during the hottest part of the day.[6] He lifted his eyes and saw three men who were standing near him. After he had prostrated himself before them, he offered them the meal cakes Sara had made, the tender and good calf he had had prepared, butter, and milk: "And he ... set *it* before them; and he stood by them under the tree, and they did eat."[7] The angels—for that is what they were—thus performed vital operations in the bodies they had assumed. Such is the formidable objection to which Saint Thomas Aquinas responds: "Properly speaking, the angels cannot be said to eat, because eating involves the taking of food convertible into the substance of the eater.... But the food taken by angels was neither changed into the assumed body, nor was the body of such a nature that food could be changed in it; consequently, it was not a true eating, but figurative or spiritual eating. This is what the angel said to Tobias: *When I was with you, I seemed indeed to eat and to drink; but I use an invisible meat and drink* (Tob. xii, 19)."[8] From that quotation, given by Saint Thomas Aquinas himself, it was obvious to him that angels ate: The meal prepared by Sara was quite "real," a calf, meal cakes, butter, milk were all truly absorbed by the three celestial visitors—an absorption everyone calls "eating." Nonetheless, in the case of the angel, that operation was an appearance, a feint, a fiction. In the mouth of the body that the spiritual creature fashioned for itself from the substance of a cloud, the mouthful of meat and the swallow of milk were vaporized in an instant; not flesh and blood, but air condensed and solidified into a dense cloud. Disappearance or mysterious assimilation?

As he personally reflected upon it, faithful to the letter of the text, he leaned toward the idea that the meat and drink had disappeared into airy bodies. Was this a fiction representative of spiritual manducation? Once more, his entry into the rarefied world of purely intelligible essences and properties led him to drift into revery, a revery where others, those great "knowers of divine wisdom," had long ago followed him. If spiritual bodies exist with spiritual sight, touch, hearing, taste, and sense of smell, as he had read, and as he himself spoke of it in everyday language ("I saw what you wanted to say"; "Let me give you a flavor of the argument"; "I hear what you're saying"; "I'm touching on the weak point in the speech"; "I taste the sweetness of that evening"), then why not conceive of the "eating" and "drinking" of pure spirits? Did not the Areopagite say that "the image of taste can be perfectly well applied to celestial powers to signify the plenitude of intellectual nourishment and the art of imbibing the fecundity of divine channels"? But the angel's words to Tobias were more bothersome and presented him with a more demanding question: "I use an invisible meat and drink." This was not a *spiritual* food or an intelligible manducation, terms that still allowed him to conceive of the angel's feigned eating and drinking as a particularly appropriate image or metaphor for the crudeness of human thought and speech. In this instance, Raphael was not speaking in figures when he evoked the food of angels, a food it was impossible to see, touch, or smell, a food without a human name, but a real food that sustained the airy body of the angel, that satisfied the hunger and thirst of the cloud he had assumed as a body, beside Tobias on the roads leading to the land of the Medes. He seemed to eat and drink when he was with him and his family: But, at the same time, he was feeding himself with a mysterious and secret food, like all angels when they have assumed bodies and eat with men. He dreamed of that secret food, imagining it as closest in its invisibility to fragments of words—there again, he rediscovered his linguistic obsessions—as the elements of a language of languages, both parts of an originary language that had long since been forgotten and the miniaturized mechanics of production for all possible languages. They were inaudible sounds like bits of silence, similar in their "material" texture to the air from which the angel's body was fashioned, but with great "nutritional" intellectual power, since they contained, at the virtual state, an incalculable number of utterances and terms, a finite but very large number of possible or real languages, that is, in the end, an infinite number of thoughts and relations among those thoughts. The angel seemed to be sharing men's meals, appeared to eat their food and speak to them, out of convivial hospitality. But, in fact, at the same moment (but what is temporal simultaneity for a being for whom time itself is a permanent present?), the spiritual creature was ingesting that same food, but at the virtual state, invisible and inaudible. That is, he was ingesting the totality of possibilities and copossibilities of edible things and expressible words. And the meal, the prepared dishes, the dialogue and the words exchanged, *realized* only a tiny part of them, a part so tiny that it was as if the angel were not truly speaking and eating but was merely producing, from the (eaten) food and the (spoken) words, representations of spiritual manducation and intelligible communication. And so it happened that he imagined the airy body of Raphael as a white and gray screen on which the silent fragments and the immaterial traces of eaten words and uttered food would appear and immediately vanish, while crackling sounds rose from this cloud with a human shape. Those sounds resembled certain human voices, but their foreign flavors and exotic aromas would have surprised his ears, would not have been what his tongue and palate expected. Or these sounds were similar to what he had heard about thunder still lurking in the storm cloud, whose music is like a beehive. It was then a short step, a slippery step of revery, to imagining that the invisible food of which Raphael spoke to Tobias was a kind of word honey, a honey of virtual, originary, honeycombed, or cellular words into which bees of thunder deposited not only their honey but also the eggs of all possible words in all possible languages.

But is the angel in a place? Do not philosophers share with Boethius the feeling that incorporeal beings are not in a place, since being in a place means being measured and contained by that place? How could the spiritual creature be localized? He found the argument decisive on this point. Thus, the opposite theses, which he read in article 1 of question 52 of the *Summa theologica*, appeared all the more moving to him, since the philosophemes gave way to poetic utterances: "*Let Thy holy angels who dwell herein, keep us in peace.*"[9] And Saint Thomas Aquinas immediately added: "It is befitting an angel to be in a place," but not in the way a body is contained in a place, a place that measures the body's quantity by the very dimensions of the container, in length, width, and depth. "But there is no such quantity [which can be measured by the dimensions of a place], for theirs is a virtual one. Consequently an angel is said to be in a corporeal place by application of the angelic power [its virtue] in any manner whatever to any place."[10] That is, he immediately added in a gloss, to this body in this place, the body the angel assumed by fashioning the air of a cloud. As a result, the question could be rephrased in another, much stranger form—and that strangeness also appealed to the somewhat deviant, or deviating, pleasures of his intelligence—that is, how can a cloud, in the shape and color of a body, thus, a cloud inhabited by the angel, be said to be in a place, since the cloud itself and its metamorphoses, between expansion and concentration, vaporization and condensation, appearance and disappearance, emergence and evanescence, being and nothingness, seemed to play with the place, with its measurements, with the way it enveloped bodies? The cloud is a creature of the horizon: not the horizon that limits and traces a borderline for the eye, but the horizon that summons the gaze beyond the circle that encloses the perceiving body, toward a "land beyond," the land of being. The cloud is a creature of space, the angel-cloud a messenger of infinite space in the closed world of measuring places and measured bodies. The angel, by virtue of the image or the sign of its airy, visible body, is the infinite creature of infinity, to be precise, the potential of infinity: "It is not necessary on this account for the angel to be contained by a place; because an incorporeal substance virtually contains the thing with which it comes into contact, and is not contained by it ... not as the thing contained but as somehow, *quoddam modo*, containing it."[11] He had to understand these difficult words; it seemed to him that he was condemned desperately to seek their meaning because they seemed to hold some decisive truth for him, concerning what he thought of man and what he thought of man's thought and of human language and of what he was saying about human language.... The angel occupies a place: He is not contained in that place; he assumes a body, he does not have a body.... The angel does not speak but emits sounds similar to those of the human voice.... The angel does not eat; he seems to do so even as he feeds himself with an invisible food.

It was in these gaps, these intervals, it was in these nuances between reality and appearance, model and imitation, that the fictions that were to introduce him to the comprehension of the great truths he was seeking were surely at play, but he also had the feeling that these fictions—these bodies that angels fashioned for themselves with the assistance of divine power, in the condensed air—were playing around with him and his will because they held a power or potentiality (*virtus, dunamis*), a virtue that went beyond him. These fictions, airy bodies emitting words, absorbing food, had no other function than to incite him to understand the mysterious, intelligible properties of spiritual substances and their innumerable communities and hierarchies; these fictions were, precisely, potentialities, virtues. They allowed him to understand all of a sudden, in a single thought, a thought as overwhelming as lightning and with the taste of the origin or end of the world, two meanings, two ideas, two notions that he could usually only conceive of as separated, opposed, and contrary: possibility and potency. For the *virtus* that the angels applied to air, to food, to speech, and, finally, to the place, was the incredible force of "suspending" not only the necessity of the relations between things and beings but also the very reality of things. That *virtus*, by means of an alarming *violence*, transformed them not into their doubles, their specters, or their appearances, all artifacts that men knew how to make or were acquainted with from the beginning of time, but into beings of another nature, capable of producing an infinity of things, but condemned, for the most part, to float at the larval state, at the borderline of "reality." And if, as it seemed probable to him, the innumerable angels, each in their order and according to their place in the hierarchy, exercised the mysterious virtue bestowed upon them on the finite set of things in this world, then that was what human beings were accustomed to call "reality," which all of a sudden moved to that larval state, with all borderlines suppressed between the real and the unreal, the world and the world beyond, the next world, multiplied into an infinity of virtualities. In a single moment (but once more, what is a moment for the spiritual powers that are familiar with all times and all aspects of time in an identical, suspended present?), reality was vaporized into clouds. It vanished into the impalpable air and moved into the pneumatic universe where myriads of airy angels, which had come to *virtualize* the world—beings, bodies, societies—disappeared. . . . The last judgment, the time and space of the world, completely traversed by invisible angels in the process of virtualizing the real, might be a pure gray surface without edges, teeming with an infinity of twinkling, luminous points, the moment when the "real" becomes an angel.

24

Neither the True Sex Nor the False

hermaphrodite, n. individual that possesses the organs of both sexes: there is no perfect hermaphrodite in the human species.
—Larousse, *Grand dictionnaire universel du XIXe siècle*

Du langage français bizarre hermaphrodite,
De quel genre te faire, équivoque maudite
Ou maudit?

Bizarre, hermaphrodite French language
What gender cursed equivocation?
—Boileau, *Satires* 12, ll.1–3, 1705

The waters of the fountain Salmacis
Have earned an evil name: the men who take them
Become effeminate or merely zero—
Certainly less than men, which is well known.
The reason why has been a guarded secret.[1]

Now here is the story.

> The infant son of Mercury and Venus
> Was nursed by niaids in Mount Ida's caves....
> When he had reached the age of three-times-five...
> He drifted toward the cities of Lycia....
> And there he found a tempting pool of water
> So clear that one could read its sandy depth.
> No swamps grew there, rank grasses, nor black weeds;
> Only the purest water flowed...
>   ... A nymph lived there
>   ... and that day saw the boy;
> O how she yearned to take him in her arms!

> ... She chose her words and spoke: "O lovely boy
> If you are not a god, then you should be one....
> Then let us find our wedding bed." She paused;
> The boy flushed red, half innocent of love....
> He cried, "Leave me or I must run away—
> Get out of here." Salmacis, shaken, said,
> "This place is yours, but stay, O darling stranger!"
> Then turned as if to leave him there alone,
> Walked slowly cautiously beyond his view,
> Looked back, dropped to her knees behind a hedge.
> Meanwhile the boy as though he were unseen ...
> Stripped off his clothes; and when she saw
> Him naked, the girl was dazzled
>   ... nor could she wait
> To hold him naked in her arms. Striking
> His arms against his sides, he leaped and dived
> Overhand stroke, into the pool; his glittering body
> Flashed and turned within clear waters.
>   ... "I've won, for he is mine,"
> She cried, clothes torn away and naked, as she
> Leaped to follow him, her arms about him fast
> Where, though he tried to shake her off, she clung
> Fastening his lips to hers, stroking his breast,
> Surrounding him with arms, legs, lips, and hands....
> The heir of Atlas struggled as he could
> Against the pleasure that the girl desired,
> But she clung to him as though their flesh were one.
> "Dear naughty boy," she said, "to torture me;
> But you won't get away. O gods in heaven,
> Give me this blessing; clip him within my arms
> Like this forever." At which the gods agreed;
> They grew one body, one face, one pair of arms
> And legs, so two became nor boy nor girl,
> Neither yet both within a single body.
>
> When tamed Hermaphroditus learned his fate
> Knew that his bath had sent him to his doom,
> To weakened members and a girlish voice,
> He raised his hands and prayed, "O Father, Mother,
> Hear your poor son who carried both your names:
> Make all who swim these waters impotent,
> Half men, half women."[2]

The myth of Hermaphroditus, recounted with refined grace by Ovid in book 4 of the *Metamorphoses*, runs the gamut between masculine and feminine, covering the entire field of relations of opposition and of complementarity deployed by gender difference, to arrive at the hybrid man-woman: Herm-(es)-aphroditus. The child of Hermes and Aphrodite, endowed with the (sexual?) attributes of his two divine parents, the *puer* who is both *vir* and *femina*, is a body *brought about* by the simple addition of two sexes and of their primary and secondary characteristics, thus *bringing about* the synthesis of opposites. He is a new being, born of the violence of love and of an imprecation in language. His name—a proper name become a common noun—has left a trace in collective memory; and the image of a scandalously appropriate contemplation of the slender, effeminate adolescent in an alexandrine statue has stirred the imagination. Yet, the narrative of the myth, in its episodes and in the poetic play of its language, questions the well-established certainties about this name and this image, destabilizes them with its tranquil obviousness, makes them fragile in the very utterances that declare them. Such is the neuter at work in the articulation of oppositions and in the declaration of syntheses, in the positing of difference itself—sexual difference—and in the graceful monster issued forth from its resolution. Neither concept nor category, the *neuter* can only be grasped as the flip side of concepts, as the gap in a relation, as the dark and unfathomable face of synthesis. In this regard, Ovid's poem soon proves to be of a frightening subtlety.

The first appearance of the child—unexpressed or virtually expressed—may be a decisive manifestation of the work of the neuter, its force of displacement. At the beginning of the poem, the child born of two gods (*Mercurio puerum diva Cythereide natum*), born like any human child of a father and a mother, from their conjoined sex organs, from the *coitus* of difference, is named only in the reference his face makes to the parental couple: "*Cujus erat facies, in qua materque paterque / Cognosci possent: nomen quoque traxit ab illis.*"

Both the mother . . . *and* the father: The two poles of sexual difference, feminine and masculine, are underscored in their *polarization* and *opposition*, in the very repetition of the coordinating particle. They can be recognized in a single face that inscribes and traces the double resemblance. And the child draws (*trahit*) his name from their portrait, a name that is proper and singular only in its repetition of the two different names in which the child has his origin. Nevertheless, the poet defers naming the child of the god and goddess from the very beginning of the narrative to the very end: He names the too-beautiful shepherd only once the strange metamorphosis has come about, or, rather, only once the union between the niaid and the child has come about. It is as if this coupling alone, in its violence, could bring the doubly divine name to the poet's lips, the name that the *puer* become *vir* bore from his birth. "Hermaphroditus" is only nameable, expressible, once the child is possessed *by* the difference between masculine and feminine, once he has entered into the double polarity of that difference, which the narrative, at its most violent moment, reasserts by inverting the power relations in the sex roles. It is the nymph who rapes the shepherd and forces him into a coitus, in which he loses his virility. It is only then that the poet remembers the name of his hero, a name that sealed his destiny, but that could be pronounced only when that destiny was fulfilled, *a name by deferred action.* The coupling with Salmacis reveals the difference between masculine and feminine, which was always present, but only in a virtual state. Only the reversal of characteristics and excess on both sides can bridge that irreparable gap: Salmacis, the woman, behaves like a male; the "heir of Atlas," the man, is treated like a woman. In acquiring a proper name in the poem at that instant, the *puer* becomes *vir*, but he does so only by losing his *virilitas*, only by having his masculinity "weakened," "tamed." Could "Hermaphroditus" be the name of that painful synthesis, of the difficult (impossible?) union of opposites, the name—neither true nor false—of the resolution of difference?

In this name that is finally declared, however, difference is clearly readable (*amborum nomen habens*). Moreover, the masculine ending *us* alters the name of the goddess of love, a name whose first letter, *A*, cuts off the final male "ending," the *es* of "Hermes," the name of the god of exchanges and transactions, making it feminine; "Hermes" enters "Aphrodite," but loses the *es*, and it is the *A* of Aphrodite that absorbs it by assimilating it into itself, by grafting itself onto it. (*Velut si quis conducta cortice ramos / Crescendo jungi.*) Finally, a last displacement affects the masculine-feminine proper name; it affects the poetic word itself, the only word to name the unspeakable in the unspeakable moment of "metamorphosis." That is, the *puer*, born, in the fourth line, of Mercury and the divine Cytherea, gets his name from both his father and his mother but, when he is finally named at the end of the poem, the Latin has become Greek, *Hermaphroditus* (and not *Mercura-venerus*). But it has become Greek *in Latin*. In this interminable oscillation of difference within difference itself, the *puissance* of the neuter—its power and its potential, its latency and its force—is revealed but never mastered.

Ovid's poem endlessly traces and uncovers what the proper name for the resolution of masculine and feminine discovers on its reverse side, that is, it traces and uncovers the unnameable work of difference, which is here called the "neuter." Hence, why is the Salmacis river *infamis* if not because its waters, through their contact, attack the very virility of the *vir* who bathes in it; if not because the perfectly transparent waves conserve the invisible memory, the inexorable trace of a strange coupling in the form of metamorphosis. Such is the memory of waters without sign or mark, *indifferent waters*, neither true nor false, waters that, however, have never ceased directing the young man's wandering like a magnet, orienting his course into the unknown: "*Videt hic stagnum lucentis ad imum / Usque solum lymphae.*" These motionless waters are so limpid in their density that surface and depth nullify each other at its edge: through these waters, the earth becomes air, or vice versa.

Hermaphroditus's lake is the "opposite" of Narcissus's lake, which relays a self-image to the gaze that is so perfect that the shepherd falls in love with the image as if it were someone else. Hermaphroditus's lake, in contrast, offers no appearance that could mislead desire; *living water, but null.* The poetic language can make this lake available to the gaze only by negating everything that might trouble or eliminate the crystal: "No swamps grew there, rank grasses, nor black weeds." This power of transparency, this calm and fascinating violence of a mirror that reflects nothing, together with the mysterious fountain of the poem, constitute the imaginary raw material for the neuter, for an absolute difference composed of the neutralization of all contraries, of all oppositions, and whose symbol is those utterly smooth waters, which are nevertheless memory through and through, waters without trace or mark of what happened earlier in them because they are, in their entirety, trace, mark, and sign, and thus also the power of impotence, the *virtus* of inadequacy, the *dunamis* of lack, the *fiasco* of totalization. In fact, what is this *semi-vir*, this half-man who is born as he emerges from the waves of the Salmacis? For his missing half does not make him a woman. And, yet, does not the shepherd in the woman's embrace, like the careless bather enveloped in the waters of impotence, feel himself becoming a half-woman, whose other, feminine half, is forever missing? And that half-femininity is not replaced by the half-masculinity left over in him. He will always live halfway between masculine and feminine; male yes, but in the fiasco of his impotence; feminine, certainly, but in the excess of her unsatisfied ardor, twice *neutralized* in the interval of difference. He will live as a man whose desire, unable to reach fulfillment, negates itself, and as a woman whose desire must remain at the painful height of nonsatisfaction. For, otherwise, how could the exact division of man and woman, masculine and feminine, come about in the son of Mercury and Venus, in order to compose the two terms, by means of addition, into heterogeneous halves? Ovid gives his attentive reader the formula for that strange arithmetic of the sexes, for the surprising calculation of difference: "*neutrumque et utrumque videntur.*" They seem to be neither one nor the other *and* both one and the other. The *neutrum* is added to the *utrumque*. The double negation of the poles of difference lies in their confrontation and their reciprocal metamorphosis: the power of the neuter, the "neither true nor false," which opens onto the abyss of a zero in the totalization of contraries where difference exhausts itself.

Masculine *vs.* feminine: *Vs.* (*versus*) is a sign or a trace. If *vs.* is a sign, it indicates the logical difference between contraries by which a determined semantic axis, that of sexuality, would find its meaning, the axis across which the myth of Hermaphroditus apparently traveled, between the masculine and the feminine pole. If *vs.* is a trace, it is the mark left behind by an operation of differentiating a totality, the trace of a gesture of cutting that separated the totality from itself, all the more so in that it allowed for the finality of the totality once more finding itself full and whole. As a result, the difference thus opened by the gesture of separation is nullified in the—originary or final—complementarity of contraries. In that case, the other is less the other than the complement of the one that, for its part, could not be the one without the other. In this, we may discover subtle variations of Aristophanes' narrative, which appears in Plato's *Banquet*. Masculine *vs.* feminine: *vs.*, the "retroactive" trace of an originary scission into man and woman, but also a "projective" index, a dotted line signaling a final union, man and woman, where the two become one flesh. There was scission; there will be union. Sexual union is thus the temporary re-union of contraries, the gauge of a final, immortal totality, but only a gauge. The division between masculine and feminine remains an original destiny; the beast with two backs evoked by Shakespeare is not like the ancient human beings in Aristophanes' story, the spherical being, masculine or feminine, self-sufficient, whose two backs are the same back, the back of the same; it is not even, like the androgyne of Aristophanes, *the being of one and the other* in the permanence of its completeness. It is, rather, the fortuitous and ephemeral moment of a union forever unmade and remade, which, in the cyclical play of time and development, corruption and death, genesis and birth, in short, in the bipolar play of sexuality, mimes the motionless and eternal sphere of Being. It is that sphere, which, in her prayer and *votum*, the nymph of the Ovidian myth wishes to constitute forever, but in real time: "Dear naughty boy, . . . to torture me; / But you won't get away. O gods in heaven, / Give me this blessing; clip him within my arms / Like this forever." The myth of Hermaphroditus narrates this imaginary bisexuality; and, yet, we have only to reread the wish of Salmacis, that violently male nymph acting against the too-feminine Hermaphroditus, to discover, in the language of the poem, the other side of bisexuality: the work of difference, the power of the neuter. Not "Make it, O Gods, that we are forever united in a single body," but "clip him within my arms / Like this forever." Such is the gesture of the neuter: The affirmation of union can be expressed only by negating the impossible desire for nondifference.

The neuter, then, is all in the gesture of cutting, but, in this instance, it is less that of a "sexion" of the bisexual totality of origin or the resolute scission of a fulfilled desire for finality than a double and unique act of nullifying the masculine *and* the feminine. Two gestures in a single stroke, which opens the double space—unfathomable, undefined, indeterminate, as Kant would say, of a nonmasculine and a nonfeminine, a nonmasculine that is not yet, that is already no longer the feminine, a nonfeminine that is not yet, that is already no longer the masculine. This is the inconceivable idea of a third gender that is not added to the other two, of a third gender that is not, properly speaking, a gender, since, on the flip side of a mythic androgyny or an ideal bisexuality, it makes possible categorical thinking in terms of gender, in terms of masculine and feminine. It makes possible a thinking about sexual difference and its poles in their complementarity.

The neuter gender—the "third" (non)gender—is, thus, at the limit, internal to the bisexual totality that the two genders, masculine and feminine, exhaust without remainder. It is in the place of the cut, the place of the double and mutual cutting into halves, but it is also outside the totality, outside sexuality. It is trans- or extrasexual, since the two halves, masculine and feminine, are instantaneously annihilated through the neuter, through its frightening power. To speak of a neuter gender would be once more to lose that power by stabilizing it in a negative concept. Apply to the neuter gender the power that this "gender" names: nongender. It is less a question of the quasi Hegelian moment of negativity in which "the nothing is incarnated and desire is fulfilled as the death of desire and the triumph over the death of desire,"[3] than the indeterminate opening of a polemical space of conflict that inexorably, repeatedly, surges forth between scission and totality, between the "sexion" of masculine *and* feminine and the union of the two halves: the space of infinity of the unnameable zero, of the "neither true nor false," on the condition that it be endlessly displaced onto the mechanisms of the representation of—sexual—difference. As he recounted the myth of Hermaphroditus in the *Metamorphoses*, Ovid was not a bad guide in that task.

End of the Road

25

Rue Traversière, no. 0

Rue Traversière has known some vicissitudes since 1672: First, in its name, which found its topographical appropriateness only in 1806, and then only on the condition that it function as a mere modifier (I like to detect in that identifying order a significant trait of the imperial administration); then, in its function; and, finally, and especially, in its use, if not in its trajectory. As Jacques Hillairet notes in the entry dedicated to it, for two centuries, the streets that were to become Rue Traversière led to the banks of the Seine, where barges brought produce and merchandise, timber in particular, destined for the constructions under way in the capital. That industrial finality has now been effaced; the loss of the ancient meaning has not found any compensation, has not acquired any new sense. A conversion into nothing: The Quai de la Rapée has become an urban highway traveled by wave upon wave of cars, and Boulevard Diderot, just as busy, interrupts Rue Traversière's course before it reaches the river. And, even if a pedestrian were to continue along it out of faithfulness to the past and to its memory, he would run up against iron grills that forbid all access to the metro lines, which, at this point, emerge from the ground, creating a new and insurmountable obstacle. One must resign oneself and accept the fact that the history of the city nullifies its own traces and contradicts the intentions of those who lived there. The conversion of Rue Traversière caused by urban development is a negative conversion: The street is henceforth without end, not because it is interminable—like Rue de Charenton in certain ways—but because the place of its end is, properly speaking, indeterminable. A conversion to nothing or, rather, a conversion of the street from its function to its name. Rue Traversière no longer crosses the city to meet the bank of the Seine and thus assure the hauling of wood for construction. It crosses for nothing, it crosses because it is called "cross," *traversière*; it does nothing but cross: a pure trajectory without beginning or end, an infinite (or gratuitous, indifferent) trajectory, without interest. The chance events of administrative decisions placed the medical-legal institute, the morgue, in a word, within view of the street, but beyond the Quai de la Rapée, Boulevard Diderot, and the metro and its iron grills, at the very edge of the river. The brick edifice, its windows covered with wire mesh, houses and refrigerates the corpses of suicides, murder victims, and the anonymous dead waiting to be recognized, waiting for names. The morgue signals the vanishing point of Rue Traversière, the sign of death, but from a place where the street-that-does-nothing-but-pass, a street that is passing away, does not go.

26

Echographies: The Crossings of a Conversion

In an inscription in the upper left-hand corner of Philippe de Champaigne's *Tolle lege*,[1] a little-known canvas by the Port-Royal painter, capital letters spell out the famous formula of Saint Augustine's conversion in a celestial ray of light. These letters, painted in yellow, seem to be on the point of effacing themselves, as if only their shadow were to remain visible to the beholder or the reader, as if the Augustinian painter of Port-Royal had found only this means to *show*, visually, the mystery of that resounding voice. Moreover, while the event of the "*tolle lege*" *here and now* is being spelled out in letters, only to be effaced in light, the Augustine depicted on the canvas, seated under a fig tree in the garden, has *already* taken the book of the apostle Paul, has *already* opened it. And, finally, the gesture of his open right hand, the thumb of his left hand inserted into the codex, his face, and his look all seem to suggest that he has *already* read.

In an engraving by Poilly on the frontispiece of Arnauld d'Andilly's translation of the *Confessions* in 1649, a cartouche takes the place of the epistles of Saint Paul; on it we read, "The Confessions of Saint Augustine." Or perhaps, in a striking instance of telescoping, this book is already the *Confessions*, the autobiographical narrative in which the scene is recounted.

That uncertainty about times and places, about the signs of writing and the images of beings (or, rather, that ineluctable transposition into the visible of what is listened to), and, at the same time, that necessary *permanence* of the instant of revelation in its representation, raise all the problems, and beyond them, the *aporias*, of the *narrative* of Augustine's conversion and those of life-writing in general: the bio-graphic.

Another detail of Champaigne's painting, not the least mysterious of all its aspects, also caught my eye. In looking closely, I read "LE LEGE TOLLE

LEGE." The frame has amputated the quotation: "TOLLE" has become "LE." In fact, it was this fortuitous repetition of LE LE that oriented my entire reading.

Saint Augustine's *Confessions* is a text in which the biographical narrative provides the woof and the invocation to "Lord God," the warp. But the narrative of self-identification is constituted and instituted in its narration only when it calls on a "you" who, in essence, knows this narrative even before its last utterance is written,[2] who promotes its narration even before its first utterance has been formulated, who stops its infinite, unfathomable reflexivity since the unattainable, direct object of the writing process and of its event "I write (that I write . . .) my life" is already there from the outset, total, entirely written, in the transcendence of the one who authorizes it.[3]

This "you," nonetheless, will never occupy the position of an "I." He will never speak—except, perhaps, one time. . . . Let us listen to that writing as it speaks: "Why do you mean so much to me? Help me to find words to explain [that is, so that I may manage to say who I am]. . . . Have pity on me and help me, O Lord my God. Tell me why you mean so much to me. *Whisper in my heart, I am here to save you.* Speak so that I may hear your words." Then I will be able to tell you what I am for you: the one to whom you have shown mercy. Then I will be able to tell you what you already know: how I *was*, what I *will be* (for you), what I *am* not and have always been. "I am here to save you." "*Dic animae meae: Salus tua ego sum.*"[4] God answers, or rather, Augustine answers in his place. He answers himself, but not by himself, rather, he responds to a double within him: "Whisper in my ear, I am here to save you." Let us read on: "*Whisper in my heart, I am here to save you.* Speak so that I may hear your words. My heart has ears ready to listen to you, Lord. Open them wide and *whisper in my heart*, I am here to save you." Augustine's writing in the text here and now is, no doubt, the only chance for that silence to manifest itself; it is the alienated sublation of the inaudibility of the voice. "I shall hear your voice and make haste to clasp myself to you." These desires for the future are triggered by that strange voice whose words "I am here to save you" were placed in God's mouth by Augustine. They immediately cease to be his own words and come back through God's mouth to the heart's ears, to Augustine. Augustine's words are strangled, made strange—strang(e)led—like a foreign voice in the process of effacing itself, the voice of someone who conceals himself in the opacity of a whisper: "Do not hide your face away from me."[5] The effaced voice brings the desire for the gaze into being, produces the possibly mortal gaze of the identification of the self as other: "I would gladly meet my death to see [your face]."[6] The "I" who is writing, and whose voice accompanies the gesture of tracing words, is thus, by that very gesture, the opening of a place, of a house, for example: "My soul is like a house . . . for you to enter [*Augusta est domus animae meae qui venias ad eam*]." And the voice circulates before or beyond the words that articulate them.[7]

In the text, the agent of the "montage" in writing is a figure that occupies the "unoccupable" place of the subject of the enunciation, a figure that represents the self's capacity for identification in its singular essence, in its truth, a truth that is never proper to it but in which the gaze returns to its own eye and in which the infinite reflexivity of autography is immobilized in death.

This figure is prosopopoeia (from *prosopon*, face, that which is before one's gaze; theater mask; grammatical person), the fabrication in language of a face that is the mask of an absence, the construction of the artifact, or rather, the simulacrum of a presence. It functions, essentially, by endowing the absent object with language:[8] language as the mark of absence, the mark of the absent one, of the dead one, of the supernatural being, but also as the mark of the presence of the artifact of writing through which the absent ones "return" to judge, accuse, seek revenge, or console.[9]

But, in the *Confessions*, the character, the *prosopon*, persona, or mask, shifts from a figure of enunciation to an enunciator, an independent, autonomous interlocutor.[10] It comes from the "outside," from the "other," and intervenes in discourse—between hallucination and free, indirect discourse.[11]

The text, in the place of its subject, will be affected by an originary and inaudible voice and will constitute itself as its echo, in the signs of language that this text inscribes.

> So, O Lord, all that I am is laid bare before you. I have declared how it profits me to confess to you. And I make my confession, not in words and sounds made by the tongue alone, but with the voice of my soul and in my thoughts which cry aloud to you. Your ear can hear them....
>
> And so my confession is made both silently in your sight, my God, and aloud as well, because even though my tongue utters no sound, my heart cries to you. For whatever good I may speak to men you have heard it before in my heart, and whatever good you hear in my heart, you have first spoken to me yourself.[12]

Thus, on the other side of the conversion fissure, Augustine sets in motion a set of oppositions and correspondences, between body and soul, seeing and listening, before and after, interior and exterior, words and voice, silence and noise, "you" and "myself"; he attempts to speak, to write, that is, to circumscribe with signs the place where the identification between the "I" and the "self" resonates in the conversion narrative.

The narrator announces the narration of a narrative. "*You have broken the chains that bound me.... I shall tell how it was that you broke them.*"[13] I shall tell—*narrabo*. This conversion is a narrative of break and liberation, a narrative whose actor, God, is posited by the narrator from the first sentence, less as the first addressee than as the witness, the spectator, or rather, the listener, a third

Echographies: The Crossings of a Conversion / 241

party or eavesdropper to an enunciation directed at "all who adore you, [who] will exclaim, 'Blessed be Lord in heaven and on earth. Great and wonderful is his name.'"[14] That is, it is directed at the Christian community of readers of the *Confessions*. This community, however, soon disappears from the text: Only the great transcendental ear remains on stage, the ear of the one who already knows the entire story because he was the sole protagonist and the stage director. The first frame of the narrative, then, consists in positioning both the addressees of the narrative and the witness to the enunciation. The second frame is a motionless painting, the self-portrait of Augustine, which takes shape in the opposition between certainty and will, speculative thought and the practice of life: "I did not ask for more certain proof of you [as incorruptible substance, life eternal], but only to be made more steadfast in you. But in my worldly life all was confusion, *omnia mutabant*."[15]

Then the narrative of conversion can begin and the story of a desire can be written. And, in that story, there is the irruption of an event, a break—a conversion? Hence, it is the story of a desire and the narrative of an event that destroys it and satisfies it.

In book 8, then, Augustine provides a schema for that event with the image of diverging paths within the Church itself: "I saw that the Church was full, yet its members each followed a different path in this world."[16] He situates himself precisely at the point of intersection. Everything he had done in the world had lost its appeal, "in comparison with your sweetness and *my love of the house where you dwell* [*iam enim me illa non delectabant prae dulcedine tua et decore domus tuae*]." He continues: "But I still held firm in the bonds of women's love." Such is the intersection, the crossing of two sources of delectation: the beauty of the divine house—we shall return to that house later—and the sweetness of woman. And it is in citing the Book, the Scriptures (Matthew 19:12), a verse presented as an unintelligible utterance, that Augustine articulates the event of the break as *self-castration*: "There are some *who have made themselves eunuchs for love of the kingdom of God.* . . . Let only those *take this in whose hearts are large enough for it.*"[17] Augustine writes that he *heard* this written and rewritten text, "*ex ore veritatis*," from the voice, the mouth of *Truth*, from the figure or the feminine prosopopoeia for the divine Word, for Jesus Christ.

Conversion is an event that cuts off continuity so meaning can come into being; the story is what fills the space and time that is thus cut off from the factual utterances. The event organizes the narrative; the story provides the facts destined to form a series of elements that receive their significance from the initial cut. The event articulates: It does not explain, but allows for intelligibility.[18] It is the starting point for comprehension but also its blind spot; it is not itself comprehended in the narrative that takes its sense from it, because it orients or grounds the successive sequences with an invisible and inexpressible finality or origin. To read book 8 of the *Confessions* is to recognize this blind point of conversion, both *terminus ad quem* and *terminus a quo*, around which, toward which, and from which all life-writing is constructed. And, through life-writing, the identification of the self is also constructed, but a self whose identity is forever lodged in the interval of that cut, in the opacity of that point, in the estrangement, the alteration of difference between self and self. Something must have happened—but what? Where to situate the "reality" of the event in the narrative we are reading? How to pinpoint, circumscribe as accurately as possible, the "something" that has happened? Augustine's narrative seems to be the staging of that something, that is, the construction, on and around this blind point, of a scene and its figures, to bring this something to meaning, to reflect it and make it understand *itself*.

The first sequence or first narrative is the visit to Simplicianus, "the spiritual father of Ambrose who was now a bishop. Ambrose truly loved him like a father, for it was through him that he had received your grace."[19] But the narrative of the visit to Simplicianus is only the "narrative" frame of an account that tells Augustine of the conversion of a famous rhetor of Rome, Victorinus. The point of articulation between the second narrative and the first is the "fact" that Augustine read the *Libri Platonicorum*, which Victorinus had translated: Victorinus "read the Holy Scriptures ... and made the most painstaking and careful story of all Christian literature."[20] Simplicianus's exemplary narrative of Victorinus's conversion is organized thematically around two axes: first, the transformation of the old Victorinus (*iste senex V.*) who defended the gods with a terrifying voice (*ore terricrepo*) into a child of Christ (*puer Christi tui*), an infant who cannot yet speak of Christ's font (*infans fontis tui*), who submitted his neck to the yoke of humility; and, second, the move from the secret, private, silent reading of the Scriptures to a public confession from a prominent place, the speaking out loud of certain sacred words learned by heart. The two axes, then, entail two oscillations: from the voice to silence, and from silence to the voice. Victorinus moves from the discourse of profane and pagan rhetoric to the muteness of Christian childhood, and from the silence of private reading to the open proclamation of faith.

The end of this first sequence is an ethical and philosophical meditation on the conflict between two wills and two laws. The dissociation of the personality Augustine has experienced is conceptualized in that way; the scission in the very identity of the self is formalized in the tension between the "self" and the "I," in the interval at work between time—and its synthesis into existence—and the position of the subject in the present moment of the free act.

Augustine takes stock of this painful quest for identity in the work of biography, that is, the troubling discovery of a transcendent synthesis of time in the empirical subject, by using the very figure of temporal difference: the figure of sleep, or more precisely, of the boundary line between waking and sleeping, the "edge" of sleep (Descartes recalls this figure at the end of his first Meditation).[21] "My thoughts, as I meditated upon you, were like the efforts of a man who tries to wake but cannot and sinks back into the depths of slumber."[22] On this borderline between waking and sleeping, the differance (with an a) of the self's identity and the impossibility for that self to occupy a place are both played out. In Augustine's text, voices provide the impetus for that strange figure of the limit between sleeping and waking. These voices or words are something like the verbal concretions of that borderline: *Verba lenta et somnolenta*, words in which it is easy to hear the echoes of a voice, *Modo, ecce modo, sine paululum*, a voice all the more inaudible in that it echoes in the soul of the sleeping man as he awakes to the words that "you, Lord" has addressed to him. "*Surge qui dormis et exsurge a mortuis et illuminabit te Christus.*"

The second sequence of the narrative of conversion is also an exemplary story of conversion: It is the narrative of the visit of a certain Ponticianus (*Ponticianus quidam*) to the small Milanese community—Nebridius, Alypius, and Augustine. During this visit, Ponticianus noticed a book on a game table that happened to be there; taking it up and opening it, he discovered (it was that of) the apostle Paul. "Then he smiled and looked at me and said how glad he was, and how surprised, to find this book, and no others, there before my eyes. He of course was a Christian."[23] "He began to tell us the story of Antony, the Egyptian monk, whose name was held in high honour." This second narrative (and the one that frames it) thus repeats the first sequence, the visit to Simplicianus, but at the same time, it transforms and displaces it.

It transforms the first narrative in that, this time, Augustine receives—he no longer knows why—the visit of Ponticianus, rather than formulating—by divine inspiration—the plan to visit Simplicianus. It displaces that narrative in that a book found by chance (picked up and opened), the book of Paul's epistles, and not a mere evocation of the name of the translator (Victorinus) of Plato's works, links the story of Antony the anchorite to the frame narrative.

That link is established almost fortuitously—"*Ortus est sermo, ipso narrante de Antonio*"—as if the story of Antony were there only to "ignite" the new narrative that is embedded in it, the story of the conversion proper. "Ponticianus continued to talk and we listened in silence. Eventually [*unde incidit*] he told us of the time when he and three of his companions were at Trêves. One afternoon, while the Emperor was watching the games in the circus, they went out to stroll in the gardens near the city walls."[24]

The third narrative emerges fortuitously from an adventitious anecdote but is connected by a very solid link to the second story, the story of Antony told by Ponticianus. It is precisely that same story, *but in a book*, the *codex in quo scripta erat vita Antonii*, which two of the four friends, who had, by chance, become separated from the others, found, by chance, in a house (*casam*) inhabited by "some servants of yours, men poor in spirit, to whom the kingdom of heaven belongs."[25]

Like Ponticianus a moment earlier (in the story Augustine tells of the visit by that same Ponticianus to Augustine and Alypius) and the book of the apostle Paul, the friend of Ponticianus opened the codex of the *Life of Saint Antony* and began to read: "All at once he was filled with the love of holiness. Angry with himself and full of remorse, he looked at his friend and said, 'What do we hope to gain by all the efforts we make? What are we looking for? . . . To be the Emperor's friends? Even so, surely our position would be precarious and exposed to much danger? We shall meet it at every turn, only to reach another danger which is greater still. And how long is it to be before we reach it? But if I wish, I can become the friend of God at this very moment.'"[26] That is the moment, the instant of conversion, told by Ponticianus and recounted again by Augustine. Let us reread the text: "*Quando istuc erit? Amicus autem Dei, si voluero, ecce nunc fio,*" or, literally, I will have wished it (future perfect), here now I have (become) it, I am it already. The present, the present instant of conversion, the *nunc* is already come at the very moment it is desired. It can appear in language, in discourse, only as the future-past instant, the tiny "hole" of the present where mortal birth comes about: "*Et turbidus parturitione novae vitae reddidit oculos paginis*" [He turned back to the book, labouring under the pain of the new life that was taking birth in him].[27] Everything has already happened, but it is as he reads the book, a biography of the holy man, as he skims over the signs on the pages, that the changes, resolutions, and metamorphoses are suddenly inscribed in time. The inexpressible moment when all time is condensed is deployed in the successive lines of signs that recount a past life, between two readings of the same book, two experiences of the same writings.[28] "*Narrabat haec Ponticianus*" [that was what Ponticianus told us].[29]

At this point, in an astonishing twisting of the time of the narration, Augustine *tells of his listening to the narrative of Ponticianus,* which he has just recounted and *written*; but he *writes an entirely different story, that of the echo of the narrative voice of Ponticianus,* itself the echo of his own voice, its reverberations and the traces of that reverberation, the written signs of his confession. He writes his own narrative as echography, the echography that precedes any birth, as it should.[30] And, yet (and this is not the least strange characteristic of that revelation of narration in reception), the narrative also tells of the metamorphosis of the "echo" into the "image": Listening to the voice as it is written and recounted becomes looking at a face, as if the catacoustical effect of the narrative voice consisted in transforming the "oral-aural" encounter between Augustine and that "other," that *Ponticianus quidam,* into an "optical-visual" encounter between Augustine and himself. Echo has been transformed into Narcissus, and, in Augustine's narrative, the agent of this reversal is none other than the "you" ("*Tu autem domine*"), whose structural, constitutive importance in life-writing in general we have already noted.

Here again, we must read the text closely to recognize the strangeness in this reversal: "*Tu autem Domine, inter verba ejus . . .*": I would go so far as to translate this phrase as "in the interval between the words of Ponticianus." ". . . *retorquebas me ad me ipsum*" [you were turning me around to look at myself], "*auferens me a dorso meo ubi me posueram dum nollem me adtendere et constituebas me ante famiem meam ut viderem quam turpis essem, quam distortus et sordidus, maculosus et ulcerosus* [for I had placed myself behind my own back, refusing to see myself. You were setting me before my own eyes so that I could see how sordid I was, how deformed and squalid, how tainted with ulcers and sores]."[31] Face to face with horror. The Narcissus of the pagan myth is not only the metamorphosis of Echo; he has himself been metamorphosed into a monster—the monster Augustine evokes a few lines later, speaking of the mysterious gap between will and power ("*Unde hoc monstrum? Et quare istuc?*" [Where did this prodigious monster come from? And why?]). "I saw it all and stood aghast, but there was no place that I could escape from myself."[32] In one sentence, Augustine describes the metamorphosis of the "echogram" into a "videogram," through an acoustical-optical reverberation of the great "you," the addressee-witness-observer of the narrative: "If I tried to turn my eyes away [*si conabar a me avertere aspectum*], they fell on Ponticianus, still telling his tale [*narrabat ille quod narrabat*] and in this way, you brought me face to face with myself once more [*inpigebat me in oculos meos*], forcing me upon my own sight."[33] Thus, we understand why, when Ponticianus stops speaking and goes home, the "you" also withdraws, and Augustine remains caught in the identificatory encounter between "I" and "myself"—*anima mea*—a silent and mortal encounter with otherness itself, *with Medusa*.[34] "*Remanserat muta trepidatio et quasi mortem reformidabat restringi a fluxu consuetudinis quo tabescbat in mortem* [It (*anima mea*) feared the stanching of the flow of habit, by which it was wasting away to death]."[35] The figure of the self, "*anima mea*," moves very close to the unoccupable place of the subject "ego," but only in order to situate the mortal difference between "I" and "myself": "It [*anima mea*] remained silent and afraid."[36]

In that tense difference of fascination and horror, in the retreat of the "you" from the text where the narrative of an "I" constituting itself into a "self" is written, let us now place the third sequence of Augustine's conversion, his "own" conversion, in which the "I" attempts the inexpressible declension, in the same place and at the same moment, of the cogito of "my" birth and "my" death.

The writing of this narrative oscillates in two different intervals, an interval of time and an interval of space. In time, first of all: On the one hand, Augustine attempts to formulate, in words, in the present moment of writing, the meaning of the states of his soul. Augustine writes of the conversation he had "today" with Alypius: "What is the matter with us? . . . These men have not had our schooling, yet they stand up and storm the gates of heaven, etc." But, on the other hand, he immediately belies the "today" and proceeds to describe the "body" of the voice. He underscores the fact that these were not the words he pronounced *at the time*: He proffered words, no doubt, but their "meaning" lay beyond them, or rather, meaning did not even reach them. The words were a mere senselessness of face and voice:

> I said something to this effect and then my feelings proved too strong [*aestus*] for me. I broke off and turned away, leaving him to gaze at me speechless and astonished [*attonitus*, as if thunderstruck, stunned, petrified, *médusé*]. For my voice sounded strange [*neque enim solita sonabam*, I vibrated with strange, inhabitual sounds] and the expression of my face and eyes, my flushed cheeks, and the pitch of my voice [*modus vocis*] told him more of the state of my mind [*animum meum*] than the actual words that I spoke.[37]

Hence, an interval of time exists between words that articulate speech and the voice—both stunned and petrifying—as a corporeal thing.

In addition to this interval of time, *in which* the narrative is written, an interval *that* the narrative writes, there is a second interval, an interval of space, an interval between two places. It is added to the first interval, or, more precisely, it intersects it in writing, in language, in the discursive "image," to the point, it seems to me, of becoming its figure, and perhaps more than its figure: its figural projection into "real" space, its figural potentiality, its figurability. That interval opens between *the house and the garden*: "My inner self was a house divided against itself [*interioris domus meae*]. In the heat of the fierce conflict which I had stirred up [*fortiter excitaveram*] against my soul [*anima mea*] in our common abode [*cubiculo nostro*], my heart, I turned upon Alypius."[38] And, a few lines later, to describe and, as it were, take stock of the opposite movement, that of tearing himself away from Alypius, Augustine posits and sets out a second scene, a second place, the garden (*hortulus*), a little garden that is part of the *hospitium nostrum*, the home where "we" had been welcomed and lodged, our place of rest. The garden was the property of the *dominus domus*, the master of the house, but his guests used it, as they did the whole house, *tota domus*, the house where the master did not live. Augustine is driven "by the tumult in my breast to take refuge in this garden where no one could interrupt that fierce struggle, in which I was my own contestant, until it came to its conclusion. What the conclusion was to be you knew, O Lord, but I did not [*donec exiret qua tu sciebas, ego autem non*]."[39] Although the *dominus* of the house does not live in it, "you dominate." "You" returns in the text that the "I" is writing, but returns, precisely, only as the one who knows the outcome, the egress, the place through which Augustine will leave the place where he has thrown himself: the little garden of the *hospitium*, uninhabited by the master of the place, the master of the dwelling. For the "you" knows the outcome of Augustine's fierce struggle with himself—the struggle between the "self" and the "I." Yet, did not Augustine himself figure that conflict, a conflict that bears his name, as the tension between two places, the *cubiculum* (room) and the *domus* (house), between "my" heart and "my" soul? He figured the tension in the difference between "I" and "myself," which is also the difference in gender between *cors meus* and *anima mea*, masculine and feminine—the woman from whom he must pull away, from whom he must decide to tear himself away.

Two intervals, then, between the language of words and the body of the voice, and between the house and the garden. But, in some sense, the second is the figurability of the first. In that double interval, "you" designates the unfathomable otherness that links the "I" and the "self" in a relation of identification *and* brings about the transcendent synthesis of time in the conjunction of "my" birth and "my" death.

Once more, let us read the text carefully: "What the conclusion was to be you knew, O Lord, but I did not. Meanwhile I was beside myself with madness that would bring me sanity. I was dying a death that would bring me life. I knew the evil that was in me, but the good that was soon to be born in me I did not know [*Moriebar vitaliter, gnarus quid mali essem et ignarus qui boni, paululum, futurus essem*]."[40] This sentence resonates in anticipation, like the echoes already evoked: "*Whisper in my heart, I am here to save you.*" Who, me? And which me?

"So I went out into the garden and Alypius followed at my heels. His presence was no intrusion on my solitude.... We sat down as far as possible from the house.... I was frantic, overcome by violent anger with myself for not accepting your will.... Yet in my bones I knew that this was what I ought to do. In my heart of hearts I praised it to the skies. And to reach this goal I needed no chariot or ship. *I need not even walk as far as I had come from the house to the place where we sat.*"[41] The conversion, that instant of presence that separates so slightly (*paululum*) the *quid mali essem* from the *quid boni futurus essem* is, in some sense, the motionless displacement, the intensification on the spot of the voice into articulated words. The displacement from the house to the garden is the necessarily "empirical" expression in space of that motionless movement. It is more than its figure, it is its figurability; it is more than the imaginary projection, it is the transcendental schematization, to use Kant's formula, which alone allows it to be inserted into space and time.[42]

Two great discourses stand as the monumental proscenium arch of this narrative of the intensification of presence in the present: on one side, the "mystery" of the scission that lies within the will and the return of the Manichees, and, on the other, the scenography of that scission and the "play" of figures that makes possible the narration of conversion. Augustine posits two protagonists, the sick, tortured "I" who twists and turns in his chains, and "you," the Lord who "in your stern mercy . . . lashed me with the double scourge of fear and shame."[43] This violent relation between "I" and "you" is soon displaced onto a double interval, in language and time on one hand, and in the movement of the body on the other. But the second is quite obviously a figure *in space* for the echoing play of the first:

> In my heart I kept saying, "Let it be now, let it be now!" [*Ecce modo fiat, modo fiat*], and merely by saying this I was on the point of making the resolution. I was on the point of making it, but I did not succeed. Yet I did not fall back into my old state. I stood on the brink of resolution, waiting to take fresh breath. I tried again and came a little nearer to my goal, and then a little nearer still, so that I could almost reach out and grasp it. But I did not reach it. I could not reach out to it or grasp it, because I held back from the step by which I should die to death and become alive to life.[44]

All the elements of this episode are played out in the instant itself: the textual scenography that distances two protagonists, "I" and "you," and attaches them by the strongest link; the echoing words *modo fiat, modo fiat*; the movements of the body and its goal; death and life; desire rising toward the *jouissance* of fulfillment and its differance (with an a). This *punctum temporis quo aliud futurus eram* is the instant when the "I" is on the point of becoming something else, the *punctum temporis* of conversion, an instant that is "defined" as the simultaneous fascination of attraction and horror. Or, to be more precise, this extreme—ever more extreme—proximity of the instant, this presence of the imminence of the occurrence, is an aversion of horror, a distancing, a turning away.

The result of these two opposing movements, the minute approach and the infinite horror, is in some sense a negative attraction, a motionless displacement, an intensification on the spot but in the manner of a negative charge: *quanto proprius admovebatur*. And the approach is also appropriation through approximation: *tanto ampliorem incutiebat horrorem* (the more it approached, the more it appropriated, and the more it appropriated, the more it struck with even greater horror, spread even greater fear). *Sed non recutiebat retro nec avertabat sed suspendebat* (but it did not turn around or turn away, but remained in suspense). The present time, the present presence of the present, is attraction and horror: It is an intensity of "negative" time, the abyssal vertigo of a suspension of time.

This is textual scenography, but it is also a staging of voices and discourse, new displacements and new metamorphoses of the echo and the image, for example, in the famous prosopopoeia of the *antiquae amicae meae* and of "Lady Continence." But, in reducing that passage to a *coup* of the master rhetorician, to a mere figurative strategy or stylistic skillfulness, we would run the risk of losing what the writing is attempting to *make heard* in the signs that inscribe the biographic, namely, the transcendental experience of time and language—

the experience of the "Other" in the identificatory ordeal between the "I" and the "self." In fact, the staging of what Augustine has just described as the constitutive interval, gap, or distance of the present, or of presence as otherness, no doubt begins with the confrontation between the "vanities of vanities" and "Continence." And that confrontation, no doubt, sets the stage for the narrative of the event of the break, the syncope, the interruption, and recovery, where the autobiographical text will try—impossibly—to ground itself.

The writing itself—on its surface and in the arrangement of its visual and auditory signifiers—announces the syncope of the life narrative, the syncope called *conversion*. It seems, in fact, that the *nugae nugarum*, the *vanitates vanitatum, antiquae amicae meae* intervene to bring Augustine back to an earlier moment, the scene of listening to the narrative of Ponticianus. That narrative, we recall, had led him from behind his own back where "I" had placed himself, so as not to see his own face. His lady friends "plucked at my garment of flesh and whispered [*submurmurabant*], 'Are you going to dismiss us? From this moment we shall never be with you again, for ever and ever. From this moment you will never again be allowed to do this thing or that, for evermore.'"[45] Something emerges here as we listen to the written text: It is not yet a rhetorical figure, but it is something more than a hallucination. It is the "properly" phantasmic moment of the voice "from behind," a voice that is foreign, other, yet that comes from oneself, from one's own body, but from that part of "my" body that "I" do not see and will never see. It comes from a place where, in these echoes from behind "me," the inexpressible neuter speaks: "*Hoc . . . illud*," this thing or that.

"But . . . I had turned my eyes elsewhere, and while I stood trembling at the barrier, on the other side I could see *Casta Dignitas Continentiae*, the chaste beauty of Continence."[46] *From behind* comes the whisper, the murmuring of the *voices* of the neuter, the inexpressible, the invisible; *facing him* is the image, the almost abstract, allegorical *icon* of Continence; *from behind*, the persistence of the faceless or unfigurable; *facing*, the prosopopoeia of the Mother, "*fecunda Mater filiorum gaudiorum.*" "She smiled at me to give me courage [*horatoria*], as though she were saying, 'Can you not do what these men and these women do?'" [*Tu non poteris quod isti, quod istae?*][47] The discourse of the allegory of Continence is a quasi discourse. Augustine writes it to create a stronger effect through the icon, an image lesson. This discourse is an *iconology*. As a result, Continence has "nothing" more to do with the *antiquae amicae meae*. They no longer belong to the same world, the same field, the same plane, even though Augustine's dramatic writing brings them together. But their confrontation, their *controversia in corde meo* is, in some sense, the transformation of the great tableau of Ponticianus's narrative, the story of his two friends' "conversion": It replicates the anchoritism they assume in reading the "biography" of Antony the hermit. The echo of that narrative in the soul and heart of Augustine has become the intolerable encounter between the "I" of desire and the "self" of aversion, through the "you" as power of reverberation.

Here, the encounter is between the "I" and an *ideal, maternal image* of the "self." The "I" is already potentially one of the *pueri* or *puellae* who rush into her circle; the *voice of woman* has taken refuge in the position that the self occupied and from which the narrative of Ponticianus had drawn it—from behind itself—as an almost inaudible, invisible whisper.

The curtain can now rise on the last moment of the narrative. First, all the images born from the depths of the self are effaced in the violence of the voices of a storm: "A great storm [*procella ingens*] broke within me, bringing with it a great deluge of tears [*ferens ingentem imbrem lacrimarum*]."[48] To let the voices of that storm [*vocibus suis*] have free rein, Augustine leaves Alypius and seeks out solitude in the garden, in the most remote part of the garden. This displacement within a single place is again marked by a voice, one of the voices of the storm: "*Nescio quid . . . dixeram in quo apparebat sonus voci meae iam fletu gravidus* [I suppose I had said something and he had known from the sound of my voice that I was ready to burst into tears]."[49] In the most remote part of the garden, there is a fig tree;[50] lying under it, Augustine is overwhelmed by the voices of the storm: "*Domine usquequo? Usquequo, domine?* [O Lord, when? When, Lord?]." But these voices spoke "not in these very words but in this strain," as an echo. "*Quamdiu, quamdiu, cras et cras? Quare non modo? Quare non hac hora finis turpitudinis meae?* [How long shall I go on saying 'tomorrow, tomorrow'? Why not now? Why not make an end of my ugly sins at this moment?]"[51] Augustine lets these echoing voices, or these echoes of voices, be heard in his writing, in its signs, indicating to the reader that these are, in fact, the voices the reader must hear. These voices lie beneath the written words, beneath or prior to the articulations of speech and writing, yet they produce the sense of these words.

At that point, from farther away, a voice reaches this most remote place outside the house deserted by its master. It comes from another, neighboring house, enters the solitude of the garden, and reaches the fig tree (and recall that it was under a fig tree that the son of God, the king of Israel, had seen Nathanael before Philip even called him),[52] the tree where, a moment earlier, Augustine had thrown himself down. Or, rather, the pitiful voices (*voces miserabiles*) that had risen up in the tears of the storm *return as a voice*, a voice that is the echo of those echoing voices, of these echoes of voices, a voice that is itself twice repetition. From the nearby house, "I heard the sing-song voice of a child. . . . Whether it was the voice of a boy or a girl I cannot say, but again and again it repeated the refrain 'Take it and read, take it and read.'" *Tolle lege, tolle lege*.[53] Not only is "take it and read" repeated twice (as Augustine writes it), but, at the center of each of the "phrases," there is an echo: "Tol(le le)ge," "lele." This voice echoes in a space before sexual difference—boy or girl?—and before musical genre—ritornello or song? And that strange, senseless stuttering within the words "*tolle lege*" fills up the instant of suspended time, fills it as *presence, but also as repetition*, a repetition of the "le" at the end and the beginning, the repetition of words as well, and, hence, opens a minuscule gap between le/le.[54] And that gap may be the response from "you, Lord" in the *Confessions*, the only response in the text, in the place of the book, where "you" is already inscribed in the words addressed to him.

And, in fact, for Augustine, that echo of a voice, of his own voice, refers to the book of the apostle Paul. He reads the Book *in silence*, without voice, reads the first chapter where his eyes happen to fall, a chapter that tells him in black and white, in the silence of writing and reading, of the advent of the "self" in the "I," an identification as the Other itself: "Not . . . not . . . not . . . but arm yourselves with the Lord Jesus Christ" (Romans 14:1).

After the "*Tolle lege! Tolle lege!*" Augustine's face changed in an instant (*statim*). This metamorphosis was the result of the face-to-face encounter with the monster and with Lady Continence: a strange, other face (*mutato vulut*). After reading the Epistle to the Romans 13, instantly (*statim*), as the last words of the sentence *echoed* in his heart, the *image* of "the light of confidence flooded into my heart and all the darkness of doubt [of differance with an a] was dispelled."[55] *Statim*, in an instant: *between* the unfathomable fissure of the present, now and always, between two letters, "le," between two voices, "le," lies the syncope of the event of conversion,[56] and, with it, the interminable work of life-writing.

This study owes a great deal to the following fundamental works: Gilles Deleuze, *Logique du sens* (Paris: Minuit, 1969), and, in particular, series 27, 217ff.; series 30, 235ff., and series 32, 261ff.; Philippe Lacoue-Labarthe, *Le sujet de la philosophie* (Paris: Aubier Flammarion, 1979), and, in particular, "L'écho du sujet," 217ff.; Arthur Darby Nock, *Conversion: The Old and the New in Religion from Alexander the Great to Augustine of Hippo* (Oxford, 1933), in particular, 254ff.; Jean-Marie Le Blond, *Les conversions d'Augustin* (Paris: Aubier 1950); Henri Irenée Marrou, *Saint Augustin et la fin de la culture antique* (Paris: Boccard, 1958).

27

The Place of the Point? Pascal

In proposing the somewhat enigmatic and redundant expression "The Place of the Point? Pascal" for the title and subject of this study, I have confined myself to extracting two terms from Pascal's texts that appear quite often, and to linking them, in the form of a question, in a relation of belonging. Sometimes, these two terms are almost identical in their use; sometimes, they are opposed to each other; and sometimes, one is included within the other. A curious relation, then, between the place and the point: sometimes inclusion, sometimes exclusion, sometimes identity, sometimes difference. In Pascal himself, the two terms can be understood *either literally*, as categories relating to space from the field of perception or geometry, *or figuratively*, as designations for terms or objects of discourse. The discourse of space and the space of discourse: Such are the two fields of study to be articulated by these two terms, the place and the point.

The only possible starting point for any discourse on Pascal's *Pensées* is to ask what we are speaking about when we speak of Pascal's *Pensées*. Of a book, naturally, a book titled some ten years after the death of its "author": *Pensées de M. Pascal sur la religion et quelques autres sujets* [Thoughts of Mr. Pascal on religion and some other subjects]. But it was never written as a book: It is, rather, the place for an open series of points. The first publishers indicated one dense point, religion, in the midst of a cloud of others, "some other subjects." A book, then, but which one? For there have been as many books under that title—books that differ from one another in their composition, their beginning, and their end—as there have been readings. And that situation continues today. There are as many places of discourses, with similar and different points arranged in different ways, as there are paths constructed from these points: notes discovered, cut, recopied, attached, cut out, and rearranged by successive readers. This book is a series of texts, the plural place of multiple readings, a book that generates an order of places to fit the itineraries that traverse it.

Who has ever read Pascal by beginning with *pensée* 1 and ending with 991? Who has ever managed to distinguish between the thoughts and the notes for the *Pensées* and the thoughts and notes for other projects? Here is a text that is constituted only through its reading, a book that is only the constructed and transitory state of a reading: To be precise, it is a plural place as the multiple arrangement of points.

Pensées is a strange work, neither completed nor yet to be completed. That is, it is made of fragments, pieces detached and isolated from the whole, as Littré says, but detached in such a way that each piece stands for the whole. It is as if each fragment and each series of fragments tended, through reading, to move toward the place where they would all come together again, as if somewhere, at the origin or the end, a proper place existed where they would all be gathered together, an originary book or a book to come of which these are the pieces or the raw material. It is as if these fragments were nostalgic for a lost totality or tempted toward a final totality, as if there were a power of the fragment resulting from a book's representation effect. The flip side of this power, however, is a kind of work of fragmentation, the effect of a force that incessantly displaces the totality, destroys it.

THE HOLE AND THE NEEDLE PRICK

The first two definitions for the entry "point" in the Littré dictionary are "a biting pain" and "the tiny hole made in a piece of fabric by a needle." It is only after these two definitions that "point" is defined as "what one conceives as the smallest part of extension." Thus, I would like to begin my itinerary of Pascalian places with a fragment on the hole and one on the prick—a hole of memory and the prick of a needle—two fragments in which there is a biting pain to Pascal's writing. From them, I will pull out the threads of my reading and seek out the place of the point.

Here is the first fragment: "As I write down my thought it sometimes escapes me, but that reminds me of my weakness, which I am always forgetting, and teaches me as much as my forgotten thought, for I care only about knowing that I am nothing."[1] And here is its variant in counterpoint: "Thoughts come at random, and go at random. No device for holding on to them or for having them. A thought has escaped: I was trying to write it down: I write in the place where it escaped me [*j'écris au lieu qu'elle m'est échappée*]."[2]

And the second fragment: "Justice and truth are two points [*pointes*] so fine that our instruments are too blunt to touch them exactly. If they do make contact, they blunt the point and press all round on the false rather than the true."[3]

The first fragment—theme and counterpoint—targets the writing of the very *pensée* in which we seize, at this point, in an instant, a syncope of writing. In the theme, we perceive how, in the fortuitous flight of what was to be written, in the moment and instant it was forgotten, the opportunity is seized for a representation of memory. Born of forgetfulness, it is the representation of an essential forgetfulness that constitutes the subject, a representation of its lack as well. *A contrario*, if I had not been affected by that accident of forgetting, if I had written what I wanted to write, I would have forgotten that I had forgotten my weakness. When I forget *my* thought, then my wish—to think and to know the self, that is, my nothingness—is fulfilled. In the counterpoint, chance is in the foreground: Forgetting and memory are only random accidents. It is no longer even *my* thought, *my pensée*; "my thought" is disappropriated and pluralized, becoming thoughts in general. Only the lawless coming and going of these fleeting thoughts is noted, events of thought that appear and disappear in a repeated *fort/da* that is no one's game and no one's art. It is neither an art of thought nor an art of memory, it neither appropriates nor conserves. There is only one diverse and lacunar thought process whose thoughts are the instantaneous effects of a force called chance, randomness. But what escapes self-presence is already occupied by what I write. *J'écris au lieu qu'elle m'est échappée* can mean either, "I write, in place of the escaped thought, the fact that it has escaped me," or "I write even though it escaped me." In the first case, the written utterance of the situation of enunciation replaces the escaped utterance and plugs the hole opened on the page. In the second, I write rather than not writing, I write as a supplement to a blank: For example, I write the first thought offered me by chance. In the theme, the accident transformed into opportunity is marked by the self-reflexivity of the subject of representation, as nothingness and as knowledge of that nothingness; in the counterpoint, in contrast, the writing of the accident, presented both as replacement for and supplement to this nothingness, is itself an accident. The reflexivity of the subject is an *event* at the very moment when writing occurs. There is no art to conserve or acquire, not even the philosophical art of the philosopher-subject as nothingness and knowledge of his own nothingness.

What, then, is the *place* of the subject? I introduce this question with the term "place" [*lieu*], which, throughout my reading, slips back and forth between noun, adverb, and preposition. And, in this place of the subject that writes—this place which is a memory lapse, a hole, where thoughts come and go—there is a point, the prick of a needle, or, rather, two. "Justice and truth are two points" so sharp, so fine, that we feel them rather than see them, so fine that our instruments—for example, the tips of our pens—are too blunt to touch them exactly, too crude to coincide with the other point. In fact, how could it coincide, since there are two points to touch? A few lines earlier Pascal had written, "our own interest is another wonderful instrument for agreeably poking out our eyes."[4] The point of our instrument is also double, but, while one marks the paper, puts a hole in it even, the point at the opposite end blinds us in pleasure. A blinding pen on one side, the side of the eye, and a groping pen on the other, the side of the writing hand, which may well manage, by chance—"thoughts come at random, and go at random"—to touch the two points of truth and justice. But then it crushes them, blunts them, and instead of a rigorous point of contact, a truthful thought, an exact practice of justice, it produces an ink blot on the paper. Instead of the double—theoretical and practical—point, there is a surface, a place where the two points are certainly somewhere, but where? From the blinded eye to the groping hand, the two tips of the pen press all about, and more on the false and unjust than on the true and just. The true and the just are certainly somewhere in the middle of this area, somewhere within the boundaries of that surface, but we will never write or think of them except under the circumstances of that double point, which we will seize only by blunting its double point to fit our ever blunted tip, in a coincidence that "comprehends" the point of truth and the point of justice, but that conceals them in the circumstances, the places, that surround them.

The question—at least, the question I would like to ask—is thus the following: What is there to say about the place of the philosophical subject, of the theoretical and practical subject, of the subject of knowledge and of action, in the fragmented writings of the *Pensées*? And what is there to say about the point of truth and justice in these writings? Can these points be determined in this place of the subject, can they be determined in all their subtlety? Can this place that envelops them come to coincide with the points and, thus, constitute itself as a subject of truth and justice, a subject of true knowledge and just acts?

THE INDIVISIBLE POINT
THE VANISHING POINT IN THE PLACE OF THE PAINTING

> If we are too young our judgement is impaired, just as it is if we are too old.
> Thinking too little about things or thinking too much both make us obstinate and fanatical.
> If we look at our work immediately after completing it, we are still too involved; if too long afterwards, we cannot pick up the thread again.
> It is like looking at pictures which are too near or too far away. There is just one indivisible point which is the right place.
> Others are too near, too far, too high, or too low. In painting the rules of perspective fix it, but who will fix it when it comes to truth and morality?[5]

This *pensée* consists in three observations: a comparison, an assertion developed and exemplified by way of comparison, and a question in conclusion. Of the three initial, entirely empirical observations, we might note that judgment, in general, as a true and just act of thought, is indiscernible from its concrete circumstances. Judgment is the effect of circumstances, or it produces those circumstances as its effects; the result is the confusion of judgment and circumstances. When is the act of thinking my own? When is it my judgment, since it is indiscernible from its circumstances? In the middle of this *pensée*, this thought in action, this judgment, there appears a topological model which consists in conceiving of a notion, a being, a term, in terms of its edges, its circumstances, the particular things in its proximity. Thus, the *pensée* asks what a "metrics" of judgment might be. How can the circumstances, the space between, be measured as a middle or mean, the happy middle, the golden mean; how can it be measured as a point, that is, as my place? How can the place of true and just judgment, the point where truth, justice, and thought coincide, be disentangled from the local circumstances that envelop it? "Limited in every respect, we find this intermediate state between two extremes reflected in all our faculties. . . . Too much noise deafens us, too much light dazzles; when we are too far or too close we cannot see properly; an argument is obscured by being too long or too short. . . . Extremes are as if they did not exist for us nor we for them; they escape us or we escape them."[6] Granted, you will say, let us confine ourselves within the limits of a prosaic and small wisdom about all human knowledge: "Once that is clearly understood, I think that each of us can stay quietly in the state in which nature has placed him,"[7] close to the limits of that narrow place. Such is the wisdom of Epicurus, according to Lucretius and Michel Serres: "The wisest man lives in that minimal gap, that space between very little and zero, the angle between the plumb line and the incline. The place of necessity and nature. . . . Everything comes back to calculating the limit, evaluating limits. Being satisfied with limitations. Building one's nest in the vicinity of the inchoate, a little garden full of figs. . . . The soul is calm in these odd places that contain no great distances. . . . It clings to the slope, it does not venture toward the ever-expanding spirals. It inhabits borderline places, odd spaces."[8]

Therein lies happiness, no doubt, and all man's unhappiness lies in not knowing (or not having known) how to stay quietly in a room, and not even in a little garden. And, if he does not (or did not) know how, it is because he cannot (or could not) do it: "Since all things are both caused or causing, assisted and assisting, mediate and immediate, providing mutual support in a chain linking together naturally and imperceptibly the most distant and different things, I consider it as impossible to know the parts without knowing the whole as to know the whole without knowing the individual parts."[9] This calculation of the exact limit, this evaluation of limits, is impossible: "We are floating in a medium of vast extent, always drifting uncertainly, blown to and fro."[10] The little garden of knowledge, of confined spaces, the practice set up just right are endlessly open to the infinite dimensions of the universe. "This is our natural state and yet the state most contrary to our inclinations."[11] The abyss is already inside the enclosure. This place is infinitely open: I cannot live in the tiny angle between the plumb line and the incline, since, however acute the angle, it stretches to the very end, and I cannot cling to the slope, stay at this one point, without dropping off in an endless fall.

That is Pascal's notion of judgment, as opposed to mind, reasoning based on principles and consequences: To judge is to apprehend the thing in its discrete and subtle elements, to sense what makes that thing singular and unique, to discern its difference, the ultimate principle that constitutes its difference. The thing lies before everyone's eyes, in its singular truth: There is no need to strain ourselves or turn our heads trying to see it. Its truth is the "last" point that makes it discernible from any other, the "end point" of its analysis: "It is only a question of good sight, but it must be good; for the principles are so intricate and numerous that it is almost impossible not to miss some. Now the omission of one principle can lead to error."[12] This thing called "thought" is made up of the infinity of its parts, its principles, an infinity that makes it *one*; and thinking *about* the thing means imagining the infinity of the circumstances that make it unique. Michel Serres posits the garden of Epicurus, the little fig garden; Pascal responds with the garden of Desargues, a garden of ripening grapes, in Condrieu, near Lyon. "We first distinguish grapes from among fruits, then muscat grapes, then those from Condrieu, then from Desargues, then the particular graft. Is that all? Has it ever produced two bunches alike, and has any bunch produced two grapes alike?"[13] If Michel Serres in the garden of Epicurus and Pascal in the garden of Desargues do not confine themselves to silently eating the figs or the muscat grapes, if they speak and write, then Pascal will tell Serres: "I have never judged anything in exactly the same way. I cannot judge a work while doing it. I must do as painters do and stand back, but not too far."[14] "How far, then?" Serres will ask. The question requires the calculation of limits, the evaluation of limits, the exact position of the point in this place. "How far then? Guess,"[15] Pascal will respond.

"I must do as painters do. . . . It is like looking at pictures which are too near or too far away. There is just one indivisible point which is the right place." If we are too far away or too near, our eyes do not recognize what the painting represents. At what distance from the painting must we stand for that recognition to take place? The question requires a rigorous response, one that will allow us to determine exactly the point of the eye in the place of contemplation, the theoretical viewpoint from which the painting is to be judged, the place of the point of truth. But what authorizes me to ask the question of theory and truth in a rigorous way and to respond exactly to it? The artifact, the work of painting, that is, an artifice, a fiction. A theoretical fiction authorizes me to pose the question of theory in a theoretical way, and to respond to that question truthfully, at the point of truth.

This viewpoint for the eye of truth is an indivisible point:

When we know better, we understand that, since nature has engraved her own image and that of her author on all things [engraved it, I would add, with a point so sharp and subtle that our instruments are too blunt to touch it exactly], they almost all share her double infinity. Thus we see that all the sciences are infinite in the range of their researches, for who can doubt that mathematics, for instance, has an infinity of infinities of propositions to expound? They are infinite also in the multiplicity and subtlety of their principles, for anyone can see that those which are supposed to be ultimate do not stand by themselves, but depend on others, which depend on others again, and thus never allow of any finality. But we treat as ultimate those which seem so to our reason, as in material things we call a point indivisible when our senses can perceive nothing beyond it, although by its nature it is infinitely divisible.[16]

The indivisible point is the point of truth in the place of the fiction, but it is also the place of the fiction of truth: its figure. Just as the primitive terms of the mathematical mind indicated the mind's natural incapacity to found an order of science that would be absolutely complete, the indivisible point marks the natural incapacity of our gaze, the limits to perception. But, from the viewpoint, we make one last point—a "vanishing" point, a point of annihilation—one last point, which we call an indivisible point. We make a name or, rather, a name makes for us what our gaze cannot make. The "indivisible point" is a powerful linguistic artifact. It performs in language what the painter-mathematician produces on the surface of the painting with the tip of his brush, in the depth of the illusory place of the painting-representation: a vanishing point. A name produces a reality, the reality of a nothingness of singular space, even though this space is infinitely divisible by its very nature. In producing reality, this performative name artificially shows the informed mind that there is a lack in its perception or conception. The name designates, within the informed man's faculties, the fluid but uncrossable limit of reason's capacity to understand; it indicates the limitations in the ability of the senses to grasp. It produces reality, but it also indicates finiteness. Finally, and all these expressions intersect, this name envelops infinity, as Pascal writes at another point. This name covers and surrounds it, comprehends and dissimulates it: It constitutes the circumstances for infinity.

The viewpoint is the theoretical place of the painted artifact's truth; the vanishing point is the place from which the illusion of depth is constructed on the surface of the painting. These two points come together in the instrumental name "indivisible point," a point between these two points, a point designed to touch the point of truth exactly. And, in that point, a figure takes shape that fictionalizes truth. It is the figure of a place where the theoretical subject coincides with the point; or, more precisely, the viewpoint and vanishing point that perspective assigns in painting is the figure that fabricates the fiction of an indivisible point in material things, a point that is only a performative name that produces reality, that indicates finiteness and that forms the circumstances surrounding infinity. It is a fiction to the second power, which truly reveals the fiction of the place of the subject and of the point of truth. In assigning this point in the art of painting, perspective institutes it at the vanishing point, as the place of the fiction of truth (of the painting). It marks the viewpoint as the place from which the gaze judges exactly what it represents; it summons the viewer's eye to the truthful discourse that names the images of things whose originals are not even worth naming. In this double point, at the place of this quasi coincidence, discourse and truth, words and reality, exchange places in the fiction, the artifacts of both language and image. This fixed, fictive place is the place of words that seize the figures of their truth and justice and that, in the effects they articulate, produce the illusion of the enunciation of the cause of those effects.

Is this the last word? No, the last word is yet to come, and it is a question. "But who will fix it when it comes to truth and morality?"[17] Who will fix that indivisible point—the true place in the art of painting—in true truth, in just justice, in that other place that is not the place of representation, in ordinary life where the principles are before everyone's eyes, where truth and justice are present, where there is no need to turn one's head or strain oneself to perceive them, but where one must have clear and penetrating vision to discern them? Is there some mechanism, some model or artifact comparable to perspective, between the projective geometry of the disciple of Desargues and painting, the art of vanity, which would allow us to fix the point where the eye is totally discerning and singularly differential? There is no response, since the fragment ends on that question. And, yet, in the question itself, a term fixes and marks a sense, a direction for response. The question is "who?" not "what?" There is not a schema, a model, a mechanism, but, rather, "someone," *a* someone we might say, an undefined, singular, unique, incomparable entity. This someone is signaled in the question itself, this someone for whom there is no definition or which any definition would obscure. This someone is a primitive term, such as that at the ultimate foundation of mathematics. However, I do not find the name of this someone in ordinary language, as space, time, motion, or number. Nor can I make this someone an "indivisible point" in material things to be perceived. This someone summons truth and justice to signify what they are through the mark he places on things in their place. He is not the subject of theory in the place of theory, but he fixes the point in its place.

Who *will* fix it? The question points neither to the present of the theoretical artifact nor to that of an enunciation of names and judgments; rather, the question points to the future gesture of fixing the point of truth and justice in that place by this someone who, perhaps here and now, has the power to make the mark, the sign. And, in counterpart, we find this fragment: "This is not the home of truth; it wanders unrecognized among men. God has covered it with a veil that keeps it from being recognized.... The place is open to blasphemy.... The issues [are] so clouded that people cannot distinguish between them."[18]

The Fixed Point

THE FIXED POINT, OR THE HARBOR
IN THE PLACE OF THE SHORE

So much for space. But there is also motion: The indivisible point is transformed into the fixed point. "Those who lead disorderly lives tell those who are normal that it is they who deviate from nature, and think they are following nature themselves; just as those who are on board ship think that the people on shore are moving away. The language is the same on all sides: we need a fixed point to judge it. The harbour is the judge of those aboard ship, but where are we going to find a harbour in morals?"[19] Here again, it is a matter of judgment and circumstances. But the question is part of a confrontation in a polemical dialogue that has a particular characteristic: The utterances that constitute it are all the same. "I am normal, I am following nature." The utterance I make to determine my correct position of enunciation is the same as that of my interlocutor. But I deny him the right to utter it, and he does the same to me. The language is the same on all sides. Hence, those who are aboard ship believe that those who are on shore are moving away, and vice versa. "We need a fixed point to judge it." How to decide between the two interlocutors, those aboard ship and those on shore who see each other retreating and disappearing in an infinite retreat? We must take a third position that is really, truly at rest as the fixed point of judgment for both parties, a shared point of arbitration: the place of the judge who pronounces justice and right. Or the place of the Cartesian mathematician who, in an arbitrary gesture, traces the axes of the coordinates determining the (fixed) point in relation to which a body can be said to be in motion. The arbitrariness of the voluntary act of mathematical reason corresponds to no true judgment, no just arbitration. It is merely a shared, popular belief, the utterance of a custom, which those who are at rest on shore formulate: "The ship is moving away toward the high seas." Those aboard ship may very well say that the shore is retreating, disappearing on the horizon; but the harbor, that shelter and haven of peace, judges that those "working toward uncertainty" have set out for the seas. Those who claim the contrary are mad or daydreaming. They exclude themselves from the common sense, the popular meanings of the community that we share when we speak to one another. "When we do not know the truth about something, it is a good thing that there should be some common error on which men's minds can fix, as, for example, the attribution to the moon of changes of seasons, progress of disease, etc. For man's chief malady is restless curiosity about things he cannot know."[20] And yet "nothing stops the volubility of our minds."

The indivisible point was that fiction of language that expressed our incapacity to perceive anything in the natural universe except in the art of figures and representations; the fixed point, in contrast, is that error—and even more paradoxical—that shared wandering (when everything moves equally, when language is the same on all sides, nothing moves in appearance, and all direct their thoughts toward the same object), a shared wandering that arrests the interminable movement of knowledge, the movement of appropriation and possession of a cause that might be the definitive reason for things. The pragmatic-practical validity of the shared error resides not in the fact that it is an error, but in the fact that it is shared. This discovery is attributed to Salomon de Tultie, whose manner of writing, like that of Epictetus and Montaigne "is the commonest, which is most persuasive, stays longest in the memory and is most often quoted, because it consists entirely of thoughts deriving from everyday conversations. For instance, when people speak of the commonly received error that the moon is the cause of everything, they never fail to say that Salomon de Tultie says that, when we do not know the truth about something, it is a good thing that there should be some common error... (which is the thought on the other side)."[21] Granted, but where will we find a harbor for morality? And who is Salomon de Tultie? And what is that thought on the other side? Where is that mysterious harbor? What is that strange thought on the other side? Who is that enigmatic author?

"*Cause and effect.* One must have a thought in the back of one's mind and judge everything by it, but go on talking like the people":[22] Such is the cunning of the cunning man. Such is the position of Salomon de Tultie, a cunning man who judges everything in terms of a thought in the back of his mind, and, yet, who speaks like the people: Yes, the moon is the cause of everything; yes, one must honor gentlemen; yes, that happens through figure and motion.... Might that be the point, then? And might that position be the place of the point, of the judgment of truth and justice? But who can fail to notice that the cunning position is cunning only because of its duplicity. It is split between utterance and enunciation: The place of discourse is the same as that of the people, a shared wandering; and yet, there is a different judgment at a distance from it. The point (of judgment) is at a distance from the place (of discourse). What is the distance between the place and the point? A question of measurement: By what yardstick should we measure it? "Guess," responds the cunning man.

But let us listen first, and once more, to the mathematician, who must know his way around the point after all. Yet, the mathematician hesitates, oscillates in an astonishing way (because he is also subtle) between the one and the zero. For the point is not one: It is a nothing, an indivisible point without space; a fixed point without motion; a zero point without number; a point-instant without time. *Un point n'est point*: The adverb "*point*," according to Littré, reinforces the negation "*ne*." A point is not one, it is nothing, that is, it is both relative and transcendent to the continuity of magnitudes. The point is the nothing that is relative and transcendent to the order of magnitude, in general, to its motion, whose miraculous property is its double infinity, a double motion toward everything and nothing, which amounts to the same thing. Every magnitude, magnitude in general, is directed in its infinite motion toward a terminus, an end, a point, but that terminus is transcendent to the motion aimed at reaching it.[23] The point is not one, it is nothing, a zero, and this nothing is precisely the infinite gap between one and zero.

The point is both the "terminus" of magnitude and the "nothing" of magnitude, it is of a different order; or it is the place of conjunction between magnitude and direction, a paradoxical articulation since it is an infinite disjunction, the uncrossable cut in the order of magnitudes (of bodies, of exteriority). And all the indivisible or fixed points are only figures for this point, of which one can speak only in figures, models, comparisons, displacements, metaphors. The point is thus the place in mathematics where the leap is made from mathematics to what surpasses it,[24] the place in mathematics where mathematics is found to be a remainder in relation to another order which I, in turn, for lack of a better word, call *sens* [both direction and sense].

I return to the cunning man, to his position between the place of his discourse and the point of his judgment, between what he says, which is just what the people say, and the thought in the back of his mind by which he judges everything.

To be cunning is, in the first place, to be disposed, apt to act, expeditious, lively and alert, ready to act in an instant. Only secondarily does the term connote knowing and being capable of applying one's knowledge to situations. Cunning, then, is feeling, the kernel of judgment, as opposed to reason. "Reason acts slowly, looking so often at so many principles, which must always be present, that it is constantly nodding or straying because all its principles are not present. Feeling does not act like that, but acts instantly, and is always ready to act."[25] The cunning man is an agile man, with a greatness of spirit, like the man who, infinitely agile, passes in an instant at infinite speed through the entire space between extremes. The effect is that produced by a glowing ember, the illusion—there again—of a continuous and unmoving line linking one extreme to the other with a motionless mark.[26] In that sense, the infinite distance between the point of the thought in the back of one's mind and the place of the shared utterance produces the effect of an infinite proximity between them, a quasi identity of the point and the place, a quasi coincidence.

The cunning position of the agile, cunning man, between the point and the place in an instant, is that of an utterance whose enunciation is infinite. There is no true, fixed, indivisible point, no true, totalizing, and instantaneous position: All these points, all these totalities are figures for the same fiction because the order of magnitude is spurred by the same movement, the same continuous flow of everything toward nothing and of nothing toward everything, never able to find repose in the nothing or the all. There is no other reason than the arbitrariness or the custom of shared wandering for positing, here or there, the indivisible, the fixed, the instant, the zero. Such is the essential discovery of Salomon de Tultie: "They never fail to say that Salomon de Tultie says that, when we do not know the truth about something, it is a good thing that there should be some common error . . . (which is the thought on the other side)." To utter ad infinitum that there is no fixed point is to posit that utterance at the point of the all or nothing, to take the leap beyond the order of magnitude to an order that is foreign to it: The thinking of infinity at the point of infinity has the effect of making any true fixed, totalizing, indivisible position indeterminate. In itself, the thinking of the infinite at the point of infinity is stripped of all determinate content: it does not think itself as content. Even though the cunning man thinks, whatever his thought may be, it is immediately dissolved, made indeterminate by its position of enunciation. He cannot maintain a discourse on his own enunciation. Even as he speaks, like everyone else (like the people), about fixed points, indivisibility, or totality, the cunning man does not adhere to them, is not fixed by them. The indivisible or fixed "point," on the one hand, and the thinking of infinity at the point of infinity, on the other, mark the dissolution of any place of theoretical or practical truth. It is both the place of the event of meaning in knowledge and the impossibility of expressing that meaning as such in a discourse dedicated to it. Meaning withdraws infinitely from its discourse.

THE DYNAMIC POINT IN ITS PLACE OF WORK

Perspective fixes the indivisible point of the theoretical eye in painting, the figure and name for a divisibility that is by nature infinite, the fixed point where the mind stops in a shared error, even though it is animated by a forever troubled wandering. Such are the utterances from the mind of the cunning man; such is the destructive mind in endless motion, which is never in the place of what it utters; such is the mind that oscillates rhythmically in a continual reversal between pro and contra. Such is the mocking spirit that speaks like the people but judges everything by a thought in the back of his mind, a thought at the infinite point of infinity, a point that, in his discourse, can be only the "all-nothing." His thoughts are never anything but effects momentarily and haphazardly distributed throughout the field of thought. The cunning man is the infinite spirit of irony that dissolves every place of rest for thought. Thus, to make a mockery of philosophy is true philosophy. The dynamic point in the place of its work of destruction, the cause of its effects, is the simultaneous conjunction and disjunction of force and direction. Such is the thought in the back of the mind.

Let us try to understand the fantastic power of that figure. For, in the end, if that thought is *in the back of* my mind [*derrière ma tête*, literally, behind my head—trans.], that means that I will never see it through reflection, through the activity of seeing-into-my-thoughts. It is a thought I do not see and cannot see as one of my thoughts, as my thought, a thought that is always at the back of my mind, that is never mine as my property. It is an attribute of my being that surges up *a tergo* and takes hold of me. And, if that thought is a back thought, always at my back, it is not merely a matter of turning my head to grasp it: It is useless to turn around and strain myself. It is a thought toward which there is no possible conversion, like the thought that inaugurates the discovery of the principles of mathematics.[27] It will always be unperceived; and, yet, I am pushed, set in motion by that thought, a strangely secret force. My judgment is the effect of that force, and my thought, the place of its manifestation in the place of my discourse when I speak like the people.

Infinitely close to both force and *sens*, and, for that very reason, extremely far away from both, the sharp and subtle point of justice makes itself felt. The bundle of fragments entitled "Causes and Effects" bears the subtitle "Sound Opinions of the People": opinions of the people, utterances of shared beliefs. And it is not by chance that most of the fragments grouped into that bundle pose the question of morality and politics, of justice and force. Causes and effects: One must judge everything by the thought in the back of one's mind, and yet one must speak like the people. "*Cause and effect*. It is then true that everyone is the victim of illusion, because the people's opinions are sound without being intellectually so, for they believe truth to be where it is not. The truth certainly lies in their opinions [place], but not at the point where they believe it to be. It is true that we should honour the gentry but not because gentle birth is a real advantage."[28] The discourse of political belief is one of the many discourses of belief, but it is also ordinary discourse itself at the conjunction-disjunction of force and *sens*; the discourse of belief is constituted through the reflection of forces in language. It is the discourse of the effects of forces, and beliefs are the representation effects of forces. Signs of beliefs are not representations of signifieds but representatives of forces that can only be grasped in their representation effects. A belief is force delegated into signs, and is, thus, itself a reflected force, a sign effect that is itself force.

In speaking, the people do not know what they are saying, and yet they are speaking the truth. Not knowing where sense lies, even though they know that the utterance makes sense, none can know the cause of the effect called "honoring the gentry." Thus, when the cunning man says, "It is true that we should honour the gentry" even while refusing to place the cause for it at the fictional point where the people place it in their own minds, he repeats what the people say and, like them, fixes wandering sense in a shared error. But, in determining the point of truth, a determination that would transform the truth of the universal illusion into the justice of a particular prescription, the discourse of the cunning man designates negatively the place of that effect of force, "but not because gentle birth is a real advantage." Where is the point of justice, the dynamic point, the reason for the effect of force, for the belief? It is not in the representation, in the descriptive statement of a quality, birth. It is elsewhere, but where? The discourse of the cunning man is not an exception to the thesis of universal illusion: His back thought merely takes any determination of the point of truth and sets it to wandering in his discourse.

Nonetheless, indeterminable sense is the inverse, in discourse, of the absolute determination of the de facto political order, force. The dynamic point is the infinite conjunction-disjunction of force and sense, of force and justice. The question of justice is inseparable from that of force. Ethics is inseparable from politics, precisely in that ethics is the force of justice and politics is the justice of force: Ethics is fortified justice; politics, justified force. Politics is ethics in reverse. Justice is annihilated force, the zero of force, or force making the leap into sense. Outside the order of magnitude and external actions, justice would be, in and of itself, force. Politics reverses this leap. It is force that seizes hold of language, signs, sense; a violence that was mute now begins to speak, to convert itself into sense outside its order, an order that represents itself through signs, in order to say that justice is unjust and that it itself is just.[29] The strongest, because he is the strongest, does things with words. He produces a felicitous performative whose situation of enunciation makes it felicitous since it is not possible to contradict him without exposing oneself to the absolute threat: "Justice is unjust, I am just, that is true or I will kill you." The discourse of the strongest who says that he is himself true and just, is the discourse of power; ethics has become politics. There is no morality, there is only politics. And the cunning man says, like the people, "We should honour the gentry." He says it because it is true and just, and he provides the sign for it: He uncovers his head (puts himself out) before a passing duke. "I am supposed not to honour a man dressed in brocade and attended by seven or eight lackeys. Why! He will have me thrashed if I do not bow to him. His clothes represent power."[30] Strange reversal.

To paraphrase: "This is not the figure of justice, for justice wanders unrecognized among men.... [This place is open to the discourse of power....] That is the source of the injustice of so-called just revolts that rise up against force." Such is the discourse of the cunning man in its infinite irony: a just judgment from the back thought, the thinking of the infinite at the point of infinity. And his thought is the effect of that thinking.

The Anagram of the Name in the Place of the Proper Name

Who is Salomon de Tultie, the cunning man?

To repeat: "But who will fix [the indivisible point] when it comes to truth and morality?" Who will set us to rest at a fixed point, a harbor, in morality? The cunning man, but who is the cunning man? How can we recognize him since he speaks like everyone else, with no external difference. "They never fail to say that Salomon de Tultie says that, when we do not know the truth about something, it is a good thing that there should be some common error... (which is the thought on the other side)." Who is Salomon de Tultie? His style "is the commonest... [the] most persuasive, stays longest in the memory and is most often quoted, because it consists entirely of thoughts deriving from everyday conversations." His style is like that of Epictetus and Montaigne.... We name him, quote him, keep him in our memories, but who is he? Perhaps you will be able to guess it from this *name* that occupies the entire space between the too close, the infinitely close, and the too far away, the infinitely distant.... Perhaps you will be able to guess it from this play of letters comparable to those you have already seen: the people's *sound* [*saines*] opinions, the people's *vain* [*vaines*] opinions; those on the *shore* [*bord*] who retreat, those in the *harbor* [*port*] who judge.... It is a play of letters, an anagram: Salomon de Tultie, Louis de Montalte—you remember, the man who, it is said, wrote letters to the provinces on the morality and politics of the Jesuit Fathers. Salomon de Tultie, Louis de Montalte, and also Amos Dettonville, that mathematician who wrote to MM. de Carcavi and Huyghens with the first elements of a calculation of infinity. Pseudonyms for a mathematician, but what sort of mathematics was he practicing? Pseudonyms for a moralist, but what kind of morality? Pascal himself, you will say. No doubt, but his name is effaced under the two pseudonyms, exhausting itself in that anagram where the two false names, their letters combined and written in a different order and a different way, suggest one final name, "as in material things we call a point indivisible when our senses can perceive nothing beyond it, although by its nature it is infinitely divisible." And what can we read in that final name into which the author, the writer, the subject in his proper name, in his true and just name, has disappeared? I read two names: Solomon, the proper name of a king, like *Louis*, a king of wisdom; and *(s)tultitia*, a common noun for nonsense, madness, like *Amos* the prophet. Epictetus is the wise Stoic; Montaigne, the Pyrrhonian philosopher; Salomon de Tultie, who dominates both of them, is the wise fool, the prophet-king of charity, a charity that is madness, whose name articulates within itself the three orders of magnitude. It articulates the magnitude of bodies, as king: of minds, as sage; and of charity, as a wisdom that is madness, a madness that is wisdom. "Our religion is wise and foolish: wise, because it is the most learned and most strongly based on miracles, prophecies, etc., foolish, because it is not all this which makes people belong to it. This is a good enough reason for condemning those who do not belong, but not for making those who do belong believe. What makes them believe is the Cross. *Lest the Cross of Christ should be made of none effect.*"[31] The order of truth and justice, the order of the heart and charity, appears in his discourse in a play of letters between proper name and common noun, between pseudonym and anagram. "I will write down my thoughts as they come and in a perhaps not aimless confusion . . . [and] will always show my aim."[32] Such is the infinite aim at the point of infinity, the thought in the back of the mind. And Salomon de Tultie shows us that point, in the place of his thoughts and even in his name: a double point, wisdom and folly, the cross of Jesus Christ, whose place he designates, for he is seized and moved by it. The subject of the discourse and the manner of writing, through the effacement of the proper name, become figures for that place.

The Last Imperceptible Point, or, Two Points in One Place

Here, then, is the last point (in my own essay as well): the indivisible point whose place is the vanity of the painted picture; the fixed point whose place is the shared wandering of everyone; the dynamic point whose place is the strange reversal of force and justice; here, then, is the last point, the indeterminable point that places the discourse of the cunning man in motion, the back thought from which he judges all things, the imperceptible point in its place of all or nothing, the point where everything is decided.

And, as a result, at that altitude and that depth of grace, everything is played out, not in the infinite gap between one and zero, but in the infinitely infinite tension between one and two. For there is one point and there are two, just as, in the anagrammed name of the cunning man, there were two names and even twice two names.

In a fragment that the editor Lafuma situates among the introductory bundles, we find: "They blaspheme against what they do not know. The Christian religion consists of two points, which it is equally important for man to know and equally dangerous not to know; and it is equally merciful of God to have given signs of both."[33] They blaspheme against what they know nothing about "because . . . God does not manifest himself to men as obviously as he might."[34] And he continues: "[The Christian religion] teaches men then these two truths alike: that there is a God, of whom men are capable, and that there is a corruption in nature which makes them unworthy. It is of equal importance for men to know each of these points."[35] And, here, contained in a phrase, is the intolerable tension between one and two: "Let us go on to examine the order of the world, and see whether all things do not tend to establish the two main tenets of this religion: Jesus Christ is the object of all things, the centre towards which all things tend. Whoever knows him knows the reason for everything."[36] Just as it is the anagram for the two false names of the mathematician and the polemicist-moralist, Salomon de Tultie is the secret anagram for Jesus Christ: the central point, the point-object and aim of the universal tension of all things, Theo-logos. "Theology is a science, but at the same time how many sciences?"[37] All sciences are enveloped in the name of theology. "I beg your pardon, sir," says Pascal to M. de Saci, "for getting so carried away by theology instead of remaining in philosophy, which was my sole subject; but that subject led me little by little into theology and it is difficult not to enter into it, whatever truth one is dealing with, because it is the center of all truths, as it appears perfectly in this case, since it so visibly contains all those that are found in these opinions."[38] Theology is the place of transit of all the truths of philosophy and the central point where they converge. And, in the end, all the truths of philosophy are two in number, two thoughts that have been proffered by the companions in writing of Salomon de Tultie, Epictetus and Montaigne: "Both possessed enlightenment about man, but one, knowing nothing of his own powerlessness, was lost in presumption, and the other, knowing only powerlessness, slipped into cowardice."[39] Could the total, totalizing philosophy consist in bringing them together, reconciling them, as one might consider bringing force and justice together? "But there would result from their assemblage only a war and general destruction, for, since one establishes the greatness of man, and the other his weakness, they destroy truth as well as each other's errors. For these wise men of the world placed two contraries in a single subject: for one attributed greatness to nature and the other weakness to that same nature, which could not hold together."[40] If the two truths of Epictetus and Montaigne can enter the single place of theology, it is only through their difference, their opposition: Montaigne in relation to Epictetus, Epictetus in relation to Montaigne. The truth of the Gospel reconciles these contraries "by an entirely divine art that consists in placing contraries in different subjects, all that is weak belonging to nature and all that is powerful belonging to grace."[41] As a result, man, the *single* subject of a *double* philosophical, anthropological discourse, finds himself in the *single* place of theology, a place that is divided in *two*. Or, more precisely, he is that place, the place of the gap between nature and grace: two opposed "subjects" whose difference makes man *himself* the infinitely infinite difference between divine greatness and human weakness. "That is the astonishing and new union that God alone could teach and that he alone could make," but "which is only image and effect of the ineffable union of two natures in the same person of a Man-God"[42] whose name is double, Jesus Christ: 1-2-1-2-1-2.

It is that rhythm and the place of its scansion that we would need to explore: the place between anthropology and theology; between the shared figures of discourse and of holy history and the proper name of truth and justice; between the fragments of the Pascalian text and the plan for the apologia of the Christian religion.

Let us merely say this to conclude: The two points of philosophical anthropology named "Epictetus" and "Montaigne" were needed to project the space of a place, the place of theology, onto another plane. That place defines its infinity only through the gap between the two writers, their opposition, their reciprocal destruction.

And, in the center of the place, in the middle, the *mi-lieu*, of that space, there lies a single point, nameable in discourse and named in history, a singular person who, in his name, his being, and his existence, is the distance between extremes and their union. He is difference itself, infinity, that is, in-difference: "Just as Jesus Christ has remained unknown among men, his truth remains among the shared opinions without difference to the outside.... Everything duplicated and the same names remaining."[43] Thus, God hid in all things and uncovered himself in all things: "When he had to appear, God still hid himself by covering himself in humanity.... And finally, when he wanted to fulfill the promise and remain among men until his second coming, he chose to remain in the strangest and most obscure secret place he could be: the Eucharist, which is without difference to the outside of common bread."[44]

Thus, paradoxically, the in-difference of the point and the place makes all the difference between the point and the place.

Thus, posing the question of the place of the point in Pascal may have been impertinent.

I do not admire the excess of a virtue like courage unless I see at the same time an excess of the opposite virtue, as in Epaminondas, who possessed extreme courage and extreme kindness. Otherwise it is not rising to the heights but falling down. We show greatness, not by being at one extreme, but by touching both at once and occupying all the space in between.

But perhaps it is only a sudden flash of the soul from one extreme to the other; perhaps greatness only ever lies in a single point, as in a glowing ember. Maybe, but at least that shows how agile the soul is, even if it does not show its range. (Pascal, *Pensées*)

Notes

♦

CHAPTER 1. RUE TRAVERSIÈRE

1. Jacques Hillairet, *Le XIIe arrondissement et son histoire* (Paris: Minuit, "Terrasse de Gutenberg," 1972). [Unless otherwise noted, quoted passages are my translation. Trans.]
2. Ibid.
3. Michel de Certeau, *The Practice of Everyday Life*, trans. Steven Rendall (Berkeley, Los Angeles, and London: University of California Press, 1988), 117.
4. Ibid.
5. Ibid.
6. Blaise Pascal, *Pensées*, trans. A. J. Krailsheimer (New York and London: Penguin Books, 1966), 37.
7. Friedrich Nietzsche, *The Birth of Tragedy*, trans. Walter Kaufmann (New York: Random House, 1967), 27.

CHAPTER 2. A SELVEDGE OF READING

1. Charles Perrault, *Histoires, ou Contes du temps passé* (Paris: C. Bargin, 1697), with frontispiece engraved by Clouzier and colored by hand, and vignettes engraved in smooth cut (original edition); *Contes de Perrault* (Paris: G. Rouger, Classiques Garnier, 1974).
2. Jacques Barchilon, *Perrault's Tales of Mother Goose: The Dedication Manuscript of 1695 Reproduced in Collotype Facsimile with Introduction and Critical Text*, 2 vols. (New York: Pierpoint Morgan Library, 1956).
3. Jacques Barchilon and Marc Soriano, "Beauty and the Beast, from Myth to Fairy Tale," *Psychoanalysis and Psychoanalytic Review* 46 (1960).

CHAPTER 3. PUNCTUATION

1. Pascal, *Pensées*, 53 [translation modified].

CHAPTER 5. JOURNEYS TO UTOPIA

1. Sir Thomas More, *Utopia*, trans. Paul Turner (Middlesex: Penguin Books, 1987), 38.
2. Ibid., my emphasis.
3. Ibid.
4. Ibid., 39.
5. Ibid.

CHAPTER 6. ARCHIPELAGO

1. Homer, *The Odyssey*, trans. Robert Fitzgerald (Garden City, NJ: Anchor Books, 1963), 3.
2. René Descartes, fifth Meditation, in *Discourse on the Method and Meditations* (New York and Middlesex: Penguin Classics, 1968).
3. Jules Verne, *The Mysterious Island* (New York: Charles Scribner's Sons, 1918), 452.
4. Jean Racine, *Andromaque*, act 3, scene 4, ll. 877–80.
5. Daniel Defoe, *Robinson Crusoe* (New York and London: W. W. Norton, 1975), 138–9, my emphasis.
6. Ibid., 39, 43.
7. Verne, *The Mysterious Island*, 53.
8. Descartes, *Discourse on the Method*, 46.
9. Ibid., 47.
10. Defoe, *Robinson Crusoe*, 43.
11. Verne, *The Mysterious Island*, 60.
12. Pascal, *Pensées*, 90–3.
13. More, *Utopia*, 69.
14. Defoe, *Robinson Crusoe*, 116.
15. Ibid., 188, Defoe's emphasis.
16. Ibid., 208.
17. Ibid., 116.
18. Ibid., 44.
19. Ibid., 45.
20. Ibid., 47.
21. Ibid., 47–8.
22. Ibid., 61–2.
23. Ibid., 78.
24. Ibid., 79–80.
25. Ibid., 86.
26. Jean-Jacques Rousseau, *Rêveries du promeneur solitaire*, in *Oeuvres complètes* (Paris: Pléiade, 1959), 1:1040–4.
27. Daniel Defoe, "Serious Reflections During the Life and Surprising Adventures of Robinson Crusoe," partly reprinted in *Robinson Crusoe* as "Serious Observations," 263.
28. Descartes, *Discourse on the Method*, 53.
29. Ibid., 53–4.

CHAPTER 7. JULIE'S GARDEN

1. Pascal, *Pensées*, 65.
2. On the tradition or topos of the garden, beginning with the Homeric landscape (for example, *Odyssey* 9.132ff., 7.112, or 5.63), all the useful examples can be found in Ernest Robert Curtius, *European Literature and the Latin Middle Ages*, trans. Willard R. Trask (New York: Pantheon Books, Bollingen Series 36, 1953), 183–202.
3. Francis Bacon, *The Works of Francis Bacon*, ed. James Spedding, Robert Leslie Ellis, and Douglas Denon Heath (Boston: Houghton Mifflin, 1872), 12:235.
4. Ibid., 235–6.
5. Ibid., 237.

CHAPTER 9. REVERIES: UTOPIAN PRACTICE AND FICTION

1. Jean-Jacques Rousseau, *The Social Contract and The Discourse on the Origin of Inequality*, ed. Lester G. Crocker (New York: Simon and Schuster, Pocket Books, 1967), 168–9 [translation slightly modified].
2. Jean-Jacques Rousseau, *Rousseau juge de Jean-Jacques*, in *Oeuvres complètes*, 1:668–72.
3. Jean Starobinski, *La transparence et l'obstacle* (Paris: Plon, 1957), 293.
4. Ibid., 294.

CHAPTER 11. THE RIGHT CHOICE AS REMAINDER

1. [The three terms in Marin's analysis are *porter* (carrying), *transporter* (transporting or hauling), and *rapporter* (fetching, in the economic sense). Hence, the last two terms are derived from the first as particular instances or methods of the action *porter*. Trans.]
2. An allusion to a song that can be read as the link between love and death for Jeanne and Nicolas, whose ass carries both:

    Adieu, cruel Jeanne; / If you love me not, / I'll get on my asss / And gallop to my death. /—Run, do not falter, Nicolas; / And above all, don't come back.

CHAPTER 12. THE LIAR

1. Descartes, *Meditations*, 110, my emphasis.
2. Pascal, *Pensées*, 245.

CHAPTER 13. GYGES

1. Herodotus, *The Histories*, trans. Aubrey de Sélincourt (London and New York: Penguin Books, 1954), 44.
2. Ibid.
3. Ibid. [translation modified].
4. Plato, *Protagoras*, rev. ed., trans. C. C. W. Taylor (Oxford: Clarendon, 1991), 14 (322c) [translation slightly modified].
5. Herodotus, *Histories*, 44.
6. Ibid.
7. Ibid., 44–5.
8. Ibid., 45.
9. Ibid., 46.
10. Ibid., 45.
11. Ibid.
12. Ibid.

CHAPTER 14. THE SUBLIME, THE OBSCENE

1. *Journal de la santé du Roi Louis XIV de l'année 1647 à l'année 1711*, notes compiled by d'Aquin (Seine-et-Oise: Société des Sciences Morales, 1862), entries for the years 1673 and 1680, 117, 135.

CHAPTER 15. THE CAESURA OF THE ROYAL BODY

1. Roland Barthes, *La chambre claire* (Paris: Seuil, 1980), 148.
2. See Ernst Kantorowicz, *The King's Two Bodies* (Princeton: Princeton University Press, 1955) and Marc Bloch, *Les rois thaumaturges* (Paris: Gallimard, 1983).

276 / NOTES

3. See Henri de Lubac, *Corpus mysticum*, 2d ed. (Paris: Aubier, 1948).
4. See Louis Marin, *La parole mangée, et autres essais théologico-politiques* (Paris: Klincksieck, 1986).

CHAPTER 16. SIMONIDES' MEMORY LAPSE

1. Cicero, *On the Character of the Orator*, trans. and ed. J. S. Watson (New York: Harper and Brothers, 1860), 2.86.352–4 (187) [translation modified].
2. See, for example, Aristotle, *De memoria* 450a.30 and b.1–10; *Rhetorica ad Herennium* 2.14.30; Quintilian, *Institutio Oratoria* 11.2.21 and, especially, 32–3. See also Marianus Capella, *De nuptiis Philologiae et Mercurii*, cited in Frances A. Yates, *The Art of Memory* (Chicago: University of Chicago Press, 1966), 51–52, and the "visual" alphabets in Giordano Bruno of the Renaissance, ibid., 118–20 and 294–5. In the same work, see the pages devoted to Leibniz, 379ff. See also Paolo Rossi, *Clavis universalis* (Milan and Naples: R. Ricciardi, 1960), 250–3. Beyond these bibliographical notes, or before them, we should note that, according to legend, Simonides was the inventor of the letters of the alphabet that were to permit a better written notation; see Jean-Pierre Vernant, *Mythe et pensée chez les Grecs* (Paris: Maspero, 1965), 77n. 98. He was also the author of the formula "the word is an image of reality."
3. See, once more, Yates's fundamental *Art of Memory* for examples that illustrate the essential opposition between imagery and writing in the arts of memory.
4. On Simonides of Ceos (556–468 B.C.E.), lyric poet "with words of honey" during the pre-Socratic era, see *Lyra Graeca*, English edition and translation, vol. 2 (Cambridge: Harvard University Press, "Loeb Classical Library," 1924), 246ff. (cited in Yates, *Art of Memory*, 27). See also Cecil M. Bowra, *Greek Lyric Poetry from Alcaman to Simonides* (Oxford: Clarendon Press, 1961), and Giuliana Lanata, *Poetica preplatonica* (Florence: La nuova Italia, 1963).
5. Quintilian, *Institutio Oratoria* 9.11–5 signals that the sources are not in agreement on the name of the person in whose honor the poem was written nor on the place where it was sung. Pharsalus or Crannon?
6. The sources even indicate he was the first to be paid for his poems.
7. See, on this point, Marcel Détienne, "La mémoire du poète," chap. 2 in *Les maîtres de vérité dans la Grèce archaïque* (Paris: Maspero, 1967), 9ff., and, in particular, on the notion of *kleos* and the status of praise, 20ff. See also the precious analyses of Nicole Loraux in *L'invention d'Athènes* (Paris: Mouton, 1981), on the political and philosophical status of the eulogy.
8. See the classical studies by Albert Bates Lord, *The Singer of Tales* (Cambridge, 1960), and G. S. Kirk, *The Songs of Homer* (Cambridge: Harvard University Press, 1962).
9. On the relation between the muses and memory, see Détienne, *Les maîtres de vérité*, 10ff., and the literary and philosophical references given there.
10. Let us also note, following the studies by Détienne in *Les maîtres de vérité*, especially 105ff., that Simonides represents a turning point in what Détienne calls the history of *Aletheia*: He begins "the process of the demonetization" of "Truth," first by making poetry a career and by obliging his contemporaries to recognize the commercial value of his art. In linking poetry to painting—he was the inventor of the formula "painting is silent poetry and poetry painting that speaks"—he makes poetry an art of deception, but one with a positive connotation. As a result, "that reflection on poetry, its function, and its proper object consummates the break with the tradition of the inspired poet who speaks the Aletheia.... The devalorization of Aletheia is intelligible only in its relation to the invention of mnemonics. From

a religious function, the foundation of the visionary poetic word, memory becomes a lay technique, the instrument of a career within everyone's reach. . . . 'Poetic revelation' gave way to a technique of fascination. Simonides condemns Aletheia and devotes himself to Apatè. . . . When he defines the art of the poet as an art of illusion whose function is to seduce by eliciting 'images,' fleeting beings that are themselves and other than themselves . . . Simonides anticipates the Sophist" (119).

11. In his version of the story, Quintilian maintains that the celebration of Castor and Pollux was a digression: "Following the common practice of poets, he had introduced a digression in praise of Castor and Pollux" (*Instituto Oratoria*, trans. H. E. Butler [Cambridge: Harvard University Press, 1958], 11.2.11 [4:217]). La Fontaine makes the same claim in his *Fables* (fable 14 of book 1, "*Simonide préservé par les dieux*"). But, for him, the digression does not fill in a memory lapse on the part of *the poet* but a blank in the genealogical, familial memory of the "hero":

> The forebears of the Athlete were unknown / His father, a good Bourgeois, with no other merit: / Infertile and petty matter. / The Poet spoke first of his Hero. / Having said of him all he could say / He went off the track, began to speak / Of Castor and Pollux.

12. Here, again, we find in Simonides the elements of that opposition between a lyric time that flows, flees, and effaces everything, and a positive time, "the wisest thing . . . because it is in that time that one learns and memorizes." See Détienne, *Les maîtres de vérité*, 3 n. 26, for references.

13. We find that equivalence and that affinity in a note, a digression, by Claude Perrault in his translation of Vitruvius. He notes that one of the three *representations* of the architectural edifice (in addition to orthography and scenography) is *ichnography*, the representation of its ground plan. The term comes from the Greek *ichnos*, which signifies imprint, trace left behind on the ground. As a result, the two dimensions of future and past are telescoped into the present of the ichnographical representation, since the ground plan, which is the first step in planning a building, is structurally equivalent to the vestige on the ground that is the last remains, the ultimate ruins of the destroyed edifice.

14. Let us note that, underlying our entire analysis at this point is the categorical opposition between spaces and places, process and order (or system). See Certeau, *The Practice of Everyday Life*, and Louis Marin, *Utopiques: Jeux d'espace* (Paris: Minuit, 1973), 257–90.

15. See Yates's remarks in *Art of Memory*, 46–9.
16. Saint Augustine, *Confessions*, book 10, trans. R. S. Pine-Coffin (London and New York: Penguin Classics, 1961), 207–52.
17. Ibid., 214.
18. Ibid., 216.
19. Ibid., 230.
20. Ibid., 230–1.
21. Ibid., 231.

CHAPTER 17. FALLS, ENCOUNTERS, AND THE *PREMIER VENU*

1. Pascal, *Pensées*, 245.
2. [*Le premier venu*, literally, "the first (to have) come," is an idiomatic expression meaning "anyone at all, just anyone." Trans.]
3. Louis Massignon, *Parole donnée* (Paris: Seuil, 1983), 353.
4. Pascal, *Pensées*, 287.

CHAPTER 18. THE SECRETS OF NAMES AND BODIES

1. See the commentary in the introduction to "Le chef-d'oeuvre inconnu," tome 10 of *La comédie humaine-Etudes philosophiques* (Paris: Bibliothèque de la Pléiade, N.R.F., 1979), 392ff., on the vogue for E. T. A. Hoffmann in Paris during the 1830s, and on the subtitle "conte fantastique" [fantastic tale], which appeared in the first publication of *L'Artiste* (31 July 1831).
2. Nonetheless, a history to come is at issue. We know the frequency of the references to the last pages of the story in the art criticism of abstract, nonfigurative painting and, in particular, in American abstract expressionism (Pollock, de Kooning, et cetera). We do not intend to evoke that history here. If it tries to be something more than a simple allusion, it is often merely the product of a retrospective illusion.
3. *Le Provincial à Paris*, 2 vols., in-8° (Paris: Gabriel Roux et Cassanet, 1847), 2:81–175.
4. By "construction," I mean, of course, not the narration of successive episodes or the enunciation of discourses on painting but the structural design of the story whose "names" designate transformations.
5. By imaginative association—and this text by Balzac has the remarkable characteristic of favoring such associations—I could easily cite some German "romantic" works.
6. Edmond and Jules Goncourt, *L'art au XVIII⁰ siècle: Watteau, Prud'hon, Boucher, Fragonard, Greuze, Debricourt, Latour, etc.* (Paris: Rapilly, 1873).
7. Erwin Panofsky, "*Et in Arcadia ego*: The Concept of Transience in Poussin and Watteau," in *Philosophy and History, Essays Presented to Ernst Cassirer* (Oxford: Clarendon Press, 1936), 223ff.
8. As René Guise notes, Balzac is anticipating here: Marie de Médicis's large order from Rubens was much later (1620). But what is the meaning of that anticipation if not to present in François Porbus an accomplished painter, a master, but one who is now "out of style"?
9. As we know, it does not appear that Frans Porbus the Younger painted a St. Mary of Egypt, even though Félibien indicates that he "made great compositions of histories," immediately adding, however, that "he had more success with portraits." See Félibien, *Entretiens sur les vies et les ouvrages des plus excellens peintres anciens et modernes* (London: D. Mortier, 1705), 3:248. In contrast, one finds in the work of another Flemish painter living in Paris, Philippe de Champaigne, a painting made for Marie de Médicis and the convent of Val de Grace, a Mary of Egypt, but in another episode of her life, when she received Holy Communion from Saint Zosimus. See Bernard Dorival, *Philippe de Champaigne, 1602–1674* (Paris: Editions des Musées Nationaux, 1965), 2:130, plate 234.
10. In St. Mary of Egypt's confession to Saint Zosimus in *The Golden Legend*, the Virgin Mary plays a decisive role in her conversion: "As I lifted my head, I saw an image of the Blessed Virgin Mary. Then I begged her with tears in my eyes to obtain pardon for my sins" (Jacobus de Voragine, *The Golden Legend*, trans. Granger Ryan and Helmut Ripperger [New York: Arno Press, 1969], 228). It is remarkable that an *image of Mary* is the source of the grace of prayer and repentance.
11. The old man agrees here with the judgment of Félibien in his *Entretiens*: "That is why we look with more pleasure at the paintings of François Porbus [over those of Fréminet], who worked in Paris at the same time; even though in truth, there is neither great fire nor force of design in what Porbus painted, but only a beauty of the brush that is pleasing to everyone" (248).
12. [In French, *trousser*, in addition to meaning "to truss up," as of poultry, signifies "to lift one's garment to prevent it from dragging on the ground." The term is also used idiomatically to mean "to possess (a woman)." Trans.]

13. Jacques Hillairet, *Connaissance du vieux Paris* (Paris, 1965), 92. Hillairet indicates that the name of the Rue de la Jussienne is a result of the deformation of "St. Mary of Egypt" ("l'Egyptienne" to "la Gipecienne"), which itself evokes the chapel built in the thirteenth century on the corner of the intersection that that street formed with Rue Montmartre. He also notes that "unmarried girls who dreaded becoming mothers secretly came to pray to Mary of Egypt to intervene."
14. See also Jacobus de Voragine, *The Golden Legend*, 228–30.
15. See Félibien, interview 8, 4:6. Henri Sauval notes that Poussin particularly admired a Last Supper painted by Frans Porbus the Younger for Saint Leu-Saint Gilles in 1618 (*Histoires et recherches des antiquités de la ville de Paris*, 3 vols. [Paris: n.p., 1724], 1:284–6). Sir Anthony Blunt writes that the painting had a great influence on Poussin's artistic development inasmuch as that Last Supper set out what Porbus had learned from the study of Titian during the nine years he spent in Italy, where he might very well have seen the *Meal in Emmaus* of the Venetian master, the property of his patron, the duke of Mantua (*The Paintings of Nicolas Poussin* [London and New York: Phaidon, 1967]). I shall limit myself here to noting that the painting by Porbus was painted for *Saint Leu-Saint Gilles*. In a distant margin of the story, the name "Gillette" in its masculine form, "Gilles," is the link between Porbus and Poussin.
16. Note that the unity that the "system" of drawing or of color gives to the painting simulates only *one of the conditions* of life. The old man's ambition is to simulate all of them and, in that way, "transmute" representation into presence.
17. Note the slippage in the hierarchies and classifications in the historical and aesthetic references to painters in particular. Raphael is placed above the Titian-Dürer opposition and later is said to be the equal of Titian.
18. Quoted in Reginald Howard Wilenski, *Flemish Painters, 1430–1830* (London: Faber and Faber, 1960), 1:564. See also, in a work no doubt consulted by Balzac, J. B. Descamps, *La vie des peintres flamands, allemands et hollandais*, 4 vols. (Paris: C.-A. Jombert, 1753–63); and idem, *Voyage pittoresque de la Flandre et du Brabant* (Paris: C.-A. Jombert, 1769).
19. At the end of the notice Gaston van Camp devotes to Grossart's *Venus and Love* (*Catalogue des Musées Royaux des Beaux-Arts de Bruxelles, Art ancien* [Brussels: Musées Royaux des Beaux-Arts, 1977], n. 27), he writes: "His *Venus and Love* escapes the classical spirit and the immobility it leads to. The mother and child are animated and their movements are inscribed in an architecture of willful asymmetry to accentuate even more their movement. This charming group in old ivory tones must have pleased the humanists, to judge by the inscription that surrounds it, which gently advises the child to spare his mother in the end so as not to perish himself."
20. For example, *Neptune and Amphitrite* in the Berlin Museum; *Adam and Eve*, Kensington Museum; *Mars and Vénus*, Antwerp; and so forth. See Wilenski, *Flemish Painters*; Martin Davies, *Early Netherlandish School: National Gallery Catalogue* (London: The Trustees, 1945); Max V. Friedländer, *Die Altniederlandische Malerei* (Berlin and Leyden: Sijthoff, 1924–57); Albrecht Dürer, *Tagebuch der Reise in die Niederlande* (Leipzig: F. A. Brockhaus, 1884). Carel Van Mander, *Heltschilderboek* (1604); et cetera.
21. In interview 8 of Félibien's *Entretiens* (4:7), we find two precise indications that Balzac might well have exploited in the "historical fiction" he proposes: "[Poussin] sought everywhere to educate himself [on his arrival in Paris in 1612]: but he encountered neither teachers nor lessons that fit with the idea he had made of the perfection of painting. Thus, he quickly left two masters from whom he had believed he could learn something. One was a painter with little skill and the other,

Ferdinand Elle Flamand, who at that time had a reputation for portraits but did not have the talent for the great designs where Poussin's genius was leading him." Ferdinand Elle Flamand or François Porbus? Félibien then adds: "He met several knowledgeable and curious persons at the Beaux-Arts who assisted him with their opinions and lent him several Raphael and Jules Romain engravings, the various beauties of which he understood so well that he imitated them perfectly. Such that, in his way of illustrating and expressing things, it already seemed he had been educated in the Raphael school from which, as M. Bellori remarked (in the *Vie* he wrote on Poussin), one could say he sucked the milk and received the nourishment and the spirit of Art as he looked at the art works."

22. In Balzac's text, this name takes two forms: the curse "Tudieu" [literally, "kill God"] and the metaphorical nickname of "the god of painting."

23. As has been noted by Panofsky in *Idea*, and later by Blunt in his *Poussin*, when Poussin formulated his theory of Beauty ("Della Idea della Belleza") in the 1640s (see his observations on painting collected by Giovanni Bellori in *Le Vita* [Rome: n.p., 1672], 460–2), he repeated a passage from the *Idea del Tempio della pittura* (Milan, 1590; repr. Rome: Colomba, 1947), by Giovanni Lomazzo, which Lomazzo had himself borrowed from Marsilio Ficino, *Sopra lo amore over convito di Platone* (Florence: Neri Dortelata, 1544). It concerns the definition of order, mood, and form, which are the "incorporeal preparatives" for Beauty in the body. Ficino notes that "order is nothing other than a harmonious distance between the parts, and that distance is either nonexistent, or empty, or an outline." He adds: "But who will maintain that lines are a body? For they are lacking width and depth, which are necessary for a body. In addition, mood is not a quantity, but a term of quantity. The terms are surfaces, lines, and points, all things that, having no depth, cannot be said of bodies. Thus, we have appearance consist, not in matter, but in the felicitous concordance of light, shadows, and lines." (Lomazzo cited Ficino, and Poussin read him in the translation by Hilaire Pader.) In this sense, therefore, the three "preparatives" of beauty are incorporeal. If we may combine history and fiction, it would appear that Poussin was recalling the remarks of Mabuse's pupil encountered in 1612-3 when he dealt with order, mood, and form, that is, with the relations internal to the figure, the relations between the figures, and the relations between the figure and the ground. But whereas Frenhofer's aim is the absolute *"trompe-l'oeil"*—which would represent the properly "fantastic," Hoffmannesque aspect of Balzac's story—Poussin's aim is to ground the art of painting, the *mimesis* of the senses, in a set of rational, metaphysically intelligible categories.

24. On the question of the *trompe-l'oeil* and mimesis, see the admirable article by Pierre Charpentrat, "Effets et formes de l'illusion," *Nouvelle Revue de Psychanalyse* 4 (1971); and the article devoted to it, written upon Charpentrat's death, Louis Marin, "Représentation et simulacre," *Critique* (June–July 1978): 373–4.

25. *Correspondance de Poussin*, ed. C. Jouanny (Paris: Archives de l'art français, 1911), 461–4.

26. On the *pose* in its relation to the notion of the present and of presence, see, in particular, the in-depth analysis of Georges Didi-Huberman in *Invention de l'hystérie* (Paris: Macula, 1982).

27. Thomas Warton, *History of English Poetry* (Hildesheim: Georg Olms Verlagsbuchhandlung, 1968), 1:120.

28. It is quite likely that Frenhofer-Balzac is evoking a precise painting by Titian: for example, the Venus of Urbino or the Venus in the Uffizi in Florence.

29. In my remarks, I have not introduced the nickname of Catherine Lescault, "La

Belle Noiseuse," which disappears from the text beginning with the edition of *Provincial à Paris*, only because Michel Serres has spoken eloquently of it in *Genèse* (Paris: Grasset, 1982).

CHAPTER 19. THE LOGIC OF SECRECY

1. [That is, an open secret, named after Punch in the Punch and Judy puppet shows. Trans.]
2. Pascal, *Pensées*, 36, 35.

CHAPTER 22. "HELLO, WHO IS THIS?"

1. Pascal, *Pensées*, 145.

CHAPTER 23. THE ANGEL OF VIRTUALITY

1. Saint Thomas Aquinas, *Summa theologica*, 5 vols. (Westminster, MD: Christian Classics, 1948), 1:265–6.
2. Ibid., 265.
3. Ibid., 266.
4. Ibid., 267.
5. Ibid., 265.
6. Ibid., 266.
7. Genesis 18:8 (King James Version).
8. Aquinas, *Summa theologica*, 1:267.
9. Ibid., 268.
10. Ibid.
11. Ibid.

CHAPTER 24. NEITHER THE TRUE SEX NOR THE FALSE

1. Ovid, *The Metamorphoses*, trans. Horace Gregory (New York and Toronto: Viking Press, 1958), 120.
2. Ibid., 120–2 (4.358–94).
3. André Green, *Nouvelle Revue de Psychanalyse* 7 (1973), 262.

CHAPTER 26. ECHOGRAPHIES: THE CROSSINGS OF A CONVERSION

1. See Jeanne Courcelle and Pierre Courcelle, "'Le Tolle Lege' de Philippe de Champaigne," *Recherches Augustiniennes* 5 (1968).
2. See Pierre Courcelle, *Recherches sur les Confessions de saint Augustin* (Paris: E. de Boccard, 1968), 13–20, and bibliography.
3. See Louis Marin, *La voix excommuniée: Essais de mémoire* (Paris: Galilée, 1981), in particular, 42–3.
4. Saint Augustine, *Confessions*, 24.
5. Ibid.
6. Ibid.
7. Ibid. See also G. Bouissac, "Rhythme et harmonie du style dans *Confessions*, I, IV, 4," in *Oeuvres de saint Augustin*, ed. Martin Skutella (Paris: Desclée and Brouwer, 1962) 652ff.; J. Finaert, *L'évolution littéraire de saint Augustin* (Paris: Les Belles Lettres, 1939), 17, 67, 77; Constantin J. Balmus, *Etude sur le style de saint Augustin dans les Confessions et La Cité de Dieu* (Paris: Les Belles Lettres, 1930); and Christine Mohmann, *Etudes sur le latin des chrétiens* (Rome: Stora e Letteratura, 1958).

282 / NOTES

8. Pierre Fontanier, *Les figures du discours* (Paris: Flammarion, 1968).
9. For illustrations of this point, which deserves further development, see *Paroles des Anciens: Apophtegmes des Pères du désert*, trans. Jean-Claude Guy (Paris: Cerf, 1993), Apophtegms Olympios 2, 119. See also the commentary by Peter Brown in *The Making of Late Antiquity* (Cambridge: Harvard University Press, 1978), 127.
10. B. Dupriez, *Gradus: Les procédés littéraires* 10/18 (Paris, 1980).
11. The phantasmic inscription may correspond to the gap between hallucination and free, indirect discourse. This point also needs to be further developed. See, in particular, Ann Banfield, *Unspeakable Sentences: Narration and Representation in the Language of Fiction* (London: Routledge and Kegan Paul, 1982).
12. Augustine, *Confessions*, 206–7.
13. Ibid., 157.
14. Ibid. Augustine is citing Psalms 71, 134, 76, and 8.
15. Ibid.
16. Ibid., 158.
17. Ibid.
18. See Michel de Certeau, *L'écriture de l'histoire* (Paris: Gallimard, 1978).
19. Augustine, *Confessions*, 159.
20. Ibid., 160.
21. The text that best accounts for this passage in the *Confessions*, it seems to me, is in chapter 5 of Jacques Lacan's *Séminaire*, book 11 (*Les quatre concepts fondamentaux de la psychanalyse*), and its analysis of dream's function in satisfying the need to prolong sleep, its notion of the encounter that makes us conceive of truth as *unterlegt, untertragen*, pending, and, finally, in the idea that the "primary process seized in its experience of break between perception and consciousness, in this . . . intemporal place . . . forces us to posit . . . another locality, another space, another scene, of *interperception and consciousness*" (55ff).
22. Augustine, *Confessions*, 164.
23. Ibid., 166.
24. Ibid., 167.
25. Ibid. See also Brown, *Making of Late Antiquity*, in particular, chap. 4.
26. Augustine, *Confessions*, 167–8.
27. Ibid.
28. See Massignon, *Parole donnée*. Massignon evokes the "blink of an eye," the instant in Muslim mysticism in which the soul perceives the laconic announcement of a decision by God, which confers on the nascent act the status that will be proclaimed on the day when the clamor of justice is heard, that is, on "the day of the Last Judgment."
29. Augustine, *Confessions*, 169.
30. ["*Echographie*" is the French term for "ultrasound." Trans.]
31. Augustine, *Confessions*, 169.
32. Ibid.
33. Ibid.
34. Marin, *La voix excommuniée*, 36–7.
35. Augustine, *Confessions*, 170.
36. Ibid.
37. Ibid.
38. Ibid., 170.
39. Ibid., 171.
40. Ibid.

41. Ibid.
42. For a completely different point of view, see the analysis by Courcelle in *Recherches*, appendix 3, "Les 'voix' dans les *Confessions*," and bibliography; and, in Pierre Courcelle, *Les Confessions de saint Augustin dans la tradition littéraire: Antécédents et postérité* (Paris: Etudes augustiniennes, 1963), the discussion in chapter 9 (165–8) of the "vicina domus" lesson (preferred to the "divina domus" lesson on *Sessorianus*) and bibliography.
43. Augustine, *Confessions*, 175.
44. Ibid., 175.
45. Ibid., 175–6.
46. Ibid.
47. Ibid., 176.
48. Ibid., 177.
49. Ibid.
50. On the fig tree, see Courcelle, *Recherches*, 193 n. 2.
51. Augustine, *Confessions*, 177.
52. See John 1:48.
53. Augustine, *Confessions*, 177. See Courcelle, *Recherches*, 188ff. and *Les Confessions dans la tradition*, chap. 7, 143ff.; and, on the form of the admonition, chap. 8, 155ff., and bibliography.
54. My colleague and friend Paolo Fabri of the University of Bologna has indicated to me the remarkable phonetic opposition of *To(le) (le)Ge* "around" the repetition of the "le."
55. Augustine, *Confessions*, 178. See André Mandouze, *Saint Augustin, l'aventure de la raison et de la grâce* (Paris: Etudes augustiniennes, 1968), 116–9, and bibliographical references.
56. It is clear that this study, which ends abruptly with the irruption of the "lux securitatis" in "the heart of Augustine" is, by that very fact, altogether inadequate. In order for the diverse themes and motifs we have introduced to be developed, if not followed to their conclusion, the following passages would have had to be analyzed: 3.11.30, which sets out, first, the fundamental relation to Alypius within "conversion" itself, and second, the visit to the mother and the memory of the dream of the rule of faith; and 9.2.4, the "weakness of the lungs" that was so painful that "my voice was husky and I could not speak for long at a time [*vocem clariorem productioremque*]" (183). That malady, which broke out before the moment of the "Tolle lege," ought to allow us to inquire into the notion of conversion, both in its spiritual or mystical dimension and in its corporeal and, more precisely, hysterical, dimension. In both cases, the relation to the voice would obviously be fundamental.

CHAPTER 27. THE PLACE OF THE POINT? PASCAL

1. Pascal, *Pensées*, 240.
2. Ibid., 218 [translation modified].
3. Ibid., 42 [translation slightly modified].
4. Ibid. [translation modified].
5. Ibid., 35 [translation modified].
6. Ibid., 92.
7. Ibid., 93.
8. Michel Serres, *La naissance de la physique dans le texte de Lucrèce* (Paris: Minuit, 1977), 227–8.

9. Pascal, *Pensées*, 93.
10. Ibid., 92.
11. Ibid.
12. Ibid., 210–1.
13. Ibid., 221.
14. Ibid.
15. Ibid.
16. Ibid., 91.
17. Ibid., 35 [translation modified].
18. Ibid., 287.
19. Ibid., 247 [translation modified].
20. Ibid., 256.
21. Ibid.
22. Ibid., 53 [translation modified].
23. Blaise Pascal, *De l'esprit géométrique. De l'art de persuader. Opuscules et lettres*, ed. Lafuma (Paris: Aubier-Montaigne, 1955), 219ff.
24. Ibid., 139.
25. Ibid., 274 [translation modified].
26. Ibid., 243.
27. Ibid., 210–1.
28. Ibid., 54 [translation modified].
29. Ibid.
30. Ibid.
31. Ibid., 290.
32. Ibid., 216.
33. Ibid., 167.
34. Ibid., 168.
35. Ibid.
36. Ibid., 169.
37. Ibid., 48.
38. Blaise Pascal, *Entretiens avec M. de Saci. Opuscules et lettres*, 87–8.
39. Ibid., 87.
40. Ibid.
41. Ibid.
42. Ibid.
43. Ibid., 253 [translation modified].
44. Blaise Pascal, *Lettres aux Roannez. Opuscules et lettres*, 98.

Index

absolute monarchy, 147. *See also* King
accident, 168, 169–72
Adam, 185, 187
Adam (Mabuse), 187, 189
Aeneas (Virgil), 27
aidôs, 126–28, 132, 134–35
Alembert, Jean Le Rond d', 15, 16, 22
alètheia, 127
Alypius, 243, 246, 250
Andelys, Les, 182
Andromaque (Jean Racine), 35–36
angels, 219–27
anonymity, 203–4
Antony, 243
aphatic, 214
apophatic, 213
Aquinas, Saint Thomas, 219–27
architecture, 160–66
Aristophanes, 233
Aristotle, 167
Arnauld, Antoine, 168, 170
Arnauld d'Andilly, Robert, 238
art of means, 5
art of memory, 159, 165. *See also* memory, theater of
Augustine, Saint: and angels, 222; and conversion, 238–51; and memory, 165–66; *uti* and *frui* in, 71
authorship, 10–11, 203–4
automatons, 68, 70, 73–74, 120–21

Bacon, Sir Francis, 57
Balzac, Honoré de, 1, 3, 179–94
banality, 168, 169
Banquet (Plato), 233
Barchilon, Jacques, 11

Barthes, Roland, 12, 144–45
Being, 95–98, 118
Benveniste, Emile, 97–98, 212
Bernardin de Saint-Pierre, Jacques-Henri, 51, 53
Beyond the Pleasure Principle (Sigmund Freud), 99
Blanchot, Maurice, 85
Bloch, Ernst, 77–78, 79, 93, 177
Bloch, Marc, 147
body, 118–21, 226. *See also* divine body; natural body; two bodies
Boethius, 226
Boileau, Nicolas, 228
Brunelleschi, Filippo, 17
brute, 78, 94
brutishness, 84
Buffon, Georges-Louis Leclerc de, 35
Butler, Samuel, 192

canopy, 154–56
carrying (*porter*), 109–10
Castor and Pollux, 158–59, 161
cataphatic, 216
catastrophe, 208–9, 211
Celestial Hierarchy (Pseudo-Dionysius the Areopagite), 221
center effect, 39–40, 41–43
Certeau, Michel de, 4–6
Champaigne, Philippe de, 238
chance, 167–74
Char, René, 77
"Chef-d'oeuvre inconnu, Le" (Honoré de Balzac), 179–94
Chuang-tzu, 87
Cicero, 158–66

Cinna (Pierre Corneille), 115
colony, 94
Confessions (Saint Augustine), 165–66, 238–51
Confessions, Les (Rousseau), 91
continence, 249
continent, 37–38
conversion, 238–51
Corneille, Pierre, 115–21
crossing, 2–3, 5–6
culture, 83
cunning man, 262–67

De doctrina christiana (Saint Augustine), 71
de facto, 80
De genesis ad literam (Saint Augustine), 222
de jure, 80
Defoe, Daniel, 36–38, 40–45
Deleuze, Gilles, 81
Delille, Abbot, 16
Desargues, Gérard, 17
Descartes, René: and automatons, 73–74; and continent argument, 37–38; influence of, on Corneille, 120–21; and the self, 68–69; and solitary meditation, 44–45
Descrittone di tutti i Paesi Bassi (Francesco Guicciardini), 185
desire, 89, 105
Détienne, Marcel, 125
Dettonville, Amos, 266
de-viation, 26, 29
diachrony, 80–81, 105–6, 110–11
dialogue, 54
diaphatic, 217
Dictionary of the English Language (Samuel Johnson), 193
Dictionnaire de botanique (Jean-Jacques Rousseau), 61–62
diegetic, 54
digression, 47, 49, 58, 61, 63, 85
discourse of others, 105, 111
Discourse on the Method (René Descartes), 37–38, 44–45
Discourse on the Origin of Inequality (Jean-Jacques Rousseau), 80–83, 99–100
divine body, 145, 147–55

Domenichino, Judith, 21
double flower, 61–62
drifting, 20–21, 26, 28, 79, 85, 92–93
Duchamp, Marcel, 168
Duprat-Duverger, L., 14
Dürer, Albrecht, 184, 186

eating, 224–26
echo, 250–51
echography, 244–45
economy of exchange, 107, 108
economy of *jouissance*, 56, 63–64, 66, 72, 73, 91–92. *See also* libidinal economy
edge, 42–43
effondement, 165–66
eidos, 125, 127–28, 132, 134–35
Elysium, 48, 55, 57, 63, 66
empty indicator, 12–13
encounter, 172–78
entrenchment, 41–42
Ephorus of Cyme, 125
Epictetus, 261, 266, 268–69
Epicurus, 257
Epistle to the Romans, 251
Essai de linguistique générale (Roman Jakobson), 212
Essay on the Origin of Languages (Jean-Jacques Rousseau), 84
ethics, 69–70, 74–75
Euryanthe (Carl von Weber), 147
Eve, 185, 187
event, 167–70, 172, 209
Examen, L' (Pierre Corneille), 116
expenditure, 91

fall, 168–70, 172, 177
feminine, 63, 127, 128, 131, 148, 229–34
Ferragus (Honoré de Balzac), 1
fetching (*rapporter*), 109–10
fiction and reality, 30–32
fixed point, 260, 267
fond, 89–90
force, 265
forgetting, 99–100
foundation, 83–84
Fraunhofer, Joseph von, 188–89
Freischütz (Carl von Weber), 147
Frenhofer, 187, 188–89, 190, 191, 193
Freud, Sigmund, 99, 134

frontispiece, 7–14, 32–33, 238–39
frui (enjoyment), 71–72, 75

Gabriel, angel, 207
garden: economy of, 52, 55–60; and *jouissance*, 47–49; as locus of writing, 53; in Pascal's *Pensées*, 257; in Rousseau's *La nouvelle Héloïse*, 46–67; in Saint Augustine's *Confessions*, 246
gaze, 123–36
Genesis, 80, 81
Georgian, 193, 194
Gillette, 179–81, 187, 188, 191, 194
Giorgion, 184, 188, 193, 194
Gorgon, 194
graft, 60–62
Grammaire de Port-Royal, 117
Guicciardini, Francesco, 185
Guise, René, 179
Guyon, Bernard, 47
Gyges, 123–36

happiness: and forgetting, 99; and *jouissance*, 90–92, 98; in Rousseau's *Rêveries*, 84, 86, 88; and rhythm, 96, 98; and utopia, 79, 81–82
Haudricourt, André G., 46
hauling (*transporter*), 109–10
Heidegger, Martin, 85
Henry IV, 181
hermaphroditism, 228–34
"Hermaphroditus," 231
Herodotus, 123–36
Hillairet, Jacques, 1, 2–3, 236
Histoire naturelle des oiseaux (Georges-Louis Leclerc de Buffon), 35
Histoires, ou Contes du temps passé (Charles Perrault), 8–14
Histories (Herodotus), 123–36
history: and the Event, 209; and narrative of origin, 158; and utopian practice, 78–80; and visibility, 125–26
History of English Poetry, Dissertation I (Thomas Warton), 192
Hjelmslev, Louis, 105
Holbein, Ambrosius, 32–33
Holbein, Hans, 32–33, 184, 186
Holophernes, 21
homeland, 87–88
Homer, 34–35

Homme, L' (André G. Haudricourt), 46
Hudibras (Samuel Butler), 192
Huon de Bordeaux, 154
Husserl, Edmund, 83
Huyghens, Constantijn, 116, 266

ideal self, 68–70, 73
identity, 242–43
immediacy, 83
indication, 87–89
indivisible point, 259, 261, 267
infinite, 17
insularity, 41, 44–45
interval, 95, 246–47
intimate journal, 144–46
island, 34–38, 86–88

Jakobson, Roman, 212, 218
Jansen, Cornelis Otto, 168, 170
Jansenists, 168, 170, 171
Johnson, Samuel, 193
jouissance: vs. consumption, 74; and garden, 47–49, 55, 58–60; and happiness, 79, 90–92, 98; and rhythm, 95–96; in Rousseau's *La nouvelle Héloïse*, 47–49, 65–66; vs. use, 71–72, 75; and utopia, 81
journey, 25–33, 48, 50, 108, 109
Jôzan, Ishikawa, 210
judgment, 255–57
justice, 265

Kantorowicz, Ernst, 147
King, 137–39, 141–43, 148, 156
Klee, Paul, 17, 18, 19
kleos (monument), 160–66

La Fontaine, Jean de, 104–14
Lacan, Jacques, 89–90
Lady Continence, 249
Lafuma, Louis, 18, 267
Lamotte, Marc-Antoine-Nicolas de, 15, 16, 22
Latham, Robert Gordon, 193
law: and the body, 146–47, 150–53, 156; and circumstance, 80; and the father, 62; and language, 152; and representation, 129–31, 134–35; in Rousseau's *Rêveries*, 89; and seduction, 126–27; and utopia, 79

Leclaire, Serge, 84
Lenfant, Abbot, 207
Lescault, Catherine, 180, 183, 187–88, 191, 193, 194
libidinal economy, 56–57, 60, 63–64, 66
Libri Platonicorum, 242
Life of Saint Antony, 244
lily, 150–53, 155
Logique de Port-Royal, 68–75
Logique du sens (Gilles Deleuze), 81
"Louis," 149–50, 156
Louis II of Bavaria, King, 144–56
Louis de Montalte, 266
Lucretius, 256
Lyotard, Jean-François, 91, 99

Mabuse, Jan, 184–87, 191
Machiavelli, Niccolò, 192
machination, 129–31
magnitude, 261, 263
Malherbe, François de, 104, 113
Malinowski, Bronislaw, 218
Manichees, 247
map, 29–31
Margaret of Austria, 184
Marie de Médicis, 180, 181–82, 187, 191
Marvell, Andrew, 55, 60
Mary of Egypt, St., 180, 181–83, 187, 191, 193
masculine, 229–34
Massignon, 177
master and slave, 113
Matthias Sandorf, 44
Meditations (René Descartes), 73–74, 120–21
Medusa, 142–43
memory, theater of, 158–66
Ménage, Gilles, 16
Menteur, Le (Pierre Corneille), 115–21
Merleau-Ponty, Maurice, 50
Metamorphoses (Ovid), 228–34
methodological fiction, 69, 70, 72–73
"Meunier, son fils et l'âne, Le" (Jean de La Fontaine), 104–14
mimetic, 54
mobility, 115
money, 161–62
Montaigne, Michel de, 261, 266, 268–69
monument of memory, 160–66
More, Sir Thomas, 25–33, 40

Mort de Pompée, La (Pierre Corneille), 115–16, 119, 120
Moses and Monotheism (Sigmund Freud), 134
Mother Goose, 10
motionless journey, 48, 52, 53, 100
"Mower Against Gardens, The" (Andrew Marvell), 60
Musset, Alfred de, 17
Mysterious Island, The (Jules Verne), 37–39

names, 163, 179–94. See also individual names; proper name
Napoleon Bonaparte, 196
narration, 9–10, 27–30
narrative, 106, 110–11
narrative of origin, 158, 162–64
natural body, 145, 147–55
nature, 62, 94
Nebridius, 243
negation, 83–84
neuter: and drifting, 92–93; and *jouissance*, 91; in La Fontaine's *Fables*, 112–13; in Ovid's *Metamorphoses*, 231–34; and rhythm, 95–96; in Rousseau's *Rêveries*, 84, 89, 92–93; and utopia, 78, 82, 86, 100
Newcastle, Marquis of, 74
"Nick," 192–93
Nietzsche, Friedrich, 6
no-place place, 82, 85, 89, 94. See also Utopia
Nouvelle Héloïse, La (Jean-Jacques Rousseau), 46–67, 82, 88
nullification, 95–96
nullity, 84

Oberon, 146, 154
objectively real, 78
Odyssey (Homer), 34–35
Oedipus, 200–204
On the Character of the Orator (Cicero), 158–66
opportunity, 168, 170–71
orality, 9–10, 13
Orient, 146, 154
originary, 81, 83–85, 94, 99–100
Other, 176, 249
outside and inside, 49
Ovid, 228–34

painting. *See* perspective in painting; representation: in painting; vanishing point; viewpoint
Panofsky, Erwin, 181
parasite, 60
Parole en archipel, La (René Char), 77
Pascal, Blaise: and chance, 167–78; and God's hiddenness, 213; and man's unhappiness, 48; and middle point, 39; nature and culture in, 88–89; notion of the self of, 121–22; and perspective in painting, 199, 255–59; and place of the point, 252–69; punctuation in, 18–19
Pascal, Etienne, 168, 170, 171
Paul et Virginie (Jacques-Henri Bernardin de Saint-Pierre), 51, 53
"Peau-d'âne" (Charles Perrault), 13, 136
Pensées (Blaise Pascal): and God's hiddenness, 213; and man's unhappiness, 48; and middle point, 39; nature and culture in, 88–89; and notion of self, 121–22; and place of the point, 252–69; punctuation in, 18–19
perfectibility, 83
performative, 145, 153
Périer, Gilberte, 167–72
Perrault, Charles, 8–14, 136
perspective in painting, 199, 255–59
phatic, 212–18
Philip, Bastard of Burgundy, 184
Physics (Aristotle), 167
place, 4–6, 252–69
Plato, 27, 97, 123, 127, 233
Poilly, 238
point, 15–18, 252–69. *See also* fixed point; indivisible point
political economy, 64, 66, 73
political power, 40–41, 128, 137–39, 141
political theory, 80
Pollux. *See* Castor and Pollux
Polyeucte (Pierre Corneille), 115
Ponticianus, 243–44, 249–50
Porbus, François, 181, 182, 183–84, 186–87
portrait, 137–38, 140, 143, 148, 156
Poussin, Nicolas, 180, 182–84, 185, 186, 187, 191
preface, 7–11
premier venu, 174–78

Principle of Hope, The (Ernst Bloch), 77–78
Problèmes de linguistique générale II (Emile Benveniste), 212
process, 105
proper name, 10, 117–19
prosopopoeia, 240, 248
Protagorus (Plato), 127
Pseudo-Dionysius the Areopagite, 221
punctuation, 15–22

quiproquo, 117

Racan, Seigneur de, 104, 113
Racine, Jean, 35–36
Raphael, 186, 187
"Raphael Hythlodeus," 27–28
rapture, 54, 63
rational knowledge, 71
reading, 9, 11–12, 18
recreation, 62, 73
remainder, 106, 108, 109–11, 114
Rembrandt, 181–82, 183, 186
representation: of angels, 220; garden and, 51, 53, 54, 65–66; and the law, 129–31; in painting, 184, 190–92, 194, 258–59; in Perrault's *Contes*, 13; and political power, 137–39, 141–42; in Rousseau's *Rêveries*, 87–88; of self, 68–69; and utopia, 99
Republic (Plato), 123
reserve, 90–92
Rêveries du promeneur solitaire (Jean-Jacques Rousseau): and island, 43–44; and *jouissance*, 66; and *La nouvelle Héloïse*, 59, 82; and utopian practice, 78–100
rhythm, 94–98
Rigaud, Hyacinthe, 148
Robinson Crusoe (Daniel Defoe), 36–38, 40–43
Rousseau, Jean-Jacques: and the garden, 46–67; and the island, 43–44; and utopian practice, 78–100. *See also* individual works
Rousseau juge de Jean-Jacques (Rousseau), 89
Rubens, Peter Paul, 181
ruse, 129–31

Saint-Cyran, 168, 170
Salmacis river, 231–32

Salomon de Tultie, 261, 263, 266–68
Satires (Nicolas Boileau), 228
secrecy game, 195–204
Secret de Polichinelle, 199
seduction, 123–36
self, 37, 40–41, 69
self/"I," 89, 172–74, 242, 245, 247, 249–50
selvedge, 7–8
Séminaire (Jacques Lacan), 89–90
sens, 262
"Serious Reflections... of Robinson Crusoe" (Daniel Defoe), 44–45
Serres, Michel, 256
sexual difference, 230–34. *See also* feminine; masculine
sharawadgi, 46, 51, 57
Shisendo property, 210
sign, 68, 72, 73, 87
sign-making, 98, 99
sign of the cross, 145–46
Simplicianus, 242
Social Contract (Jean-Jacques Rousseau), 81
social pact, 94
Soriano, Marc, 11
space, 4
space between, 108, 154
spectacle, 51, 54, 139. *See also* representation
Stendhal (Henri Beyle), 19–22
stroll, 48, 50, 52, 53
subject, constitution of, 168, 169–70, 172. *See also* self; self/"I"
sublime, 138
Suite du menteur, La (Pierre Corneille), 116, 120, 121
Summa theologica (Saint Thomas Aquinas), 219–27
Sun King, 146, 156
symbolic, 77, 79
symbolic object, 78, 93, 99, 100
synchrony, 80–81, 105–6
system, 105

tata effect, 7, 13
telephonic. *See* phatic
Temple, William, 46, 51
"Thinker as Poet, The" (Martin Heidegger), 85
third term, 107–8, 112
thought in the back of one's mind, 261, 262–64

Titania, 154
Titian, 184, 186, 187
Tobias, 27, 220, 224–25
"Tolle lege," 238, 250–51
Tolle lege (Philippe de Champaigne), 238
transport, 54, 63
travel narrative, 4–5, 29
trompe-l'oeil, 190–91, 194
truth, 127–28, 130
tuchè, 175
two bodies, 147–48, 150–55. *See also* divine body; natural body

Ulysses, 27
"Upon the Gardens of Epicurus" (William Temple), 46
use (*uti*), 71–72, 75
Utopia (Sir Thomas More), 25–33, 40
utopia: in Ernst Bloch, 77–78; garden as, 64–65; and happiness, 79; and history, 80; journey and, 26–28; and neuter, 93; time and space in, 26
utopian practice, 78–100

vanishing point, 17, 258–59
variation, 116–17
Verdad sospechosa, La (Don Juan Ruiz de Alarcón), 116, 117
Verne, Jules, 37–39
Veronese, Paolo, 184, 186
Vespucci, Amerigo, 28, 30
Victorinus, 242
Vie de feu M. Pascal, La (Gilberte Périer), 167–72
Vie de Henry Brulard, La (Stendhal), 19–22
viewpoint, 17, 257–59
Virgil, 27
virtuality, 19, 227
visibility, 130, 132–33
Vitruvius, 8
Voltaire, 16

Wagner, Richard, 148
Warton, Thomas, 192
Watteau, Antoine, 180, 181
wax tablet, 159–60
Weber, Carl von, 146, 154
Wieland, Christoph Martin, 146
window, 120